FROM SEA TO SHINING SEA

The Story of America

Make a joyful noise unto the Lord, all ye lands!
Serve the Lord with gladness!
Come before his presence with singing!
Know ye that the Lord he is God;
It is he that hath made us and not we ourselves;
We are his people, and the sheep of his pasture.
Enter into his gates with thanksgiving,
And into his courts with praise.
Be thankful unto him, and bless his name.
For the Lord is good;
His mercy is everlasting;
And his truth endureth to all generations!
                                        —Psalm 100

Volume 5

FROM SEA TO SHINING SEA

The Story of America

Contributor to Volume 5

Christopher Zehnder

General Editor

Rollin A. Lasseter

Produced and developed by:

Catholic Schools Textbook Project

In cooperation with:

Ave Maria University

Ignatius Press   San Francisco

Project Manager: Douglas Alexander

Editing: Patricia Bozell, Bridget Neumayr, and Christianne Thillen

Design and Production: Hespenheide Design, Lindsey Altenbernt, Stephanie Davila, Gary Hespenheide, Randy Miyake, Leslie Weller, and Patti Zeman

Acknowledgments: to all of our spiritual, intellectual, and material benefactors, especially Leslie Alexander, Dr. Dominic Aquila, Mr. and Mrs. William Burleigh, Sr. John Dominic Rasmussen, O.P., Fr. Joseph Fessio, S.J., Dan Guernsey, Dr. James Hitchcock, Dr. Ken Kaiser, Helen Lasseter, Ruth Lasseter, Ron Lawson, Mother Assumpta Long, Luke Macik, Esq., Jan Matulka, Fr. Marvin O'Connell, Dr. Andrew Seeley, Mary Ann Shapiro, Mr. and Mrs. Charles Van Hecke, Jessie Van Hecke, and Karen Walker (StudioRaphael). In memoriam, Jacqleen Ferrell and Hal Wales, Esq.

Also, gratitude is due the following organizations for their contributions: Ave Maria University, Dominican Sisters of Nashville, Sisters of Mary Mother of the Church, Sisters of Mary Mother of the Eucharist, The Moran Foundation, and St. Augustine Academy, Spiritus Sanctus Academies, Ville de Marie Academy

Cover Credits: Father Junipero Serra © Robert Holmes/CORBIS; George Washington © Francis G. Mayer/CORBIS; Kateri Tekakwitha © Fr. John Giuliani; Abraham Lincoln © James P. Blair/CORBIS; United States Supreme Court © Joseph Sohm ChromoSohm Inc./CORBIS

Photo Credits: p. vi and p. 52 Our Lady of Guadalupe Abbey; all other images supplied by Corbis: p. 1 Richard Cummins; pp. 2–8 Bettmann; p. 9 Ted Spiegel; p. 11 Academy of Natural Sciences of Philadelphia; p. 12 Historical Picture Archive; pp. 13–22 Bettmann; p. 25 Archivo Iconografico, S.A.; p. 26 Gianni Dagli Orti; pp. 27–29 Bettmann; p. 31 Charles & Josette Lenars; p. 35 Archivo Iconografico, S.A.; p. 37 Blaine Harrington III; p. 39 Bettmann; p. 42 Tom Bean; p. 45 Bettmann; p. 46 Historical Picture Archive; pp. 48–50 Danny Lehman; p. 51 Archivo Iconografico; p. 53 Charles & Josette Lenars; p. 54 Reuters NewMedia Inc.; p. 56 Danny Lehman; p. 57 Archivo Iconografico, S.A.; p. 58 George H. H. Huey; p. 60 L. Clarke; p. 63 Philip James Corwin; p. 65 Bob Krist; p. 66 Lowell Georgia; pp. 69–70 Bettmann; p. 71 above, Academy of Natural Sciences of Philadelphia; p. 72 Gianni Dagli Orti; pp. 74–75 Bettmann; p. 81 Richard Cummins; pp. 83–9 Bettmann; p. 92 John Farmar; Cordaiy Photo Library Ltd.; p. 93 Gianni Dagli Orti; p. 94 Bob Krist; pp. 95–6 Bettmann; p. 97 The Mariners' Museum; p. 99 The Mariners' Museum; pp. 100–102 Bettmann; p. 103 Farrell Grehan; p. 106 Bettmann; p. 107 above, Museum of the City of New York; pp. 108–9 Bettmann; p. 111 Gianni Dagli Orti; pp. 112–16 Bettmann; p. 117 Francis G. Mayer; p. 118 Buddy Mays; pp. 122–32 Bettmann; p. 132 below, Paul A. Souders; pp. 137–44 Bettmann; p. 145 The Corcoran Gallery of Art; p. 146 Bettmann; p. 148 Tom Bean; p. 149 Wally McNamee; pp. 150–53 Bettmann; p. 154 Kevin Fleming; p. 155 Franklin McMahon; p. 160 above, Bettmann, below, Lee Snider; p. 162 Steve Crise; pp. 164–67 Bettmann; p. 168 Joseph Sohm; p. 169 Bettmann; p. 170 Stapleton Collection; pp. 171–81 Bettmann; p. 182 Bob Krist; pp. 187–91 Bettmann; p. 192 Dallas and John Heaton; p. 193 Joseph Sohm; ChromoSohm Inc.; p. 194 Bettmann; p. 195 above, Alan Schein Photography; p. 195 below, Royalty-Free; p. 197 Peggy & Ronald Barnett; p. 199 Dennis Degnan; p. 202 Bettmann; p. 203 Kevin Fleming; p. 204 Wally McNamee; p. 207 Roger Ressmeyer; p. 208 Archivo Iconografico, S.A.; pp. 209–11 Bettmann; p. 212 Ron Sanford; p. 214 Bettmann; p. 215 Kevin Fleming; p. 217 Bettmann; p. 218 Gianni Dagli Orti; pp. 219–27 Bettmann; p. 228 Joseph Sohm; p. 229 Bettmann; p. 230 Richard T. Nowitz; pp. 232–36 Bettmann; p. 238 Philippa Lewis; Edifice; p. 245 James Leynse/Corbis SABA; pp. 247–50 Bettmann

Credits continue on page 451

Table of Contents

Preface

As an educator I have often noted a serious struggle in Catholic education—Catholic educators lack Catholic textbooks. Secular textbooks are attractive and rich in illustrations and maps but unsuitable for Catholic schools. These books often carry an anti-Catholic bias by presenting Catholic contributions in an unfavorable light, or downplaying them. The alternatives to secular texts are old Catholic texts, but these also prove inadequate. Since no distinctively Catholic textbooks have been published since the 1960s, teachers are forced to use old copies of these texts or rely on photocopies. Even the original editions of such Catholic texts lack the graphic quality of the new secular texts, and thus they fail to attract students accustomed to the allures of a media culture. More importantly, old Catholic history texts, especially American history texts, are outdated, and they suffer from a parochialism in which Catholics felt they had to prove their Americanism. Thus, these texts generally do not address the intellectual and cultural needs of today's Catholic students.

I am not alone in my assessment of the situation. Other educators have also noted a defect common to both secular and Catholic texts: they are written in a style that fails to capture the drama of history. History, as its name indicates, is, first and foremost, a story—a story as riveting as any fictional tale and as full of tragedy and comedy, of despair and hope as any novel or epic. Its characters are real human beings like each one of us; some are heroes, others are villains; some are exceptional, but most are average people trying to work through the unique circumstances of their time and place. Since history has the character of story, it must be told as a story, especially to young readers. History texts should draw us into the hopes and fears, the struggles and victories of men of past times. They should help us meet historical characters as real people of flesh and blood.

For over a decade, the Catholic Schools Textbook Project has been working to produce textbooks pleasing to the eye, accurate, interesting to read, and imbued with Catholic tradition. This volume, *From Sea to Shining Sea*, has been written in view of these goals. In it, the foundations of America are told as a series of interesting stories that form one great story. The text relays to students the necessary "secular" historical knowledge, while giving due place to the contributions of Catholics and of the Catholic Church in the settlement and foundation of the nations of North America. The text shows how central the Catholic faith has been to the entire European American experiment, and, without exaggeration and without whitewashing, how important it is to the continuation of that experiment.

In telling the story of America, our text, *From Sea to Shining Sea*, remains true to the Catholic vision of history as set forth in the Second Vatican Council's guiding document *Lumen Gentium*. It also fills a void in the histor- ical education of young people, who know little or nothing of the contributions of past ages to our civilization and religion. This vacuum of historical knowledge is not our true heritage. Ours is a culture of life and of hope, of faith, vast and deep, and rich achievements for the common good. May this textbook be one con- tribution to the full restoration of that culture.

—Michael J. Van Hecke, M.Ed.
President
The Catholic Schools Textbook Project

Introduction

Since the Second Vatican Council, Catholics have been aware of the deficiencies in religious education which afflict the Church at all levels, from kindergarten to graduate school, and some efforts have been made to correct these.

But the faith is more than theology. Because the Second Person of the Trinity became man, entered human history, that history must have deep religious significance for believers. The Judaeo-Christian tradition sees historical events as governed by Divine Providence, while at the same time warning believers against thinking that they are able to read the meaning of that Providence.

It is not insignificant that the Gospels were written not as theological treatises but as historical narratives, nor is it coincidental that the most radical attacks on Christianity have been on its historicity.

Just as Catholics have been deprived of much of their authentic theology over the past forty years, so also they have been deprived of their history, a deprivation which has been much less noticed. This has several damaging effects. Catholics now have little sense of their tradition, little understanding of how the faith can and should permeate a culture and serve as a leaven in that culture. They have little sense of what the lived faith was like through the centuries. Indeed they are extraordinarily present-minded, with little understanding of the faith as anything beyond their own immediate communities. They have little sense of the Communion of Saints—that they are intimately linked with all those who have gone before them with the sign of faith. They have little sense that history itself has a religious meaning.

The Catholic Schools Textbook Project is one of the most promising enterprises of the post-conciliar era, with its determination to once more make available to Catholics an understanding of "secular" subjects which helps illumine the richness of the faith.

The curricula of the Catholic schools prior to Vatican II has often been criticized for its alleged parochialism, the assumption that there was such a thing as "Catholic mathematics," for example, or the tendency to look at the past exclusively through apologetic eyes. These mistakes, to the extent that they were real, will not be made by the Catholic School Textbook Project. As this volume shows, it will be a series which on the one hand honors the Catholic faith and on the other is not afraid to be honest and comprehensive in its treatment of the past. It is a project which deserves the support of every serious Catholic.

—James Hitchcock
St. Louis University

Chapter 1 A New World

A Saintly Explorer

"What are the three things God loves, Mother?" the young boy asked. "Child," the holy nun replied, "God loves the true faith that comes from a pure heart. He loves the simple religious life and the generous kindness of Christian love."

"And what does God hate?" the child then asked.

"Three things He hates," she replied. "God hates a scowling face. He hates stubborn wrongdoing, and too much trust in money."

Thus, St. Ita taught the young boy, Brendan. It was a lesson he learned well. So great was his faith that he took on the religious life of a monk. Though he lived in poverty, Brendan was joyful. He loved neither riches, nor comforts. He lived a life of penance, and what little he had, he generously shared with the poor. When the good Bishop Erc ordained him a priest, Brendan took on a most heroic task: he left his homeland and friends and traveled to foreign lands to spread the Gospel of Jesus Christ.

Statue of St. Brendan

Brendan lived in fifth-century Ireland. It was a dangerous time. Small kings and chieftains continually waged wars against each other. Bandits infested the roads and highways, and pirates terrorized those who sailed on the seas. Most of Europe was still not Christian, and pagan warriors had no respect for priests or monks or nuns. A small band of monks, traveling by land or water, could be enslaved or even killed. Nature, too, posed many threats. Small boats could be wrecked in rough seas; violent weather and wild beasts endangered those who traveled over land. Brendan was not daunted by such dangers. Instead, he listened to the promise of Our Lord: "Every one that hath forsaken father or mother or sister or lands for my sake shall receive a hundredfold in the present and shall possess everlasting life."

coracle: a small boat used by Irish fishermen, made of hides stretched over a wooden frame

Emboldened by this promise, Brendan built himself a boat. This boat was unlike any most of us are used to seeing. It was, of course, not built of steel, nor even of wood planks. It was a **coracle,** a small vessel used by Irish fishermen. It looked rather like a bowl or an upside-down umbrella. To build it, Brendan constructed a wood frame, over which he stretched tanned oxen hides. To keep the water from soaking through the hides, he smeared them with animal fat.

This old illustration shows a sea monster attacking a ship.

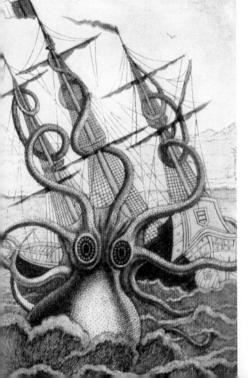

Taking with him a handful of monks, Brendan set sail for the "Land of Promise of the Saints." This land, which lay westward across the ocean, was said to be most beautiful. There, tall, stately trees rose majestically toward heaven, and rich grasses grew by streams of clear, sweet water. To reach this Land of Promise, though, Brendan and his monks had to pass through many dangers and many strange lands. Sometimes they came across other monks on distant sea islands, for Irish monks had long been sailing west to found new monasteries. Eventually, though, Brendan and his monks would arrive in lands that had never before seen European men.

Did Brendan Really Land in America?

Many people have long doubted the story of St. Brendan's voyage. Not only have they questioned the many fabulous occurrences recorded about the voyage, but they could not believe that a coracle could sail across the stormy Atlantic Ocean. However, in 1976, a British navigation scholar named Tim Severin proved that a coracle could sail from Ireland to North America by making the journey himself! He also showed that St. Brendan's giant crystals, the island of birds, and even the friendly whales could have a basis in everyday facts.

In a coracle built according to the description of Brendan's boat, Severin set sail from Ireland. The coracle followed the ocean currents that flowed northward and westward along the coast of Scotland. North of Scotland, Severin reached the Faroe Islands, where, on one island, he saw hundreds of sea birds. Could this have been the "Paradise of Birds"? Severin also noted that the word *Faroe* means "island of sheep." The ocean current took Severin farther westward in a great half-circle, until he reached Iceland. There, like Brendan, he spent the winter. Iceland is known for its volcanoes.

Could this have been the origin of the "flaming, foul smelling rocks" cast by the inhabitants of an island Brendan passed on his voyage? Severin also noted that the whales he found at sea were quite friendly. They would sometimes swim around the coracle, even swim under the boat and gently bump it from below.

Severin landed on Newfoundland in North America on June 26, 1977. Following the ocean currents, the journey had taken Severin only a few months. To return to Ireland, though, would take far longer, because the coracle would have to go against the currents. St. Brendan might possibly have followed the current as far south as Virginia; on his return to Ireland he would then have had to fight the currents for an even longer distance. This could explain why the legends say St. Brendan's voyage lasted seven years.

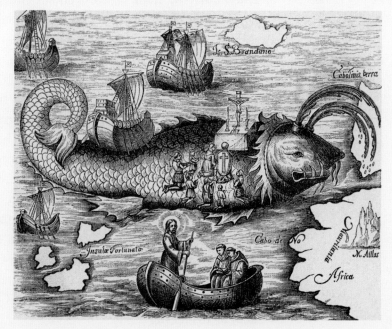

Many are the wonders told of Brendan's voyage. Not far north of the northern tip of Scotland, the monks came to a group of islands. Brendan called these islands the Paradise of Birds, because he found so many white seabirds there. The largest of the islands held such a great a number of sheep that the monks called it the Island of Sheep. Sailing farther north and west, the monks, so says the legend, "passed by crystals that rose up to the sky." Soon they reached an island whose inhabitants pelted them "with flaming, foul smelling rocks."

While at sea, on the feast of St. Paul the Apostle (June 30), Brendan's companions grew fearful; Brendan was chanting the prayers for that feast so loudly, they said, that he would wake the dangerous sea monsters. Brendan laughed at their fears. "Where is your faith?" he asked his companions. "Fear nothing but Our Lord, and love him with fear." Brendan then said Mass with great reverence. While he sang the Mass prayers, lo! sea monsters rose from the depths, and began playing merrily around the boat. Thus they frolicked until nightfall, when Brendan ended the prayers for the feast. The monsters then sank again into the salty depths of the sea.

Yet another story is told of Brendan's voyage. As Easter was approaching, his monks told Brendan that he should find land where they might celebrate the holy feast. "Brothers," said Brendan, "Our Lord can give us land anywhere he wishes." On Easter day, God, indeed, gave the brothers land: a great white sea monster rose from the depths and made an island of his back. There the brothers celebrated Easter for one day and two nights. Finally, Brendan and his monks reached the Land of Promise, where they remained for a time and then returned to Ireland.

Brendan's voyage to and from the Land of Promise lasted seven years. It is said that the holy man lost no one from his crew, nor did any suffer from hunger or thirst during the long voyage. Returning to Ireland, Brendan founded more monasteries and built churches. He died at the monastery he founded at Clonfert on May 16, the day kept as his feast.

Viking Explorers Discover a New World

Eric the Red

Winter was bitterly cold in Greenland. In the Viking farmsteads that dotted the coast of this Arctic wilderness, families gathered for warmth around great fires built in the middle of their long houses. Viking houses were unlike our own. The entire family lived in one long hall, or main room. They had no bedrooms, but slept on an earthen ledge along the walls; some slept in small boxes like closets. On a large stone called the "hearth," the great fire burned; its smoke rose upward and escaped through a round hole cut in the roof. Sometimes, when the wind blew through the hole, smoke filled the long house, stinging the eyes of those who lived there. The only light came from the fire, and from torches placed along walls. The flickering flames cast a dim, moving light over the faces and forms of the family members.

Like other families, Eric the Red (so called because of his fiery red hair), his wife, Thjodhild (pronounced THYOHD·hild), and their children spent the evenings before going to sleep listening to stories. These stories, called **sagas,** told of great Viking heroes and their deeds, of Viking families and their adventures. Sometimes, they listened to stories told by travelers who had crossed to **Greenland** over the cold seas that separated Greenland from other Viking lands in Norway, Scotland, and Iceland. The Vikings were great sailors; in long, curved boats with figures of dragons' heads on their prows, they crossed many oceans and sailed up many great rivers. Vikings had settled such faraway lands as Russia and northern France, and had even crossed into the Mediterranean Sea. The Vikings were pagans who conquered and terrorized Christian settlements

sagas: the heroic tales told by the Vikings

Greenland: an icy island discovered by Eric the Red and settled by Vikings; it lies between Iceland and Canada.

throughout Europe. Some Vikings went into battle without armor, even without shirts! These warriors were called "berserkers," which meant "bare-chested ones."

On one such winter night, Eric the Red and his family perhaps heard the story told by Bjarni Herjolfsson (BYAR•nee HAIR•yohlfs•son), or Bjarni, the son of Herjolf. Bjarni told how his ship had been blown off course on a journey from Iceland to Greenland. Pushed across the waves far to the west, Bjarni had seen a new land unknown to the Vikings. The tale of this new land awakened Eric's interest; here was a country to be discovered and, perhaps, settled.

Eric the Red had, himself, been a discoverer. Eric's father had fled from Norway to Iceland after he had killed a man. Raised in Iceland, Eric became a great seafarer and had a farm in the western part of Iceland, at Breydafjord (BRY•dah•fyohrd). According to a saga written about him, Eric lent two carved poles to a friend. When the friend neglected to return the poles, Eric went to his house and took them. This insulted his friend, and he sent two of his sons to attack Eric. Eric fought with the two young men and killed them; for this the court of Iceland, called the *Thing*, declared Eric an "outlaw," and told him to leave Iceland for three years. If Eric remained in Iceland, any of the young men's relatives had the right to kill him.

Eric left Iceland and set sail for the north and west. There he discovered the cold shores of a land before unknown to the Vikings. For three years he sailed along the eastern and western coasts of this

A Viking battle

land and found the dwellings of an unknown people. These people, he discovered, paddled the sea waters in boats made from stretching animal skins over wooden frames and used tools made from stones. When the three years of his exile were over, Eric returned to Iceland and told the people there of this new land. Though it was colder and more barren than Iceland, Eric called the new land "Greenland" in order to attract settlers.

Many Icelanders decided they would move to Greenland. Around the year 985 or 986, about 25 ships filled with colonists left Iceland for Greenland. Only about 14 ships survived the ocean crossing. The survivors settled along the eastern and western coasts of Greenland, where they established farms and raised grain, cattle, hogs, and sheep. They also lived by hunting large, wild animals, such as bear and caribou. Eric the Red moved his family to Greenland and set up his farmstead on the eastern coast.

So it was that Bjarni Herjolfsson's story about a new land farther west than Greenland piqued Eric's interest. He could not go to sea himself, so he decided to send his son, Leif (LIFE). Leif Ericsson was known far and wide as a masterful seaman.

9/15

Leif the Lucky

A saga says that Leif Ericsson was "a big, strapping fellow, handsome to look at, thoughtful and temperate in all things, as well as highly respected." No one knows where he was born, but Leif grew up on his father's farm in Greenland. There he learned the art of sailing from his father, from whom he also inherited the desire to find new lands.

While still a young man, Leif set out on the long voyage to Norway. Such a voyage was common to young Viking men, who were ambitious to serve great kings and lords. Leif arrived at the court of Norway's king, Olaf Tryggvason (Trig•VAH•son). King Olaf, the first Norse king to become a Christian, was working to convert his people to the Christian faith. Spending the winter of the year

999–1000 at King Olaf's court, Leif himself became a Christian. When Olaf asked him to return to Greenland to convert the Vikings there to the Faith, Leif joyfully agreed. In the spring, Leif set sail for home, accompanied by a priest. Olaf sent two other priests to Iceland, to preach the Gospel there.

Leif and the priest were successful in bringing many Greenlanders into the Church. Thjodhild, Leif's mother, gladly accepted the Faith, though his father, Eric, clung to the old Norse religion that worshipped the one-eyed god, Odin, and the god Thor, who with his giant hammer rocked the skies with thunder. Thjodhild built a small church some distance from their farmstead where she and other Christians could come to worship Christ and receive the sacraments.

Thus, perhaps to found a Christian settlement, Leif set sail to see if he could find Bjarni Herjolfsson's land in the west. The first land he reached was not very encouraging. It was flat and stony, and Leif named it "Flat-Stone Land." This land was probably Baffin Island. Sailing southward, Leif came upon a level country, densely covered with forests. This country, which was probably part of Labrador, he named "Forest Land." From Forest Land, Leif continued southward until he came to a land of rich grasses, towering trees, and large, rushing rivers filled with salmon. Because so many grape vines grew in this region, Leif

Leif Ericsson off the coast of Vinland

named it **Vinland,** or "Wine Land." He and his men built several stone houses near the seashore and then returned home.

It is thought that Vinland is on the northern tip of Newfoundland. There, hundreds of years later, archaeologists discovered the ruins of stone houses built by Vikings. The sagas, though, seem to say that Leif went even farther south and landed on what is today Prince Edward Island. The news of this new land, of its fertile soil and abundant timber and water, was welcome to the people of frozen, barren Greenland. It was not long before a small group of adventurers formed to try their hand at settling the new country.

Vikings Settle Vinland

Thorfinn Karlsefni (THOR•fin•Karl•SEF•nee) was the first Viking to attempt to settle Vinland. Receiving Leif's permission to use the houses he had constructed in Vinland, Thorfinn set sail. With him went 160 men and 5 women. The adventurers clearly wanted to form a permanent settlement because they brought livestock with them.

Thorfinn followed the same route as Eric, landing first at Flat-Stone Land, then at Forest Land. Farther south he came upon a large bay, which could have been the Bay of Fundy. Sailing even farther south, the Vikings discovered a large river with an island at its mouth. There they built their settlement.

Thorfinn and the settlers discovered that this land was already inhabited by people, whom they named **Skraelings** (SKRAY•leengs). This was the same name the Vikings gave to the native inhabitants they had found in Greenland (Inuits and Eskimos). Thorfinn tried to be friendly with these people and began trading with them. At

Vinland: the place of Viking settlements on Newfoundland in Canada, or on Prince Edward Island, farther south

Skraelings: the Viking name for the natives of Vinland and of Greenland

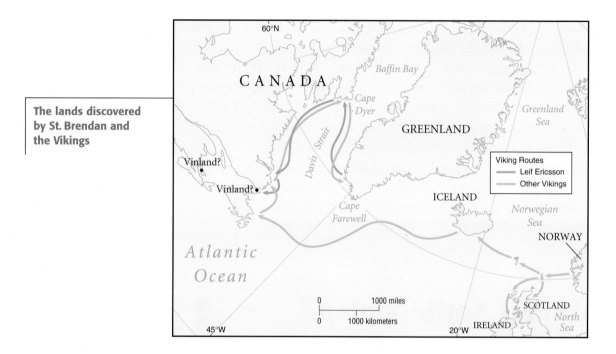

The lands discovered
by St. Brendan and
the Vikings

first the Skraelings and the Vikings lived at peace with one another, and Thorfinn baptized two Skraeling boys from Forest Land. The Vikings settled down to raise their cattle and to trade with the natives. During the first autumn, Thorfinn's wife, Gudrid, gave birth to a son, whom they named Snorri. He was the first European born in North America.

But the Vikings and the Skraelings did not long remain at peace. War broke out between them, and though the Vikings were brave, stout fighters, the Skraelings far outnumbered them. Thorfinn realized that if he stayed in Vinland he would always be at war, and so after about three years he and his people decided to return to Greenland.

During the next twenty years or so, the Vikings made three more attempts to settle Vinland. All were failures. In 1121, a bishop from Greenland named Eirik Gnupsson (EYE•rik GNOOP•son) set sail to bring the Gospel to Vinland. Nothing is known of his voyage, nor do we know if he ever returned to his people.

White Indians

It is said that about 50 years after Bishop Eirik Gnupsson set sail for Vinland, another brave seafarer crossed the Atlantic to find a new world.

There was a king in Wales named Owain Gwynedd (GWIN •ed), who had 17 sons and two daughters. When King Owain died in 1170, his sons could not agree which one of them should be king. War broke out among the brothers. So sad and miserable a place did Wales become that one of King Owain's sons, named Madoc, decided he would set sail across the ocean to find a new home. This home, he hoped, would be free of all war.

According to tales told many years after the voyage, Madoc crossed the Atlantic Ocean into what is now the Gulf of Mexico. Sailing along the coast of present-day Florida and Alabama, Madoc found a great bay. So warm was the air, and so green and fair were the lands around the bay that Madoc decided he had found the land he had been searching for. He returned to Wales and told of the new land across the sea. Many who were as tired of war as Madoc decided to brave the great ocean with him. After bringing the first group of Welsh settlers to his new land, Madoc returned to Wales for more settlers. Again Madoc crossed the ocean, never again to return to Wales.

Mandan Indian chief

This is all that European writers tell of Madoc and his Welsh settlers. What happened to them? Were they killed by Indians? Did they eventually return to Wales? No one knows. Many historians doubt that Madoc's voyage to the new world ever happened. It is *just legend,* they say. Yet, if you were to follow the Alabama River, which flows into Mobile Bay in Alabama, you would find along its banks the ruins of an old fortress that some say the Indians could not have built. In fact, the fortress looks very much like castles found in Wales. Another such fortress can be found at Fort Mountain in Georgia, and a third (with a moat around it) near Manchester, Tennessee. Some people claim to have found Welsh helmets and armor, as well as Roman coins, in Kentucky and Ohio. Were these things left by Madoc's people?

In a letter he wrote in 1810, John Sevier, then governor of Tennessee, perhaps sheds more light on the fate of Madoc and the Welsh. Governor Sevier wrote that, in 1782, a Cherokee Indian chief named Oconostota told him that "white people" had built the fortresses in Alabama, Georgia, and Tennessee. Asked what these white people were called, Oconostota said his grandfather and father had called them "Welsh."

Mandan Indian boats

What had happened to these "Welsh"? Oconostota told Governor Sevier that Indian enemies had forced the Welsh to abandon their first fortress at Lookout Mountain in Tennessee. Going up the Coosa River, the Welsh next settled in Georgia, building a fortress atop the 3,000-foot Fort Mountain. Once again the Indians forced them to move on, and the Welsh stayed for a time in the area of Chattanooga, Tennessee.

For many years, said Oconostota, his people, the Cherokee, fought with the Welsh. Finally, the Welsh made peace with the Cherokee and agreed to leave the Duck River area. According to the chief, the Welsh followed the Tennessee River to the Ohio, and floated down the Ohio to the Mississippi. When they reached the Missouri River, which flows into the Mississippi, Oconostota said the Welsh followed that muddy water into the west. What happened to them after that? "They are no more white people," said the chief. "They are now all become Indians, and look like other red people of the country."

In the 1700s and into the early 1800s, French, English, and American explorers told of an Indian tribe called the **Mandans,** many of whom looked more like Europeans than Indians. The Mandan language, some said, was similar to Welsh; at least many of its words were very close to Welsh words. The Mandans' boats, too, were similar to Welsh boats. They looked like teacups without handles! And Mandan villages had streets and squares, much like European vil-

Mandans: members of a Dakota Indian tribe, said to have resembled Europeans in their looks, language, and ways

lages. Are these stories true? Were the Mandans descended from Madoc's Welsh? Unfortunately, we shall never know for sure, because in the early 1800s, a disease called smallpox killed off most of the Mandan tribe.

Admiral of the Ocean Sea

Westward, across the Sea

If Madoc sailed to America, few remembered his voyage. The story of Leif Ericsson and Vinland was little known outside Iceland and Scandinavia. All of Europe, though, knew the legend of St. Brendan, and none knew it better than the Portuguese. In the early 1400s, Prince Henry the Navigator, the son of the king of Portugal, had sent ships westward into the Atlantic Ocean to discover where "St. Brendan's Isles" lay. Though on these voyages the Portuguese discovered the Azores and the Cape Verde Islands, they were not satisfied. St. Brendan's Isles, they believed, lay farther west.

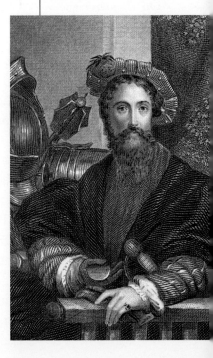

Christopher Columbus

One young man named Christopher Columbus heard all the stories about St. Brendan's Isles and believed them. A seafarer had told Columbus about three islands he had sighted far out in the Atlantic Ocean. These surely must be St. Brendan's Isles, Columbus thought. Columbus was very interested in news of islands that lay westward across the sea, for he had a great dream. He wanted to prove that he could reach the rich lands of India and China by sailing directly west across the sea.

Columbus was not from Portugal, but from the seafaring city of Genoa in Italy. Columbus went to sea when he was a young man and sailed throughout the Mediterranean. In 1476, he was shipwrecked off the coast of Portugal. After being rescued, he decided to remain in that country. In those days, Portugal was the best place for a sailor to live. Aboard Portuguese ships, Columbus sailed to the Canary Islands, the Azores, and the Cape

The port of Lisbon in Portugal

Christopher: name that means "bearer of Christ"

Verde Islands, and even voyaged as far north as England and Iceland. As a Portuguese sailor, Columbus learned how to sail on the rough and tempest-tossed Atlantic.

Doubtless, after so many voyages, Columbus thought he was well prepared to take on the quest of sailing westward across the "Ocean Sea" (as men then called the Atlantic) to the far-off "Indies." Columbus knew that great riches were in store for anyone who found such a route, for the Indies held spices, silks, and perhaps even gold!

Yet Columbus was not thinking just of riches in making his plan. A devout Catholic, Columbus believed God had chosen him to bring the Gospel of Christ to unbelievers overseas. After all, his name was **Christopher,** which means "bearer of Christ." He also hoped that riches obtained from the Indies could be used to fund a crusade to retake Jerusalem from the Muslims.

Columbus first offered his plan to King John II of Portugal. Would his majesty be interested in funding such an expedition? The king was indeed interested, but said no. For three years Columbus hoped the king would change his mind, but he never did. In 1488, a Portuguese captain named Bartolomeu Dias found a route to the Indies. He did so not by sailing west, as Columbus proposed, but by sailing south. Dias sailed along the coast of Africa until he came to the tip of Africa, called the Cape of Good Hope. With good hope, Dias then sailed eastward across the Indian Ocean, and so reached India.

Unable to interest the king of Portugal in his quest, Columbus turned to Spain. He laid out his plan to Queen Isabella, who said she would have a group of scholars study it. But finding a route to the Indies was the least of Isabella's concerns. She and her husband, King Ferdinand, were busy fighting a war with Granada, a Muslim kingdom that controlled the southern tip of Spain. For the next several years, the "Catholic Monarchs" (as Ferdinand and Isabella were called) said nothing to Columbus about his plan. Then, in 1491, after five years of waiting, Columbus received word that Isabella's scholars had rejected his plan!

Queen Isabella and King Ferdinand of Spain

If it had not been for an old friend, a Franciscan priest named Father Juan Perez (HWAHN•PAIR•ez), Columbus would have left Spain then and there. Father Juan asked Isabella to meet again with Columbus, and the queen agreed. Columbus once again laid out his plan to Isabella, and the queen again asked her scholars what they thought of it. On January 2, 1492, Columbus heard from the Catholic Monarchs. They again refused to fund his expedition!

After this second rejection, Columbus packed his bags, saddled his mule, and set off for the city of Cordova. From there he would set off for France. Perhaps the French king would take an interest in his plan, he thought. He had traveled only about four miles when he was met by a messenger from the queen. Isabella, he learned, had changed her mind; she and Ferdinand would fund Columbus's expedition to the Indies.

Voyage into Unknown Waters

It took some courage for sailors to set off westward across the Ocean Sea. In those days, few sailors had ventured far out to sea, but had always kept close to the coast. Sailors did not fear sailing off the end of the world, for most people knew the Earth was round like a ball. They did fear that they might sail so far out to sea that the winds that blew them west would not blow them back home again. And who knew how far the Indies really were? What if they sailed and sailed, and found no land? This, indeed, was a frightening thought! They might end up stranded in the middle of the ocean, where they would run out of food and fresh water, and so would die a slow and painful death.

Santa Maria: Spanish for "Saint Mary." Columbus's flagship was named for the Mother of God.

Columbus and his crew set sail from Spain on August 3, 1492, in three small ships. Columbus's "flagship," the ***Santa Maria*** (SAN•tah Mah•REE•ah), was a small vessel; the other two ships, the *Niña* (NEE•nyah) and the *Pinta* (PEEN•tah), were even smaller. In these small craft the sailors were to brave the great and violent Atlantic Ocean.

The vast Ocean Sea was a wondrous place. Needless to say, the sailors kept a weather eye out for the sea monsters, about which many stories had been told. Whether they saw any, nobody can say. In late September, the three small ships moved through a sea covered with a carpet of seaweed. Then, for several days, no wind blew. The sea below them was like glass. Only the swimming sailors caused ripples to disturb the water.

Every day the men on Columbus's ships would greet the morning with prayer. At daybreak, a sailor would sing this song to waken his mates:

Replicas of Columbus's three sailing ships: the *Niña,* the *Pinta,* and the *Santa Maria*

Bendita sea la luz	Blessed be the light
y la Santa Veracruz	And the Holy Cross;
y el Señor de la Verdad	And the Lord of Truth
y la Santa Trinidad;	And the Holy Trinity;
bendita sea el alma,	blessed be the soul,
y el Señor que nos la manda.	and the Lord who guides it.
Bendito sea el día	Blessed be the day
y el Señor que nos lo envía.	And the Lord who sends it to us.

But the evening song was reserved for Blessed Mary Virgin. It was the ancient and beautiful "Salve Regina."

Salve Regina,	Hail Holy Queen,
Mater Misericordiae,	Mother of Mercy,
vita, dulcedo, et spes	Hail, our life, our sweetness, and
nostra, salve.	our hope.
Ad te clamamus, exsules	To thee do we cry, poor banished
filii Evae.	children of Eve.
Ad te suspiramus,	To thee do we send up our sighs,
gementes et flentes	mourning and weeping
in hac lacrimarum valle.	in this valley of tears.
Eia ergo, advocata nostra,	Turn then, most gracious advocate,
illos tuos misericordes oculos	thine eyes of mercy
ad nos converte.	toward us.
Et Jesum, benedictum	And after this our exile,
fructum ventris tui,	show unto us the blessed
nobis post hoc exsilium ostende.	fruit of thy womb, Jesus.
O clemens, O pia, O dulcis	O clement, O loving, O sweet
Virgo Maria.	Virgin Mary.

By the end of September, Columbus's sailors were getting restless and fearful. They had sailed far into the west, but saw no land. What if the Indies were farther away than Columbus thought? What if the ships became stranded in the middle of the sea and could not return to Spain? On September 25 the captain of the *Pinta* cried out that he saw land; but neither the next day, nor the next, did any land appear. Five days passed, and still no land. On October 10 the crew threatened to mutiny, and Columbus had to promise that if they discovered no land in three days, they would return to Spain.

One day passed, and then another. No land appeared. But on the third day, long before sunrise, Columbus heard the cry that he had so long hoped for. "Land! Land!" cried the sailor on watch. Dawn came; then the sun rose. In the full light of day, across the blue-green water, the sailors could see an island! They had reached land, indeed! That day, October 12, 1492, Columbus and his men rejoiced to feel solid earth beneath their feet.

Columbus ordered the planting of the royal standard on the island that he named **San Salvador** ("Holy Savior"). With the flag of Spain in one hand, and a sword in the other, Columbus knelt and claimed the land for the Church and for the Catholic monarchs, Isabella and Ferdinand.

Columbus claims San Salvador for the Church and Spain.

San Salvador: Spanish for the "Holy Savior," Our Lord Jesus Christ

In Search of Japan and China

Columbus had no idea that he had reached a new world—or that before him lay two great continents that were in no way part of Asia. Of course, Europeans had heard, at least, of the voyage of St. Brendan. But some thought the saint had found only some islands in the sea, while others (like Columbus) thought he had landed in Asia. Columbus believed that San Salvador must be some small island off the coast of that great continent. He was convinced that if he sailed only a little farther west, he would, perhaps, discover the fabled land of Japan. Once he found Japan, discovering the route to China would be simple.

Columbus had read about Japan and China in the writings of another Italian explorer named Marco Polo. About two hundred years before Columbus's voyage, Marco Polo had traveled east across Asia, into China, and over the sea to Japan. Marvelous were the tales Polo told about these lands! Both China and Japan were ancient, civilized societies. Besides the spices and rich silks one could find in those lands, there was gold! Marco Polo wrote that houses in Japan had roofs of gold.

Columbus discovered that the native people on the island of San Salvador were nothing like the highly civilized Chinese and Japanese. The people of San Salvador (called the *Taino* TYE•noh) lived in houses built of sticks and leaves. They wore few clothes, only a cloth around their loins. The Taino made pottery and were farmers, growing corn, yams, and other root crops.

Two days after landing at San Salvador, the *Niña, Pinta,* and *Santa Maria* set sail in search of Japan. After sailing amid many small islands, Columbus and his men came upon the coastline of what was clearly either a large island or part of the coast of Asia. Columbus thought this might be Japan; but sailing up and down the coastline, he discovered no great cities, no gold. In early December, Columbus left this land behind (it was the island of Cuba) and sailed east. He found another large island and, more importantly, the first signs of gold.

The Taino natives on this island (today called Hispaniola) wore gold ornaments. Where did they find this gold, Columbus asked them? Guacanagri (Gwah•cah•nah•GREE), one of the Taino chieftains, told him that gold could be found on the island, in a place called Cibao (see•BAH•oh). Rejoicing at this news, Columbus planned to set sail for Spain to tell Isabella and Ferdinand of his discovery.

But before Columbus could set sail, the *Santa Maria* hit a reef and sank. With the help of the friendly Taino, Columbus and his men built a fortress for *Santa Maria*'s crew on the coast of Hispaniola. Since it was Christmastime, Columbus named this fort "Navidad" (Nativity).

On January 16, 1493, Columbus set sail for Spain. The news he brought would turn the world upside down.

Settlement of the "Indies"

King Ferdinand and Queen Isabella honored Columbus as a hero after he returned to Spain. Soon they were planning another voyage for him. This time, instead of 3 ships, they would give him 17. The Catholic Monarchs commanded Columbus to establish a trading settlement and to return with gold; but his more important task, they said, was to bring the Gospel of Christ to the natives overseas.

Columbus returned to the Indies along a different route. When he reached Hispaniola, he discovered that Navidad had been destroyed

King Ferdinand and Queen Isabella send Columbus to America.

Sharing the New World

Columbus had not been home long before news of his discoveries traveled over all Europe. Since everybody thought Columbus had found a route to China, Japan, and India, they called the new lands the "Indies," and the people who lived there, "Indians." The king of Portugal heard about the voyage, and probably was not happy with himself for not having given Columbus ships when he had asked for them. To make sure no war broke out between Spain and Portugal over the newly discovered lands, Pope Alexander VI, on a map, divided the Atlantic with a line. All lands discovered east of that line should belong to Portugal, said the Pope; all lands west of the line should belong to Spain. The Pope told both kingdoms that their first duty was to bring the Catholic Faith to the "Indians."

by the Taino. The Indians had destroyed the settlement because the Spaniards there had mistreated them. Columbus set up another settlement, calling it Isabela. Columbus had trouble with the settlers at Isabela; because they were so interested in finding gold, they spent no time in building homes, raising cattle, and farming.

On his second voyage Columbus again failed to find any signs of China or Japan. What's more, he returned to Spain in 1496 without much gold.

In 1498, Columbus returned to the Indies and this time discovered a great continent. Though he thought it was part of Asia, it was really South America. So beautiful to Columbus was the coastline of this continent that he thought he had found the Garden of Eden! This voyage, though, brought Columbus great sorrow. Blamed for the bad condition of the settlement on Hispaniola, Columbus was chained like a prisoner and shipped back to Spain.

Columbus was not long in Spain before Queen Isabella released him. In 1502 she sent him again to the Indies. On this voyage, Columbus sailed along the coast of Central America, looking for a sea passage to India. Again he failed. He returned to Spain in 1504, where he spent the last two years of his life. Columbus died on May 20, 1506, still believing that the lands he had discovered were a part of Asia.

Other Spanish Explorers

Spain sent other explorers to the Indies besides Columbus. In 1499, one group of explorers, which included an Italian named Amerigo Vespucci (Ah•MAIR•ee•goh Ves•POO•chee), explored the northern coast of South America. There they found the mouth of a mighty river, which they named the Amazon. They also explored the coast of Florida and the eastern coast of North America. Because of a book that told of Amerigo Vespucci's voyages to the Indies, people in Europe came to call all the new lands **America.**

America: the name the Europeans gave the New World after reading about Amerigo Vespucci's voyages

One Spaniard became an explorer because he fell in love. Juan Ponce de León (Hwan PON•say day lay•OHN) was an older man who loved a beautiful young girl named Beatriz. Desiring to be young again so Beatriz would love him, Ponce de León went in search of the fountain of youth which, he heard, was on an island called Bimini. He landed on Bimini on Easter Sunday in 1513, and named it Florida, since, in Spain, Easter Sunday was called *Pascua Florida* ("Flowery Sunday"). He explored the eastern coast of this island (which is really a peninsula), but, alas, found no fountain of youth. Several years later, Ponce de León tried to found a settlement in Florida, but the Indians drove him off. Instead of finding youth in Florida, Ponce de León found death. He died from a wound he received in a battle with the Florida Indians.

In 1513, the Spanish captain Vasco Núñez de Balboa (VAHS•coh NU•nyez day Bal•BOH•ah) and his men climbed a high peak in Darien (now known as Panama) and to the west saw a new ocean. This ocean, which Balboa called the "South Sea" (we call it the Pacific), clearly separated the "Indies" from Asia. Of course, Balboa could not see Asia across the South Sea, for that

Amerigo Vespucci

Balboa discovers the Pacific.

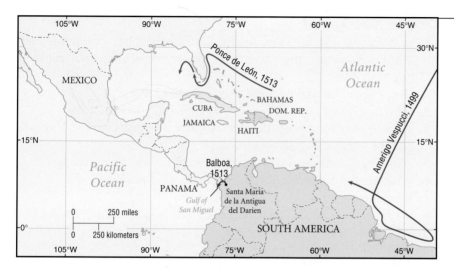

105°W   90°W   75°W   60°W   45°W

30°N

Ponce de León, 1513

Atlantic Ocean

MEXICO

BAHAMAS
CUBA   DOM. REP.
JAMAICA
HAITI

15°N   15°N

Pacific Ocean

Balboa, 1513

Amerigo Vespucci 1499

PANAMA   Santa María de la Antigua del Darien
Gulf of San Miguel

0   250 miles
0   250 kilometers

SOUTH AMERICA

0°

105°W   90°W   75°W   60°W   45°W

Routes of Spanish explorers in the Americas: Amerigo Vespucci (1499), Ponce de León (1513), and Vasco Balboa (1513).

continent lay thousands of miles to the west. Balboa's discovery showed that Columbus had not discovered a new route to the rich lands of China, Japan, and India, but something far more important. Columbus had discovered a New World.

Chapter 1 Review

9/18

Summary

- Legends and ruins tell us of early explorations of America. St. Brendan of Ireland's fabled voyage was successfully reenacted in recent years. Stories tell us of the voyages and settlements of Leif Ericsson of Greenland and Madoc of Wales, and stone ruins in Newfoundland and the American South match these legends.
- In 1492, Christopher Columbus sailed under the banner of Spain, for Ferdinand and Isabella. While searching for the Asian Indies, he discovered the Americas, but died thinking he had wandered near Asia and had failed to find the treasure of Japan, China, and the Indies.
- Later explorers saw awesome sights and learned that America was its own continent. Balboa discovered the Pacific Ocean, and Ponce de León ventured into Florida. These explorers soon learned that while the treasures of Asia were far, far away, they had found something more important—land for their home countries to settle and colonize!

Chapter Checkpoint

1. St. Brendan, Leif Ericsson, Madoc, and Christopher Columbus each sailed west across the Ocean Sea. Name something each explorer hoped to find.
2. How did our continent come to be named America?
3. Who discovered the South Sea (now called the Pacific Ocean)?
4. What evidence supports the stories about Brendan's voyage, Vinland, and the Welsh colonists?
5. Which king and queen sponsored Christopher Columbus's voyage?
6. What are the *Santa Maria*, the *Niña*, and the *Pinta*?
7. What happened on October 12, 1492?
8. What year was South America discovered? Which explorer found it?
9. What did Ponce de León discover on Easter Sunday, 1513? What does the name of that land mean?
10. Were explorers afraid they would fall off the Earth if they sailed across the Ocean Sea?

Chapter Activities

1. Think about why St. Brendan sailed west. Legends told of a "Land of Promise of the Saints," which lay westward across the ocean. Where do you think these legends came from? Do people still think of America as a Land of Promise?
2. Christopher Columbus died thinking he was a failure, because he had not found Japan and China. In fact, he has been remembered ever since for discovering America. What are some places and things that have been named after him?

The American Larder

Columbus took back maize (the Indian word for corn) to the Europeans. Until his voyage, maize had never been tasted in Europe. On November 5, 1492, Columbus wrote in his journal: "There was a great deal of tilled land sowed with a sort of beans and a sort of grain they call 'Mahiz,' which tasted good baked or dried, and made into flour."

9/21

Chapter 2 # Conquest of the New World

Hernán Cortés

To Mexico!

Hernán Cortés

Stories told in Spain of the New World drew many men across the Ocean Sea. Some of these men shared the dream of Queen Isabella and journeyed over the many dangerous ocean miles to teach the Indians about Jesus Christ and the Catholic Faith. Many of these men were missionary priests and brothers. Other men, though, came for the gold that could be found in the lands they called the Indies. These wealth-seeking adventurers were not always bad men (though many of them were), but they were not so concerned about what was good for the Indians. As they went about conquering the islands in what is now called the Caribbean, they enslaved the Indians living there, forcing them to work in gold mines the adventurers established. Because they had come to the New World to conquer it for Spain, these

An artist's view of Tenochtitlán, capital of the Aztec Empire

conquistadors: Spanish adventurers who wanted to conquer the New World for Spain

Hernán Cortés: the conquistador who defeated the Aztecs and ruled New Spain

adventurers were called **conquistadors** (con•KEES•tah•dohrs). Because of the bad treatment they received from the conquistadors, many Indians died.

One of these conquistadors was **Hernán Cortés** (air•NAHN cor•TEZ). No one expected much of Cortés because he had been a wild young man. After coming to the Indies, Cortés joined in the conquest of the island of Cuba. In return, the governor of Cuba, Diego Velasquez (dee•AY•goh vel•AHS•kez), gave Cortés land on the island, along with a gold mine and Indian slaves. Cortés soon became the mayor of Santiago, a Spanish town in Cuba. It looked as if the young adventurer would settle down to become a wealthy Spanish gentleman.

But such a quiet life could not satisfy Cortés. When he heard that a Spanish captain had discovered lands to the west of Cuba, Cortés asked Governor Velázquez for ships and men. Cortés told Velázquez that he wanted to explore these lands and conquer them for the king of Spain. Velázquez allowed Cortés to have 11 ships and more than 600 soldiers and sailors. But Velázquez did not like Cortés. Before Cortés set sail, the governor sent orders to remove Cortés as commander of the expedition. Cortés heard about Velázquez 's plans and set sail before he officially received the governor's orders. Cortés's bold act made the governor very angry.

Though Cortés was eager to win honor for himself and to find gold in the lands to which he sailed, he saw himself as a kind of missionary to the Indians. With him went two Dominican missionaries, whose task it would be to bring the Catholic Faith to the Indian people and to baptize them in the name of the Holy Trinity. Cortés saw himself not only as a conqueror for Spain, but for the Kingdom of Christ as well.

When Cortés and the fleet landed on the coast of what is now Mexico in February 1518, they found that the Indians of this new land were different from the primitive Indians the Spaniards had encountered on the Caribbean islands. For one thing, the numerous Indians dwelt in cities surrounded by well-cultivated fields of maize, or Indian corn. Instead of living in houses made of sticks and grass, the Indians of Mexico had houses made of stone, as well as great buildings and pyramids of the same material. They were also warlike. On the coast of Tabasco, 40,000 Indians attacked Cortés and his men. The Indians would have destroyed the Spaniards had it not been for their guns and great warhorses. The Indians, of course, had no guns; and never having seen horses, they were terrified of these strange creatures.

Montezuma, king of the Aztecs

But more powerful than the Indians Cortés met on the coast were the Aztecs. To reach the land of the Aztecs, one had to cross the hot, swampy coastal plains, and climb high, snow-capped mountains. In a high valley in these mountains lay the great Aztec city, named Tenochtitlán (te•NOCH•tit•lan).

Montezuma: the
Aztec king

Aztecs: Indians who
lived in the moun-
tains of central
Mexico

Though the Aztec king, **Montezuma** (mon•te•ZOO•mah), ruled over many cities and tribes, Tenochtitlán was his capital. And a beautiful capital it was! Built in the middle of a lake on which lay floating islands bright with flowers, the city of Tenochtitlán was a storybook land of great temples and palaces. The **Aztecs** also made fine ornaments and had a written language in which they recorded their beautiful poetry.

But despite all this beauty and grandeur, the Aztecs had an ugly and cruel religion. Atop the great pyramids that were their temples, Aztec priests offered up human sacrifices to their gods. Plunging sharp obsidian knives into the chests of their victims, the priests cut out the beating hearts, which they then cast into the mouth of a terrible stone idol. When Aztec armies went to war with neighboring tribes, they captured enemy warriors alive in order to sacrifice them. Aztec priests sacrificed about 20,000 victims every year.

With such an enemy as the Aztecs awaiting them, it was no wonder that some of Cortés's men wanted to return to Cuba! Cortés, though, had decided to stay in Mexico and conquer Montezuma's mighty city. Hearing that some of his men were planning to mutiny, Cortés ordered the burning of all but one of the ships that had brought him and his men to

Montezuma welcomes Cortés at Tenochtitlán (Mexico City).

Mexico. The cowards, said Cortés, could return to Cuba on the remaining ship; he himself would stay even if only one man remained with him. Seeing their commander's bravery, most of the army, their courage rekindled, cried, "To Mexico! To Mexico!"

Cortés had strengthened their weak spirits; they would follow wherever he led.

Cortés orders the scuttling of his ships.

The Return of the White God

9/22

Fear had filled the heart of the Aztec emperor Montezuma when he heard of the coming of the Spaniards.

The Aztec legends told of a god called **Quetzalcoatl** (kweh•zahl•coh• AH•tul), who had once ruled over men and taught them how to farm and to govern themselves. Quetzalcoatl's rule, said the legends, was a period of great peace and happiness that ended when another god drove Quetzalcoatl from his kingdom, forcing him to flee eastward across the great Ocean Sea. The legends also said that Quetzalcoatl would one day return from over the sea, from the east, and that when he came, he would abolish human sacrifice and restore justice. Quetzalcoatl, it was said, looked very different from the dark-skinned, beardless Aztecs; according to legend, he had white skin, dark hair, and a flowing beard.

According to the reports Montezuma had received, the Spaniards had white skin and flowing beards and had sailed eastward across the ocean on great winged vessels. Could the leader of these strange men, this Cortés, be Quetzalcoatl? After all, according to reports Montezuma had received, Cortés released prisoners held for human sacrifice in every village he entered. If Cortés were the god, Montezuma knew that he had to treat him with great

Quetzalcoatl: the fair-skinned Aztec god who had ruled wisely and was supposed to return to restore justice

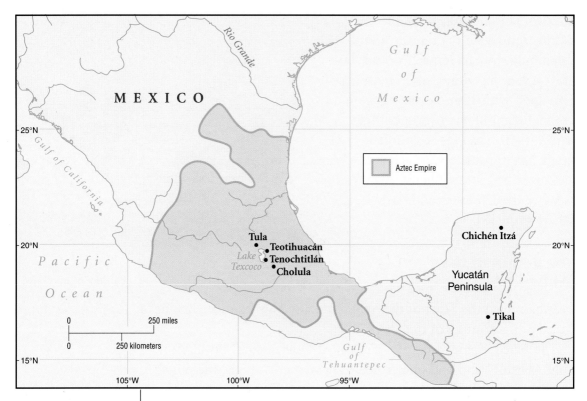

The territory of the Aztec people

respect. But if Cortés were not the god, he might be an invader against whom Montezuma would have to protect himself and his kingdom. The king was uncertain what he should do.

As Cortés and his small army came ever closer to Tenochtitlán, Montezuma sent messengers out to greet them. At one point, Montezuma changed his mind and ordered the Indians in the city of Cholula to destroy the Spaniards. Cortés discovered the plot, and beat the Indians back with great slaughter. Soon, Indian tribes— enemies of the Aztecs—joined Cortés. Montezuma decided that he had no choice but to welcome Cortés into the city of Tenochtitlán.

Montezuma was most gracious toward Cortés and his army, which consisted of about 400 Spaniards and about 6,500 Indian allies. With kingly hospitality, Montezuma allowed Cortés and his men to behold all the beauties of the city. Though the Spaniards admired the buildings and gardens of Tenochtitlán, the signs of human sacrifice in the temples appalled them. They thought the religion of the Aztecs was devil worship, indeed.

Though Montezuma was outwardly kind, Cortés feared him. Reports had reached Cortés from the coast (where he had left some of his men) that an Aztec chief had killed two Spaniards. Indian prisoners taken by the Spaniards laid the blame for the killings on Montezuma. Cortés, surrounded by his soldiers, appeared before Montezuma and asked why he had done this treacherous deed. Montezuma denied having anything to do with the killings. Cortés did not believe the king and ordered his men to take him prisoner. Cortés said he would hold Montezuma prisoner until the king punished the guilty chief.

Though he was Cortés's prisoner, Montezuma still acted as king of Tenochtitlán. As king, he swore allegiance to King Charles I of Spain. (Ferdinand and Isabella had died and their grandson, Charles, now ruled their kingdoms.) Montezuma also divided up all his treasure among the Spaniards and allowed Cortés to turn one of the Aztec temples into a Catholic church.

Ruins of an Aztec temple

But Cortés soon heard some disturbing news. Governor Velázquez had sent ships and soldiers to Mexico to capture Cortés and bring him to Cuba to stand trial for disobeying the governor's commands when he sailed to Mexico. Cortés wasted no time. Gathering 70 men, he left the city of Tenochtitlán and marched to the coast where Velázquez's army had landed. He left Pedro de Alvarado in command of the rest of the Spanish soldiers in the city.

With Cortés gone, Alvarado feared that the Aztecs would rise up and destroy his army. One night, unarmed Aztecs gathered to celebrate a religious festival. Fearing the Indians had gathered to attack the Spaniards, Alvarado ordered his men to attack the Indians, killing many of them. Seeing the slaughter of their people, the Aztecs attacked the Spanish quarters. Then Montezuma appeared on the walls of the Spanish quarters and asked his people to cease their attack. The Aztecs obeyed, but they would not allow the Spaniards to leave their quarters.

Meanwhile, Cortés had not only defeated Velázquez's men on the coast but persuaded them to join him! Cortés returned to the city of Tenochtitlán with more than 1,000 Spanish soldiers and 2,000 Indian allies. The Aztecs allowed him to enter the city; but as soon as Cortés joined his men, the Aztecs attacked the Spanish quarters. In the middle of a bloody battle, Montezuma again appeared on the walls of the Spanish quarters to beg his people to let the Spaniards leave the city. This time, the Aztecs only threw stones at their king, striking him several times. Montezuma was removed to his room, where he soon died.

Gathering his men around him, Cortés attacked the Aztecs. Capturing the great temple where

Montezuma, the Aztec ruler, meets Hernán Cortés and his men at the edge of Tenochtitlán.

so many men, women, and children had been sacrificed, the Spaniards tore down the bloody altar to the Aztec god. But Cortés knew that he could not remain in the city of Tenochtitlán. On the night of June 30 to July 1, 1520, the Spaniards left their quarters under cover of darkness.

Great dangers awaited Cortés and his men as they made their way through the streets of the city. Since Tenochtitlán was built in the middle of a lake, the Spaniards had to cross over a long, narrow land bridge to the opposite shore. While crossing this land bridge, the Spaniards could be surrounded and destroyed by Aztecs in canoes on the lake. If only the Spaniards and their Indian allies could escape the city unnoticed!

This was not to be. As the soldiers moved themselves along with their horses and cannon onto the land bridge, war drums sounded from the great temple in the city. The Aztecs had discovered their escape! Soon the Indians were attacking the Spaniards from all sides. Hundreds of Spaniards and their Indian allies died from the Aztec assault; the Indians captured others alive to sacrifice them to their war god. Despite the bitter assault, Cortés and his men moved on across the land bridge until they reached the far side. They called that night *La Noche Triste,* "the Night of Sorrows."

Cortés and his army then faced the long march to reach the lands held by their Indian allies. Seven days after the Night of Sorrows, a large Aztec force attacked the Spaniards at a place called Otumba, but after several hours of fighting, Cortés defeated them. The Spaniards continued their march. A few days later, they reached their Indian allies and could rest from their labors.

La Noche Triste: Spanish for "the Night of Sorrows," when the Aztecs massacred the Spaniards and Indians escaping from the city of Tenochtitlán

The Conquest of Mexico

Most men might have given up after such a defeat, but not Hernán Cortés. No sooner had he gotten his small army to safety than he began planning a return to Tenochtitlán. Soon Cortés's troops were reinforced by more Indian allies and by Spaniards from Cuba. Cortés ordered the building of small ships so that Tenochtitlán could be attacked from the lake. About seven months after the Night of Sorrows, Cortés was ready to return to the city of Tenochtitlán.

Three days after Christmas, 1520, the Spanish began their long, hard return to the city of Tenochtitlán. As the soldiers marched or rode, many could probably still hear Cortés's words ringing in their ears, calling them to deeds of courage and honor. The cause they were fighting for was a just one, Cortés had told his soldiers. The Aztecs and all the Indian tribes worshipped demons; the Spaniards, he said, were fighting to overthrow the rule of the demons and to establish the throne of Christ in Mexico. The Aztecs were also traitors, Cortés had declared, for Montezuma had sworn allegiance to King Charles I of Spain, and now the Aztecs were rebelling against his majesty.

Between December 31, 1520, and April 1521, Cortés's armies conquered the cities that surrounded the lake of Tenochtitlán. On April 28, Cortés ordered the assault on Tenochtitlán itself to begin. By capturing the land bridges to the city and sending out his small ships to prowl the lake around the city, Cortés had completely encircled Tenochtitlán by May.

But conquering Tenochtitlán was a different matter. For three months the Spaniards slowly pushed their way into the city, fighting for every inch of ground. The Aztecs were stout and courageous warriors. Though they suffered from hunger and sickness, the new king, Guatemozín (gwa•teh•moh•ZEEN), and his people refused to surrender. Finally on August 13, Cortés led an attack on the marketplace where the Aztecs made their last stand. The Indians fought fiercely but were finally defeated by the Spanish and their Indian allies. King Guatemozín tried to escape by canoe across the lake but was captured by the commander of Cortés's lake ships.

Tenochtitlán had been conquered; the once beautiful city lay in ruins.

9/23

The Rebuilding of Mexico

After the conquest, King Charles made Cortés governor of the city of Tenochtitlán and of the areas surrounding it, down to the sea. The Spanish called this region **New Spain.** As governor of New Spain, Cortés rebuilt the city of Tenochtitlán (which became known as Mexico City). With its new cathedral and other beautiful public buildings, Mexico City (some said) was as beautiful as any city in Europe; that was saying much, for Europe had many beautiful cities. Cortés encouraged Spaniards to settle in Mexico, and many came to the New World. Some Spaniards married Indians. The children that came from these marriages were neither Spanish nor Indian, but a mixture of the two. Most people in Latin America today are a mixture of Spanish and Indian.

More important than rebuilding Mexico City, Cortés saw to it that the Indians were taught the Catholic Faith. A small band of Franciscan friars crossed the sea to New Spain in 1524. Dressed in

> **New Spain:** the area around Mexico City, extending to the sea

Map of New Spain (1576)

rough habits and carrying wooden crosses, they made the long journey from the seacoast to Mexico City. The Indians who came out to see these strange men kept repeating, *"Motólinia! Motólinia!"* (Moh•TOH•lee•NEE•ah). One of the friars, Toribio de Benavente (Toh•REE•bee•oh day Bayn•ah•VAYN•tay), hearing this word, *motólinia,* asked someone what it meant. "It means 'poor man,'" he was told. "So I don't forget this word," said Fray Toribio, "it shall from now on be my name!" From that day until his death many years later, Fray Toribio called himself Motólinia, the "poor man."

More surprising to the Indians than the poor clothing of the friars was how Cortés greeted these "beggars." Because Cortés had conquered their mighty empire, the Aztecs had great respect for him. Some Indians even thought him a god! What a wonder was it for them, then, to see the great conqueror Cortés kneel down before these friars and kiss their hands! Turning to the Indians, and seeing their wonder, Cortés said that they too should show respect to the friars, who had come to teach them about the love of God.

Inca: the Indian king of Peru

The Quest for Cities of Gold

Many leagues south of Mexico, in the tall and cold Andes Mountains, there reigned another Indian king as powerful as Montezuma. This king, called the **Inca** (EEN•cah), ruled over a great kingdom called Peru. Like the land of the Aztecs, Peru had cities with great and beautiful temples and grand public buildings. Peru also had gold—an abundance of gold! Stories of Peru's gold reached the ears of the Spaniard, Francisco Pizarro (pee•ZAHR•oh), and his brothers. In January 1530, with a small band of adventurers, they set sail for Panama; a year later, they

Territory of the Inca Empire

Inca Empire

0   500 miles

0   500 kilometers

embarked from Panama to Peru in hopes of conquering it as Cortés had conquered Mexico.

With the Pizarro brothers went a young man named **Hernando de Soto.** Since coming to the New World several years before the conquest of Mexico, De Soto had fought in many Indian wars in Darien (Panama), Honduras, and Nicaragua. As Pizarro's second-in-command, De Soto discovered the capital of the Inca and helped in capturing that mighty ruler. Receiving a share of the Inca's treasure, De Soto returned to Spain a very rich man.

Hernando de Soto seemingly had everything a man could want. He was immensely rich, owned a great estate, and had a beautiful wife. Even King Charles borrowed money from him! But De Soto was not content. He missed his life in the New World. He longed for adventure. He desired, once again, to do great deeds. Hearing stories of the great riches to be found in the land of Florida, De Soto asked King Charles to allow him to explore and conquer

Hernando de Soto: the conquistador who explored Florida; he also discovered the Mississippi River, and evangelized the Indians in Arkansas

Inca ruins at Machu Picchu, Peru

De Soto lands in Florida.

that land. King Charles granted his request, and in 1538, De Soto set sail for Cuba.

De Soto remained in Cuba only long enough to outfit his expedition. In May of 1539, he set sail for Florida with nine ships and 1,000 men. Landing at what is today Tampa Bay (De Soto called it *Espiritu Santo* [ay•SPEER•ee•toh SAHN•toh], or "Holy Spirit Bay"), De Soto and his men explored the wilderness of western Florida. De Soto soon learned how fierce the Florida Indians, especially the Apalachee, were. Though the Apalachee were not easy foes to overcome, De Soto eventually subdued them. Then, turning northward toward what is now the state of Georgia, De Soto and his men followed the rumors of gold.

Pushing into northern and eastern Georgia, De Soto found some pearls, but no gold. As in Florida, the Indians were proud and warlike. They did not take kindly to De Soto's habit of forcing warriors to carry his baggage. Finding no gold, De Soto again turned south, leading his men into what is today Alabama.

Near Mobile Bay (where hundreds of years before Madoc may have landed) Indians invited the Spaniards into their village, which was surrounded by a high wood stockade. One of De Soto's men warned him that it might be a trap, but De Soto was too proud to refuse the invitation. De Soto should have listened to the soldier, for it was a trap, and the Spaniards barely escaped from the village alive.

Forming up his men outside the village, De Soto met the Indian attack. It was a fierce, nine-hour battle. The Spaniards tried to push their way into the stockade, but the Indian defenders kept them at bay; even Indian women and children came out to defend their village. Finally, the Spaniards seized the stockade and the battle ended. About 2,500 Indians lay dead, and about 20 Spaniards.

So far, De Soto's expedition had been a failure; but, brave and stubborn, he would not accept defeat. Instead of heading east to where ships awaited that would take his army home, De Soto turned his march northwest. From December 1540 to April 1541, Indians attacked De Soto and his men nearly every night; but, still they marched on. On May 21, 1541, De Soto and his men reached a wide, muddy river. It was the Mississippi. Crossing this greatest of North American rivers, the Spaniards marched into Arkansas.

There, De Soto showed that he did not care for gold and adventure alone, but also for the Catholic Faith and the salvation of souls.

De Soto discovers the Mississippi River.

Raising a tall cross, the conquistador preached to the Indians about how God, who had made the world, became a man and died on the cross for their salvation. He told how Christ had risen from the dead and ascended into heaven. Christ, he said, waited with open arms to receive anyone who would believe in him.

The Spaniards spent the winter in Arkansas and returned the following spring to the Mississippi River. De Soto was exhausted and filled with disappointment. His dream of finding gold had come to nothing; his expedition, he now knew, had been a failure. The proud conquistador came down with a fever. He suffered from pain and disappointment, but no word of complaint passed his lips. On May 20, 1542, he confessed his sins and begged his men to pray for him. The next day, Hernando de Soto died. His men buried him in the broad Mississippi, the river he had discovered exactly one year before.

The adventure had ended for De Soto, but not for his men. Under their new leader, Luis de Moscoso, they built small ships and floated down the Mississippi. Though Indians attacked them continually from the riverbanks, the Spaniards finally reached the Gulf of Mexico. They passed down the coast of Mexico until they arrived at the Mexican town of Panuco. The first thing the adventurers did after coming ashore was to find a church and hear Mass. With the priest, they raised their prayers of thanksgiving to God for their deliverance from danger and death.

The Seven Cities of Cibola

While De Soto wandered through "Florida" in search of gold, farther west, a Franciscan friar, Fray Marcos de Niza, set out on a similar expedition. The viceroy (king's representative) in Mexico, Don Antonio de Mendoza, was eager to establish a Spanish settlement in the far north of New Spain. He sent Fray Marcos to explore these lands and report on what he found there.

When he returned to Mexico, Fray Marcos told a fabulous story. Far to the north, he said, lay the "Seven Cities of Cibola," where the buildings were covered in gold! If this were true, then these cities would be as great a discovery as the empires of the Aztecs and the Inca, so Mendoza was eager to discover the truth of Fray Marcos's tale. Mendoza gathered 436 soldiers and settlers and many heads of cattle, sheep, and pigs. He placed the soldiers and settlers under the command of Francisco Vásquez de Coronado. In true Spanish fashion, Mendoza ordered Coronado to establish a settlement in the north and, if necessary, conquer the natives there. Above all, Mendoza charged Coronado to see to it that the Gospel was preached to the pagan Indians. Five Franciscan friars were to accompany the expedition for this purpose.

Marching north, Coronado's expedition crossed dry desert lands populated mostly by wandering Indian tribes. In what is today south-

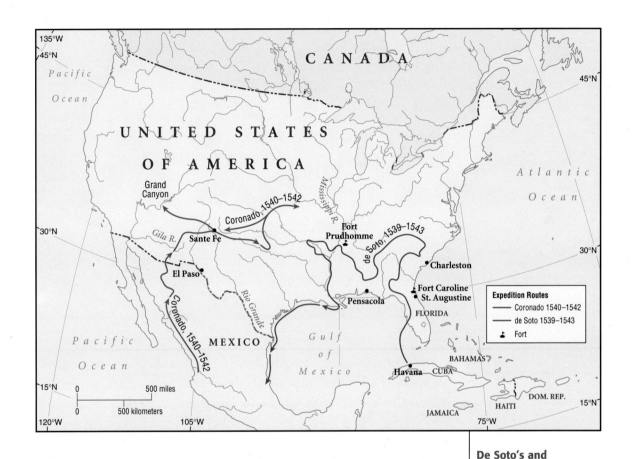

De Soto's and Coronado's expeditions in the Americas

ern Arizona, Coronado came across the San Pedro River and followed it to where it flowed into the Gila (HEE•lah) River. Soon they came to mountainous country with springs and forests of fir trees. Passing through this country, they discovered the first of Cibola's seven cities. But, to the Spaniards' disappointment, it was only a walled settlement of baked brick houses without even a glimmer of gold.

This was Hawikuh, a *pueblo,* or town, of the Zuñi (ZOO•nyee) Indians. Though Hawikuh's houses were not covered with gold, Coronado thought he might find gold within its walls. More importantly, he might find food there for the famished soldiers and settlers who followed him. The Zuñi, however, were not friendly; just a year before they had killed Estéban, one of Fray Marcos's

pueblo: a Spanish word meaning "town"; used to refer to the towns of the Zuñi and other tribes

Ruins of a pueblo
in Arizona

companions. When Coronado demanded that the Zuñi surrender to the Spanish king, the Indians responded with a shower of arrows and stones. But armed with guns and mounted on horses, the Spanish were too powerful for the Zuñi. Spanish soldiers charged the walls of the pueblo, driving off and killing their Indian foes. Though wounded by a flying stone, Coronado entered Hawikuh in triumph.

To his disappointment, Coronado found no gold in Hawikuh. The conquistador then organized three expeditions to explore the land to the north and east. One, under Garcia López de Cárdenas, journeyed far to the north and west and discovered an awe-inspiring sight: the Grand Canyon. The second expedition under Hernán de Alvarado and Fray Juan Padilla (pah•DEE•yah) wandered far to the east, into the flat plains of northern Texas, where great herds of wild buffalo grazed. Coronado himself led the third expedition over the dry lands of what is now northern New Mexico until he came to the valley of the Rio Grande (REE•oh GRAHN•day). There they found more pueblos, but no gold.

While in the Rio Grande valley, Coronado heard more tales of cities of gold. An Indian the Spaniards named "El Turco" told Coronado that far to the north and east lay the city of Quivira (kee•VEE•rah), where, El Turco said, an abundance of gold metal could be found. (Quivira lay in what is now Kansas.) After a long journey, Coronado reached Quivira, but it was merely a village of round wooden houses with grass roofs. Though he found no gold in Quivira, Coronado did find another gold-colored metal: copper. He returned, disappointed, to the Rio Grande valley.

Coronado was not the only one disappointed with the expedition into the land he named New Mexico. The settlers who had come with Coronado from Mexico found life in the Rio Grande valley too difficult; they wanted to return to Mexico. So, in spring of 1542, Coronado led the settlers and soldiers back into Mexico.

But not everyone returned to Mexico. Fray Juan Padilla and other missionaries had not come with Coronado to find gold, but to bring the treasure of Christ to the pagan Indians. Though Coronado's quest had ended in failure, Fray Juan believed his own mission had just begun.

Chapter 2 Review

9/25

Summary

- Hernán Cortés and his band of conquistadors landed on the coast of Mexico and battled their way to the land of the Aztecs, where his men grew afraid of the Indians' savage ways and longed to return to Cuba. Cortés burned his ships, met the fearsome king Montezuma, and after the awful defeat of the Night of Sorrows, conquered the city of Tenochtitlán.
- After the conquest of the city of Tenochtitlán, Cortés rebuilt New Spain. Mexico City (Tenochtitlán's new name) and its surrounding lands became a reminder of Old Spain, with arch-laden, elegant buildings, fountains and wide plazas, bell towers and cathedrals. These old and beautiful cities of the Americas still survive today.
- Spanish explorers traveled to Peru and found gold, and then went north into what is now the United States searching for gold. To their

disappointment, they found no gold in the north; but they discovered lands and Indian tribes, which the missionaries intent on preaching Christ found much more interesting!

Chapter Checkpoint

1. Twice Diego Velázquez wanted to stop Cortés. What did he try to do each time?
2. What was the legend of the Seven Cities of Cibola?
3. Name two good things and two bad things about Atzec civilization.
4. Why did Montezuma welcome Cortés?
5. How did Cortés conquer Tenochtitlán?
6. Was it important to the Spaniards to convert the Indians?
7. When Hernando de Soto went to look for the cities of gold, what did he find?
8. Who was Francisco Vásquez de Coronado?
9. Who was Fray Juan Padilla?
10. Who discovered the Mississippi River?

Chapter Activities

1. Hernán Cortés and Hernando de Soto became rich young men and could have settled down to a quiet, wealthy life. What made them seek adventure? More wealth? Glory? A desire to convert the Indians? If you had been Cortés or De Soto, would you have retired or sought adventure?
2. Make a list of some of the modern adventures that Catholic boys and girls can look forward to. Some of these are daring and others quiet, but they are all exciting. Which adventures do you feel called to while you are young? How about when you are grown up?

The American Larder

When the Spaniards arrived in Mexico, they discovered ball courts in all of the major cities of Mexico and Central America. These ball courts were used for a contest between captive slaves playing on opposing teams. Each team tried to win by making goals with a tightly wound ball of rubber (the rubber tree grows in Central and South America). After the contest, there was a feast. Unlucky was the team that lost because the losers were killed and eaten.

Conquistadors of Christ

9/28

Defender of the Indians

When he first came to the New World in 1502, Bartolomé de Las Casas behaved like any other Spanish colonist. Las Casas had come over the sea from Spain with Nicholas Ovando, the new governor of Hispaniola, who gave him land along with Indian servants to work on it. These Indians were not considered slaves, but they had no choice but to work for Las Casas. He, in turn, had to care for the Indians and to teach them the Catholic Faith. In this way he would help them become members of the Church and good subjects of the Spanish king.

Fray Bartolomé de Las Casas, "Defender of the Indians"

Though Las Casas was probably a kind master to his Indians, other Spanish landowners were not so kind. Some landowners would use the Indians as one would use cattle; sometimes, they treated Indians worse than cattle. Often they neglected to teach them the Catholic Faith. Such treatment of the Indians was against the law of the Spanish monarchs, Isabella and Ferdinand; but they were far away across the sea and so found it hard to enforce their own laws in America.

A Turning Point for Las Casas

Though he became a priest in 1510, Las Casas did not give up his lands, nor did he cease forcing Indians to work for him. But at some point in the years after his ordination, Las Casas changed. We do not know when exactly, or why, but change he did. Perhaps he changed on account of a sermon preached by a Dominican friar named Antonio de Montesinos in 1511 in a small church, roofed with straw, on the island of Hispaniola. "Are these Indians not men?" cried Fray Antonio to the congregation of Spanish landholders. "Do they not have rational souls? Are you not obliged to love them as you love yourselves?"

Bartolomé de Las Casas came to the conclusion that he and his fellow Spaniards were not loving the Indians with the love of Christ. Forced to do labor that was too hard for them, thousands of Indians were dying. Soon, it appeared, few or maybe no Indians would be left alive in the Caribbean Islands. Padre Las Casas realized that in order to love the Indians he had to treat them with

Battle between Spanish conquistadors and the Indians

justice. He came to the frightening conclusion that "when we preach to the Indians about the humility and poverty of Jesus Christ, and how He suffered for us, and how God rejoices in the poor and in those the world despises, [the Indians] think we are lying to them." Las Casas freed his Indians and began a lifelong crusade to defend all Indians from the greed and cruelty of the colonists.

The Padre at the Spanish Court

Las Casas returned to Spain in 1517 to inform the court how badly the colonists were treating the Indians in America. Queen Isabella had been dead for thirteen years, and King Ferdinand had died in 1516. Cardinal Ximenes (hee•MEH•nez) now held the throne until Charles, who was Ferdinand and Isabella's grandson, could be crowned king. The cardinal listened to Las Casas's complaints and took them to heart. Ximenes gave Las Casas the title of "Protector of the Indians" and appointed a commission of priests to investigate how Indians were being treated in America.

But even though Cardinal Ximenes, and later King Charles, were concerned about how the Indians were treated, little changed after Las Casas returned to Hispaniola. Padre Las Casas came to believe that the only way to help the Indians would be to place them under the protection of the Church.

In 1519, the Spanish government gave Las Casas permission to set up a colony made up only of Indians and Spanish farmers; but this colony, Cumaná, on the coast of Venezuela, was a failure. Spaniards in a nearby settlement so angered the Indians in Las Casas's colony that they rose in revolt, killing as many Europeans as they could find. Disappointed, Las Casas returned to Hispaniola. He entered a Dominican friary and, in 1522, became a Dominican friar.

Though his colony had failed, Fray Bartolomé de Las Casas did not give up fighting for the rights of Indians. He traveled back and forth to Spain to plead with the king for the Indians. He wrote pamphlets arguing that the Spanish government had no right to conquer the Indians, and certainly no right to enslave them. Missionaries, said Las Casas, should go to the Indians without soldiers accompanying them.

Some missionaries disagreed with Las Casas. The Franciscan priest "Motólinia" thought the ideas of Las Casas were not practical. Though a few missionaries could be cruel toward the Indians, Motólinia was not. He simply thought that without the soldiers protecting them, missionaries would be killed by the Indians. And, then, who would preach the Gospel to them? Sadly, Motólinia was often right, as we shall see in the story of Fray Juan de Padilla.

The Priest Who Lived Like a Beggar

Motólinia was well loved by the Indians because of his great charity and holiness. Whatever he received, he gave to the Indians. Sometimes this meant he had no food for himself. Motólinia lived like a *motólinia* (a "beggar") indeed, for the love of Christ and of souls.

King Charles Helps the Indians

Though Las Casas found fault with how the Spanish behaved in the New World, King Charles I did not try to silence him. Instead, the king took everything Fray Bartolomé said to heart. Like Isabella, Charles was a devout Catholic and cared more for the justice of Christ than for worldly riches. King Charles passed laws to help better the lives of the Indians. In 1544 he even made Las Casas the bishop of Chiapas, a region in southern Mexico. As bishop, Las Casas refused to give communion to any colonist who treated his Indian workers as slaves. Many Indians in Chiapas came into the Church because the bishop used peaceful ways to convert them to the Faith.

Native Indian women in Chiapas, Mexico. King Charles I of Spain made Las Casas the bishop of Chiapas in 1544.

In 1550 King Charles did a most surprising thing. He ordered an end to all conquests in the New World until a conference of theologians could decide whether it was right to conquer the Indians. Las Casas had come to Spain in 1547, and it was largely because of him that the king had called the conference. But the commission did not entirely agree with Las Casas's opinions. They said Spaniards must first try to convince the Indians to obey the king of Spain. But they also said that force could be used if the Indians refused to obey, or if they threatened to harm missionaries who came to work among them. No one, said the commission, was allowed to make the Indians slaves. The commission's decisions were finally made part of Spanish law in 1573.

Though he was unable to get everything he wanted from the king, Las Casas still did much to help the Indians. Queen Isabella, King Charles, and the kings of Spain that followed them looked upon the Indians as their subjects, equal to their Spanish subjects. Though they wanted the wealth that could be found in the New World, their chief concern was that the Indians hear and accept the Gospel of Christ. The monarchs did not wish to be cruel, but they made many mistakes in dealing with the Indians. Bartolomé de Las Casas helped the monarchs see their mistakes. More importantly, he showed how they might improve the conditions under which the Indians lived. To this day, Indians in Latin America look upon Bartolomé de Las Casas as one of the great friends of their race.

Empress of the Americas

The Bishop and the Men of Blood

Fray Juan de Zumárraga was troubled. Being a bishop is never easy, but being the bishop of New Spain (it seemed) was a task beyond the power of any man. Indeed, Fray Juan had not wanted to be bishop. For over 30 years he had lived the quiet life of a Franciscan friar. He had prayed and fasted; he had said Mass, administered the sacraments, and preached to the people. Then one fatal day, in 1527, King Charles I had stopped at the Franciscan convent in Valladolid (vah•yeh•duh•LEE), in Spain. The king was so impressed by Fray Juan, who directed the life of the convent, that he wanted him to serve as the first bishop of New Spain. Fray Juan, the son of poor parents, did not think himself worthy of that great office; but his religious superior told him that he had to obey King Charles. So it was that one year later, Fray Juan found himself in the city of Mexico, the bishop of pagans, new Christian converts, and half-civilized Spanish adventurers.

The task of ruling such a diocese would have been hard enough under normal conditions, but Fray Juan had to fight against evil and oppression. Since the conquest of Mexico in 1521, Hernán Cortés had governed New Spain. On the whole, Cortés had been a good governor. He had rebuilt Mexico City and, for the most part, had treated the Indians with kindness. King Charles, though, had heard rumors that Cortés had wanted to take New Spain and rule it for himself. Half believing the rumors, Charles told Cortés to return to Spain. In place of Cortés, the king sent three men—Nuño de Guzmán (NOO•nyoh day gooz•MAHN), Juan Ortiz de Matienzo (HWAN ohr•TEEZ mah•tee•EHN•zoh), and Diego Delgadillo (dee•AY•goh del•gah•DEE•oh) to rule New Spain and to see if the rumors about Cortés were true. With these men, called the "Royal Audience," Charles sent Fray Juan, who would serve not only as bishop, but as "Protector of the Indians." The king wanted to make sure the Indians were being treated with justice.

The Royal Audience became Fray Juan's most bitter enemies. Guzmán,

- A detail of a Mexican historical mural shows missionaries with local Indians.

Matienzo, and Delgadillo were cruel men. They forced the Indians to pay heavy taxes. They branded them with red-hot branding irons. They stole their wives and daughters, and they enslaved the Indian men. As Protector of the Indians, Fray Juan did all he could to oppose the Royal Audience; but Guzmán, Matienzo, and Delgadillo would not listen to him. The bishop wrote letters to the king complaining about the Audience, but these letters never reached Charles. The Audience seized the letters before they could leave New Spain.

Bishop Zumárraga, though, finally outsmarted the Audience. With the help of a sailor, he placed a letter in a block of wax, which was cast into a barrel of oil. So hidden, the letter crossed the Atlantic and reached King Charles. When Charles read about the evil deeds of the Audience, he was filled with anger. He sent a new Audience to New Spain to take the place of Guzmán, Matienzo, and Delgadillo. With the Audience went Cortés, whom the king had confirmed as Captain General, but not governor, of New Spain.

Though, by 1531, Cortés and the new Audience were in power, all was not well in New Spain. The conquest and three years of cruelty had made many Indians think that the God the Spanish priests told them about did not love them. To many Indians, Jesus was the white man's god; they thought he did not care about the brown-skinned natives. Bishop Zumárraga loved his Indian flock. How could he convince them that God loved them as well as he loved the Spaniards? Many evils, many cruelties were still part of life in New Spain. What could he as bishop do to stop them?

One cold day in December of 1531, Bishop Zumárraga, busy at work, received a visitor. Before him knelt an Aztec man, clad only in a loincloth and a cloak called a *tilma,* made from cactus fibers. The bishop received many visitors, so this man was not unusual. Perhaps Fray Juan was only half listening as the man, named Juan Diego, told his story.

Aztecs in this illustration wear the loincloth and tilma.

tilma: a cloak made of cactus fibers

Our Lady of Guadalupe

Juan Diego said that he had set out from his village at break of day to hear Mass in the city. Passing by the hill called Tepeyac (TEH•puh•yak), a hill he had passed many times before, Juan Diego heard the singing of birds. He was most surprised, for at that time of the year one did not hear songbirds. He stopped, and looked east toward the hill. Suddenly the singing ceased and, instead, he heard a voice calling his name: "Juanito, Juan Diegito," it said.

Juan Diego said he felt no fear, but climbed to the hilltop from where the voice came. There he saw a most beautiful lady dressed in garments that shone with the brightness of the sun. Then the lady spoke, and beautiful was the sound of her voice! "I am the Virgin Mary, Mother of the true God who created all things," she said. "Go tell the bishop of Mexico that I wish a church built here on this hilltop in my honor. From this church I will show the people of this land that I am merciful to all who call upon me in faith."

Bishops cannot believe everything they are told, and Juan Diego's story sounded fantastic, indeed. Perhaps this Indian had made up the story because he himself wanted a church built and was afraid to ask for it himself. But Bishop Zumárraga was not harsh to Juan Diego, telling him, "Come again another time, my son. When you come I will give further thought to what you have to say." Then dismissing Juan Diego, the bishop turned again to the affairs that had occupied him since morning.

Roses in December

Juan Diego was disappointed by his meeting with the bishop. At sundown he returned to Tepeyac hill, where the resplendent Lady awaited him. Falling on his knees, Juan Diego told the Lady that he feared the bishop did not believe his story. "I am a lowly man," he told the Lady. "Send someone else, someone important, to give your message to the bishop. Me he will not believe." The Lady, however, said she had chosen Juan Diego, and it was he who must go. Gladly Juan Diego obeyed. The next day, Sunday, he said, he would return to the bishop and deliver the Lady's message.

After Mass the next day, Juan Diego went to the bishop's palace. As on the previous day, he waited long before he could get in to see the bishop. Juan Diego, with tears in his eyes, told the bishop of the Lady's request. It seemed to Zumárraga that Juan Diego was not a liar; still, he could not be certain that the Virgin had appeared to the Indian. "You must bring me a sign that the Virgin has appeared to you," he told Juan Diego. When Juan Diego left his presence, the bishop ordered two of his servants to follow him. They set out after Juan Diego, but as they approached the hill of Tepeyac, they lost sight of him. Angry that he had escaped them, the servants returned to the bishop. "That Indian is a liar," they said. "Do not believe him."

The image of the Madonna appears on Juan Diego's tilma, which is filled with roses.

Meanwhile, Juan Diego had climbed the hill of Tepeyac. "Return here tomorrow," the Lady told him, "and I will give you a sign that will convince the bishop. I will richly reward you for your service to me." Juan Diego promised to return the next day. He then returned home.

But reaching his home, Juan Diego found that his uncle, Juan Bernardino, had fallen sick. The next day, Monday, Juan Diego spent caring for his uncle; he did not return to Tepeyac hill as the Lady had commanded. That night, Juan Bernardino was so sick that he feared he would die. He asked Juan Diego to fetch him a priest who could give him the last rites. Full of sorrow, Juan Diego set out Tuesday morning for the city to find a priest to minister to his uncle.

Approaching Tepeyac hill, Juan Diego tried to take a different way than the one he normally took. He was afraid the Lady might see him and delay him from fetching a priest for his uncle. But the Lady saw him, and descending the hill, asked him,

"Where are you hastening to, my son?" Juan Diego told her of his uncle, and promised that he would return to her tomorrow. "Now," he said to the Lady, "I must find a priest who will hear my uncle's confession and absolve him."

The Lady was not angry with Juan Diego. Instead, promising him that his uncle was already healed of his sickness, she told Juan Diego to climb to the summit of the hill. He obeyed her, and at the place where the Lady had first appeared to him, Juan Diego found many varieties of beautiful roses. Imagine his surprise at this sight, for Juan Diego knew that no roses grew in December. Filling his tilma full with fragrant blossoms, Juan Diego brought them to the Lady. Removing the roses from the tilma, the Lady again replaced them. "Take these roses to the bishop," she told Juan Diego. "They are the sign he asked for. Seeing them he will know that I have appeared to you and that he must do as I requested." Full of joy, Juan Diego continued his journey to the city. He was certain the bishop would this time believe him.

The First Indian Saint in the Americas

For Catholics, there are few places in the world as sacred as the Mexico City basilica, which honors the Virgin of Guadalupe, Mexico's patroness. On July 31, 2002, Juan Diego was canonized (proclaimed a saint) in the basilica by Pope John Paul II. As many as a million people lined the route taken by John Paul to the basilica on the morning of July 31. As the Pope rode past in his "popemobile," people cheered, mariachi bands played, children sang and danced. Many in the crowd traveled hundreds, even thousands, of miles to get to the basilica for the canonization. Some pilgrims, dressed in the traditional garb of the Aztecs, shook clam rattles and blew on conch shells; the festive and joyful service lasted about three hours.

Pope John Paul II prays during the Mass for Juan Diego's canonization in Mexico City.

A Great Miracle

The day was already growing old when Bishop Zumárraga heard a frantic knocking at his door. Opening it he found two of his servants, their faces pale with astonishment. "That Indian, Juan Diego, has returned," they told the bishop. "Seeing he had something wrapped up in his tilma we asked that we might see what it was. When he opened his tilma, lo! it was full of roses, fresh as if they had been plucked in the spring. We tried to touch them, but every time we reached our hands toward them they disappeared into the cloth." Hearing this marvel, the bishop ordered his servants to bring Juan Diego into his presence.

Entering the bishop's chamber, Juan Diego fell on his knees. "I have returned, lord bishop, with the sign you requested," said Juan Diego. He opened his tilma and a flood of roses fell to the floor. To Juan Diego's surprise, the bishop and all those in the room fell to their knees. The bishop wept as he prayed, "Lady, forgive me for not fulfilling your request." Juan Diego wondered what all this could mean; then looking down at his tilma, he understood. For on the rough white cloth he saw the image of the Lady, just as she had appeared to him on Tepeyac hill.

The next day, Juan Diego led Bishop Zumárraga and others to Tepeyac hill so they could see the place where the Lady had requested her church be built. When Juan Diego asked the bishop's permission to return to his village to see how his sick uncle fared, Zumárraga gave him his blessing, but said he should not return alone. Surrounded by those who had come with him to Tepeyac hill, Juan Diego returned to Juan Bernardino. The great bishop, friend of God and the king, was paying a great honor to poor, lowly Juan Diego! The Lady had worked another wonder. She had exalted the humble and made the great the companion of the lowly.

When they all reached the village, they found Juan Bernardino recovered from his sickness. The Lady, he told them, had appeared to him as well and had cured him. "She said I must go to the bishop

Pilgrims make their way toward the modern Basilica of Our Lady of Guadalupe in Mexico City. The original eighteenth-century basilica stands in the background.

to tell him that she wished her image should bear the name, Our Lady of Guadalupe," said Juan Bernardino.

Bishop Zumárraga fulfilled his promise and erected a church in honor of Our Lady of Guadalupe on Tepeyac hill. There he placed Juan Diego's tilma that bore the image of the Lady. In this image, the Lady appears dressed not as a Spanish woman, but as an Aztec princess. She stands before the sun, her two hands pointing, in Aztec fashion, toward the heavens where her Son, Jesus, reigns as king. The Aztecs understood the message. They were no longer to worship the sun god but the more powerful God of the Christians. They also understood that the Lady and her Son loved the Indians as well as the Spanish. Millions of Indians, who had feared the Spaniards' God, now accepted baptism and became Christians.

Our Lady had answered Bishop Zumárraga's prayers.

Missions and Martyrs

Martyrdom in Kansas

They marched forth with the spirit of conquistadors. Fearless, they braved the wilderness and the wrath of savage peoples. They went neither for gold nor silver nor to win great kingdoms for themselves. These men, the missionaries of the New World, wanted only to win a kingdom of souls for their king, Jesus Christ.

Among the most zealous of these courageous men was the Franciscan friar, Juan de Padilla. When he arrived in New Mexico with Coronado, Fray Juan de Padilla had already been successful as a missionary to the Indians in Mexico. When King Charles I had sent the new Audience to Mexico City in 1529, Nuño de Guzmán, with a band of conquistadors, fled toward the Pacific coast. With them went Fray Juan de Padilla, who served as chaplain. Fray Juan protected the Indians from the cruelty of the bloody Guzmán.

For about ten years, Fray Juan labored among the Indians in what are now the Mexican states of Colima (coh•LEE•mah) and Jalisco (ha•LEES•coh). Though he had become the superior of a Franciscan convent, Fray Juan gave up this position to follow Coronado into New Mexico. With Coronado, he crossed the wide plains in search of the city of gold, called Quivira. Unlike Coronado, though, Fray Juan was not disappointed that the city was merely a village with a little copper instead of gold. It was just for such Indians as those of Quivira that he had come to New Mexico. It was just for such as these that he remained in New Mexico when the conquistador returned to Mexico in 1542.

Sculpture of Juan de Padilla in prayer

Two other Franciscans remained with Juan de Padilla in New Mexico, as well as a handful of soldiers. The Franciscans labored among the Pawnee and Guia tribes, and many Indians came into the Church. But Fray Juan's zeal would not let him rest. He wanted to go farther east (into the lands then called the **Gran Quivira,** but now Kansas). Unfortunately, though, the tribes to the east were enemies of the Guia and Pawnee and so would probably look on Fray Juan as an enemy also. Captain Pedro Castañeda de Najera (cah•stah•NYAY•dah day nah•HAIR•ah) warned Fray Juan of the dangers that awaited him in the Gran Quivira, but to no avail. With Fray Luis de Ubeda, the soldier Andres Ocampo, two Indians named Lucas and Sebastián, and two other Mexican Indians, Fray Juan marched into the plains of Kansas.

Gran Quivira: the former name of lands in the present-day state of Kansas

It was autumn and the days were growing cold on the vast, treeless plains. Day after day, the missionary adventurers could see nothing around them but endless miles of grass. Above them clouds scudded across a deep blue sky. We know little of Juan de Padilla's journey, except its sad but courageous ending. One day in November 1542, a band of Indians appeared over the horizon. Seeing only lost souls in need of Christ, Fray Juan raised high a rough-hewn wooden cross. The Indians, though, belonged to an enemy tribe of the Guia. They let fly a barrage of arrows that pierced the good friar, who knelt to the ground, still holding aloft the cross, and then fell. Only in death did Fray Juan de Padilla let fall the sacred sign of our salvation.

Fray Juan's companions were able to escape death from the Indians. Later they returned to bury Fray Juan de Padilla. After many months of wandering, weary and hungry, they reached Mexico City, where they told the story of the death of the man who was the first to shed his blood for Christ in lands that would one day become part of the United States of America.

The Lady in Blue

The king of Spain did not abandon New Mexico after Coronado failed to found a settlement there. Fifty-eight years after Juan de Padilla met his death in the Gran Quivira, a new band of settlers crossed the Rio Grande into New Mexico. With these settlers came some Franciscan friars who, by the end of 1598, had established three missions for the Indians.

But the Indians of New Mexico, who lived in pueblos (small towns of adobe dwellings, protected by adobe walls), wanted nothing to do with the Spaniards or with their religion. In 1598 the Indians of the Acoma pueblo ambushed and killed a small band of Spaniards. Vicente de Zaldivar, whose brother was among those killed, led a

Ruins of mission San Gregorio de Abo, New Mexico

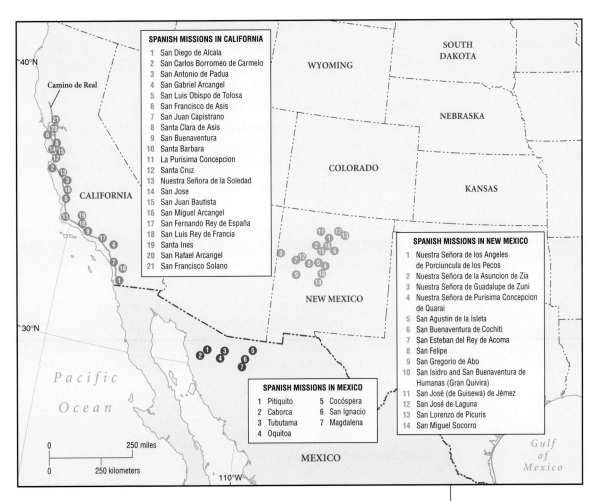

SPANISH MISSIONS IN CALIFORNIA

1 San Diego de Alcala
2 San Carlos Borromeo de Carmelo
3 San Antonio de Padua
4 San Gabriel Arcangel
5 San Luis Obispo de Tolosa
6 San Francisco de Asis
7 San Juan Capistrano
8 Santa Clara de Asis
9 San Buenaventura
10 Santa Barbara
11 La Purisima Concepcion
12 Santa Cruz
13 Nuestra Señora de la Soledad
14 San Jose
15 San Juan Bautista
16 San Miguel Arcangel
17 San Fernando Rey de España
18 San Luis Rey de Francia
19 Santa Ines
20 San Rafael Arcangel
21 San Francisco Solano

SPANISH MISSIONS IN NEW MEXICO

1 Nuestra Señora de los Angeles
   de Porciuncula de los Pecos
2 Nuestra Señora de la Asuncion de Zia
3 Nuestra Señora de Guadalupe de Zuni
4 Nuestra Señora de Purisima Concepcion
   de Quarai
5 San Agustin de la Isleta
6 San Buenaventura de Cochiti
7 San Esteban del Rey de Acoma
8 San Felipe
9 San Gregorio de Abo
10 San Isidro and San Buenaventura de
    Humanas (Gran Quivira)
11 San José (de Guisewa) de Jémez
12 San José de Laguna
13 San Lorenzo de Picuris
14 San Miguel Socorro

SPANISH MISSIONS IN MEXICO

1 Pitiquito   5 Cocóspera
2 Caborca   6 San Ignacio
3 Tubutama   7 Magdalena
4 Oquitoa

Spanish missions in Mexico, New Mexico, Kansas, and California

force of Spaniards against the pueblo. Acoma was built atop a flat-topped mountain, called a *mesa* (MAY•sah—"table") in Spanish. The steep, sheer walls of the mesa made it very difficult to attack Acoma, but de Zaldivar and his men, using ropes, scaled the mesa walls and took the pueblo, capturing 500 Indians. Many years would pass before the Pueblo Indians again waged war against the Spanish.

Though the settlers were not pleased with New Mexico, the king of Spain, Philip III, would not allow them to return to Mexico. He feared that, without the Spanish settlement, the Indians of New

Santa Fe: city in New Mexico named after the Holy Faith

Mexico would never hear the Gospel. After a time, New Mexico began to prosper. The Spanish founded the city of **Santa Fe** (meaning "Holy Faith"), and the Franciscans established many missions. In less than 90 years after the martyrdom of Juan de Padilla, 60,000 Indians were practicing Catholics.

Texan legend tells of a group of Indians from Texas who arrived in Santa Fe in 1629, requesting baptism. The friars who questioned these Indians were surprised to learn that they knew Christian prayers and the teachings of the Church. When the friars asked the Indians how they knew so much about the Faith, the Indians said that a beautiful lady dressed in blue had many times come to them and taught them. When she last appeared, she commanded them to go to Santa Fe to receive baptism from the priests there.

Who this lady in blue was remained a mystery to the friars who traveled the 200 miles to preach to the Indians in Texas. Then, in 1631, some of the friars from New Mexico returned to Spain. There they found a convent of sisters who wore blue habits. The head of this convent, Sister Maria de Jesus, told the friars that when she was in prayer God had made her appear to Indians in distant America. Could it have been she who had taught these Indians how to pray?

New Mexico Burning

Though the Spanish colony and the Indian missions were making progress, all was not peaceful in New Mexico. Only three years after Indians arrived in Santa Fe seeking baptism, the Indians of Hawikuh pueblo killed the missionary priest, Fray Francisco Letrado. Though pierced by many arrows, Fray Francisco died with a crucifix in his hand, praying for his murderers.

Though many years passed with little violence after the death of Fray Francisco, some pagan Indians only awaited the day when they could drive the Spaniards out.

Reconstruction of a Navaho dwelling near a mesa in Arizona

Indian **shamans,** or "medicine men," were angry over the many Indians who had become Christian. For many years, few Indians would listen to these shamans; but, then, things started to go wrong in New Mexico. Wild Indian tribes attacked the pueblos, enslaving the Indians who lived there. A long drought and sicknesses caused many Indian deaths. The shamans began to say that these evils had come because the Indians had abandoned their old gods to worship this new god called "Christ." Many pueblo Indians believed the shamans and returned to pagan worship.

shaman: an Indian medicine man

A Sioux shaman

Other Indians were angry because the Spanish governors of New Mexico had mistreated them. The governors demanded that the Indians pay tribute to them and labor for them. In 1675, Governor Juan Francisco de Treviño (tre•VEE•nyoh) discovered that some Indians were planning to revolt against the Spanish. Imprisoning their leaders, he sentenced them to death. Later he changed his mind and, instead of executing the Indian leaders, had them whipped.

Whipping was, in some ways, worse than death to the proud Indian; it was a serious insult. Because he had been so insulted, Popé (poh•PAY), a shaman from Taos pueblo, laid plans to overthrow the Spanish. For ten years he worked to unite all the pueblos against the Spanish. By 1680 he had gathered a force of Indians strong enough to challenge the Spanish power.

Spanish settlers and Christian Indians did not expect the storm that fell on them on August 10, 1680. Throughout New Mexico, the Indians rose and slaughtered men, women and children. Both Spaniards and Christian Indians died in Popé's rebellion. Priests suffered cruel tortures. Many Spaniards and Indians found refuge in the **presidio** (fortress) in Santa Fe. For eleven days the Spanish soldiers were able to defend the presidio; but when the rebel Indians cut off the presidio's water supply, the defenders knew they had to leave. On August 21, one thousand men, women, and children, escorted by a small band of Spanish soldiers, fled from Santa Fe. The Spanish colony of New Mexico and its missions had been destroyed.

presidio: a fortress

One pueblo, though, remained faithful. This was Isleta, which welcomed the refugees from Santa Fe. But the governor of New Mexico knew he could not remain in Isleta, and so he led the settlers 200 miles south to El Paso on the Rio Grande. The refugees suffered so from their 90-mile summer journey across the burning desert that they called it *Jornada del Muerto* (hor•NAH•dah del MWAIR•toh), the "journey of death."

For twelve years New Mexico remained under the control of Popé and other Pueblo Indian leaders. These were not good years. The Indians did not like the new government their leaders set up. Besides, without Spanish arms to protect them, the pueblos suffered attacks from the Comanches, Apaches, Utes, and Navajos. Finally, some Indians went to El Paso to ask the Spanish governor to return to New Mexico. In August 1692, Governor Diego de Vargas with 300 soldiers and Spanish and Indian colonists set off north towards Santa Fe. Having taken Santa Fe, Vargas spent the next year bringing all of New Mexico again under Spanish rule. Most pueblos surrendered without a battle; others resisted but were finally conquered.

In the years following the reconquest, New Mexico grew and prospered. New settlers came north from Mexico as well as missionaries who founded new missions to the Indians. Though some Indians revolted again in 1696, they could not overthrow the Spanish who had returned to New Mexico to stay.

Into California

Miracle on St. Joseph's Day

Day after day, for nine days, the small man in gray robes climbed to the summit of the little hill and looked anxiously out to sea. Day after day, he had been disappointed. Below him lay the bay like a long finger of water thrust into the land. Beyond the bay lay the sea; nothing but the sea. No sails could he see coming up over the horizon, no ship sailing into harbor. Nothing but the deep, blue sea.

Fray Junípero (hoo•NEE•pe•roh) Serra, the small man in gray, desperately wanted to see a ship. Without the supplies of food the ship would bring, the new settlement of San Diego, with its mission, could not survive. Don Gaspar de Portolá, commander of the Spanish troops in San Diego, had told Fray Junípero that the settlement had to be abandoned. But Fray Junípero asked Portolá to wait only nine more days, until March 19, the feast of St. Joseph. Fray Junípero said he would pray a novena prayer to St. Joseph; if no supplies came by St. Joseph's day, the friar said he would agree to leave San Diego.

Twenty years before, in 1749, Junípero Serra had left his home on the island of Majorca in the Mediterranean to serve as a missionary in Mexico. With his fellow Franciscans, Fray Junípero had worked among pagan Indians in the Sierra Gorda region, 175 miles north of Mexico City. In 1767, he became the father-president of the Franciscan missions in Baja California. Two years later, Fray Junípero joined Portolá in an expedition into **Alta California,** as the modern state of California was then called. Spain had discovered Alta California more than 200 years before but had never settled it. Portolá was to lead the military force that would protect Fray Junípero and his band of Franciscans as they set up missions in the new land.

Alta California: Spanish term for the territory north of the Mexican state of Baja California

The journey north had been difficult for Fray Junípero. When he first came to Mexico he injured his leg, and the wound had never healed. The journey into California was long and difficult, and Fray Junípero's leg swelled and gave him continuous pain. But so great was his desire to bring the Gospel to the Indians of Alta California that Serra would not be left behind. Despite the great pain in his leg, the friar continued the long journey into the north.

The mission church of San Diego de Alcala

Mission Indians in Southern California make baskets and hair ropes.

Serra had stayed at San Diego, the first Spanish settlement in California, while Portolá continued his exploration to the north. Things had not gone well at the settlement during the six months Portolá was away. The expected supply ship had not arrived. Fray Junípero had made no converts. The Indians were unfriendly. They stole from the Spanish camp and even tore strips of cloth from the sails on the Spanish ships. When the Spanish fought back, the Indians attacked them with arrows, killing some of the settlers. When he returned in January 1770, Portolá saw how badly off the settlement was. He was certain it could not continue.

What must Fray Junípero have thought when, climbing the hill on the morning of the last day of the novena, he saw no ship? It was St. Joseph's day, and it seemed the saint had not answered Junípero's prayers. He descended the hill, probably certain that he must abandon California. But the day had not ended. That afternoon, someone sighted a ship under full sail. It was the *San Antonio,* coming from Mexico with supplies for the San Diego settlement. St. Joseph had answered Fray Junípero's prayers after all.

The California Missions

Monterey: Spanish for "king's mountain"; the name of a bay in California. Today it is the name of a city on the peninsula at the south end of Monterey Bay.
San Francisco Bay: bay in California named after Saint Francis of Assisi

Don Gaspar de Portolá had gone north to find a bay that, over 100 years before, the Spanish explorer Sebastián Vizcaíno had discovered. Vizcaíno had named this bay **Monterey,** meaning "king's mountain." There, the first Mass to be said in California was offered. But in seeking Monterey, Portolá discovered a much larger bay than either San Diego or Monterey. This was **San Francisco Bay,** named after St. Francis of Assisi, the founder of Fray Junípero's order.

Fray Junípero joined Portolá on his second journey to Monterey in April 1770. On the feast of Pentecost, the day on which the Church celebrates the descent of the Holy Spirit on the apostles, Serra and Portolá took possession of Alta California for the king of Spain. More importantly, Serra claimed Monterey for the King of Heaven. Hanging a bell from a great tree, Fray Junípero joyfully rang it. "Come, Gentiles!" he cried. "Come to the Holy Church. Come and receive the Faith of Jesus Christ!" At Monterey, near the modern-day city of that name, Fray Junípero established his second mission, calling it *San Carlos Borromeo de Carmelo* (Saint Charles Borromeo of Carmel).

In the years that followed, Fray Junípero established seven more missions up and down the coast of California. In these missions, the friars not only instructed the Indians in the Faith, but taught them how to farm and do various crafts, such as carpentry, leather tanning, and masonry. The Indians also learned how to play European musical instruments. The friars formed small orchestras of Indian musicians who played many difficult pieces written by European composers. As in other parts of Spanish America, the friars' goal was to teach the California Indians how to live in a Christian and Spanish society.

This was rather difficult, for the California Indians were very primitive. They lived by hunting and gathering acorns and other nuts. California had many small tribes, which fought bloody feuds with each other. Their weapons were made of bone or stone, since they did not know how to smelt iron. Indian homes were small, dome-like structures made of willow branches and reeds. Their greatest art was baskets that had beautiful, intricate designs. These baskets were so tightly woven that they could hold water. The Indians boiled water by heating up stones in the fire and then dropping the hot stones into the water-filled baskets. But though their culture was primitive, the California Indians were quick to learn

Mission San Carlos Borromeo de Carmelo

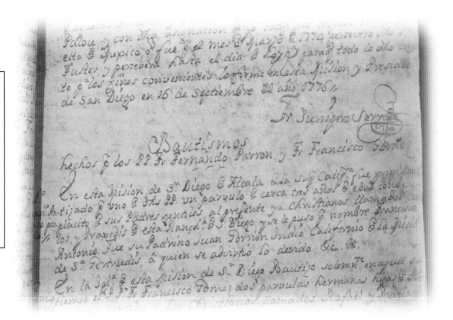

California's Mission San Diego de Alcala was founded by Father Junípero Serra in 1769. Father Serra kept all his own records written in longhand. This is a section of one of his original documents that records the founding of the mission.

the arts the friars taught them. The friars themselves commented on how intelligent the Indians were.

But not all was peaceful in Alta California. Fray Junípero argued with the Spanish governor over the cruel way the soldiers sometimes treated the Indians. Then there was the problem that many Indians were dying from European diseases, for which they had no immunities. Though they tried to help the sick Indians, the friars did not fully understand why they were dying from diseases that killed so few Europeans.

Wild tribes, too, encouraged mission Indians to rebel. When, in 1775, the friars at San Diego Mission disciplined two Christian Indians who had been caught stealing, the Indians fled from the mission to the tribes that lived in the hills to the east of San Diego. On the fourth of November, 600 Indians attacked the mission and killed one of the priests there—Fray Luis Jayme (loo•EES HIGH•may). Then they shot his body full of arrows and pounded his head and face with stones and hunting sticks.

But Fray Junípero showed his charity in asking the governor to pardon the Indian who had been chiefly responsible for Fray Luis's death. The murderer should be punished, Serra told the governor, but he should not be executed. "Let him live," pleaded Fray Junípero, "in order that he should be saved. Give him to understand . . . that he is being pardoned in accordance with our law which commands us to forgive injuries."

Fray Junípero Serra spent the remainder of his life in California, visiting the missions he had established, preaching the Gospel, administering the sacraments, and protecting the rights of the Indians. In 1784 he began to feel pains in his chest, and he knew his end was near. After receiving last rites, Fray Junípero died on August 28. Both Spaniards and the Indians he so loved came to his funeral. So loud was the weeping of the Indians at the funeral that it was hard to hear the friars sing the office of the dead.

Fray Junípero was buried in the sanctuary of the mission church of San Carlos de Borromeo on the Monterey peninsula.

Chapter 3 Review

Summary

- Mistreatment by the Spanish made the Aztecs believe that the true God's love did not extend to them—or even worse, that the Spaniards' god was no more real than their gods! Our Lady of Guadalupe helped her beloved Aztecs, appearing to Juan Diego as an Aztec princess and sending him to the bishop with a miraculous tilma. After knowing that God loved the Aztecs, the Mexican people quickly converted to the Faith.
- In the north things were more difficult, and Spanish missionaries were martyred by the Indian tribes. Fray Juan de Padilla was the first American martyr. The missions in New Mexico were destroyed during Popé's rebellion, but Diego de Vargas saved Santa Fe in 1691 and reunited New Mexico.
- Fray Junípero Serra built California's famous missions, whose friars taught the Indians their faith and a new way of life that included farming and crafts. The orange-roofed adobe missions still dot California's landscape, reminding us of Fray Junípero's labors.

Chapter Checkpoint

1. Who was the defender of the Indians?
2. How did some of the conquistadors mistreat the Indians?
3. Why did the Royal Audience come to New Spain? Why were Guzmán, Ortiz, and Delgadillo sent back to Spain?
4. Who was the bishop of Mexico when Our Lady of Guadalupe appeared to St. Juan Diego?
5. Retell the story of Our Lady of Guadalupe. Why does Our Lady's appearance mean so much to Mexican Indians?
6. Who was the first martyr in what is now the United States?
7. What was Popé's rebellion? Where did it happen?
8. What priest is famous for establishing the California missions?
9. What did the California Indians learn in the missions?

Chapter Activities

1. California is famous to Americans as a place where people seek wealth. Miners flocked there during the Gold Rush, and would-be movie stars flocked to Hollywood when film was invented. What would Fray Junípero Serra want California to be famous for today? How can America carry on the work he started in those long-ago missions?
2. Ask your family and friends if they know who was the first martyr in the United States. Tell them the story of Fray Juan de Padilla.

The American Larder

With only a donkey and a bag of seed corn for planting, the sixteenth-century Franciscan missionaries went into the harsh, dry lands of Texas to baptize and catechize the Indians who lived along the San Antonio River. The Franciscans taught the Indians to farm and instructed them in the Spanish language. Together, they built five or so missionary churches. These missions served as the first foundations of Christianity to Indians who were so miserable that they were derided as the "dung-eaters" by the other inhabitants, the cannibal Caddos on the Gulf Coast, and the ferocious Comanches to the west. No one but the Franciscan missionaries seems to have been interested in these indigenous peoples of the San Antonio area; they were just too pitiful to bother raiding.

Chapter 4 France in the New World

10/5

The Founding of New France

Spain's Rival

Spain's success in the New World was bound to make other European nations jealous. Francis I, the king of France, was already fearful of Charles I. Charles was not only the king of Spain, but also, as Charles V, the Holy Roman Emperor and king of Germany. Charles's lands surrounded France on three sides. Now with all the gold and silver from the New World, King Charles was very powerful indeed. King Francis I wanted some of that wealth, and began scheming to get it.

Francis tried using **privateers.** Privateers were really only pirates; but because they worked for a king, they were thought to be respectable pirates. Their job was to attack and rob the Spanish ships that brought gold and silver from America to Spain. This was not a very good way to take Spanish treasure, as King Francis probably knew. Spanish ships were not weak opponents at sea, and though

Jacques Cartier, a French privateer

privateer: a pirate hired by a king or queen to steal treasure from another country's ships

69

**Giovanni da Verrazano,
an Italian privateer**

some treasure was lost to pirates, most of it still reached Spain and the coffers of King Charles. No, Francis would have to find a different way to get New World gold. He would have to send someone to America to find it. The man the king chose was Giovanni da Verrazano.

Giovanni da Verrazano was born near Florence, Italy, 10 years before Christopher Columbus sailed to America. Verrazano had much experience at sea; he had sailed throughout the Mediterranean and had even lived in Syria and Egypt. Having served as a privateer for King Francis, he had firm knowledge of the Atlantic. Verrazano was the perfect one to send on a voyage of exploration to America.

King Francis told Verrazano that he wanted him not only to sail to America, but to find a northwest passage through America to the Indies. With this goal, Verrazano set sail in the *Dauphine* in January 1524. For less than two months he was at sea, sailing northwest to avoid Spanish lands in America. In March, Verrazano landed on the coast of what is today North Carolina. He then sailed north and found a great opening into the sea. It was New York harbor. From this harbor, Verrazano sailed northward along the coasts of what would one day be Massachusetts, Rhode Island, and Maine, and then proceeded on to Newfoundland.

Verrazano returned to France in July. Though he encouraged King Francis to send colonists to America, the king did nothing. He was at war with King Charles and had no time to think about colonies.

But 10 years later, King Francis again turned his thoughts to America and the northwest passage. Again he chose a privateer to make the voyage, one Jacques Cartier (ZHOCK car•tee•AY) of Saint-Malo on the northern coast of France. With two small ships and only 61 men, Cartier set sail for America in April 1534. It took Cartier only 20 days to reach the coast of Newfoundland where, fearful of the great icebergs in the sea, he sailed into a bay. From Newfoundland, Cartier sailed farther north; but seeing only barren, cold lands, he again turned south. Sailing past Newfoundland, he found beautiful Prince Edward Island and then a great inlet that he thought might be the northwest passage. It was not that fabled passage but the large Chaleur Bay. After trading with the Indians of Chaleur Bay for beaver, fox, and marten furs, Cartier returned to France.

Martens

Eight months later, Cartier was again on the sea. Returning to the area around Chaleur Bay, Cartier saw the great St. Lawrence waterway. Learning from local Indians about a land of gold far up the St. Lawrence, Cartier pushed his way upriver. Sailing as far as the present site of the city of Montreal, Cartier found no gold. Disappointed, he returned to France.

Six years passed before King Francis sent Cartier on another voyage. This time Cartier was under the command of Lord Roberval, who had been told by the king to establish a colony in Canada. The colony failed. Since winters in that region were so cold, far colder than in France, many colonists fell sick and died. Those who survived returned to France in 1543.

The Founding of Canada

He wanted to be a navigator, not a soldier. Born in a little seaport town in France about 1567, Samuel de Champlain (sam•wy•EL duh sham•PLAIN) was, certainly, more fitted to the sea than to the military camp. France, though, was in the midst of a great civil war between French Protestants (called Huguenots) and French Catholics. Champlain, like other young men of his country, took up arms. When the war ended, Champlain returned to his home and joined his uncle on a voyage to Spain. While in Spain, Champlain was given command of a vessel

Samuel de Champlain, a French explorer

bound for the West Indies. Thus, in 1599, he was able to fulfill a long dream of his—to cross the Atlantic and explore the New World.

Over 60 years had passed since France had sent explorers over to America. The new French king, Henry IV, wanted to take over where King Francis I had left off. In 1603, King Henry commissioned an expedition to return to the regions explored by Verrazano and Cartier and establish a settlement there. On this expedition, as second in command, went Samuel de Champlain. Crossing the cold Atlantic, the expedition reached the St. Lawrence, which the French called the "**River of Canada.**"

River of Canada: the name for what is now the St. Lawrence River

With a companion, Champlain set off up the St. Lawrence to explore the lands farther inland. For many miles the St. Lawrence is very wide, but at a place the Indians called *Quebec*, it grows suddenly narrower. There, on the north side of the river, loomed a large hill, which, Champlain thought, would be a good site for a fortress. Champlain went even farther up the St. Lawrence to the place where rapids disturb the river, just west of where the city of Montreal stands today.

Champlain not only explored the lands about the St. Lawrence, but he also came to learn about the Indian tribes that dwelt there. The Indians of Canada were not as civilized as the Aztecs of Mexico nor the Incas of Peru. Instead of stone dwellings, the Canadian Indians lived in villages in dwellings made of wood and tree bark. Though, like many other Indian tribes, the Canadian Indians went on hunting forays, they also engaged in farming. Among the crops they grew were maize (corn), squash, beans, and tobacco.

Many tribes lived in Canada. Among these were two great tribes, the Hurons and the Algonquin. These tribes were closely related and fought alongside each other

An Iroquois Indian

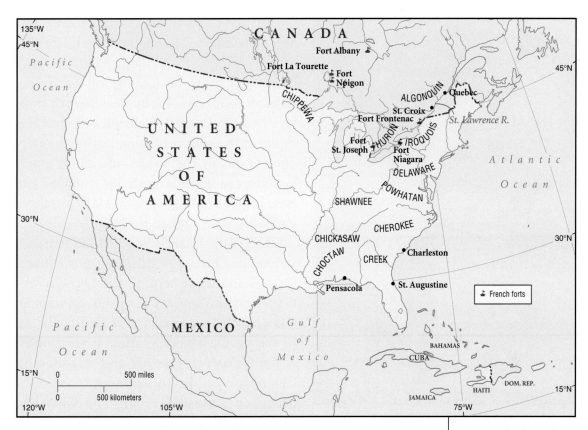

Indian tribes in North America and French forts and settlements in Canada

against their enemies: the Mohawk, Onondaga, Oneida, Cayuga, and Seneca tribes. These five tribes or "nations" formed a league with each other and together were called the Iroquois. The Iroquois were powerful and bitter enemies. Beginning about the time Champlain was exploring the St. Lawrence, the Iroquois began waging war on surrounding tribes. Eventually, as we shall see, the Iroquois became the enemies of Champlain and the French.

Champlain returned to France in August 1603. In 1604, and again in 1608, Champlain returned to North America, seeking a site for a settlement. In 1608, at Quebec, Champlain built a dwelling and a storehouse. The storehouse would house the pelts of beaver, marten, and fox that, instead of gold, would become France's source of wealth in the New World. Though Champlain wanted

Fur traders

men to settle as farmers around Quebec, few did. Frenchmen seemed to prefer the free life of a fur trapper. Paddling their canoes along the many rivers of Canada or wandering through its forests of lofty trees, French trappers not only captured valuable pelts but also explored the wild continent. Loving the freedom found in the wild lands, the trappers became fast friends with the Indians and even began to live like them. Many a trapper took an Indian woman for his wife.

Champlain himself was not content just staying in Quebec, watching it grow into a fortress and settlement. Longing to discover new lands and sources of wealth, Champlain followed the rivers that flowed into the St. Lawrence. On one expedition, having joined a war party of Hurons and Algonquins, Champlain paddled up a river he named the Richelieu (rea•shul•YEU). The Richelieu River, Champlain discovered, flowed out of an enormous body of water, a long lake that stretched southward, beyond sight. This was Lake Champlain, which lies between the modern states of New York and Vermont.

Champlain passed down this great lake until it gradually narrowed, over a hundred miles to the south. On a peninsula jutting into the lake, called Ticonderoga, Champlain and his French joined the Hurons and Algonquins in a battle against the Iroquois. Though they could probably have defeated the Hurons and Algonquins by themselves, the Iroquois could not overcome the French. The Iroquois never forgave the French for joining forces with their enemies. In the years to come, the Iroquois would remain foes of the French.

In 1612, the king of France appointed Champlain to be lieutenant general of "**New France,**" as Canada was called. In 1615, Champlain joined a war party of Indians and found lakes even larger than Lake Champlain—**Lake Huron,** and **Lake Ontario.** These lakes were two of the inland freshwater seas we call the **Great Lakes.**

After this expedition, Champlain settled down at Quebec to oversee the settlement's growth. Quebec grew slowly, so that by the late 1620s it had only about 100 settlers. In 1629, English pirates, under the pay of the king of England, captured Quebec and imprisoned Champlain. For three years, Champlain remained their prisoner. In 1632, he was released and once again took over governing Quebec. He died three years later, in 1635.

> **New France:** a translation of the French name for modern Canada
> **Lake Huron:** a Great Lake between Canada and Michigan
> **Lake Ontario:** a Great Lake between Canada and New York
> **Great Lakes:** great inland freshwater seas that divide Canada from various states

10/6

The Cross in the Wilderness

Labors of the Blackrobes

After four years spent laboring in the wilderness, one would have thought Father Jean de Brébeuf (ZHON duh bray•BEUF) would have been happy to be home, in France. Father Brébeuf had been one of three Jesuit priests whom Samuel de Champlain had invited to come to Quebec in 1625. They had not remained in the French settlement but had gone to live among the Indians, to live like Indians. Dwelling in wigwams, Brébeuf and his brother Jesuits braved the cold Canadian winters. With Father de Noüe (noo•AY), Brébeuf had traveled by canoe to Lake Huron to bring the Gospel to the Indians there but was unable to convert anyone.

A priest speaks to an Indian council.

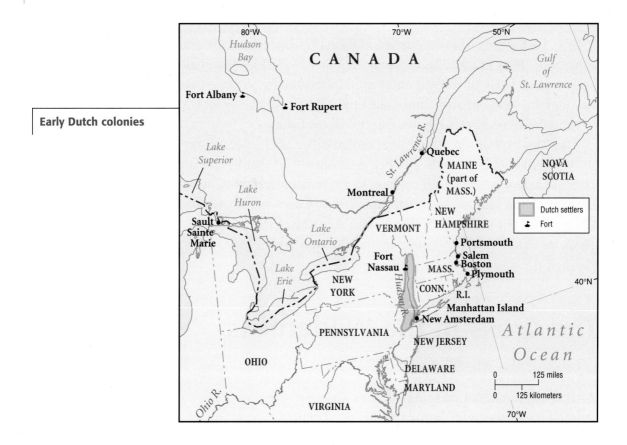

Early Dutch colonies

Then, in 1629, when the English seized Quebec, Brébeuf was forced to leave Canada. Back in France, far from all the hardships and disappointments of his life in Canada, Father Brébeuf waited eagerly for the day he could return and, once again, minister to the Indians.

Not until 1633 was Father Brébeuf finally able to return to Canada. With another Jesuit, Father Daniel, Brébeuf left Quebec and traveled 30 days through the wilderness to the country of the Hurons, along the banks of Lake Huron. The priests faced not only such wilderness dangers as wild animals but also the threat of hostile Indians, for their journey took them through the country of the Iroquois, who hated the French. But finally Fathers Brébeuf and Daniel reached Lake Huron. Father Brébeuf would spend the next

16 years there, living a life of great suffering, ministering to the Hurons. To the Indians, Brébeuf and his fellow Jesuits would be known as **blackrobes** because of the long, black robes (or cassocks) the priests wore.

Three years later, in 1636, another Jesuit missionary, Father Isaac Jogues (ZHOG), arrived in the regions in which Brébeuf and Daniel labored. The same love of God and zeal for souls that Father Brébeuf possessed had brought Father Jogues to the savage and dangerous country around Lake Huron. Along the banks of the great lake, Father Jogues, with other Jesuits, including Father Charles Garnier (garn•YAH), wandered until they came to Sault Sainte Marie on the banks of the St. Mary's River. Father Jogues longed not only to convert the Indians around Sault Sainte Marie but to go even farther west to the Sioux Indians, who lived at the very beginnings of the great Mississippi River.

The early 1640s was a dangerous time for the missionaries, for the warfare between the Hurons and Iroquois had grown more bitter. The Iroquois had become even more powerful, for they had obtained guns from the Dutch, who had established the trading colony named **New Amsterdam** far to the south on Manhattan Island. Since they were establishing settlements all along the Hudson River, the Dutch needed to be on good terms with their neighbor, the Iroquois.

The first missionary to suffer from the Iroquois was Father Isaac Jogues. He was returning to Sault Sainte Marie from the French settlement of Trois-Rivières on the St. Lawrence when he was captured by a band of Mohawks. The Mohawks took Father Jogues to their village on the Mohawk River, about 40 miles north of where Albany, New York, is today. The Mohawks treated Father Jogues like a slave and tortured him by biting or burning off several of his fingers. Jogues bravely bore his sufferings for a year and a month. Finally, he was rescued by Dutch settlers, who took him down the Hudson River to New Amsterdam. From there he returned to France.

blackrobes: the Indian name for French priests, who wore black cassocks

New Amsterdam: a Dutch colony on Manhattan Island

Despite the brutal suffering he had undergone, Father Jogues longed to return to the missions. Only a few months after returning to France, he was again in Canada. Never flinching in the face of danger, Father Jogues decided to bring the Gospel to the very Indians who had tortured and enslaved him. It was not a good time to go among the Mohawk. Sickness had struck many of the Iroquois, and blight had ruined their crops. The Indians believed the missionaries were sorcerers who brought all these troubles on them.

With only one companion, Father Jogues entered the Mohawk lands. The Indians captured him and, stripping him naked, slashed him with sharp knives. Finally, they felled the priest with a blow from a tomahawk. Cutting off Father Jogues's head, they placed it on a pole. His body they threw into the Mohawk River.

Meanwhile, the Iroquois were gradually destroying the Huron nation. Not only did the Huron themselves suffer, but the missionaries as well. Though now at peace with the French, the Iroquois tortured and killed French missionaries who worked among their enemies. On March 16, 1649, Iroquois warriors captured Father Jean Brébeuf.

The Iroquois build a boat.

Henry Hudson

The French were not the only ones looking for a shorter route to the Indies. Nor were they the only ones who envied the wealth Spain found in the New World. A group of Dutch merchants in the Netherlands, who had formed the Dutch East India Company in 1602, hired an English navigator named Henry Hudson to find a passage to the Indies that did not go around the horn of Africa. The merchants knew that both the French and the English had been unsuccessful in finding a northwest passage. So the merchants asked Hudson, instead, to find them a northeast passage.

With a Dutch and English crew, Hudson set sail from Amsterdam in the *Half Moon* in April 1609. He first tried to sail eastward along the north coast of Russia; but this was the region of the North Pole, and the waters soon became choked with ice. When he became convinced that he could go no farther eastward, Hudson changed course and began seeking for a northwest passage instead. Setting his course somewhat south and west, Hudson crossed the Atlantic and landed on the coast of Newfoundland. Hudson sailed southward along the coasts of what would be Nova Scotia, Maine, and Massachusetts. When he reached what looked like a great water passage into the mainland, Hudson turned the *Half Moon* up the passage. Passing a long island that the Indians called Manhattan, Hudson continued northward up the water passage; he thought, perhaps, he had found the northwest passage to the Indies. Of course, he had not. By the time he reached the site of the future city of Albany, New York, Hudson discovered that his northwest passage was only a great river. Turning south once again, he sailed down the river that would one day bear his name: the Hudson River.

The merchants of the Dutch East India Company were very interested in the news Hudson brought back to Amsterdam of the rich furs that could be trapped along the shores of the Hudson River. In 1610 the company began sending fur-trading ships to the country Hudson had discovered. So much wealth was gotten from the region that, by 1618, the Dutch had established two trading settlements on the Hudson. The first was **Fort Nassau,** on the site where Albany, New York, now sits; the other, later named New Amsterdam (1625), was on the southern tip of Manhattan Island. In the coming years Dutch settlers would settle in this region, and a new colony would be born—New Netherland.

Poor Henry Hudson, though, ended his life sadly. In 1610 some English merchants sent him on another voyage to see if he could discover a northwest passage to the Indies. Reaching Newfoundland, this time Hudson sailed north instead of south. Passing between Newfoundland and Baffin Island, he entered a wide body of water that he thought might be the Pacific Ocean. It was not that ocean but a great bay, whose water—as he discovered—turns to ice in winter. From November to June, Hudson and his crew were stuck in ice. In summer, when the ice finally thawed, Hudson wanted to sail farther into the west to see if he could reach the Indies. But, tired and starved, his crew did not want to hear of any more voyaging. Putting Hudson and a few others in a small boat along with a gun, some powder, a cooking pot, and other supplies, the crew sailed off, leaving Hudson on the bay that one day would be called Hudson Bay. The ship returned to England, but Henry Hudson was never heard from again.

> **Fort Nassau:** a Dutch colony that occupied the site of modern Albany, New York

Though the tortures that followed his capture were horrible, Father Brébeuf never uttered a groan. When the Indians beat him with clubs, Father Brébeuf did not cry out. Tying him to posts, the savages kindled a fire at his feet and slashed him with their knives; still, Father Brébeuf did not beg for mercy. The Indians next poured scalding hot water over Brébeuf's head as if they were baptizing him. And if all these tortures were not enough, the Indians tied around Brébeuf's neck a collar of red-hot tomahawk heads and drove a red-hot iron rod down his throat. When Brébeuf finally lay dead, the Indians cut out his heart and ate it. He had been a brave enemy and the Indians desired a part of his spirit. They thought they could get this by eating his heart.

By 1649, the year Brébeuf suffered martyrdom, the Iroquois had destroyed the Huron nation. They next turned their attention to other tribes, including the Tobacco nation. Since 1646, Father Charles Garnier had been working among the Tobacco people and had made many converts. Though a frail man, Father Garnier had endured many hardships in the wilderness. So patient was Garnier that he was known as the "lamb" of the missions. Without fear he awaited his own martyrdom, which he knew was not far off. With simple faith Father Garnier commended himself to Our Lady, whose Immaculate Conception he had once vowed to defend.

He had not long to wait. Garnier's village of St. John's was but one of the Tobacco settlements that the Iroquois attacked with savage fury. Thinking nothing of himself, Father Garnier encouraged his people not to forsake Christ in their hour of trial. Finally, Father Garnier was himself so wounded that he knew he would surely die. Still, he thought not of himself, but of his suffering flock. Father Garnier dragged himself across the ground toward a dying Indian to give him absolution. As he raised his hand in blessing, Garnier received his deathblow from another warrior. The good priest died in the very act of giving another eternal life. The date was December 7, 1649, the eve of the feast of the Immaculate Conception.

10/7

Lily of the Mohawk

It sometimes seemed that the missionaries who roamed New France suffered much but made little progress among the Indians. It was very difficult to convert the wandering tribesmen of the forests. The Indians who did become Christian often died from disease or were killed by their enemies, the Iroquois. Though the Indians came to love the blackrobes, it seemed that the French missions were mostly a failure.

But Jesuit missions did produce one success: a Mohawk Indian girl named Kateri Tekakwitha. Kateri's mother and father had died from smallpox when she was a young girl. After their death, she went to live with her uncle, who was the chief of the Turtle clan of the Mohawk tribe. Kateri first heard of the Christian faith from the French missionary, Father Jacques de Lamberville (ZHOCK duh LOMB•er• VEEL). When only 11 years old, she became a Christian, though she had to delay receiving baptism.

Kateri Tekakwitha so deeply loved God that she wished to give herself to him entirely. She did not want to marry, but to remain consecrated to Christ as a holy virgin was very difficult in Indian society. All alone she faced many temptations to deny Christ, but she did not fall into sin. Finally, at the age of 18, Kateri received baptism from Father Lamberville.

The Mohawks, most of whom were not Christian, could not understand why a woman would remain unmarried. They so pressured Kateri to abandon the life of chastity she had embraced that she finally fled from her home to a village of Christians on the St. Lawrence River. There she spent the few remaining years of her life doing good works. All who lived around her marveled at her holiness. At her death she became an object of veneration to the Indian peoples of the northlands. So beautiful had been her life and so holy had been her death that she was ever after known as the "Lily of the Mohawk."

Mission figurine of Kateri Tekakwitha

New Lands for King Louis

The Adventurer and the Blackrobe

Louis Joliet (ZHOL•y•ay) might have become a priest, but the wild lands of New France called to him; instead, he became a fur trader and adventurer. Born in Quebec in 1645, Joliet studied at the Jesuit school there, where he was known as a good mathematics scholar. At the age of 17 he received minor orders (which means he was being trained to be a priest); but within a few years he was far from Quebec, trading with Indians and roving through the forests and along the wilderness rivers of Canada.

Jacques Marquette, a missionary explorer

Joliet was not the only French adventurer to hear Indian stories about a great river that flowed into the sea far to the south. These stories had crossed the ocean and reached the court of King Louis XIV in Paris. King Louis needed a lot of money, because he wanted to expand the power of France in Europe. He hoped that this great river might reach to the Pacific Ocean and so allow him to get his hands on Mexican silver. King Louis told the governor of New France to find someone who could explore this "great water," as the Indians called the river. The governor knew just the "someone" to choose—the fur trader, Louis Joliet.

Joliet chose an old schoolmate for his companion on this expedition of discovery. Jacques Marquette (ZHOCK mar•KETT) had also studied under the Jesuits in Quebec, and like Joliet, he had taken **minor orders.** Unlike Joliet, though, Marquette became a priest. As a Jesuit missionary, Marquette became an expert in Indian languages and even wandered into the same backcountry that Joliet loved so much. When Joliet asked Father Marquette if he would join the expedition, the priest was working among Huron and Ottawa Indians on Mackinac Island on Lake Huron. Both of these tribes had been driven from their homelands by other tribes. They were downtrod-

minor orders: members of the clergy below the order of deacon, including acolyte, exorcist, and subdeacon

den and unwilling to accept baptism. Hoping to have better luck among the Indians along the great water, Father Marquette joined Joliet's expedition.

It was in May 1673 that Joliet, Marquette, and five others left Mackinac Island on their quest to find the great water. Paddling through the straits of Mackinac in birchbark canoes, the explorers entered the fourth of the Great Lakes, **Lake Michigan.** It was spring, but a chill still lay on the lake. Following old well-used Indian paths, the explorers crossed Lake Michigan and entered Green Bay, in what is now eastern Wisconsin. From Green Bay, they followed the Fox River upstream until they reached Lake Winnebago. From Lake Winnebago they continued westward, following the Fox River.

Both trappers and Jesuits had visited the region around Lake Winnebago before, but of the country beyond the lake they knew little. When Joliet and Marquette's party entered a swamp, they did not know what to do. Many channels of water led in different directions. Which would take them to the great water? Here, Father Marquette's skill in languages came in handy. He spoke with Indians of the region and learned that the Wisconsin River lay only a short distance from the Fox. The explorers had only to carry their canoes a short distance overland, and they would find it. The

Lake Michigan: one of the four Great Lakes; it is surrounded by the states of Michigan, Wisconsin, Illinois, and Indiana.

Jacques Marquette and Louis Joliet, missionary explorers, travel with Indians down the Mississippi River, 1672.

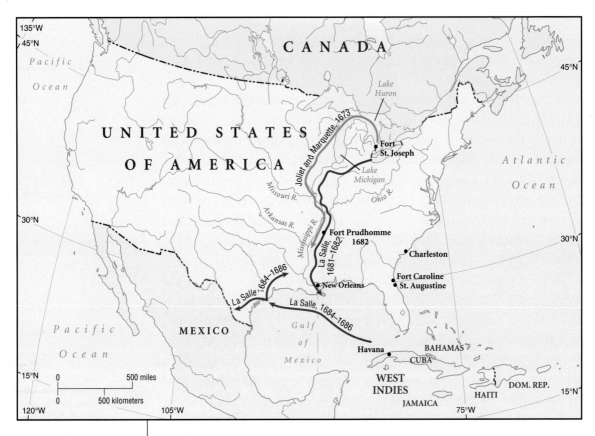

**Joliet and Marquette's
and La Salle's voyages
in North America**

Wisconsin River, the natives said, flowed eventually into the great
water, far to the west.

The Wisconsin did, indeed, flow into the great water—the river
we call the Mississippi. Joliet and Marquette were far to the north
of the place where Hernando de Soto had come upon the same
river over a century earlier. It was June and the summer air grew
ever warmer as the explorers floated down the river. Soon they
came into the country of the Illinois Indians, whose great fields of
corn grew along the banks of the river. The Illinois proved friendly
to the explorers. The Indians asked that Marquette remain among
them, but the priest replied that he first had to complete the expedition. But afterwards, he said, he would come to live and work
among them.

Southward, ever southward floated Joliet and Marquette down the great river. On their right, they passed a river, a great muddy river, swift and wild, that carried large tree trunks and floating islands into the Mississippi. This was the Missouri, which rose about 2,700 miles to the west, in the Rocky Mountains, and crossed wide plains before it poured into the Mississippi. So great was the Missouri that Marquette thought they had found the northwest passage to the Indies. Further downstream, the explorers passed another great river, the Ohio, that flowed into the Mississippi from the east.

South of the Missouri, the explorers entered into warm and humid lands, where draping mosses hung from trees like long, green beards. Coming to where the Arkansas River flows into the Mississippi, the explorers went ashore. An Indian tribe that lived along the river entertained Joliet and Marquette and their party with a meal of cornmeal cakes and roasted dog. This was little to the Frenchmen's liking; but having good manners, they ate it anyway. The Indian chief explained to them that he would have served them buffalo meat, if his tribe had any. But the Indian tribes living on the plains to the west had guns, and they would not let his tribe hunt buffalo.

From the chief's story, Joliet and Marquette learned they had entered Spanish territory—since only the Spanish could have given the Indians guns. Both explorers feared that if they went any farther south, they might be captured by the Spanish, and then they could never bring to King Louis what they had learned about the great water. Besides, now they had seen enough to know that the Mississippi did not flow into the Pacific. If anything, it flowed into the Caribbean Sea, right into the heart of Spanish America.

From the Arkansas River, the exploring party again turned northward. Retracing their way, they came at last to Marquette's mission on Mackinac Island. There, Joliet left the priest and returned to Quebec to report to the governor of New France.

A year later, Father Marquette, to keep his promise, returned to the Illinois Indians. Spending the winter of 1674–1675 near the present site of the city of Chicago, Marquette grew very ill.

Nevertheless, in the spring, he pushed south to the country of the Illinois people. There he said Mass for the people, but being so weakened by sickness, he could not remain among them. After only three weeks, he began his return journey to Mackinac Island. He would never see his mission again; Marquette died near the Marquette River on May 18, 1675. He was only 38 years old.

Voyages of the Lord of La Salle

There were many differences between Louis Joliet and René de La Salle (ren•EH•duh•la•SAL). While Joliet was born in America and was the son of a poor wagon maker, La Salle was born in France and was the son of a nobleman. La Salle's full name was René-Robert Cavelier, Sieur de La Salle (which means René-Robert, Knight, Lord of La Salle), a very noble name, indeed. But Joliet had no other name except Louis. Yet, despite their differences, Joliet and La Salle were very similar. Both had been educated by Jesuits, and both had thought of entering the priesthood. Both, too, had abandoned the priesthood in favor of exploring the wilds of America.

René de La Salle first came to America in 1666. He received a grant of land outside the settlement of Montreal but soon found that the life of a farmer was not for him. Like so many other Frenchmen, he left the plow to become a fur trader, exploring the Great Lakes and the many rivers that flowed into them.

Around the time Joliet and Marquette were exploring the Mississippi, the governor of New France came up with a plan that included La Salle. The governor was afraid that the coming of the Dutch and the English to America would put New France in danger. To protect New France, he thought he would build forts and missions up and down the rivers of New France, including the newly discovered Mississippi. The governor sent La Salle to France to convince King Louis XIV of this plan. After two years, the king agreed. Not only that, but Louis said he wanted La Salle to explore the Mississippi all the way to its delta. In return, he would give La Salle control of all the lands he should discover, as well as control of the fur trade in those lands.

La Salle, with a party of 54 adventurers that included woodsmen and Indian guides as well as 10 Indian women and three children, set out in the winter of 1681–1682 to explore the Mississippi. The winter was bitterly cold, and the party dragged their canoes on sleds down the frozen waters of the Chicago and Illinois rivers. Except for the cold, La Salle's exploring party suffered no mishaps on their journey. Because La Salle had a peace pipe, he was able to make friends with the Indians he met along the river. He might have benefited from the fact that the French had a very good reputation among the Indians. Unlike the Spanish, the French established few permanent settlements in the New World, and neither the fur trappers nor the missionaries threatened the Indian way of life.

La Salle claims the Mississippi Valley for France.

La Salle's party passed beyond the Arkansas River into lands where winter never came. Like De Soto's men long before, the French explorers entered the swampy delta of the Mississippi. La Salle dreamed of building a city in the delta, on the spot where the Mississippi made a wide bend. This city, thought La Salle, would become the Paris of the New World.

On April 9, 1692, when La Salle reached the mouth of the Mississippi, where the great river poured into the Gulf of Mexico, he claimed the entire river and all the lands on either side for King Louis XIV of France. He also gave these lands a new name, in honor of the king; he called them **Louisiana.**

Louisiana: the name given to all the lands on either side of the Mississippi River

Though La Salle had no trouble from Indians on his journey, he soon found he had plenty of trouble from the French. New France had a new governor who did not like La Salle's control over the great river. This governor was joined by several French merchants who were also jealous of La Salle. La Salle finally had to return to France to seek the king's support against his enemies. Louis listened to La Salle, and once again named him governor of Louisiana.

La Salle had already erected some forts and trading posts on the Mississippi. Now, with the king's blessing, he wished to return to the Mississippi delta to build his New World Paris. In 1684, with four ships and 400 men, La Salle set sail from France, bound for the Mississippi delta. Unfortunately, when his small fleet reached the West Indies, it was attacked by the Spanish. La Salle then fell sick and had to stay on a West Indian island until

La Salle takes possession of Louisiana.

he recovered. By the time he recovered, most of his men had deserted him.

When La Salle was finally able to set sail again, only 180 of his men remained with him. More misfortunes were to come. Sailing north and west, La Salle completely missed the Mississippi delta. He ended up hundreds of miles to the west, in Matagorda Bay on the coast of Texas. La Salle knew he had missed the Mississippi, and he set out on an overland expedition to find out just where he was. When this first expedition failed, he set out on another, only to be killed by his own men in March 1687.

Though La Salle had failed to build his new Paris and establish a great empire for France in the Mississippi River valley, his work continued after his death. Under King Louis XIV, forts and missions, along with French settlements, were built all along the Mississippi. In 1717, the city of La Salle's dreams was established on the very spot he had chosen for it. Called New Orleans, this city would become the most important trade and cultural center of the deep South. Even today it remains a center of French culture in the United States.

Chapter 4 Review

Summary
- France began exploring the New World because Spain was powerful in Europe and in the New World. France's wealth would come not from gold, but from the precious warm furs of the plentiful animals that roamed the northern forests.
- Canada was founded and settled by the French, who built some farms, trapped furs in the woods, and continued exploring the vast midsection of the North American continent. The French missionaries, called black-robes, labored among the Indian tribes, converting some like St. Kateri Tekakwitha, but often shedding the blood of others like Saints Isaac Jogues and Jean de Brébeuf.
- The French explorers Joliet, Marquette, and La Salle ventured into the United States to explore the great water. Joliet and his translator, Father Marquette, found the northern waters of the Mississippi. La Salle claimed all the lands along the Mississippi River for his king, naming

them Louisiana in honor of King Louis. This increased the territory of New France, making France a great power in the New World.

Chapter Checkpoint

1. What did King Francis I do?
2. Who was Giovanni da Verrazano? What lands did he find?
3. What did Jacques Cartier discover?
4. Which French explorer has a lake named for him, between New York and Vermont?
5. Name the tribes that made up the Iroquois alliance.
6. What tribes were enemies of the Iroquois and friends of the French?
7. Who were two great blackrobe martyrs? Which one died near Albany, New York?
8. After her holy death, what was St. Kateri Tekakwitha called?
9. How did Father Marquette help Louis Joliet discover the Mississippi? What might have happened if he had not been on the expedition?
10. Although René La Salle explored the Great Lakes, he is most famous for his trip down the Mississippi. What did he do at the end of this trip?

Chapter Activities

1. Since the United States was founded by English colonists, we often forget the French roots in this country. Take a map of the United States and look at the states that were parts of the original territories of Louisiana and New France (i.e., Louisiana, Alabama, Mississippi, Arkansas, Missouri, Illinois, Iowa, Wisconsin, and Michigan). How many names of towns, rivers, cities, and states remind us of the French? Do you see the names Joliet, Marquette, or La Salle anywhere?
2. Tell someone you know—your parents, grandparents, or friends—about the saints of New France.

The American Larder

Among the Iroquois Indians, there was a mythological story about three inseparable sisters; these three sisters were the food staples of squash, corn, and beans. Corn, beans, and squash were usually planted together in a mound and usually eaten together. When the plants began to grow, the corn grew tall and straight; the bean plants then used the corn for a trellis, and the squash with its huge leaves trailed down the mound, keeping weeds down. When did the planting of these inseparable sisters take place? When the young leaves of the oak tree were about the size of a squirrel's ear, the Indians said.

Chapter 5 England Comes to America

If England Had Discovered America . . .

Christopher Columbus was not the only seafarer to dream of reaching the Indies by sailing west. Another sailor from Genoa, Giovanni Caboto, also believed one could reach far-off China and Japan by sailing west. What's more, he came to this idea about the same time Columbus did. Who knows? If Queen Isabella had refused to fund Columbus's voyage, it might have been Giovanni Caboto who discovered America. And it would not have been Spain who first settled the New World, but England.

It might have been England, for Giovanni Caboto moved to that great island in 1484. John Cabot (as the English called Caboto) tried to convince the merchants of the seafaring town of Bristol to pay for an expedition to discover a westward route to the Indies.

John and Sebastian Cabot depart from Bristol harbor.

91

Did the merchants think him crazy? Not at all! Since they had often crossed the cold Atlantic to Iceland, they had heard stories about the "Island of Brazil" and of the "Seven Cities" that lay to the west. The merchants sent Cabot to explore westward to find these islands, but always without success. Finally, in 1493, came news of Columbus's discovery of the "Indies." It was no longer any use searching for islands, Cabot and the merchants thought. They should just get to the Indies as quickly as possible.

The *Matthew:* the first English ship to sail for the New World

Cabot approached King Henry VII of England. Would his majesty approve an expedition to discover a route to the Indies? King Henry did approve, but being somewhat stingy, he told Cabot that he had to pay for the exploration himself. On May 2, 1497, Cabot and a crew of 18 men set sail from Bristol harbor in the **Matthew.**

John Cabot's tall ship, the *Matthew,* is re-created here in full sail. John Cabot left Bristol to discover Newfoundland, in North America.

It took Cabot only a little over seven weeks to cross the northern Atlantic. On June 24, 1497, the feast of the birth of St. John the Baptist, Cabot landed on Cape Breton Island and claimed it for King Henry of England. Cabot, who was certain he had landed in the Indies, sailed north again to see what more he could discover. Though he skirted

the coast of Newfoundland, Cabot found no signs that he was in Asia. But still believing that he had reached the Indies, he returned to England, landing at Bristol on August 6.

Though Cabot had not returned to England with gold or spices, King Henry approved another exploration to the Indies. The king even offered to pay for the effort! In May 1498, Cabot with 300 men in two ships, set sail again—this time to find a northwest passage to the Indies. Cabot first set his course for Greenland. From Greenland, he crossed to cold, forbidding Baffin Island. Finding that land little to his liking, Cabot turned south, sailing along the coasts of Newfoundland, Nova Scotia, Maine, and Massachusetts. He made it as far south as Maryland when his dwindling supplies forced him to return to England. He arrived in Bristol in the autumn of 1498.

King Henry VII did nothing further about Cabot's discoveries. His son, Henry VIII, who became king in 1509, didn't seem at all interested in the Indies or the New World. In fact, the king seemed more interested in how to divorce his wife, Catherine of Aragon (daughter to Ferdinand and Isabella), than in spices or gold. When the Pope refused to allow Henry to divorce Catherine, Henry decided to leave the Catholic Church. To excuse his disobedience, the king said that he himself, not the Pope, was the head of the Church in England. He also conveniently found an archbishop in his new church who would allow him to divorce Catherine. So was the "Church of England" founded, a church split from the Catholic Church.

King Henry VIII

Under the reigns of Henry VIII's son, Edward VI, and of Henry's daughter, Queen Elizabeth I, the Church of England began rejecting many other Catholic doctrines. It became a Protestant church. So, who knows? If England had first discovered America, perhaps the first settlements in the New World would have been Protestant and not Catholic. The history of the world might have been very different, indeed.

A Pirate's Life

The Queen's Dragon

It was a warm, muggy night. Guided by the lights of the town, the men quietly sailed their boats into shore. They had come to this little Spanish town on the coast of Panama to rob it. They were pirates, hungry for Spanish silver and gold.

They found bars of silver in this town, called *Nombre de Dios* ("Name of God"), but they were unable to take much of it. The attack had gone off well, but their leader, Francis Drake, had been shot by one of the few Spanish men who defended the town. Fearful that the Spanish might gather and attack them in turn, the pirates withdrew from the town.

Francis Drake

Though Francis Drake had fainted from loss of much blood, he soon recovered. He began making more raids on Spanish settlements on the Panama and South American coast—the region called the Spanish Main. Black slaves who had run away from their Spanish masters joined the pirates, as did French "privateers." The jungles of this region made it easy for them to hide. From the cover of the jungle, Drake and his men one day were able to ambush the mule train bringing silver from the mines to Nombre de Dios. Defeating the Spanish guard, Drake and his men seized much silver. On August 9, 1573, they sailed into Plymouth harbor in England, very rich men indeed.

Pirate though he was, Francis Drake did not have to hide what he had done from Queen Elizabeth, for she had sent him to the New World to steal Spanish silver. Drake was a privateer. Elizabeth was so pleased with Drake for bringing so much silver back home that she commissioned him to set sail on another and greater voyage. Drake, said the queen, was to try to sail all the way around the world.

Of course, the queen wanted Drake to raid Spanish settlements and attack Spanish ships on his trip. In his ship, the *Golden Hind,* and with a small fleet of four ships, Drake set sail in December 1577 for the coast of South America. Four months later, Drake reached the coast of Brazil. From Brazil he sailed south along the South American coast until he reached the Straits of Magellan between the tip of South America and Antarctica. So harsh was the weather in the straits that it took 16 days for Drake to pass them and round the tip of the continent.

Francis Drake and California Indians

Sailing northward along the west coast of South America, Drake attacked Spanish ships and pillaged Spanish settlements. Though he did not harm the people living in these settlements, he did steal their wealth—especially their gold and silver. Being a Protestant, Drake had no respect for Catholic churches but stole their sacred vessels (which were made of gold) and smashed their sacred pictures and crucifixes. It was for this reason that the Spanish called him *el Draco,* "the Dragon."

el Draco: Spanish for "the Dragon"; Francis Drake's nickname

Drake's voyage took him as far north as the coast of California. Somewhere along this coast he came ashore and claimed the land for Queen Elizabeth. From this region, which he named "New Albion," Drake sailed along the coast to the Olympic Peninsula in what is now the state of Washington. From there he crossed the wide Pacific, passed through the Indian Ocean, rounded the Cape of Good Hope, and sailed up the coast of Africa. Finally, on September 26, 1580, Drake arrived in Portsmouth harbor. The queen was so pleased with Drake that she came to Portsmouth to meet him. On board his ship, the *Golden Hind,* Queen Elizabeth knighted her "dragon." He was, from then on, known as *Sir* Francis Drake.

In the coming years, Sir Francis would continue to serve his queen. When war finally broke out between Spain and England, Drake led a fleet to the West Indies, where he captured the Spanish towns of Cartagena on the coast of Colombia, San Domingo on the island of Hispaniola, and Saint Augustine in Florida. Drake finally met his own death in 1596 on another expedition against the Spanish in the West Indies. Placing his body in a lead coffin, his men threw it into the waters near Nombre de Dios.

Sir Walter Raleigh spreads his cloak over a mud puddle for Queen Elizabeth.

The Queen's Favorite

Walter Raleigh certainly knew how to charm a queen. According to one story, he spread his cloak over a mud puddle so Queen Elizabeth could walk across it without getting her feet dirty. Whether this story is true or not, Walter Raleigh did become Elizabeth's favorite. As such, he was able to interest her in something that very much interested him. Walter Raleigh wanted to establish settlements in the New World.

Raleigh himself had never been to America. In 1584, he sent an expedition under Philip Amadas and Arthur Barlowe across the ocean to explore sites for a possible settlement. The expedition arrived back in England several months later after sailing along the coasts of what is today Florida, Georgia, and North Carolina. Barlowe and Amadas had many interesting things to show the queen: furs, a pearl necklace, and two Indians named Manteo and Wanchese. Elizabeth was very pleased, especially with the Indians; but what made her even happier was Raleigh's announcement that he wanted to name the new lands in America after the queen. Because Elizabeth had never married, she was called the "Virgin Queen." Raleigh thus named the new lands **Virginia,** in her honor.

Virginia: the colony Sir Walter Raleigh named after Queen Elizabeth, the "Virgin Queen"

English settlers arrive in Virginia.

After Amadas and Barlowe's successful voyage, Raleigh was able to get enough money to fund a settlement in America. In 1585, he sent Sir Richard Grenville with 108 settlers to Roanoke Island off the coast of what is now North Carolina. With the settlers sailed the Indian, Manteo. The settlement called **Roanoake** was not a success. The settlers could not plant any crops because they arrived on Roanoke Island too late in the year; moreover, seawater spoiled all their seeds. Grenville sailed to England for supplies; but when he returned to Roanoke Island, he found nobody there. Sir Francis Drake, stopping at Roanoke Island, had already brought all the settlers back to England.

Raleigh did not give up after this failure, but he was convinced that the swampy Roanoke Island was no place for a colony. So, in 1587, he sent about 120 men, women, and children under John White to Virginia and told them to settle on the Chesapeake Bay instead. But the sailors who brought the settlers over had other ideas. Landing the settlers at Roanoke, they refused to take them any further north. So, once again, the colony had to be founded on Roanoke.

Roanoke: the first English settlement in Virginia; it disappeared without a trace.

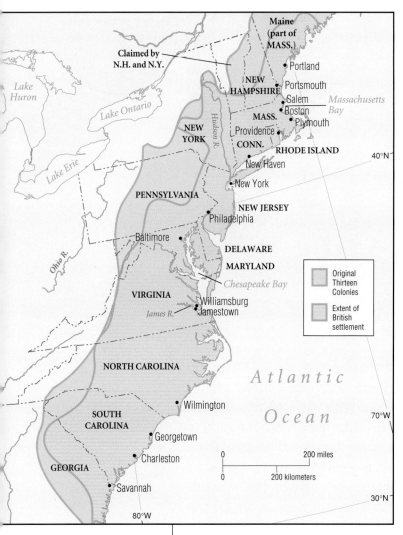

The 13 original colonies

It was on Roanoke Island that John White's daughter, Elinor Dare, gave birth to a daughter, the first English child born in America. But the child, named Virginia Dare, never lived among English people. Shortly after her birth, John White set sail for England to fetch supplies for the colony. Because England was at war with Spain, White was unable to return to the colony for three years. When White finally did return to Roanoke in 1590, he found no English settlers. Even their houses had been dismantled. All that remained was a wall of logs on which was carved the word "Croatoan," the name of an island off the coast of North Carolina. John White was never able to discover whether his daughter, granddaughter, and the other settlers had gone to that island, or whether they were living or dead. To this day, no one knows what happened to Virginia Dare and the Roanoke colony.

After 1587, Raleigh did nothing more to colonize Virginia. He had had a stroke of bad luck; he was no longer the queen's favorite. She had even imprisoned him for a while in the Tower of London. Raleigh had even more bad luck in 1603, when James I became king of England. King James thought Raleigh was a traitor and imprisoned him in the Tower of London for 13 years.

After his release from the Tower, Raleigh set sail for Guiana, on the coast of South America, to find a gold mine there. King James allowed him to go, but warned him not to fight with the Spanish. Off the coast of Guiana, Raleigh had another stroke of bad luck. Having fallen sick, he allowed his men to go ashore and explore without him. Unfortunately, when they returned they told him they had fought with the Spanish. They also told Raleigh that his son had been killed in the battle. Even worse, when Raleigh returned to England, the king ordered him to be executed for fighting with the Spanish.

Raleigh faced his death with great dignity. Asking to see the axe with which they would behead him, Raleigh said, "This is a sharp Medicine, but it is a Physician for all diseases." Then, placing his head on the chopping block, he calmly awaited his death.

The Land Where Tobacco Was King

The Adventurer and the Indian Maid

A few days before Christmas in 1606, three ships set sail from England. They were the *Susan Constant,* the *Godspeed,* and the *Discovery,* bound for Virginia. Bartholomew Gosnold promoted this expedition that brought 105 men to the New World in the hopes of, at last, founding a permanent colony there.

Models of the *Susan Constant, Godspeed,* and *Discovery*. **The original three colonist ships landed at Cape Henry on April 26, 1607. Their passengers established Jamestown, the first permanent American colony.**

Captain John Smith

Captain Gosnold might have wished that the number of colonists would drop to 104 before the end of the voyage. There was one man on board that some of the voyagers would willingly have thrown overboard. This was Captain John Smith, who many thought a proud and boastful man.

According to the stories he told about himself, John Smith had lived a very adventurous life. Since leaving home at the age of 16 in 1596, Smith had served in the French army, had been to sea as a merchant, and had fought with the Austrian army against the Moslem Turks. It was the Austrians, he said, who had made him a captain. In 1602, Smith was wounded in a battle against the Turks, who captured him and made him a slave.

The Turk who bought Smith sent him to the city of Istanbul as a present to his girlfriend. The Turkish woman, seeing the handsome slave, fell in love with him (at least, that's what Smith said). She sent Smith to her brothers so that he could be trained to serve as a fighter for the Turkish sultan. This gave Smith his chance for freedom. Killing one of the brothers, Smith fled to Russia. From there, passing through Poland, he eventually rejoined the Austrian army in Transylvania.

Captain John Smith had arrived back in England in time to join Gosnold's expedition to Virginia. Though the Virginia Company (London entrepreneurs who funded the expedition) had wanted Smith to be one of the governors of the new colony, Gosnold and others refused to give him a place on the governing council. They thought Smith had been plotting against them on the voyage.

So, not as a governor but as just a colonist, Smith sailed into the Chesapeake Bay and up the broad river that the colonists named the "James" after the king of England. The colonists chose a site for their settlement on a small peninsula sticking out into the James River. There they built a fort, calling it "Jamestown." The new site had many advantages; it could be protected from Indian attack and was surrounded by tall trees that could be cut down for timber. But Jamestown had one serious problem; it was built too near swampy ground. During the hot and muggy summer, many colonists, including Gosnold, died of swamp fever.

Jamestown also faced another threat: Indian attacks. Indians raided the camps, stealing supplies, guns, and gunpowder. On an overland expedition in search of supplies in December 1607, Captain John Smith was captured by Algonquin Indians who brought him to their powerful chief, Powhatan. At first Powhatan appeared friendly. After admiring Smith's compass (which the chief called a "magic crystal"), Powhatan invited him to a feast. But in the middle of the feast several braves grabbed Smith and stretched him out on a rock; other braves stood nearby with clubs, ready to beat him. While Powhatan enjoyed his little game, a young Indian girl suddenly ran into the circle of braves and threw her arms around Smith's head. Laying her own head on his chest, the Indian maid begged Powhatan not to kill the brave white man. The great chief could not refuse the girl, for she was his daughter, Matoaka, whom everyone called **Pocahontas** (meaning "playful one"). Powhatan ordered his braves to release Smith and made him a subchief of his tribe.

Pocahontas not only saved Smith's life, but she also saved Jamestown colony. The Algonquin Indians grew friendly toward the

Pocahontas: Algonquin Indian name, meaning "playful one"

Pocahontas saves John Smith's life.

Settlers in Jamestown

colonists on account of Smith. The Indians began visiting Jamestown, bringing with them game and other food. They also brought Pocahontas, who was always eager to visit her friend, Captain John Smith. Smith also enjoyed these visits. The 10-year-old Pocahontas, he said, was the most beautiful and intelligent of all Powhatan's people.

If it hadn't been for the food brought by the Indians, the Jamestown colonists might well have starved. Most of the colonists were nobles who, while in England, had never worked a day of their lives. Even in Virginia they refused to work, and so fields went unplowed and barns remained unbuilt or unrepaired. The arrival of 120 more settlers in January of 1608 did not help matters. Only one man was capable of saving the colony. This man was Captain John Smith.

Though many of the original colonists still did not like him, Smith became the governor of Jamestown on September 10, 1608, elected to serve a one-year term. As governor, Smith drove the colonists to save themselves. Whether they were willing or not, Smith forced everyone to work in the fields and build new storage barns for crops. So successful was Smith that by the summer of 1609, it looked as if the colony of Jamestown might survive.

However, because he was so hard on the colonists, Smith made many enemies. Some of these returned to England and complained about him to the merchants of the London Company (who funded Jamestown). Smith, they said, had been too harsh with the colonists and had not sent valuable cargoes to England. Hearing these complaints, the merchants decided to remove Smith as governor of Jamestown. In July 1609, a ship arrived at Jamestown with letters stating that Smith was to be replaced as governor.

Smith remained in Jamestown throughout the summer and into the autumn of 1609, because the new governor who was to replace him was late in arriving from England. That autumn, Smith suffered a serious accident; some gunpowder exploded and he was badly burned. When Smith departed for England, the colonists had already gathered a bountiful harvest into barns, a harvest they would not have had without the efforts of Captain John Smith.

Smith was unable to say farewell to the young Indian girl who had saved his life. Pocahontas had been told about Smith's accident, but nothing else. She mourned for her friend, believing he must be dead. Not for many years would Pocahontas know that Smith had returned alive, though not well, to his homeland across the sea.

Jamestown Saved

The colonists at Jamestown waited a long time for a governor to replace Captain John Smith. Autumn passed and winter approached, and still the new governor had not arrived. When winter came, it was an especially cold one. Though the harvest had been

10/14

Re-creation of the Jamestown settlement

good, many colonists starved. With the coming of spring, only 60 of about 220 colonists remained alive.

Sir Thomas Gates had been sent ahead by the new governor, Lord de la Warr, to bring supplies to the Jamestown colony. Unfortunately, Gates's ship had been wrecked in the Bermuda Islands, and he and his crew were forced to remain there for the winter. Just before Gates finally arrived at Jamestown on May 1610, the colonists had given up all hope. Burying their armor and guns, they planned to abandon Jamestown; then Gates and the much-needed supplies arrived, and hope returned. Jamestown had been saved.

Gates's ship brought to Virginia something even more valuable than supplies. A man named John Rolfe had sailed with Gates and had spent the winter with him in the Bahamas. While there, Rolfe obtained seed for the kind of tobacco the Spanish grew on the Caribbean islands: rich, sweet, full-bodied tobacco, the very best tobacco to be found the world over. Only the Spanish grew this kind of tobacco, and they sold it to the English at very high prices.

The people of Virginia had been looking for something that would make them money, and everything had failed. Tobacco, John Rolfe thought, was the answer. The English had grown very fond of tobacco smoking, and John Rolfe figured that if Virginia grew tobacco, it could be sold in England for less than the Spaniards' tobacco. Rolfe and some others planted the tobacco. When they harvested it, they found that it was almost as good as Caribbean tobacco. Soon, the

An eighteenth-century illustration shows the curing, airing, and storing of tobacco.

smokers in England agreed on its quality, and tobacco growing became for Virginia the chief way of making money. Once again, the colony had been saved.

John Rolfe brought the treasure of tobacco to Virginia; in turn, Virginia held a treasure for him. Rolfe had not been long in the colony before he fell in love with the Indian woman, Pocahontas. Pocahontas had been living at the new English settlement of Henrico as a captive. After Captain John Smith returned to England, war had broken out between the English and Powhatan. The chief had captured several Englishmen, so the English kidnapped Pocahontas. The English said they would exchange Pocahontas for the captive Englishmen.

Pocahontas returned John Rolfe's love, but he was troubled. He could not bring himself to marry Pocahontas, for he was a Christian and she, a pagan. But it soon became clear that a marriage between Rolfe and Pocahontas would bring peace between the English and the Indians. Pocahontas, who had been allowed to return to her people, told her father that the English had treated her well. She also told him that she loved John Rolfe and wanted to marry him. Powhatan agreed to the marriage. Pocahontas was baptized and took on the Christian name, Rebecca. On April 5, 1614, she and John Rolfe were married.

John and Rebecca Rolfe had a son, whom they named Thomas. Shortly after the child's birth, the Rolfes sailed to England. What must have been Rebecca Rolfe's wonder when she saw the great buildings, the churches, and the swarms of people in London! How very different it was from Virginia! In London, the Rolfes were presented to the king and the royal family. In London, too, Rebecca met, once again, her old friend, Captain John Smith. But Rebecca Rolfe's wonder and joy were not to last. She fell sick, and in March 1617, Rebecca Rolfe, Pocahontas, the daughter of the great chief Powhatan, died. She was only 22 years old.

John Rolfe laid his beloved wife in the cemetery in Gravesend, England.

Plymouth and Massachusetts Bay

A Haven for the Saints

In a city in Holland called Leyden lived a colony of Englishmen. These English men and women had come to live in Holland for only one reason: they wanted the freedom to practice their religion without interference from the government or anyone else. In England they had feared persecution from the king's government because they refused to attend the services of the king's church. In Holland no one would make them attend any church; Holland allowed its citizens to worship in any church they chose.

But even though they enjoyed freedom of religion, the English men and women, who called themselves the "Saints," were not happy. They did not like it that their children were beginning to act more like Dutchmen and less like Englishmen. After 10 years in Leyden, the Saints decided they had to move elsewhere. But where would they go?

Why not Virginia? In those days, Virginia stretched from the Hudson River southward, so the Saints had plenty of choice places to settle. The Saints approached merchants in London to see if they could help them obtain some land in Virginia, around the mouth of the Hudson River. The merchants asked King James what he thought of allowing the "Saints" to settle in Virginia, and he thought it a fine idea. The king would allow them to settle along the Hudson River, or wherever else they wished, and he wouldn't force them to be members of the Church of England. What more could the Saints want?

The Mayflower Compact

It was on September 6, 1620, that the Saints set sail from Plymouth harbor in England in a ship called the *Mayflower*. The Saints were not the only ones on the long sea crossing; in fact, most of the others were not Saints at all. This caused some troubles, for the Saints thought that their fellow passengers were not very saintly and worried that this might cause problems when they tried to form a colony in Virginia. To make sure the others would behave themselves in their new home, the Saints wrote out laws to govern their colony. The Saints and the other settlers together signed on to this list of laws, which became known as the **Mayflower Compact.**

After a two-month voyage, the *Mayflower* finally landed in America. Unfortunately, it was not Virginia where they anchored, but a land even farther north than the Hudson River country. It was a land colder than the lands around Jamestown, far colder than anything the colonists had known in England. November had arrived, and the colonists had hardly enough time before winter came to set up their settlement (which they named Plymouth). None of them had ever known so bitter a winter. By its end, nearly half of the Plymouth colonists had died.

The pilgrims land in Plymouth.

Mayflower Compact: list of laws the Saints drew up to govern their new colony

Unlooked-for Help

One day in March 1621, after the worst of winter had passed, the Plymouth colonists were surprised to see two Indians come into their settlement. Up to then, the colonists had had no contact with Indians. What was their surprise, then, when one of the Indians spoke to them in English! This Indian was named Samoset. Many years before, he had been taken captive by an English captain and

Massasoit, chief of the Wampanoag Indians, meets with the pilgrims.

The first Thanksgiving

sold as a slave in Spain. Samoset later escaped and came to London. From London he had returned to the lands of his people.

Samoset told the colonists that he would introduce them to Massasoit, the chief of the Wampanoag tribe, who lived around Plymouth. Samoset arranged a meeting between the colonists and Massasoit. The Indians and the English signed a peace treaty. Moreover, the powerful Massasoit told his people to befriend the English. The Indians taught the colonists how to farm in the new country that was now their home.

That summer, the colonists planted the crops that gave them an abundant harvest in the autumn. In October the colonists prepared a harvest feast in order to give thanks to God for all his blessings. Massasoit and other Indians came to this feast. It is this feast Americans today remember on Thanksgiving Day.

10/15

The Founding of New England

Pilgrims: our name for the Saints of Plymouth

The Saints of Plymouth (whom, today, we call the **Pilgrims**) were not the only ones to settle the area around Plymouth. In 1628, another group of English Christians called Puritans (whose beliefs were very much like those of the Saints) also left England bound for America. Under their leader, John Endecott, they settled farther north, forming a colony they named Salem. In 1629 the new English king, Charles I, allowed another group of Puritans to settle on the Massachusetts Bay. They built a settlement between

Salem and Plymouth and called it Boston. The Puritans, like the Saints, were hard-working folk. They soon established other colonies, pushing ever westward into what is now the state of Massachusetts.

Though both the Puritans and the Saints had come to America to escape being persecuted for their religious beliefs, they persecuted those in their colonies who were not Saints or Puritans. The Puritans passed laws against Baptists and Quakers; they also did not allow Catholics to settle in their colonies. Quakers, especially, suffered for their religion; they were often whipped, imprisoned, branded with hot irons, or driven out into the wilderness.

Some people who disagreed with the Puritans and the Saints went off and founded their own colonies. One of these was a woman named Anne Hutchinson. She left the Massachusetts Bay colony and went south to Narragansett Bay. There, she and her followers set up the colony of Portsmouth on Rhode Island. Another inhabitant of Boston, named Roger Williams, believed it was wrong for the Puritans to persecute other people for their religious beliefs. He, too, went to Narragansett Bay and set up a colony he named Providence. Williams' Providence granted religious freedom to everyone—Protestants, Catholics, and Jews.

But not everyone who left Plymouth or Massachusetts Bay did so for religious reasons. Some just began feeling cramped in the older colonies. They went farther west into Massachusetts. Others followed the Connecticut River southward into what is today Connecticut, where they set up the colonies of Hartford and New Haven. All of these colonies became part of what was known as New England.

After a while, the Indians of New England resented the white

The pilgrims at Plymouth listen to the first sermon ashore.

Face-off between colonists and Native Americans during King Philip's War

King Philip's War: a year-long battle between the New England Indians and the settlers

people for moving onto their lands. In 1637 the powerful Pequot tribe rose up against the whites and was nearly destroyed. More successful was an uprising led by Metacom, the chief of the Wampanoag tribe. Over 50 years had passed since the Saints and Massasoit, chief of the Wampanoags, had signed their peace treaty. Since that time, the Indians had suffered ill treatment. Metacom, whom the whites called "King Philip," was angry over this ill treatment of his people. On June 24, 1675, he led warriors in an attack on the settlement of Swansea. This was the beginning of what became known as **King Philip's War.**

Other Indian tribes soon joined King Philip and the Wampanoags. Throughout the summer of 1675, the Indians attacked and destroyed all the English settlements in the western part of Massachusetts, burning down houses and murdering any whites they could find. For a time it looked as if the Indians might drive all the Europeans out of Massachusetts.

But then came the Great Swamp Fight, so called because it was fought in a swamp near South Kingstown, Rhode Island. In this battle, men from Plymouth defeated a large force of Indians. In April 1676 the chief Canonchet was captured and executed. When his captors told him he was about to die, the brave chief replied: "I like it well; I shall die before my heart is soft and I have done anything unworthy of myself." But the war continued until King Philip himself was captured and killed on August 12, 1676.

Our Lady's Haven

Searching for Religious Liberty

In 1625, Sir George Calvert did a rather surprising thing. He became Catholic. Though becoming Catholic might not seem so strange to us today, in seventeenth-century England it was strange indeed, and dangerous! England had laws against attending Mass and spreading the Catholic Faith. Priests caught saying Mass in England were killed. The English government said that because Catholics obeyed the Pope, they served a foreign king; and England's greatest enemy, Spain, was a Catholic country. Besides, the king of England wanted to have control of all religion in his country, and that meant everyone had to belong to his church—the Church of England—whether they wanted to or not.

King James I of England

Of course, Sir George Calvert was never in too much danger. His good friend was King James I, who was rather fond of Catholics. James's mother was Mary, the Catholic Queen of Scotland, who was overthrown by Protestants when James was only a baby. Mary had fled to her cousin, Elizabeth I, for protection; but Elizabeth had had Mary imprisoned in the Tower of London and later executed. James became king of England only because Elizabeth had no children and his family, the Stuarts, was the next in line to the throne. James could not be king of either England or Scotland and be Catholic, but he was friendly to Catholics; he made George Calvert a nobleman, naming him Baron Baltimore.

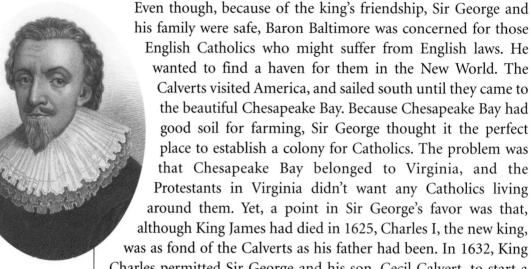

Lord Baltimore

Even though, because of the king's friendship, Sir George and his family were safe, Baron Baltimore was concerned for those English Catholics who might suffer from English laws. He wanted to find a haven for them in the New World. The Calverts visited America, and sailed south until they came to the beautiful Chesapeake Bay. Because Chesapeake Bay had good soil for farming, Sir George thought it the perfect place to establish a colony for Catholics. The problem was that Chesapeake Bay belonged to Virginia, and the Protestants in Virginia didn't want any Catholics living around them. Yet, a point in Sir George's favor was that, although King James had died in 1625, Charles I, the new king, was as fond of the Calverts as his father had been. In 1632, King Charles permitted Sir George and his son, Cecil Calvert, to start a new colony on Chesapeake Bay.

When Sir George died in 1632, Cecil Calvert, the second Lord Baltimore, took over the task of settling the new colony. The king allowed Cecil to make all laws for the new colony. Neither Lord Baltimore nor the king could say openly that Catholics were allowed to practice their religion freely in the new colony, but the king quietly allowed it. Lord Baltimore also could not say openly why he named the new colony Maryland. Although he said that it was in honor of the queen, whose name was Henrietta Maria, he really named it in honor of the Blessed Virgin Mary, Mother of God.

Religious Liberty Found and Lost

The colony of Maryland was open to both Protestants and Catholics. When, in the late fall of 1633, two ships, the *Ark* and the *Dove,* set sail for Maryland, they carried Protestant and Catholic settlers. Leonard Calvert, Lord Baltimore's brother, went with the settlers as the governor of the colony. In the spring of 1634, after landing at the mouth of the Potomac River, the settlers founded their first settlement, which they named St. Mary's.

For at least the first 15 years of the colony's history, Catholics and Protestants lived together in harmony. Whether Catholic, or Anglican (Church of England), or Puritan, or Baptist, or whatever affiliation, a man was free to practice his religion in Lord Baltimore's domains. For Catholics this was especially good, for they could now have their priests, attend Mass, and receive the sacraments without fear of persecution. Lord Baltimore so wanted peace between Protestants and Catholics in Maryland that he made it illegal for either group to criticize the other in public.

But early on, there was some trouble in Maryland. This came from a Virginian named William Claiborne. Claiborne was angry because he had been forced off his land on Chesapeake Bay when the Maryland colony was formed. For this he wanted to take his revenge on Catholics, whom he blamed for his troubles. In 1645, Claiborne joined with a Puritan pirate named Richard Ingle and kidnapped

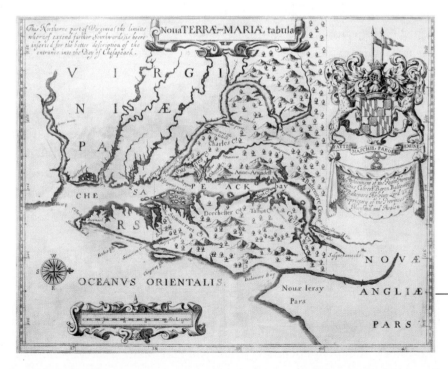

Old map of Chesapeake Bay and the Potomac River

Oliver Cromwell dissolves Parliament.

two Jesuit priests in Maryland. Claiborne and Ingle took the priests to England where, according to the laws, they could be executed. Fortunately for the priests, the English court ruled that since they had come to England against their will, they had to be released. The priests left the country and eventually returned to Maryland.

But Claiborne was to cause more trouble for Catholics in Maryland. In 1649, a Puritan general in England named Oliver Cromwell overthrew King Charles I, had him beheaded, and took over the government of England. Knowing that Cromwell hated Catholics, Claiborne and another Virginian named Richard Bennett gathered a force of men and invaded Maryland because, they said, the government of Maryland was not loyal to Cromwell. The invaders drove Governor William Stone from Maryland and began making laws against Catholics.

This was a bitter time for the Catholics of Maryland. Many priests were placed in irons and shipped to England to meet their fate. Those who could escape had to flee into the wilds of Virginia, where they lived in huts built into pits in the ground. It was Lord Baltimore who came to the rescue of Catholic Marylanders. A prudent and influential man, Cecil Calvert convinced Cromwell to recognize his lordship over Maryland. Claiborne and his party were driven out of the colony, and Maryland was again ruled by her old laws.

After Cromwell died, the Stuart family once again ruled England. Under the next two kings, Charles II and his brother, James II (who was a Catholic), Catholics in Maryland continued to enjoy the freedom to practice the Faith. When James II was overthrown, the new king, William III, ended Maryland's religious freedom until America's independence. In 1692, King William decreed that all

Marylanders had to support the Church of England. He excused only Puritans and some other Protestants who were not members of the English Church. Now that most Marylanders were Protestant, laws were passed forbidding the saying of Mass and punishing parents who taught their children the Catholic Faith. The new laws said that a Protestant who converted to the Catholic Church could be killed.

These new anti-Catholic laws were not always enforced, yet Catholic laymen and priests lived in fear of them. The priests who remained in Maryland lived like gentlemen on private estates, and Catholics came to them secretly to hear Mass and receive the sacraments. The priests' Protestant neighbors doubtless knew who they were and what they were doing, but most of the neighbors said nothing. Yet, for many years Catholics lived in fear of persecution from their Protestant neighbors.

Other Colonies

A Present to the Duke of York

On August 18, 1664, four English ships under the command of Richard Nicolls sailed up the Hudson River into the harbor of New Amsterdam. This little Dutch trading settlement on Manhattan Island was the port for many trading ships, but the English ships that sailed up the Hudson that day had not come to trade. They were war ships. Nicolls sent a message to the Dutch governor, demanding that he surrender New Amsterdam to the king of England.

Peter Stuyvesant, the Dutch governor, did not want to give up New Amsterdam without a fight. The problem was that the inhabitants of New Amsterdam didn't like Stuyvesant. The peg-legged Stuyvesant had a bad temper and had raised taxes. The Dutch complained that he

10/16

Governor Stuyvesant destroys the summons to surrender New Amsterdam.

ruled them as if he were their king. So it was that when Stuyvesant called his people to arms, nobody did anything. The English were able to take New Amsterdam without firing a shot.

By October, the English took not only New Amsterdam but other Dutch American colonies as well. The king of England, Charles II, gave all these territories a new name: New York. The settlement of New Amsterdam became New York City. King Charles called this new colony New York because he had given it to his brother James, the duke of York. James made all the laws for the new colony, but after a time he allowed New Yorkers to elect an assembly that would pass laws.

Though New York was now an English colony, the original Dutch colonists remained very important. Some of the richest and most powerful people in the Hudson River Valley, from New York City to Albany, were Dutch. These families would be very influential in the government of New York for many years to come.

Governor Stuyvesant surrenders New Amsterdam to the British in 1664.

The Woods of William Penn

Sir William Penn was not very pleased with his son. Sir William was an admiral in the British navy and a very powerful man, and he wanted his son (also named William) to grow up and be like him: a powerful man. Admiral Penn had sent William Jr. to some of the best schools in England, and when he was old enough, to Oxford University. It was at Oxford that young William got himself in trouble. King Charles II and the Parliament had passed laws requiring all students at Oxford to attend Church of England religious services, and William refused. For disobeying the king's law, William was expelled from the university.

Young William Penn refused to attend Anglican Church services because he had come under the influence of the members of the

Society of Friends, also called the Quakers. Quakers claimed that believers did not need to go to a church or even to the Bible to find out what God had said. Believers, they thought, were taught directly by the Holy Spirit. Quakers had no priests or ministers in their church services. They sat in silence, waiting for the Spirit to speak to their hearts. If someone felt the Spirit had a message for the others, he would stand up and speak. Sometimes they would start shaking and trembling, which is how they got the name "Quakers."

Quakers were pacifists; that is, they did not believe it was ever right to fight in war. They also believed that everyone should be free to practice whatever religion he wanted and that no one should force another to practice a religion he did not believe in. So it was that the young William Penn refused to attend Anglican chapel services. His disgusted father, the admiral, sent William to France and then to Ireland, to get him as far away as possible from the Quakers. Unfortunately, William found a colony of Quakers in Ireland and became a full-fledged Quaker himself.

William Penn traveled throughout Europe preaching Quakerism. Everywhere he went, he found that governments persecuted Quakers. He dreamed of establishing a colony in America where the Quakers could practice their religion in peace. Unlike the Puritans, though, Penn wanted religious freedom not only for Quakers, but for everyone. Although he didn't like them, Penn wanted his colony to accept even Catholics, if they wanted to come.

Quaker though he was, William Penn could influence the king. Admiral Penn had died in 1670 and his wealth went to William Jr. In 1675, King Charles II made

English Quaker leader and founder of Pennsylvania colony, William Penn, establishes friendly relations with Native American tribes during his visit in 1682.

young Penn the governor of the colony of New Jersey, and Penn settled many Quakers there. But the king owed William Penn money. Penn requested that, instead of money, the king give him land. Charles agreed, and in 1681, he gave Penn a large tract of land stretching northward from the boundary of Maryland to New York, and from New Jersey westward. Penn wanted to call this tract of land *Sylvania* (meaning "forest land"), but the king had other ideas. Charles added Penn's name (in honor of his father) to Sylvania, and so the colony became known as **Pennsylvania,** or "Penn's Woods."

The news of a colony in America that welcomed anyone of any religion attracted many settlers from both Great Britain and Europe. Of course, Quakers flocked to Pennsylvania; but so did German **Mennonites,** who founded Germantown and later became known as the "Pennsylvania Dutch." Catholics, too, came to Pennsylvania and practiced their religion in peace. As a symbol for his religious ideals, William Penn founded a new city on the Delaware River, calling it Philadelphia, the "city of brotherly love."

William Penn tried to act justly toward everyone. Though the Pennsylvania colony allowed men to own African slaves, Penn wanted the colonial assembly to pass laws allowing slaves to receive an education and to marry. (Slaves were not generally allowed to

Pennsylvania: "Penn's Woods," the colony given to William Penn by King Charles II
Mennonites: a Protestant group similar to the Amish; also noted for plain dress and simple living

The Pennsylvania Dutch use horse-drawn carriages.

get married.) But the colonial assembly would not pass these laws that would have made life easier for the poor slaves.

Penn also wanted to make sure that Indians in Pennsylvania were treated with justice. He was saddened that so many Indians learned bad behavior, like drunkenness, from people who called themselves Christians. Penn made treaties with the Indians and kept them. The Indians, in turn, did not raid settlements in Pennsylvania.

Though things did not always run smoothly in Penn's Woods, the colony grew and prospered. Hard-working settlers from all over the world settled in the colony. At least one-third of Pennsylvanians were Germans who established and ran productive farms. Philadelphia grew and became—with Boston, Massachusetts—the most cultured city in the English colonies. It was the only city besides Boston that, by 1700, had a printing press. It also had the best hospitals in the colonies.

William Penn served as governor of Pennsylvania for most of his life. But as he grew older, he grew sickly. William Penn died six years later, at the ripe old age of 74.

Chapter 5 Review

10/19

Summary

- English exploration began with John Cabot, but its major achievements began when Queen Elizabeth I sent the privateer Francis Drake to raid the Spanish colonies and Walter Raleigh to explore sites for colonies.
- The first English colonies—Roanoke and Jamestown—were in Virginia. Jamestown survived because of an Indian maid called Pocahontas, and a crop called tobacco that gave the Virginians a product to sell abroad. Other colonies—New England, Maryland, and Pennsylvania—sprang up because people desired freedom of religion.
- The Saints who settled Plymouth signed the Mayflower Compact, the first document of self-government in the British colonies. While the British wanted colonies for wealth, the colonists had the desire for freedom of religion and government—two wishes that would lead to the American Revolution.

Chapter Checkpoint

1. What religion might have dominated the New World if John Cabot had discovered America?
2. Who was the queen's pirate who sailed around the world?
3. Who was the first English child born in the New World?
4. Why is Sir Walter Raleigh important in American history?
5. Was the region known as Virginia the same area as the modern state of Virginia?
6. How did Lord Baltimore ensure religious freedom for his colony?
7. Which kings or queens supported religious freedom in the colonies? Which did not?
8. What is Rebecca Rolfe's more famous name?
9. Did the Saints and Puritans intend to settle Massachusetts?
10. What laws did William Penn establish in Pennsylvania? Who came to his colony?

Chapter Activities

1. How would the English colonies have been different if the Church of England had allowed religious freedom at home?
2. Class activity: Find out about the daily life of the English colonists. What did they eat? What kinds of homes did they live in? How did they decorate their homes? What were the perils of American life?

The American Larder

The food of the sailors who came to America did not include fresh vegetables and fruits; in the long voyages, the sailors often came down with scurvy. Scurvy, which was caused by malnutrition, was a dreadful disease which made the sailors weak and sad. Worse, their wounds would not heal, their joints and muscles ached, and their gums bled. Sometimes the sailors bled internally or even from the roots of their hair. The Indians of the far north treated scurvy with an extract of spruce needles, which is high in vitamin C and fights scurvy. Later, it was discovered that citrus—lemons, limes, and oranges—was the best cure for scurvy, and these fruits began to be part of a long voyage. The British sailors ate so much citrus that they came to be called Limeys.

Chapter 6 The Battle for North America

10/20

Queen Anne and King George Go to War

Blood and Fire at Ayubale

The Spanish missions in Florida were in peril. Yes, Florida had missions, very successful ones, founded by Franciscan missionaries. In the 1560s, King Philip II of Spain had heard that French **Huguenots** had started a settlement on the coast of Florida. King Philip did not want Frenchmen, especially not Protestant Frenchmen, settling on lands that belonged to Spain. So it was that in 1560, he sent missionaries and settlers to Florida. They founded the settlement of Saint Augustine and set about driving out the Huguenots. When that was accomplished, the Spanish Franciscans founded missions that extended up the Atlantic coast into what is today the state of Georgia.

An Indian rebellion in the early 1600s destroyed the missions in Georgia. After the rebellious Indians were subdued, more missionaries came

Huguenots: French Protestants who followed the teachings of John Calvin

Colonists lay out the streets of St. Augustine, Florida. They use string to measure, and dig with shovels and pickaxes.

121

and rebuilt the missions. They pushed westward into the interior of Florida and founded more missions among the Timucuan and Apalachee Indians. Two more Indian rebellions broke out in Florida in the 1600s because the Indians felt that the Spanish governors had treated them badly. But by 1655, about 26,000 Indians had been baptized and lived and worked around the Florida missions.

However, these missions would not remain at peace for long. English settlers in Charleston, 60 miles up the coast from the Georgia missions, wanted the Georgia mission lands. In 1670, King Charles II of England had allowed these English, along with Scots and French Huguenots, to settle in what is now South Carolina. The men of Charleston were mostly trappers, and they wanted to look for furs in the lands occupied by the missions. They also saw that they could make some money by capturing mission Indians and selling them as slaves.

The people of Charleston (called Charlestonians) often used pagan Indians to do their dirty work. In 1680, a band of pagan Indians attacked a Catholic Indian settlement on St. Simons Island on the St. Johns River in Florida. But Christian Indians and Spanish soldiers drove off the invaders. A short time after this attack, Charlestonians led a group of 300 pagan Indians against Mission

Spanish settlers, having arrived at St. Augustine, are being escorted by natives.

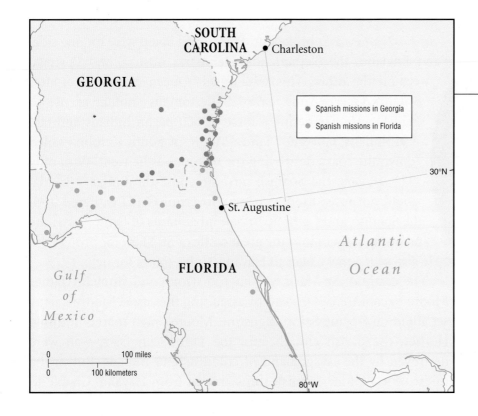

SOUTH CAROLINA
• Charleston

GEORGIA

Spanish missions in Georgia
Spanish missions in Florida

30°N

• St. Augustine

Atlantic Ocean

FLORIDA

Gulf of Mexico

0   100 miles
0   100 kilometers

80°W

Spanish missions in seventeenth-century Georgia and Florida

Santa Catalina de Guale. Again, they were driven off, but this attack was a sign of worse things to come. For the next four years, the Georgia missions suffered attacks by land from Charlestonians and pagan Yamassee Indians, and by sea from pirates. Finally, the Spanish governor of Florida decided he could no longer defend the missions and ordered the missionaries and Indians to abandon them. The missionaries and the Christian Indians fled south across the St. Johns River into Florida.

With the Georgia missions gone, the Charlestonians and their Yamassee allies now turned their attention to the missions in western Florida. Fierce bands of pagan Indians and so-called "Christian" settlers overwhelmed the missions, enslaving Catholic Indian men, women, and children. The captives were forced to work as slaves on plantations in South Carolina and in the British West Indies islands.

Queen Anne of Great Britain and Ireland (1665–1714)

In 1702, a new war broke out. France and Spain were on one side, and England, the Netherlands, Denmark, Austria, and Portugal were on the other. This war, called "Queen Anne's War" after Britain's Queen Anne, gave Charlestonians another excuse to raid Florida. Gathering a force of 600 pagan Indians and 600 Carolinians, Governor James Moore of South Carolina sailed down the coast, destroying the missions as he went. With only 323 soldiers, the Spanish governor, José de Zuñíga y Cerda, could not resist Moore's army. Governor Cerda gathered both the Spanish and Catholic Indian inhabitants of Saint Augustine and brought them into the great castle of St. Mark for protection. He also sent a messenger to Havana, Cuba, to ask for help.

The castle of St. Mark was far too strong and stout for James Moore to capture. So, instead of assaulting the castle, Moore's army set about destroying Saint Augustine. Moore's men spared nothing. Houses, the parish church, and the Franciscan friary—all were destroyed by the savage band of colonists and Indians. But in the midst of it all, four Spanish ships arrived from Havana. Unable to resist the new arrivals, Moore burned all his own ships (so that they would not fall to the Spaniards) and fled from Saint Augustine by land. With him went 500 captives, all Catholic Indians, whom Moore sold as slaves in Charleston.

Persisting in his cruelty, James Moore led another force of 50 Carolinians and 1,000 pagan Creek Indians into western Florida one year later. The Franciscan priest at mission Concepción de Ayubale, Fray Angel de Miranda, went about his normal duties on the morning of January 25, 1704. He had no warning of the danger that awaited him and his flock. Suddenly, through the clear morning air, came the chilling war cries of Indians. Unprepared for an attack, Fray Angel gathered as many of his Apalachee Indian warriors as he could into the parish church. The small band of defenders held off Moore's savage attacks until Spanish soldiers under Captain Alonso Dias Mejía arrived from a nearby mission. With only 30 Spanish soldiers and 400 Apalachee braves, Mejía was able to drive the Creeks and the

Indian Martyrs in Florida

Many a Catholic Apalachee gained a great victory on that terrible day in January 1704—not as warriors, but as martyrs. Encouraging each other in their faith, they cried out to their torturers, "Do what you want, we will soon appear before God! Make more fire so that our hearts may be allowed to suffer for our souls."

Carolinians from Ayubale twice. But by evening, Mejía and his men ran out of ammunition and surrendered.

Even though the mission had been surrendered, Moore, with the Carolinians and Creeks, initiated the cruelest work of the day. They began slaughtering their now helpless and terrified foes, sparing no one. They beheaded and butchered another Franciscan friar, Fray Juan de Pargo Araujo. They murdered Apalachee men, women, and children in cold blood, scalping them and mutilating their dead bodies. But 1,000 other Apalachee men, women, and children did not die that day; Moore dragged them to Carolina as slaves.

Over the next six months James Moore's Indians and Carolinians laid waste to the missions and Spanish settlements in the Apalachee region of Florida, killing the inhabitants and enslaving those who survived. In July 1704, the Spanish decided to abandon Apalachee. Those Indians who were able to escape came to Saint Augustine or to the French colony on Mobile Bay. In all, 13 missions were lost and about 4,000 Apalachees were killed or enslaved in Moore's war on western Florida.

Queen Anne's War was not fought only in Florida. Battles of British forces and colonists against the French also occurred along the St. Lawrence River. The war finally ended in 1713. Though Spain did not lose any of its colonies in America, the French had to surrender the Hudson Bay territory, Acadia (now called Nova Scotia),

People mill in the street of St. Augustine, Florida, an early American settlement.

and Newfoundland to Great Britain. Florida remained Spanish, but its once-great missions were destroyed, never again to be rebuilt.

The War of Jenkins' Ear

10/21

Robert Jenkins was an English sea captain. Like other English captains, Jenkins used his ship to carry goods to Spanish colonies and to bring Spanish-made goods to other parts of the world. Jenkins ran into some bad luck in his trading with the Spanish colonies. By Spanish law, only Spanish ships could trade with Spanish colonies. In 1739, the Spanish captured Jenkins and punished him in a most savage way. They cut off one of his ears, and set him sailing back to England. The members of Parliament were so distressed at Jenkins' treatment that they declared war on Spain. The English called this war the "War of Jenkins' Ear."

This War of Jenkins' Ear was a part of what seemed to be one long war between the English and the Spanish and the English and the French. The kingdoms of Spain and France always fought together against England, for the kings of Spain and France belonged to the same family. These wars were fought both in Europe and in America.

In the War of Jenkins' Ear, colonial general James Edward Oglethorpe fought the Spanish in Florida. King George II of England had allowed General Oglethorpe to settle colonists in the territory where many Spanish missions had stood. This territory belonged to Spain, but King George II claimed it for England, calling it "Georgia" after himself. The Spanish tried to drive Oglethorpe and his settlers out of Georgia, but failed.

A Man Named Washington

English colonists, especially in Virginia, wanted to be able to cross the Appalachian Mountains and settle in the great Ohio River valley. The problem was that the French claimed this valley as part of their territory. Just like the English, the French, too, wanted control of

King George II of England

North America. To keep English settlers from coming to the Ohio Valley, the French governor began building forts along the upper Ohio River. Governor Robert Dinwiddie of Virginia was not pleased with this, for Virginia claimed this region as part of its territory. In 1753, Dinwiddie sent the French commander a message saying that the French should stop building forts on the Ohio River. Dinwiddie chose a young Virginia gentleman, a major, to deliver the message. This 21-year-old was George Washington, who had served as the adjutant of one of Virginia's four military districts. So it was that Washington was sent by Governor Dinwiddie to deliver his message to the French commander on the Ohio River.

Washington delivered Governor Dinwiddie's message, but the French commander ignored it. In the spring of 1754, Dinwiddie sent Washington again to the Ohio River, but not with a message. The Virginia governor told Washington to drive the French from the Ohio Valley.

George Washington's Family

George Washington's family had been in Virginia since 1657. George's father, Augustine Washington, was the owner of six plantations, so George grew up learning the secrets of tobacco growing and cattle raising. Later he became a surveyor and wandered the wild western lands of Virginia, where he learned resourcefulness and endurance. In 1752, George inherited his brother Lawrence's Mount Vernon estate on the Potomac River. It was there that George settled down to the life of a Virginia gentleman and a most successful tobacco grower. A tall young man with large hands and broad shoulders, George Washington excelled in sports and was fond of horseback riding, dancing, and wrestling.

Fort Duquesne:
the French fortress
near the junction of
the Allegheny and
Monongahela Rivers,
the site of modern-
day Pittsburgh,
Pennsylvania

**George Washington
reads prayers
in his camp as a
lieutenant colonel
in the French and
Indian War of 1754.**

When Washington reached the Ohio Valley, he learned that the French had already erected **Fort Duquesne** near the junction of the Allegheny and Monongahela Rivers. Washington built a log stockade, not far from the French fort, at a place called Great Meadows. On May 28, 1754, Washington and his 350 men made a surprise attack on a small detachment of French troops, killing their commander and nine others. Washington took the rest of the French soldiers prisoner.

Washington's attack greatly angered the French commander. Gathering about 700 men, he marched against Washington. When Washington heard that the French were approaching, he ordered his Virginians to retreat to their fort at Great Meadows. There they fought a day-long battle. Unable to resist so large a force of French, Washington finally surrendered on July 4. The French did not take any of the Virginians as prisoners. Instead, after disarming them, they allowed the Virginians to return to their homes.

Though Washington had been beaten, Governor Dinwiddie made him a lieutenant colonel. About his first experience of war, Washington wrote, "I have heard the bullets whistle; and believe me, there is something charming in the sound."

The French and Indian War

War on the Virginia Frontier

George Washington's battles in the Ohio Valley turned out to be the first in a long series of battles that Americans called the **French and Indian War.** This war was the most important one yet fought in the colonies between Great Britain and France. The outcome decided which of these kingdoms would control North America.

After his defeat at Great Meadows, Washington remained a military commander in Virginia until October 1754, when he resigned. Washington had not resigned because he was ashamed of what had happened at Great Meadows, but because he was not being paid enough for his services. More important, he felt insulted because the British government had declared that all colonial officers had to

> **French and Indian War:** the colonial name for the war against New France and the Indians in America

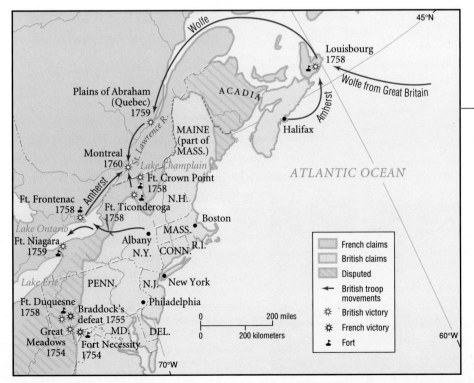

Battles and forts of the French and Indian War

obey British officers. It did not matter if the colonial officer was a general or a colonel or a lieutenant; he had to obey. Washington thought this was an insult to all colonial officers. Like most Virginia gentlemen, Washington could not tolerate insults.

Washington changed his mind in February 1755, when British General Edward Braddock arrived in Virginia with an army of British **Redcoats.** General Braddock, who had heard of Washington, asked him to serve as his personal assistant. Washington was eager to go to war and gladly accepted Braddock's offer. Washington, however, was no cowardly servant to Braddock. When the general criticized the Virginians, calling them lazy and dishonest, Washington boldly defended them. In the end, Braddock took Washington's advice on how to conduct the coming campaign against the French in the Ohio Valley. Unlike Washington, Braddock had never fought in the dense forests that covered Virginia and the Ohio Valley.

With a force of about 1,500 Redcoats and colonials, Braddock marched westward toward Fort Duquesne. It was still early summer and the green-shaded woods were beautiful, but they hid dangers. Washington was at Braddock's side on July 9, 1755, when the woods along the Monongahela River erupted in gunfire. A force of 72 French officers and regular soldiers, along with 150 French Canadian militia and 637 Indian braves, ambushed the large British force. Neither British nor colonial soldiers could see their enemies, who were hidden in the green shadows of the dense forest. When Braddock was mortally injured, it was Washington

> **Redcoats:** the nickname for British soldiers, who wore red uniforms with white breeches

Bravery under Fire

Though he was very ill at the time, Washington did not shy from the woodland battle near Fort Duquesne in 1755. With General Braddock, he rode back and forth among the terrified British and colonials, encouraging them to stand firm. With bullets whizzing by him from every side, it was a wonder that Washington was not injured. As it was, two of his horses were shot from under him, and four bullets pierced his clothes without injuring his flesh.

General Edward Braddock is carried off the battlefield (left) after defeat in the French and Indian War in 1775.

who rallied the soldiers and saved them from complete destruction. Still, the battle was a great defeat for the British. General Braddock died from his wound, with George Washington at his bedside.

The defeat of Braddock's army left western Virginia open to French and Indian attacks. In August 1755, Washington was appointed commander of all the Virginia troops. His assignment was a difficult one—protecting the Virginia frontier with only 700 men. These were all colonial farmers with no military discipline. It was difficult for Washington to get them to obey him, and the wilderness life was hard to bear. Still, Washington did his duty and learned many lessons that would be of use in the years to come.

On to Quebec

For three years after Braddock's defeat, the war did not go well for the British. In 1755, Massachusetts Governor William Shirley unsuccessfully attacked the French Fort Niagara; he was unable to take it. On September 8, General William Johnson defeated the French on Lake George but he could not drive them from Lake Champlain. There the French built Fort Ticonderoga. In 1756, French forces captured British forts on Lake Ontario and on Lake George.

But things changed when William Pitt became prime minister of Great Britain. Pitt thought that the best way to defeat the French in North America was to keep them from bringing in more troops. That meant the British had to use their navy to break off all contact between France and its colonies. Pitt's strategy worked. The British fleet controlled the seas, and without the arrival of more French troops, the war began to go in favor of the British. Pitt made General Jeffrey Amherst commander in chief of all British forces in North America.

Pittsburg, Pennsylvania, today

A Colonial City Is Named

Washington fought alongside Brigadier General John Forbes when he finally captured the troublesome Fort Duquesne in 1758. In honor of Prime Minister Pitt, Forbes renamed Fort Duquesne, calling it Fort Pitt. Later, it became known as Pittsburgh.

Battle for Quebec

On the morning of September 13, 1759, the French commander Montcalm, with 4,000 French troops, faced General Wolfe and his men on the Plains of Abraham. The brave French, clad all in white uniforms, gave their cry, *"Vive le Roi!"* (Long live the king!) and advanced on the British. When the French approached, General Wolfe forbade his men to open fire. The French came ever closer, but the British ranks remained silent.

Wolfe and Montcalm face each other in the Battle of Quebec.

Finally, when the French were only 40 yards away, Wolfe gave the command, "Fire!" The British guns spoke, and black smoke hid the oncoming enemy. Again Wolfe cried, "Fire!" and hundreds of Frenchmen fell dead to the earth. Then Wolfe commanded a bayonet charge. With a loud cry, the British with their shining bayonets rushed against the French, who were now fleeing before them. Though he had been seriously wounded, Wolfe commanded his men to keep the French from retreating into Quebec. With this last command, General Wolfe breathed his last.

But the greatest victory belonged to General Amherst's energetic brigadier general, James Wolfe. Wolfe's goal was to capture the strongly held French position at Quebec on the St. Lawrence River. If he could take Quebec, Wolfe could sail up the St. Lawrence and seize the French settlement of Montreal. The British forces would then control the entire St. Lawrence waterway. It would be a great deed; the challenge was in how to do it.

Quebec was well defended. The fortress perched on cliffs on the north bank of the St. Lawrence River; from this height, its cannon could easily fire on any ships that sailed past on the river. What's more, the Marquis de Montcalm, the French commander at Quebec, had 14,000 men under his command. Two miles upriver, General Wolfe had only 4,000 men.

Quebec was well defended, but Wolfe noticed one place that Montcalm had left unguarded. This was a narrow passage up the cliffs, leading to a plateau called the Plains of Abraham just outside the walls of Quebec. In the dark of early morning on September 13, 1759, Wolfe led 1,700 British troops up this narrow passage, overcoming the few French who guarded it. In the next few hours, boats quietly brought more and more British. When the sun rose that morning, the startled French beheld 4,500 British, drawn up in ranks on the Plains of Abraham. That day, the British were victorious, although it cost General Wolfe his life. A wounded Montcalm surrendered Quebec. With Quebec taken, the St. Lawrence River, from Montreal to the sea, belonged to the British.

The Fall of New France

In July 1759, France's old enemy, the Iroquois Indians, joined the British in successfully attacking **Fort Niagara,** which lay at the gateway to Lake Erie. The British captured the fortress and so opened the Great Lakes to British control. With both Fort Niagara and Quebec in their hands, the British marched against the French city of Montreal in 1760. British General Amherst completely surrounded Montreal and forced the French governor to surrender on September 8, 1760.

The capture of Montreal ended the fighting between the British and French in North America, but it did not end the French and Indian War. Along the banks of Lake Erie lived the Ottawa Indians. **Chief Pontiac,** their leader, hated the British. The French had allowed the Indians to practice their ancient ways pretty much undisturbed. But Pontiac knew that under British control his people would lose their lands to English settlers.

Chief Pontiac had a plan. In 1762, he sent messengers to all the Indian tribes

Fort Niagara: the site of present-day Buffalo, New York
Chief Pontiac: the Ottawa Indian chief who united the tribes along the frontier against the British and colonials

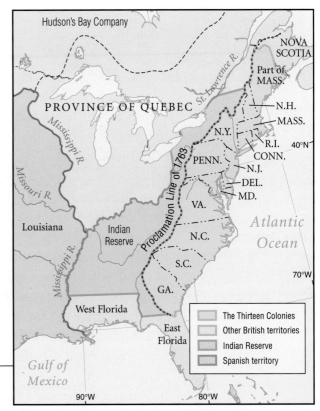

Colonial possessions of France, Spain, and England after the French and Indian War

The Death of Chief Pontiac

Chief Pontiac had hoped that the French would help him against the British. But when he heard that the French had signed a peace treaty with the British, he knew his cause was hopeless. On July 25, 1766, Pontiac signed a treaty of peace and friendship with the British at Oswego, New York. Pontiac returned to his lands on the Maumee River in Illinois, but he did not live long in peace. In 1769, an Illinois Indian, hired by a British merchant, murdered Pontiac. So angered were other tribes by Pontiac's death that they attacked and nearly destroyed the Illinois tribe from which the assassin came.

Fort Detroit: the site of present-day Detroit, Michigan

living between Lake Superior and the lower part of the Mississippi. Bearing red-stained tomahawks and wampum war belts, the messengers carried Pontiac's call to war. At a meeting of tribal chiefs in April 1763, Pontiac called on all the Indian tribes to unite against the British and drive them out of tribal lands. Pontiac said that in May the united tribes should attack all the British forts from the Mississippi to Lake Superior. When these forts were destroyed, the tribes could go on to destroy all undefended British settlements.

In May, Pontiac launched his bloody plans and almost carried them out. He led his Ottawa and the Ojibwa and Potawattomi tribes against **Fort Detroit.** Pontiac had hoped to surprise the garrison in the fort, but an Indian girl warned the British commander at Detroit of the attack. So it was that Pontiac on May 9 was forced to lay siege to the fort, in a struggle that lasted for five months. The defenders could not drive the Indians away, nor could the Indians capture the fort. Elsewhere the Indians captured 8 out of 12 British forts and massacred most of their garrisons. When British relief forces marched out to help, the Indians destroyed them all. Pontiac's Indian allies controlled the frontier.

In 1763, in the middle of this Indian war, the British and the French signed the **Treaty of Paris,** which ended the war between them. The treaty gave all of Canada to the British. Except for a few islands off the coast of Newfoundland and in the West Indies, France lost all its New World colonies. Great Britain now ruled New France.

Treaty of Paris: the agreement that ended the French and Indian War, giving Canada to the British

Chapter 6 Review

10/23

Summary
- Attacks in Georgia, James Moore's bloody massacres in Florida during Queen Anne's War, and General Oglethorpe's crushing occupation of Georgia and Florida ended Spain's hopes for strong Catholic colonies and missions on the East Coast. Catholic Indians from this area became slaves for the British colonists. Many, however, were massacred in their missions, becoming martyrs for the Faith.
- George Washington served the British valiantly during the French and Indian War. Charmed by the whistle of the bullets, Washington learned frontier warfare, discipline, and leadership.
- In the French and Indian War, the French lost Canada to the British, and Louisiana to the Spanish. The Indians, under Chief Pontiac, united against the victorious British, aiming to drive them off the frontier through warfare and murder. Pontiac's cause was hopeless, and he made peace with the British at Oswego, New York, in 1766.

Chapter Checkpoint
1. Where were the enslaved Indians forced to work after the Georgia and Florida missions were raided?
2. Name the Indian tribes that lived in the Spanish missions in Georgia and Florida. Name the pagan tribes that fought against them.
3. Name the countries that fought on each side of Queen Anne's War. What happened to the Spanish colonies? What happened to the French colonies?
4. Where was Fray Juan de Pargo Araujo martyred?
5. What war led the British to claim the Spanish territory in Georgia?
6. What Virginia farmer was told by Governor Dinwiddie to drive the French from the Ohio Valley?
7. Name the important British and French generals in the French and Indian War.

8. When did the British gain control of the Great Lakes?
9. Who did Chief Pontiac want to drive out of the tribal lands from Lake Superior to the Mississippi?
10. Where were the two treaties signed that ended each part of the French and Indian War?

Chapter Activities

1. Today, there is a city named Pontiac, Michigan. There has also been a brand of car made by General Motors that was named after Chief Pontiac. As a class, find out how the city and the car got their names. Did people want to honor Chief Pontiac? Why? Do you think it is right to honor him? Why or why not?

2. The French and Indian War is a forgotten war in American history, but it is important. Write two paragraphs about this war. In the first, explain why this war is important to the United States. In the second, explain why it was important to Canada. In each paragraph, think about how this war changed these two nations.

The American Larder

Pocket soup was a necessity for early American travelers and soldiers of the eighteenth century. Pocket soup was made by boiling a leg of veal (calf), bones and all, in water. Neither seasonings nor vegetables were added to this soup, because this would make it spoil more quickly. It was allowed to boil down until very thick, like jelly, and then turned onto a clean flannel cloth and cut into squares, or, "cakes." Wrapped in flannel, these cakes could then be put into a saddlebag or coat pocket. The cakes kept well, too; for several weeks, travelers could make a meal just by adding boiling water to a chunk of this pocket soup.

Chapter 7 If This Be Treason . . .

10/26

The Colonists Protest

The Colonies Must Pay

Not long after he helped the British capture Fort Duquesne, George Washington resigned from the colonial militia. The 26-year-old Washington was about to take on new responsibilities: marriage and family. On January 6, 1759, he married Martha Dandridge Custis, a widow with two children. Martha not only brought happiness to Washington, but, because she was one of the richest women in Virginia, she brought him wealth. Though he and Martha never had children of their own, Washington was very attentive to Martha's two children, Patsy and John Parke Custis.

Along with his own Mount Vernon estate on the Potomac River, Washington was an able overseer of the Custis White House plantation on the York River, near Williamsburg, the capital of colonial Virginia. A very successful tobacco farmer, Washington practiced crop rotation so as not to ruin the soil. He

Mount Vernon

The Pastimes of George Washington

Because he loved dancing and the company of friends, Washington threw many parties at Mount Vernon. He was fond, too, of hunting and fishing. Though not a formally educated man, Washington was cultured. He rarely missed an opportunity to see plays at the theater in nearby Alexandria or in Williamsburg. He was especially fond of William Shakespeare and could quote many passages from his works. Washington seemed content living the life of a farmer, having gained the reputation of being, in the words of a fellow Virginian, "a young man of an extraordinary and exalted character."

House of Burgesses: the lawmaking body of the colony of Virginia

also raised peach and apple orchards and grapes for Madeira wine. With his own produce, Washington fed his many dependents; being a large colonial landowner in Virginia, he had many slaves. He cared for them all, seeing to it that they were well dressed, fed, and housed; when they were sick, he obtained medical care for them.

As one of the great men of his colony, Washington had been elected to Virginia's lawmaking body, the **House of Burgesses,** in 1758. Every year, he traveled to Williamsburg to attend the meetings. Outside of spending these few weeks each year at the House of Burgesses, the young Washington had little interest in politics. But in 1765, all this changed for him and many others. Washington attended the meeting of the House of Burgesses in May of that year and heard ominous words, foretelling an end to peace and calm in England's American colonies. Patrick Henry, another young burgess, had risen to speak. In most solemn tones, Henry declared, "Caesar had his Brutus. Charles the First his Cromwell, and George the Third . . ."

"Treason!" cried several burgesses, interrupting Henry's speech. They knew what was he was driving at. Brutus had killed Caesar in the Roman Senate. Cromwell had beheaded Charles I. What was Henry saying about the British king, who also was king of Virginia and the other colonies?

Martha Custis Washington

Anger over the Stamp Tax

Today, we use stamps on all posted mail. Why were the colonists so upset over such a little thing as a stamp tax? Because, until 1765, Parliament in far-off England had never made the colonists pay any tax on their day-to-day activities. Colonists had paid taxes on goods imported from Europe, but their own local representatives—like the members of the House of Burgesses in Virginia—had decided what sort of taxes their people would pay. The colonists had representatives in their own assemblies, but they had none in the English Parliament. Patrick Henry and others were angered because they had no voice, no representation, in the Parliament—a faraway government that was imposing taxes on them.

Patrick Henry

"George III," said Henry after a pause, "may profit by their example." The uproar in the hall rose, but then slowly died down. When all was quiet again, Patrick Henry defiantly added, "If *this* be treason, make the most of it!"

Not only Patrick Henry, but many other colonists were angry over a law passed by the British Parliament in 1765 and called the Stamp Act. This law required that the colonists pay a tax on all legal documents, diplomas, licenses, newspapers, and other documents. The British government collected this tax by requiring that all these documents be printed on paper marked with a special seal or stamp, and that the colonists had to pay for the paper.

Parliament passed the Stamp Act tax to pay for the French and Indian War, which had been very expensive. For the same reason, Parliament passed other laws. For example, Parliament passed a law to keep New England merchants from smuggling in molasses (that is, sneaking it into port without paying a tax). Royal officials, Parliament declared, could obtain permission from the colonial

The Sons of Liberty

Some colonists resisted the Stamp Act in more violent ways than by merely protesting. In every coastal town from Massachusetts to Georgia, bands of men calling themselves the **Sons of Liberty** seized the printed stamp paper and destroyed it. They also stirred up mobs to attack anyone they thought was an enemy of liberty.

In New York, one mob attacked the house of a British officer, who had been heard to say that he would "cram the Stamp Act down the colonists' throats." The mob burned his furniture, tore up his garden, and drank all his liquor.

Sons of Liberty:
colonial revolutionaries, who used pamphlets and even false stories to make the colonists rise up against the British

Stamp Act Riots

courts (whose judges were controlled by the king) to search warehouses for smuggled goods. All merchants caught smuggling, Parliament declared, were not to be tried by a jury of their own peers, but in "admiralty courts" operated by the British navy. Trial by jury was an ancient English right, and here the colonists were being deprived of it.

Some colonists protested, saying that such laws violated the English constitution and were even opposed to the natural rights of man. They reasoned that, although they were colonists, they were *English* colonists. They should possess all the rights that other Englishmen enjoyed under the law. The colonists also believed that only their local assemblies could tax them, since no Englishman could be taxed without representation. They concluded that they might be within their rights to refuse to pay any tax Parliament laid

This publication, issued on October 31, 1765, was filled with cartoons and articles opposing the Stamp Act, a revenue law passed by the English Parliament. It claimed that, since the colonists were not represented in Parliament, any tax Parliament imposed on them without their consent was unconstitutional.

on them. The colonists began to ask themselves, "Should we obey such laws, if they are unjust?"

The Stamp Act brought the colonies together for the first time. In October 1765, representatives from nine colonies met in New York City for a Stamp Act Congress. The congress protested the Stamp Act, saying Parliament could not tax the colonies because it did not represent them. The congress also declared that trial by jury was a right belonging to every British subject, and neither the king nor Parliament could take it away.

The Declaratory Act

The Declaratory Act said that Parliament had absolute control over when and how it taxed the colonies. Most colonists either knew nothing of the Declaratory Act or simply ignored it. But other, more radical colonists understood what the Declaratory Act was all about. They wanted to stir up rebellion, for they believed that Parliament had no right at all to tax the colonists.

Sam Adams

The Liberty Tree

Something was needed to stir up the colonial people against the British. As the head of Boston's Sons of Liberty (and with money from the rich young merchant John Hancock), Samuel Adams threw big parties around a great elm tree in Boston. Around this "Liberty Tree," as Sam Adams and the Sons of Liberty called it, people were invited to dance and drink free rum. Sons of Liberty, wearing "liberty caps," hung effigies of the "enemies of liberty" from the branches of the Liberty Tree, made speeches, and sang patriotic songs.

In March 1766, Parliament repealed the Stamp Act. When the news reached the colonies, there was great rejoicing. George Washington was among those who had protested the Stamp Act; he, doubtless, hoped that Parliament would never attempt anything of the kind again.

Radicals Fight Parliament

radicals: people with revolutionary ideas about how governments should be run and how people should live in society

Most colonists were not **radicals**. After the repeal of the Stamp Act, most American colonists hoped everyday life would return to the way it was before the French and Indian War. They were happy under British rule and proud to be subjects of King George III. Things seemed to be going well, and the king was very popular. The short-lived Stamp Act had not changed this. But the colonists might have felt differently had they known that at the very same time that Parliament had repealed the Stamp Act, it had passed the Declaratory Act.

After the repeal of the Stamp Act, the colonists just settled back into their old ways and no longer worried about British tyranny. As long as everything seemed to be going all right, and people were comfortable, few cared about such threats to freedom as the Declaratory Act. Samuel Adams of Boston, however, did care. He did not have to wait long for Parliament to anger the colonists again.

In August 1766, new men came to power in the British Parliament. One of these, Charles Townshend, was made Chancellor of the Exchequer, which meant he had the power to tax. Townshend wanted to punish the colonists for their rebellion against the Stamp Act, so in June 1767 he came up with new taxes. The acts, called the Townshend Acts, placed new taxes on English manufactured items sent to the colonies. The Townshend Acts also placed a tax on tea imported into the colonies by the British East India Company.

The colonists wrote many pamphlets and letters giving reasoned arguments why Parliament's activities violated the colonists' rights as Englishmen. One such letter issued by the Massachusetts assembly protested the Townshend Acts; it said Parliament could not tax the people without their consent. This letter angered Lord Hillsborough, who was British secretary for the colonies. He ordered the Massachusetts assembly to take back what was said in the letter; if they did not, he would order the assembly to disband. When the Massachusetts assembly refused to obey Hillsborough, he carried out his threat. He declared that members of the assembly must disperse and return to their homes. They no longer had any authority to make laws.

However, Massachusetts was determined not to give in to Parliament. When a mob in Boston attacked a British customs official, British troops were sent into Boston. This only angered the colonists more. Sam Adams and other radicals at a Boston town meeting said Massachusetts should organize a convention to decide what to do. Adams himself wandered through the streets of the city calling on citizens to arm themselves against the British army. But despite these calls for **revolution,** Bostonians remained peaceful. The Massachusetts convention that did meet told colonists not to do anything violent; the British army, they warned, was too powerful.

revolution: a war begun within a country to overthrow the existing government

Then, in 1770, Parliament again seemed to back down. In March, the new prime minister of England repealed all but one of the Townshend Acts. He kept the tax on British East India tea to show the American colonists that Parliament still claimed the right to tax them without their consent.

The Boston Massacre, according to Paul Revere's engraving

Boston Massacre: Sam Adams's name for the incident when British soldiers fired upon a violent mob and killed three colonists

The Boston Massacre

Ever since British troops had arrived in Boston, Sam Adams and the Sons of Liberty had been spreading false stories about the soldiers. These stories stirred up some Bostonians to threaten the British soldiers, whom they called "lobster-backs" for their red uniform coats, and even to attack them when they were alone.

On the evening of March 5, 1770, a jeering crowd of men and boys began throwing snowballs and ice balls at a British soldier standing guard before the Customshouse on State Street. It quickly became a mob of several hundred, and the main guard of about 20 British soldiers was called out to help their unfortunate comrade. Fixing their bayonets, the guards did not attack, even though they were being pelted with snowballs, ice, and cobblestones. But, when one member of the mob struck a soldier with a club, the soldier fired into the crowd. Against orders, other soldiers also fired into the crowd, and when all was done, three members of the mob lay dead, while two more were mortally wounded.

Samuel Adams and the Sons of Liberty called this bloody act the **Boston Massacre.** They began spreading pamphlets, claiming that the "massacre" was another example that the British were tyrants who cared nothing about the colonists. Another member of the Sons of Liberty, the silversmith Paul Revere, made an engraving (a drawing etched on a metal plate) of the event; it shows a small number of respectable Boston citizens being fired upon by British troops. The engraving was inaccurate, but it stirred up many colonists against the British. As luck would have it, when the British troops and their commanding officer came to trial, it was Sam Adams's cousin, John Adams—the future president of the United States—who was the only lawyer in Massachusetts willing to take the case of the British.

John Adams loved justice and knew that the British soldiers were being deprived of it. At their trial, he argued persuasively that they had been provoked by a mob, that the soldiers were not so much to blame as the English government. The British soldiers were successfully acquitted, but John Adams lost many of his colonial friends and supporters because he had taken the soldiers' case.

Tea Served in Boston Harbor

Yet, in spite of the Boston Massacre, most American colonists were not ready for revolutionary action. This frustrated radicals like the Sons of Liberty. They needed *something* to stir up the colonists. As it turned out, they did not have to wait long for that something, and it was a tea party. It was not a pretty little tea party with china and cookies; it was a humorous name given to a violent act of defiance. The **Boston Tea Party** was the event that threw the colonials into war with England. This is how it came about.

John Adams

For years, the British East India Company had been allowed to sell its tea only to British merchants, who in turn sold it to the American colonies. This, plus the Townshend tax mentioned earlier, made the tea quite expensive. In fact, many Americans drank smuggled tea, which they could get for less money. This all changed in May 1773, when Parliament allowed the British East India Company to sell its tea directly to the colonies. Without having to use British merchants, the company was thus able to sell its tea for even less than smuggled tea. Moreover, the East India Company was allowed to sell its tea only to colonial merchants who had no ties with the Sons of Liberty, some of whom were smugglers or had ties to the smugglers.

The Sons of Liberty and other radical groups protested this new act of Parliament. By allowing only certain merchants to sell East India tea, they said, the Parliament was playing favorites, and that was unjust. The tea issue so stirred up the colonists that in New

Boston Tea Party: a protest during which the Sons of Liberty dumped 343 boxes of British tea in Boston harbor, leading to a severe British reaction that would prompt a united revolution

York and Philadelphia, they kept the East India Company's tea ships from entering the harbor. But in Boston (the most radical city of all) the tea ships were allowed to enter the port.

Sam Adams called a meeting at the Old South Meeting House in Boston (a "meeting house" was a Puritan church) on December 16, 1773, to protest the entry of the tea ships into Boston harbor. The Sons of Liberty and their leaders, who gathered that night, sent a message to Massachusetts Governor Thomas Hutchinson. The message demanded the governor to force the tea ships to leave the harbor. When Samuel Adams received the expected news that Governor Hutchinson had refused the demands, he ended the meeting with the words, "This meeting can do nothing further to save the country."

The meeting disbanded, and a sign was given. Immediately, a band of colonial men, disguised as Mohawk Indians, ran with whooping yells past the meeting house. They were soon joined by other men, some of whom were dressed like Indians; others had darkened their faces and masqueraded as black slaves. Gathering at the city wharf, these men, numbering about 150, rowed out to the tea ships in Boston harbor. Without opposition, they began emptying all the boxes of tea into the harbor. By the time they were done, 343 large boxes of tea lay floating in the salty brine.

A Colonial Song about the Boston Tea Party

We made a plaguey mess of tea
In one of the biggest dishes,
I mean we steeped it in the sea
And treated all the fishes.
Tol-le-lol-de-riddle, Tol-le-lol-de-ray,
And treated all the fishes.

10/28

Parliament Strikes Back

Boston Pays the Price for Tea

As it turned out, Boston Harbor water made a very bitter cup of tea, indeed. The dumping of the East India tea was not to the taste of Parliament, and its members showed their displeasure by passing some nasty laws against Boston and the colony of Massachusetts. Despite the urging of some members for less severe punishment, the majority in Parliament in March 1774 ended up passing the Boston Port Act, which ordered the closing of Boston harbor until all the spilled tea was paid for. This meant that no ships were allowed into port or out of port. With the harbor closed, Boston merchants and fishermen would be unable to earn a living or to bring any goods to the city. To make sure the port stayed closed and that no smuggling went on, the British navy would blockade the port while British Redcoats occupied the city. The private citizens of Boston, Parliament later declared, would have to "quarter" (that is, house and feed) the British soldiers that were forced upon them.

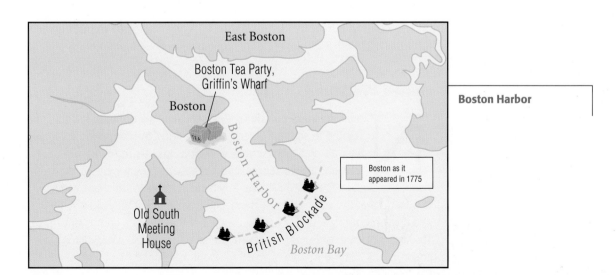

Boston Harbor

Reenactment of a military drill. The Redcoats are dressed in full historical dress uniform of red coats and tall black hats.

The outraged members of Parliament did not stop there. Not only did they pass laws restricting Boston's trade, they also made another law, the Massachusetts Government Act, restricting the freedom of all the people of Massachusetts. The Government Act stated that certain government offices, which the local inhabitants had always voted for, would now come under the power of the royal governor. Thus, all lower-court judges, justices of the peace, and sheriffs would no longer be elected offices, but appointed offices. The Government Act had the effect of turning not only the Bostonians, but all the people of Massachusetts against the British government.

In Boston, citizens called a meeting at Faneuil Hall (pronounced "FAN•yell") to decide what to do about the new laws. They drew up what they called a Solemn League and Covenant not to export goods

United We Stand

Not all colonists outside of Massachusetts were sure they wanted to sign the Solemn League and Covenant; it would, after all, cost them money as well as lose them many comforts and conveniences. However, many others were willing to stand with Boston against Parliament. In Virginia, George Washington wrote to a friend that the colonies must stand with Boston; for, if they did not, he said, Parliament might take away the liberties of the colonies one by one. The Virginia House of Burgesses was of the same mind with Washington, and in May 1774 the members voted to adopt a "resolve" that condemned the "hostile invasion" of Boston.

Founding of the Minutemen

When British General Thomas Gage and his Redcoats arrived in Boston, Gage found that holding Boston would not be the difficult part of his job. But as the newly appointed governor of Massachusetts, Gage would have to enforce the Government Act, and this he found impossible to do. In the countryside, the people threatened any royal officials Gage sent out to them and would not allow courts to open. Instead of royal judges, an illegal colonial assembly, with John Hancock as president, gathered in Concord and passed laws and levied taxes. This assembly formed "committees of safety" to go out and gather arms and ammunition. A colonial militia, made up of farmers and tradesmen, also began military training at Concord. Though these men did not leave their homes and jobs, they would be ready to fight at a minute's notice if the British marched against them. Because of this, the members of the militia became known as **Minutemen**.

Minutemen: the Massachusetts militia, who were ready to fight at a minute's notice

to, nor import goods from, Great Britain. The Bostonians asked the other colonies to join them in this Solemn League, hoping that if all the colonies refused to trade with Britain, Parliament would have to repeal its "tyrannical" acts.

The royal governor of Virginia was not pleased with the decision by the House of Burgesses to stand with Boston, and so he dissolved the assembly. Since the government house was closed to them, the members of the Virginia legislature and other former burgesses met at the Raleigh Tavern in Williamsburg to decide what to do next. Not only did they decide to join Massachusetts in the Solemn League and Covenant, but they called on Virginia and the other colonies to join in a "continental congress" of all the colonies. The first Continental Congress was, therefore, scheduled to meet in Philadelphia in September 1774.

**The First
Continental Congress**

Tories: the nickname
for colonists loyal to
Great Britain

The Continental Congress and Parliament

The colonies sent representatives who gathered in Philadelphia on September 5, 1774, for the First Continental Congress. Though they all thought that Parliament was unjust in its dealings with the colonies, they did not all agree on what should be done about it. Most colonists wanted to stay in the British Empire, but some were in favor of independence and the creation of a new country altogether. Those who wanted to remain British subjects, though with certain rights and considerations, called themselves loyalists (their opponents called them **Tories**). Those who supported American independence called themselves patriots.

The Continental Congress was united enough to issue its own Declaration and Resolves. In this document, the congress declared that the colonists had certain rights, which they received from the British constitution and from the royal charters that established the colonies. These rights, stated the Declaration and Resolves, came not only from charters and constitutions but also from the "laws of nature." That is, the colonists had these rights simply because they were human beings. No government could justly take away such "natural" rights, the congress said. The Continental Congress adopted the "Declaration and Resolves" on October 14, 1774.

Rough Times for Tories

The division among the colonists was great. Many loyalists left and returned to England to live. The radical patriots, like the Sons of Liberty, could be very harsh on those loyalists who remained. They spied on people to find out what they really thought. Were they loyalists or were they patriots? The radicals threatened the loyalists. Some of the punishments were mild, such as publicly shaming those who drank British tea. But some "Tories" had their houses burned or otherwise lost their property; others even lost their lives.

Further, the Continental Congress challenged Parliament to repeal the Boston Port Act and the Massachusetts Government Act, or the colonies would begin to block all imported goods coming from Great Britain as well as the exports going out. This threat of a trade war worried many colonists, who feared that it might lead to open war with Great Britain.

Though loyalists (or Tories) were a minority in the colonies, so were those in favor of the bold challenge to England by the Continental Congress. The vast majority of colonists were largely content with the way things were. Not only would loyalists refuse to

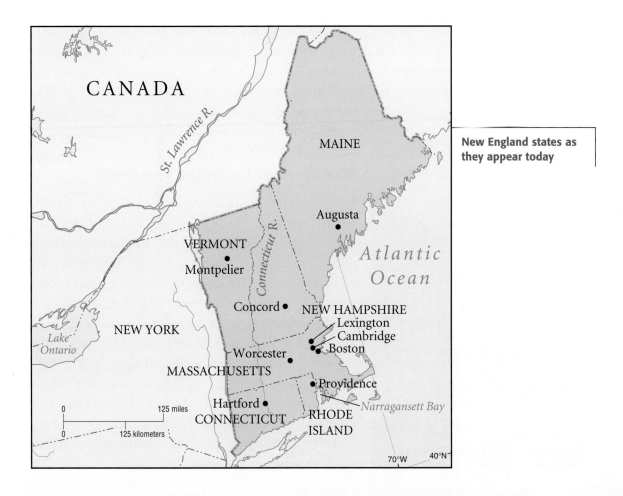

New England states as they appear today

go along with the proposed blockade, but most of the colonists would refuse, as well.

Among the British, there was widespread popular sympathy with the American colonists for their treatment by "Mother England." There was talk in Parliament of giving in to some or all of the demands of the Continental Congress. However, most members of Parliament, and King George, were in favor of getting even tougher. Harsh laws against the New England fishermen were passed—and even harsher trade laws, too, which said that the New England colonies could trade only with England and Ireland, but with no other countries.

Such parliamentary acts chipped away at the colonists' loyalty to Great Britain. Still, these acts were not enough to make the colonists want to break away from their mother country. Most Americans remained loyal to King George, and though they lived far across the sea, they still thought of themselves as Englishmen. It would take more than even harsh acts of Parliament to make them want to break away.

Boston's Old North Church

Bloodshed at Lexington and Concord *10/29*

Loyalists in Boston were growing impatient. British general Thomas Gage, who had been in Boston for almost 11 months, had done nothing about the radical patriots in the Massachusetts countryside, in Middlesex County, who had set up their own rebel government and were training a militia. Meanwhile, General Gage and his army of about 3,500 men sat idle in Boston. General Gage knew what the loyalists were thinking; he knew he had to do something. He learned that the rebels were storing arms in the towns of Worcester and Concord. Since Concord was closer to Boston, Gage thought he could more easily send soldiers there to seize the illegal arms.

The radical patriots, through their own system of spies, found out that General Gage was planning to seize the guns stored at Worcester and Concord. General Gage was also hoping to capture the rebels assembled at Concord. The patriots decided to send out couriers to warn the countryside when the British began to move. They also decided to place a signal lantern (or two) high in the tower of Boston's Old North Church to warn the people in Charlestown, across the bay, of the coming of the British. If one signal were hung, that meant the British were marching by land into Cambridge; if two, then the British would be coming "by sea," that is, across the bay. On the night of April 18, 1775, two lanterns were hung in the Old North Church tower; the Redcoats were coming by sea.

Boston's Paul Revere was to be one of the couriers; he was to cross the bay into Charlestown and from there take a horse and ride to

Paul Revere's Ride

The opening of a long poem called "Paul Revere's Ride," by Henry Wadsworth Longfellow, goes like this:

> Listen my children and you shall hear
> Of the midnight ride of Paul Revere,
> On the eighteenth of April, in Seventy-five;
> Hardly a man is now alive
> Who remembers that famous day and year.
> He said to his friend, "If the British march
> By land or sea from the town to-night,
> Hang a lantern aloft in the belfry arch
> Of the North Church tower as a signal light, —
> One, if by land, and two, if by sea;
> And I on the opposite shore will be,
> Ready to ride and spread the alarm
> Through every Middlesex village and farm,
> For the country folk to be up and to arm."

Lexington. It was near midnight when Revere began paddling a rowboat across Boston harbor. He was in considerable danger; he had to pass by several British ships, and if their night watchmen noticed him, they would capture him. But though he came close enough to hear voices aboard the British ship *Somerset*, he passed unnoticed. Landing at Charlestown, Revere mounted a horse and began his "midnight ride." For a time two British officers pursued him, but Revere was able to elude them. All along the 12-mile road to Lexington, he roused the local people with the cry, "The British are coming!"

A reproduction of the original Old North Bridge crosses the Concord River at the site where the colonial Minutemen fought the British on April 19, 1775.

Remembering the Minutemen

On July 4, 1837, 62 years after the Battle of Concord Bridge, a battle monument was dedicated at the North Bridge. American poet Ralph Waldo Emerson, whose own grandfather was in Concord during the battle, wrote this poem for the dedication. The poem, originally written as a song, is called "The Concord Hymn":

By the rude bridge that arched the flood,
Their flag to April's breeze unfurled,
Here once the embattled farmers stood
And fired the shot heard round the world.
The foe long since in silence slept;
Alike the conqueror silent sleeps;
And Time the ruined bridge has swept
Down the dark stream which seaward creeps.
On this green bank, by this soft stream,
We set to-day a votive stone;
That memory may their deed redeem,
When, like our sires, our sons are gone.
Spirit, that made those heroes dare
To die, and leave their children free,
Bid Time and Nature gently spare
The shaft we raise to them and thee.

The Battle of Lexington

Throughout the early morning hours of Wednesday, April 19, Minutemen gathered on the town green in Lexington. Warned by their commanders not to fight unless the Redcoats fired the first shot, these patriots remained grimly silent even when, in the early light of day, they saw advancing Redcoats. The first contingent of British soldiers was approaching, led by Major John Pitcairn. As Pitcairn turned into Lexington, he saw a band of armed men blocking the road to Concord. Ordering his own men to halt, Pitcairn cried out, "Ye villains, ye rebels disperse! Lay down your arms!" Then, after a pause, "Why don't ye lay down your arms?"

The rebels did not answer but began to retreat behind a stone wall that ran alongside the road. When Pitcairn sent a detachment of soldiers to stop them, a few shots rang out, wounding a Redcoat and hitting Pitcairn's horse. Against Pitcairn's orders, the Redcoats then fired a murderous volley at the rebels. When the smoke cleared, ten of the rebels lay dead; nine were wounded.

News of the slaughter at Lexington spread quickly across the countryside, enraging the people against the British. When they finally marched into Concord, four miles from Lexington, the Redcoats were met by two battalions of armed Minutemen. As the British slowly advanced, the militia slowly retreated. Crossing the Concord River by the North Bridge, they settled into position on a ridge northwest of the town. The British followed the militia over the bridge and halted before the ridge. For two hours the two sides faced each other without firing a shot. Finally, the British commander realized that he was in a dangerous position; there was a river, with only a small bridge to cross it, behind him. So when the militia began to advance against him, he ordered a retreat. The militia, seeing the Redcoats withdraw, opened fire on them, killing seven British and wounding five others.

The Redcoats did not stop in Concord, but continued their retreat toward Lexington. All along the road, an unseen enemy fired on the British from behind trees and stones. Whenever the Redcoats attempted a counterattack, the enemy retreated into the woods. The British grew tired and were filled with despair. When they reached Lexington, they met another contingent of British troops and reformed their ranks. But 12 miles still lay between them and Boston, 12 miles of the same murderous fire. When the British finally reached the safety of Boston, they had heavy losses—73 killed and 200 wounded. Of the Americans, 49 had been killed and 41 wounded.

It was not long before news of the Battles of Lexington and Concord spread to the other colonies. Soon, men from other colonies began streaming into Massachusetts and joined the militia, which was now laying siege to Boston. From Connecticut they came, from Philadelphia, New York, and New Hampshire.

So was war begun between the American colonists and England. Though some rejoiced at the news, others were deeply troubled and grieved. No one knew what the future held. One thing seemed clear, though: the colonies must either fight on and win this war, or lose all the rights that they held so dear.

10/30

Chapter 7 Review

Summary
- The British decided that the colonists must pay the bills from the French and Indian War. This led Parliament to pass many acts levying heavy taxes on the colonists.
- The colonists had no representatives in Parliament, and resisted the idea of taxation without representation. Formal organization of the Continental Congress and the Massachusetts assembly, coupled with the activities and riots of Samuel Adams's Sons of Liberty, paved the way for revolution.
- The first battles of the American Revolution were fought as colonists stopped British troops from reaching and destroying the colonists' arms in Concord. Lexington, on the road to Concord, was a defeat for the Americans. But the Americans regrouped along the Concord River, defeating the British soundly and driving them back to Boston.

Chapter Checkpoint
1. What was the name of George Washington's wife? Did they have any children of their own?
2. Make a list of the acts of Parliament that angered the colonists. Name each act, the date it was passed, what it ordered, and why the colonists resisted.
3. What is "taxation without representation"? How did the colonists want to solve this problem at first? What did they later decide to do?
4. What did Patrick Henry say in his famous speech to Virginia's House of Burgesses in 1765?
5. Why was Parliament taxing the colonies?
6. Who was Samuel Adams? Name three important things he did that led to the American Revolution.
7. Why did the Boston Tea Party happen? How did the British react?
8. When and where was the First Continental Congress? What document did it issue?
9. Write six sentences describing the battles of Lexington and Concord. Be sure to mention General Gage, Paul Revere, Major John Pitcairn, the Concord River, the North Bridge, and the number of Redcoats and Minutemen killed.

Chapter Activities

1. Make a list of some of the many reminders of the American Revolution and the early patriots all around us. Coins, state names, schools, mascots, towns, national monuments, and so forth carry memories of the revolution. How many reminders can you list?

2. Revolutions are very serious matters. If they fail, countries will be in a worse state. If revolutionaries want change for the wrong reasons, countries will be worse off. Think about what would have happened if the Americans had lost the revolution.

3. What do you think made the colonists brave enough to fight a war on their own soil, knowing their homes and farms might be destroyed?

The American Larder

The pineapple was not known in Europe until it was taken back there from the Caribbean islands by the early explorers. It quickly became a great favorite in Europe and America, and the early colonists especially loved pineapple. In colonial America, the pineapple became a symbol of hospitality and prosperity. When a guest came to visit a wealthy home in colonial Virginia, the host gave a pineapple to the guest upon his or her arrival. But if the guest stayed too long, he or she was given another pineapple as a polite sign that the welcome was wearing a little thin. The pineapple can be seen in many designs, jewelry, and decorations of this period. The colonists would export a cargo of tobacco to the Caribbean islands where the pineapple grew and there trade their tobacco for pineapples.

Chapter 8 The Revolutionary War

11/2

The Road to Independence

A Step Beyond

Benedict Arnold, a merchant of New Haven, Connecticut, wanted to do great things for the colonial cause and his own reputation. But by the end of the Revolution, he did grave harm to the colonials, and his return to England as a Tory has earned him forever the name of traitor and turncoat. It all began when Arnold, in search of glory, set his sights on the strongest British fort in North America—Fort Ticonderoga, on the southern shore of Lake Champlain. Not only did Fort Ticonderoga hold a great supply of armaments, but it lay on the water route the British might take to invade the colonies.

At the same time, a rough frontiersman named Ethan Allen, then living in the Green Mountains in Vermont, had decided it was high time to attack Ticonderoga, too. Though Arnold had received a military commission from the Massachusetts assembly, Ethan Allen had his Green Mountain Boys, who would follow no one else but him. Arnold and Allen argued over who should take command of the expedition. Finally, they came to a compromise: they would lead the expedition together.

Benedict Arnold

159

Ethan Allen

Marching side by side, Allen and Arnold led their 83 men to the shores of Lake Champlain. Crossing the lake in the early morning hours of May 9, 1775, the Americans were surprised to find the gates of Fort Ticonderoga flung wide open as if in welcome. Without firing a shot, the Americans simply marched right into the fort. Striding confidently, Ethan Allen marched up to the commanding officer's quarters and shouted, "Come out you old rat!" and demanded the surrender of the fort.

The British officer, doubtless surprised and offended by this rude command, asked in the name of whom or what this unkempt frontiersman demanded surrender.

"In the name of the Great Jehovah and the Continental Congress," replied the plucky Allen. That must have been good enough, for the British commander surrendered Fort Ticonderoga to the colonials. Soon, through swift military activity in the area, not only Ticonderoga but all of Lake Champlain came under the control of the Americans.

Having dealt with the British, Benedict Arnold wanted to take the command of the troops at Ticonderoga from Allen. Daily, more and more recruits joined Arnold's forces. Then, foolishly, Allen led his Green Mountain Boys in an invasion of Canada. The invasion was unsuccessful, and furthermore, when Allen returned he found that Arnold had taken full control of the American forces on Lake Champlain. The merchant from New Haven had outsmarted the frontiersman from the Green Mountains.

Many old cannons rest around the South Barracks at Fort Ticonderoga, New York.

Bunker Hill

The members of the Massachusetts assembly rejoiced when they heard the news of Arnold and Allen's victories on Lake Champlain. The same could not be said of the men who had gathered to form the Second Continental Congress. These men, who were representatives from each of the thirteen colonies, had come to Philadelphia to decide what the colonies should do about the siege of Boston. They included some of the most famous and talented men in British America: from Boston, John Adams, and from Virginia, Patrick Henry, Thomas Jefferson, Richard Henry Lee, and George Washington. The congress members approved of what the colonists had done at Lexington and Concord. After all, the men of Massachusetts were merely defending themselves against a British attack. But taking Fort Ticonderoga and other holdings on Lake Champlain was different; *that* was not self-defense, but an attack on the authority of King George III.

They debated what to do. Should Fort Ticonderoga be abandoned? Most of the members of congress were not ready for war on England. But if war came, the colonies would need guns and ammunition if they were to defend themselves against the army of Great Britain. Fort Ticonderoga had plenty of both guns and ammunition. Further, if the British were going to invade the colonies, they would come down Lake Champlain and, from there, cross to the Hudson River. If the British made it to the Hudson, it would be clear sailing to New York City, and the New Yorkers did not like the idea of their largest city falling to the British. So the congress members decided not to abandon Fort Ticonderoga.

The congress also decided to make George Washington commander in chief of the so-called army of the United Colonies. They sent Benedict Arnold to Maine to organize an army for military action in Canada. The congress hoped that French would join the colonies in their struggle against Great Britain.

It was only after he had left Philadelphia on June 23, 1775, to take up his command that George Washington learned his army, called

Statue of Colonel William Prescott at Bunker Hill

the Continental army, had fought another battle with the British outside of Boston. The British had sent General George Howe to Boston to replace General Gage as the commander of the British forces there. General Howe was bound and determined to destroy the motley rebel forces outside of Boston. He planned an attack on the town of Cambridge and the Dorchester Heights, which lay just outside of the port town. But unfortunately for Howe, the colonials got wind of his plans and were prepared to meet his attack.

On June 16, 1775, the officer in charge, Colonel William Prescott, decided he would meet the British attack by placing men and artillery on Bunker Hill, just outside of Boston. From there the colonials could lob bombs onto the British forces in Boston. But the artillery, which was brought from Lake Champlain, did not arrive in time, and Prescott's men made a mistake. They occupied Breeds Hill instead of Bunker Hill. Still, when the sun rose the next morning, the British were surprised to see a stockade atop Breeds Hill and trenches dug along its base. Colonial militia, their gun barrels and bayonets glistening in the sunlight, awaited the British.

But General Howe was not daunted by the colonists. Why should he be? There were very few of them, they had little ammunition, and their artillery had not arrived. Surely the mighty British army with its powerful guns and smart military discipline could drive off that ragged band of farmers and craftsmen! With cool confidence, Howe ordered the British ships in Boston harbor to open fire on Breeds Hill. He then ordered British grenadiers and light infantry to drive off the Massachusetts, Connecticut, and New Hampshire men lined behind a stone wall and rail fence they had hastily built behind Breeds Hill and at the foot of Bunker Hill.

The colonials watched with fear and dread as the ranks of red-coated soldiers slowly advanced toward them. The whistling of cannonballs, shot from British warships and from an artillery battery on Copps Hill in Boston, filled the air. In the distance, on the other side of Breeds Hill, the town of Charlestown had been struck many times by these missiles, setting many buildings blazing. Great tongues of fire licked the sky. Great billows of smoke rose above Breeds Hill.

As the British drew nearer, the artillery fire ceased. The colonials heard only the beating of British drums and the thud-thud-thud of British feet. "Don't fire until you see the whites of their eyes!" Prescott shouted, and the men held their fire. The British were 200 feet away—then 100—then 75. Still, the colonials held their fire. When the British were only 50 feet away, the colonials could see the whites of their eyes. "Fire!"

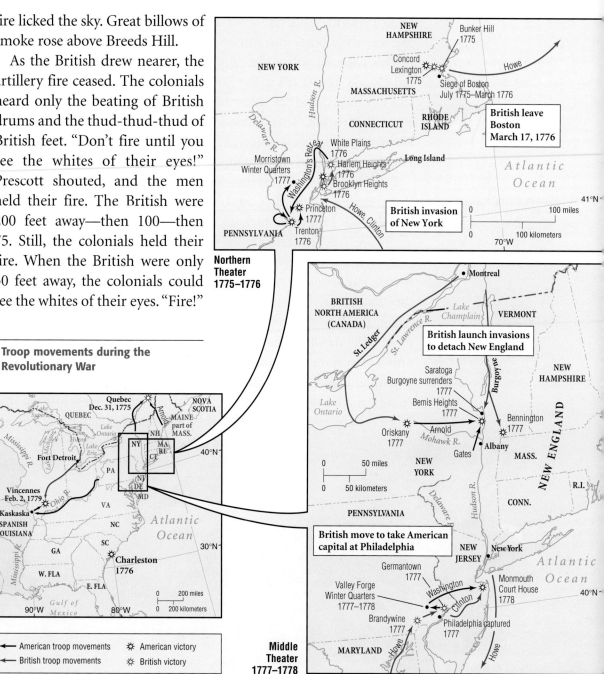

Troop movements during the Revolutionary War

Northern Theater 1775–1776

Middle Theater 1777–1778

British leave Boston March 17, 1776

British invasion of New York

British launch invasions to detach New England

British move to take American capital at Philadelphia

← American troop movements
← British troop movements
✷ American victory
✷ British victory

cried Prescott. And the colonials fired a blazing volley, wrapping themselves in black gun smoke.

This colonial volley tore into the advancing British, and many a red-coated soldier fell to the ground, dead or wounded. The British still advanced, and the colonials continued their point-blank fire. More British fell. Then came a force of grenadiers led by General Howe himself. They, too, were riddled by colonial fire, and fell. Finally, panic filled the remaining British, and they fled.

But Howe was not beaten. He reorganized his troops and, this time, British grenadiers and marines advanced directly against Breeds Hill. From the stockade and from the trenches the colonials again opened fire. The British fell in great numbers. But the colonials were running out of ammunition. Howe's third assault against Breeds Hill was able to drive the colonials from their positions, and they fled before the victorious British.

Yet, the British were not so victorious. Of the 2,200 British who fought that day, 1,054 had been killed and wounded. The colonists lost only 444 men out of 3,200. The **Battle of Bunker Hill** (which was actually fought on Breeds Hill) gave the colonists confidence that they could stand up to the British. The battle, too, taught the British that the colonials were tougher than they had thought; it was a dearly bought victory. "Another such," said a British general, "would have ruined us."

Battle of Bunker Hill: an important battle in which the Massachusetts militia fought bravely, although they lost. The strong American effort gave the colonists confidence that they could win against the British.

Battle of Bunker Hill

11/3

The Colonies Declare Independence

General Washington Takes Command

The New England militiamen who formed the army of the United Colonies were tough and scrappy fighters, but they were not soldiers. These Minutemen were just too independent. They would leave their farms to fight when they were needed, but as soon as the battle was over, they wanted to return to their farms. Most of the militiamen had signed up to fight for only six months, and when that time was up, they expected to return to their homes. How were the colonies supposed to fight a war against the mighty British army when most colonial militiamen would just up and leave when their periods of service were over?

This was one of George Washington's problems when he arrived at the Boston lines. His other problem was how to turn these undisciplined militiamen into soldiers. His first problem was solved when Congress allowed him to enlist men for three-year periods. The other problem would take more time; but later, with the help of a German baron with the amazing name of Friedrich Wilhelm Augustus Heinrich Ferdinand von Steuben, Washington was eventually able to whip his new army into shape.

Virginians and New Englanders were very different sorts of people, and since he was an aristocratic Virginian, Washington sometimes found it hard to deal with the rough and unruly Yankee farmers and mechanics. Yet, Washington was just the man for the job. His devotion to the colonial cause and his stern self-control

George Washington and his troops

filled the men with confidence. They also learned that their new general genuinely cared for them. When supplies ran short in the army, Washington drew resources from his own estate to feed and clothe his men.

Washington won his first victory without even firing a shot. In March 1776, his army occupied the Dorchester Heights, which overlooked Boston. Seeing that Washington's move had isolated his army on the peninsula on which Boston sat, General Howe decided to abandon Boston. On March 17, the British army and all the loyalists in the city boarded ships and set sail for Nova Scotia. With the British gone from Boston, Washington and the army of the United Colonies marched in triumph into the city.

Free and Independent States

Despite Lexington and Concord, and despite Bunker Hill, most patriots believed that King George was on their side. It was Parliament, they believed, that was causing all the trouble. Thus, except for a few like Sam Adams and the Sons of Liberty, most colonial patriots wanted to remain part of the British Empire. They sim-

Signing of the Declaration of Independence, July 4, 1776

ply wanted their rights respected. All this changed because of the publication of *Common Sense,* which changed the colonists' minds.

Common Sense was published in January 1776 anonymously (that is, the author did not give his name). Later, a young man named Thomas Paine was known to be the writer. Soon, people all over the colonies were reading the writer's revolutionary new thoughts. The colonies should be independent, for only by being independent could they be free, declared *Common Sense.* Further, since the king of England was a tyrant (one who used the colonists for his own benefit), the colonists owed him no loyalty or obedience. Finally, *Common Sense* declared that a free America could become the only truly free nation on earth. It could become the home of freedom for all mankind.

George Washington had remained faithful to the King—toasting George III's health every night at dinner. But then, Washington read *Common Sense* and

COMMON SENSE:

ADDRESSED TO THE

INHABITANTS

OF

AMERICA,

On the following interesting

SUBJECTS.

I. Of the Origin and Design of Government in general, with concise Remarks on the English Constitution.

II. Of Monarchy and Hereditary Succession.

III. Thoughts on the present State of American Affairs.

IV. Of the present Ability of America, with some miscellaneous Reflections.

Written by an ENGLISHMAN.
By Thomas Paine

Man knows no Master save creating HEAVEN, Or those whom choice and common good ordain.
THOMSON.

PHILADELPHIA, Printed
And Sold by R. BELL, in Third-Street, 1776.

embraced the cause of independence. So did many members of the Second Continental Congress; yet many still were not convinced. Throughout the spring of 1776, the congress debated whether the colonies should declare their independence from Great Britain. Delegates from the New England colonies and from Virginia were in favor of independence, and soon the other southern colonies voiced their support. The middle colonies of New York, New Jersey, Maryland, Delaware, and Pennsylvania were opposed.

Excerpt from the Declaration of Independence

"We, therefore, the Representatives of the united States of America, in General Congress, Assembled, appealing to the Supreme Judge of the World for the Rectitude of our Intentions, do, in the Name, and by Authority of the good People of these Colonies, solemnly Publish and Declare, That these United Colonies are, and of Right ought to be, Free and Independent States; that they are absolved from all Allegiance to the British Crown, and that all political Connection between them and the State of Great Britain, is and ought to be totally dissolved; and that as Free and Independent States, they have full Power to levy War, conclude Peace, contract Alliances, establish Commerce, and to do all other Acts and Things which Independent States may of right do. And for the support of this Declaration, with a firm Reliance on the Protection of divine Providence, we mutually pledge to each other our Lives, our Fortunes, and our sacred Honor."

Declaration of Independence: the Continental Congress's declaration that the American colonies were free states over which Britain had no control

After months of debate and disagreement, the congress decided to bring the question of independence to a vote. On July 2, 1776, the representatives of all the colonies except New York voted for independence—New York's representatives did not vote *against* independence; they just did not vote at all. Two days later, on July 4, the congress approved what would become the most important document in the history of the United States, the **Declaration of Independence.** On that day John Hancock (who presided over the Continental Congress), along with the delegates, signed this famous document declaring the thirteen American colonies to be free and independent states.

Though the congress had appointed a committee of five men to compose the Declaration of Independence, only one of them did most of the writing. The main author was Thomas Jefferson of Virginia, but he was influenced by his friend and colleague, John Adams. Jefferson's declaration was more than a simple statement that the colonies had separated themselves from Great Britain; it was a statement of beliefs that would inspire Americans from Revolutionary War days to our own: "We hold these truths to be self-evident," said the Declaration of Independence, "that all men are created equal, that they are endowed by their Creator with certain unalienable Rights, that among these are Life, Liberty, and the pursuit of Happiness."

Governments come into being, said the declaration, "to secure these rights"; and these governments must be formed by the people who will be governed by them. The declaration further said that whenever a government acts against the natural rights of mankind, that government must be changed or abandoned for a new government. The government of Great Britain had violated the rights of the American colonists, said the declaration, and so the colonies had the right to form their own independent governments.

Having declared their independence, the new states had to fight a long war to keep it.

King George III: the British king at the time of the American Revolution

Loyalists Fight Back

Despite the Declaration of Independence, a large number of colonists did not think that **King George III** was a tyrant. These people called themselves loyalists because—like all the colonists—they had taken solemn oaths of loyalty to the king, and they thought it was wrong to go back on what they had promised to God and man. The patriots thought these loyalists were betraying the colonial cause and called them Tories. (In England, a Tory was someone who supported the idea of a strong king.) But some patriots did more than call the loyalists names. The radicals, like the Sons of Liberty, often treated loyalists cruelly; they humiliated them, they scourged them with whips, they tarred and feathered them. Despite this treatment, many loyalists refused to back down; instead, they formed their own militias and went to fight for the British.

A Famous Highland Lass in North Carolina

The beautiful wife of the highlander colonel Allan Macdonald was a zealous loyalist. She was also a Scottish heroine; she had saved "Bonnie Prince Charlie" from the British. ("Prince Charlie," the grandson of King James II, had led a revolution against British rule in Scotland in 1745, and failed.) Now, in America, Flora Macdonald, mounted on a noble snow-white horse, rode throughout the Scottish settlements of the Carolinas, calling on her people in both English and Gaelic to take up arms for King George. Many responded to her call. Clad in kilts and marching to the blaring music of the bagpipes, 1,700 loyalist highlanders marched out to join the British forces. Unfortunately for Flora Macdonald, the British were defeated by the patriots in a battle near Wilmington, North Carolina. Her husband was taken prisoner and his land was seized. At her husband's urging, Flora Macdonald fled to the Isle of Skye in Scotland, never to return to America.

Men from the highlands of Scotland, who had settled in the western part of North Carolina, had long looked upon the rich plantation owners in the eastern part of the colony as enemies; in fact, back in 1771, the highlanders had fought a war with these eastern, or "tidewater," plantation owners. Because these plantation owners had joined the patriot cause, the Scots highlanders joined the British. Their leaders agreed to help drive the patriots from North Carolina.

Scottish highlanders

After July 4, 1776, loyalists suffered more at the hands of patriot colonists. Some Catholic Scottish highlanders, who had sworn loyalty to King George after fighting against him under Bonnie Prince Charlie, had settled in the Mohawk Valley in what is now upper New York State. When they refused to take up arms against the king, the radical patriots drove them and their priest, Father John McKenna, from New York.

Throughout the Revolutionary War, patriots and loyalists committed many cruel acts against each other. Since so many colonists fought for the British cause, the American Revolution could also be thought of as the first American civil war.

War in the North

Trenton and Princeton

While the Continental Congress was debating whether the colonies should declare their independence from Great Britain, the British general Sir William Howe was transporting his army from Halifax, Nova Scotia, to the city of New York. Getting wind of what General Howe was up to, General Washington led his army of 18,000 men from Boston to New York. By August, Washington and his men were encamped on Long Island, at Brooklyn Heights, while the British army held New York City and the British fleet controlled the harbor.

New York City was a good base for General Howe. For one thing, the city was filled with loyalists, and for another, it had about the best harbor in the colonies. From New York, Howe could sail up the Hudson River to

11/4

George Washington shakes hands with a military official.

**British General
William Howe**

BY HIS EXCELLENCY

WILLIAM HOWE,

MAJOR GENERAL, &c. &c. &c.

AS Linnen and Woolen Goods are Articles much wanted by the Rebels, and would aid and affiſt them in their Rebellion, the Commander in Chief expects that all good Subjects will uſe their utmoſt Endeavors to have all ſuch Articles convey'd from this Place: Any who have notOpportunity to convey theirGoods under their own Care, may deliver them on Board the Minerva at Hubbard's Wharf, to *Crean Bruſh*, Eſq; mark'd with their Names, who will give a Certificate of the Delivery, and will oblige himſelf to return them to the Owners, all unavoidable Accidents accepted.

If after this Notice any Perſon ſecretes or keeps in his Poſſeſſion ſuch Articles, he will be treated as a Favourer of Rebels.

Boſton, March 10th, 1776.

attack American forces on Lake Champlain. Or, he could send the navy southward around New Jersey and up the Delaware River to Philadelphia, the capital of the United States, while his army marched there overland.

The fact that Washington's army was over on Long Island did not bother Howe at all. On August 27, 1776, Howe had fought a battle with Washington and roundly beaten him. Washington was forced to flee up the Hudson River, on whose banks he built two forts. But what were these puny forts to the mighty British army? Howe, surely, could crush them and the ragtag army of the United States as well.

General Washington was certain that Howe would march against Philadelphia; the only question was, when? To defend Philadelphia, Washington needed to get between that city and the British. To do this, he had to be the first to cross a bridge over the Raritan River in New Jersey. He could not delay. If he did not beat Howe over the bridge, nothing would stand between the British and Philadelphia.

Washington did not delay. Taking all but 5,000 of his men, he marched them from the Hudson to the Raritan and crossed over, while Howe dilly-dallied in New York. Although he had a good chance to destroy the small force of 5,000 men Washington had left on the Hudson and then to march against Washington's remaining army, Howe did nothing. On December 13 he decided he and his men would remain in New York City until the spring. Meanwhile, Washington had crossed the Delaware River into Pennsylvania from Trenton, New Jersey.

Except for the one battle on Long Island, which had been a defeat, Washington's army had done nothing except move about the countryside. This moving about was important, but it did little to encourage the soldiers. Washington knew he needed a battle victory to lift the spirits of his men. Without a victory, many would abandon the army, since their enlistment times were nearly up.

At Trenton, New Jersey—on the other side of the Delaware River from where Washington was encamped—there lay an

Washington crosses the Delaware River.

encampment of soldiers who were fighting under the pay of the British government. These mercenary soldiers were not British but Germans. Mostly they came from the small German principality of Hesse; therefore, they were called Hessians.

Christmas day, 1776, was upon them, and Washington knew that the Hessians would spend the holy day drinking, singing, and generally having a good time. They would not be prepared to meet an attack from the Americans that day, nor even the next, since they would then be worn out from their yuletide celebrations.

So on Christmas night, Washington made a bold move with his ragtag militia. He and his poorly clothed, half-starved army set out by night and crossed the Delaware River back into New Jersey. In the early morning hours of December 26, the Americans attacked the Hessian camp. The Germans, as Washington expected, were still asleep; so the attack came as a complete surprise. The drowsy Hessians briefly fought back, but soon surrendered.

This victory at Trenton not only encouraged Washington's men, but inspired more men to join his army. With a larger army, Washington marched against British forces at Princeton, New Jersey, in January 1777. This was a harder fight, since this time the Redcoats were prepared to meet the rebel attack. The British might have driven the Americans from the field that day had it not been for Washington. The sight of their commander standing firm and encouraging his men not to waver or retreat so inspired the Americans that they routed the British and took Princeton.

The Victories of Benedict Arnold

General Horatio Gates: the commander of the American army in New York. He was a poor commander, and his appointment to lead the army angered Benedict Arnold.

Although Benedict Arnold had shown himself to be a brilliant tactician and a talented general, the congress inexplicably gave the command of the American army in New York to another general, **Horatio Gates.** Gates was a poor commander. It was lucky for him, and for the United States, that Benedict Arnold still marched with the American army. Without Benedict Arnold, the colonial rebels

One Bright Spot for the Patriots

Congress had sent Benjamin Franklin, a Philadelphia printer and well-known scientist , to Paris to convince **King Louis XVI** to join with the colonies against Great Britain. Because of his scientific experiments, Franklin was well respected in Paris. The French aristocrats were also interested in what the Americans were doing, not only because they were fighting France's old enemy, Great Britain, but because they were fighting for freedom and a republican government. French aristocrats were wild for such ideas. One French aristocrat, the **Marquis de Lafayette,** had even come to America to fight for the rebels. In 1777, Congress made him a major general in the American army. So it was that Benjamin Franklin was able to convince King Louis to sign a treaty of friendship with the colonists on February 6, 1778. France would send ships and troops to America to help in the cause of independence. But another three years would pass before the Americans, with French help, could do anything against the victorious British.

King Louis XVI: the king of France, who helped the Americans win freedom from Great Britain. He was later executed during the bloody French Revolution.

Marquis de Lafayette: a French aristocrat who fought as a major general in the American army

would have lost an important battle, and they may even have lost the war.

The Americans met a much larger British force on September 19, 1777, near Saratoga, New York. It was Benedict Arnold who led his brigade in the attack against the British, and it was Benedict Arnold's skill that defeated them. But when General Gates wrote up his report of the battle for the congress, he failed to mention Benedict Arnold at all. Understandably, it angered Arnold that Gates was taking all the credit for winning the battle. Arnold protested, but Gates would not change his report. Instead, in retaliation, General Gates removed Arnold from the official command of his New England brigade. But Arnold remained in the army, and it was a good thing. In fact, he took unofficial command of the New England troops in a second battle, on October 7, during which the Americans, under Arnold's command, routed the British. New England and New York had been saved.

Horatio Gates

Valley Forge

Like an old bear coming out from his den after hibernation, British general William Howe roused himself to fight the Americans in the spring of 1777. With a few yawns and stretches, Howe organized his army, sending 5,000 up the Hudson to join more British soldiers. With the remaining 18,000, Howe himself set sail from New York harbor, bound for Chesapeake Bay. From Chesapeake Bay, Howe's army pushed up the Delaware River, landing 50 miles south of Philadelphia in early September.

Only Washington's army of 12,000 men stood between Howe's Redcoats and Philadelphia, then the capital of the United States. The men in the rebel army had no uniforms, wore raggedy clothes, and were always short of food. Yet, despite these hardships, they had hope. When they marched into battle against the British at Brandywine Creek on September 11, 1777, the patriots wore sprigs of green in

George Washington meets with Marquis Lafayette at Valley Forge, where the Continental army suffered through the cold winter during the American Revolution.

their caps as symbols of hope. They were, however, no match in open battle against the well-fed, well-disciplined, and well-armed British host. In the battle of Brandywine Creek, the colonial rebels lost 1,000 men. Washington was forced to retreat to the north; and the congressmen, with the British at their doorstep, packed up their papers and fled from Philadelphia to Lancaster, Pennsylvania.

On September 26, General Howe marched in triumph into Philadelphia. Two weeks later, on October 5, 1777, Howe's Redcoats again defeated Washington, this time at Germantown, Pennsylvania. The capture of Philadelphia was just the beginning of worse things to come for the Americans. For the next four years the rebels would suffer one defeat after another. Beaten a second time in one month, and with winter coming on, Washington led his men to Valley Forge, Pennsylvania. There, cold and hungry and discouraged, they barely survived the bitter winter; meanwhile, Howe and his British soldiers, warm and housed, feasted and played in Philadelphia.

The War Moves South

11/5

Many Defeats

The British now set their sights on targets farther south. The city of Savannah, on the coast of Georgia, fell to British troops in December 1778. From Savannah, the British marched inland to Augusta, the state capital, and took it. By the spring of 1779, all of Georgia belonged to the British.

With Georgia conquered, the British moved with an army of loyalists and Cherokee Indians into South Carolina. Their target was the city of Charleston, but they moved slowly while destroying and looting as they passed through South Carolina. On April 8, 1780, the British general, **Lord Charles Cornwallis,** surrounded the city by sea and land. The American commander in Charleston had no choice but to surrender the city to

Lord Charles Cornwallis: the British general who commanded troops from Charleston, South Carolina. He surrendered his entire army to George Washington after the battle of Yorktown.

the British. By July of 1780, all of South Carolina belonged to the British. On August 16, 1780, Cornwallis defeated the American general Horatio Gates at Camden, North Carolina.

The defeat at Camden was not the end of the bad news for the colonial rebels. In September came the news that Benedict Arnold had turned traitor to the Americans and gone over to the British. Arnold had never gotten over the insulting way General Gates had treated him after the fighting at Saratoga, New York. The final straw came in February 1779 when Congress received charges that Arnold had committed various crimes. Congress decided that he had to face a court-martial to answer the charges. The court-martial, which met from December 1779 to January 1780, decided that Arnold was guilty of two of the minor charges and would receive a reprimand from Washington. Though Arnold's punishment was small, the very fact that he had been accused at all was too much for his proud spirit to take. Because he thought the Continental Congress did not appreciate his services, Benedict Arnold switched his allegiance to the British and planned to betray some important American military posts to them.

Unaware of Arnold's intended treachery, General Washington made him the commander of the fortress of West Point in August

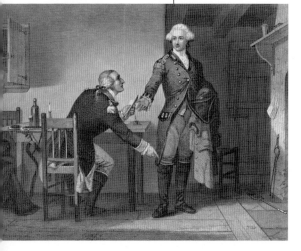

Benedict Arnold persuades Major John André to hide the secret plans to turn West Point over to the British.

1780. This was an important fortress, for if the British gained control of it, they could control the entire Hudson River Valley in New York. On the night of September 21, 1780, Benedict Arnold met secretly with one Major John André, who represented the British. André returned from the meeting carrying papers that contained plans for the plot to hand West Point over to the British. But the rebels captured André before he could cross the British lines, and the plot was discovered. Hearing of André's capture, Benedict Arnold was able to make his escape to the British, who made him a brigadier general in the king's

King's Mountain: A Long-Awaited Victory

After defeating Horatio Gates at Camden, General Cornwallis decided to conquer the rest of North Carolina as well. He sent a ruthless leader, one Major Patrick Ferguson, along with over 1,400 loyalists—including highlanders and other colonial settlers who had been forced into the British army—to attack the rebel settlements in western North Carolina. Ferguson sent a challenge to the settlers west of the Blue Ridge Mountains that unless they came over to the loyalist side, he would "march his army over the mountains, hang their leaders, and lay their country waste with fire and sword." Knowing Ferguson's reputation for cruelty, the mountain patriots (without military training or uniforms, without pay, and without orders) organized themselves into a militia of about 1,000 men. Nearly half the rebel force was made up of the east Tennessean and southwestern Virginian Overmountain Men. Fighting with rabbit rifles and hatchets, and using the woods as cover, the patriots stormed the loyalists at King's Mountain, North Carolina, on October 7, 1780. They killed or took prisoner every last man. Ferguson himself was killed in this battle, which lasted little more than an hour. The 800 loyalist prisoners were "lost" by their rebel countrymen, and both sides returned to their respective homes. Without Ferguson's support, Cornwallis called off his invasion of North Carolina. It was this battle that is credited with turning the tide of the Revolutionary War.

army. In losing Arnold, the Americans lost one of their most brilliant generals. His betrayal saddened many patriots, including General Washington, who had put great trust in him.

From Defeat to Victory

By the time the winter of 1781 rolled around, the Continental Congress had learned its lesson. All through the war it had been appointing generals, like Horatio Gates; most had been dismal failures. Realizing that Cornwallis would again invade North Carolina in the spring, the congress finally delegated the job of choosing generals to General George Washington, who really understood the business of war.

Washington's choice to lead the American forces against Cornwallis was Major General Nathaniel Greene. Greene was an expert at strategy, and his men loved him. Though in his battles with Cornwallis, through the spring and summer of 1781, Greene was always the one to retreat, it was Cornwallis who always lost the most men. So it was, in the autumn of 1781, that Greene was able to march into South Carolina and force British and loyalist forces to take refuge in Charleston. Cornwallis himself, with only 1,400 troops, moved into Wilmington, North Carolina.

Southern Theater 1780–1781

← American troop movements
← British troop movements
☀ American victory
☀ British victory

British troops attempt to push through the Carolinas and Virginia

In April, Cornwallis left Wilmington for Virginia, where Benedict Arnold, leading 1,700 loyalists, had been winning victories. In Petersburg, Virginia, Cornwallis and Arnold joined forces.

On July 6, Cornwallis's Redcoats and Benedict Arnold's loyalists entered Yorktown, a town in Virginia, on the James River. Cornwallis wanted to gather a large force of British and loyalist soldiers in Yorktown and lead them in a conquest of the Southern states. But British General Henry Clinton, hundreds of miles away in New York, refused to bring his army to join Cornwallis's small force in Yorktown. Instead, he sent a small number of reinforcements, increasing the number of Cornwallis's army to only 7,000 men. General Clinton later regretted this decision.

Victory at Yorktown

By the spring of 1781, the Continental army was in a sad state. The men wore torn and tattered clothing and shoes with gaping holes in them (or often no shoes at all). They were cold and hungry in winter, hot and hungry in summer. Because the states had not been sending contributions to pay for the army, the soldiers received no pay. Many had not been paid for two or three years. Yet despite these hardships, these men fought on, for they loved their brave and patriotic commander, General Washington, and the cause of freedom.

In the summer of 1781, Washington received good news. King Louis of France had sent Admiral Count de Grasse with 20 ships to the aid of the Americans. These ships sailed first to the West Indies, where they picked up 3,000 French soldiers and four more ships. From the West Indies, de Grasse sent an emissary to General Washington to discuss whether the combined French and American armies should attack General

General George Washington fires the first cannon in the bombardment of the British works at Yorktown.

Men dressed as American Revolutionary soldiers march during an historical reenactment of a battle at Yorktown, Virginia.

Clinton's army in New York or General Cornwallis's army at Yorktown, Virginia. They agreed that they would attack Cornwallis at Yorktown. The trick was to keep General Clinton from getting wind of their plans, for if he found out, he might send Cornwallis more troops. Washington saw to it that Clinton received false reports that the Americans and French were about to attack New York. Fooled by these reports, Clinton kept all his men in New York; not one Redcoat did he send south to help Cornwallis.

On August 31, Washington and the French general Rochambeau began marching south to Yorktown. Meanwhile, de Grasse had set sail from the West Indies. On September 5, the French fleet met a British fleet of 19 ships near Cape Charles, which lay at the entrance of Chesapeake Bay. In the sea battle that followed, the French fleet defeated the British fleet so badly that it was forced to flee to New York for repairs. Yorktown no longer had a navy to defend it.

Cornwallis's army was in a dangerous position. Yorktown lay on a peninsula. Without ships, Cornwallis could not escape by sea. On September 28 he found that his narrow land route was blocked by Washington and Rochambeau's combined French and American army, which was over twice as large as the British and loyalist army. For about two weeks, de Grasse's navy and Washington and Rochambeau's army laid siege to Cornwallis. On October 17, 1781, realizing that he could not escape and that Clinton would send him no help, Cornwallis finally sent out a white flag of surrender.

Two days later, Cornwallis surrendered his entire army to Washington. To the British tune, "The World Turned Upside Down," the British troops marched out of Yorktown and stacked their guns in the presence of Washington and Rochambeau and their armies.

The War's End

In many places throughout the states, people greeted the news of Cornwallis's surrender at Yorktown with rejoicing. Washington's victory, they believed, meant that the long war was over; the United States were truly free and independent. Yet, another year passed before Great Britain formally acknowledged the independence of the American states.

Finally, the long-awaited day arrived. On **November 25, 1783,** the British army, its soldiers dressed in their bright red uniforms, bearing their gleaming weapons, evacuated New York City—never to return. With the British army gone, General Washington led his tattered troops into the city.

Washington remained in New York for only a few more days. At a farewell meal with his officers, Washington lifted his wineglass in a toast. "With a heart full of love and gratitude," he said, "I now take my leave of you. I most devoutly wish that your later days may be as prosperous and happy as your former ones have been glorious and honorable."

Leaving New York, Washington returned to his home at Mount Vernon to spend Christmas with his wife, Martha, and her grandchildren.

November 25, 1783: the day the Revolutionary War finally ended, as the British troops evacuated New York City and George Washington led his troops into New York

The surrender of British troops led by General Cornwallis at Yorktown, Virginia, on October 19, 1781. The French fleet, commanded by Admiral de Grasse, is in Chesapeake Bay.

11/6

Chapter 8 Review

Summary

- Early battles of the Revolutionary War, including those at Saratoga, Bunker Hill, and Trenton, gave the American colonists hope that they could defeat the British and establish a country.
- After these early battles, the colonies began to unite behind the Revolution. General Washington, assisted by Baron von Steuben, turned the New England farmers into a real, fighting army. Thomas Paine's pamphlet *Common Sense* convinced many colonists that the King of England was a tyrant. And on July 4, 1776, the Continental Congress signed a Declaration of Independence, uniting all the colonies behind the fight for independence.
- Many hardships faced the country during the Revolution. The war pitted colonial loyalists and colonial patriots against each other, so this Revolution could be thought of as our first civil war. Moreover, the Americans lost many lives, and seemed for several long years to be one step away from defeat. But the British grew overconfident, and were surprised when the French and Americans defeated the unprepared British at Yorktown. Lord Cornwallis surrendered all his troops to George Washington, and two years later—on November 25, 1783—the British finally evacuated New York City.

Chapter Checkpoint

1. What did Benedict Arnold do to help the Americans? If he had succeeded in giving up West Point, what would have happened to New York?
2. Who was Ethan Allen?
3. What did the American general William Prescott say to his troops at the Battle of Bunker Hill? How many men did he lose that day? How many did the British lose?
4. Who trained the colonial militiamen to fight like real soldiers?
5. What was the name of the pamphlet that turned many loyalist colonists into patriots? Who wrote it? What did it say?
6. Write a paragraph about July 4, 1776. Answer the following questions: What was signed that day? What group signed it? Who wrote it? Who was the first person to sign it? What important things did it say?

7. Who was Flora Macdonald? What brave thing did she do in Scotland? What did she do in North Carolina?

8. What did King Louis XVI of France sign on February 6, 1778? When did French help for the States finally arrive?

9. Was General Cornwallis overconfident after winning so many battles in the South? How was he taken by surprise at Yorktown?

Chapter Activities

1. Divide the class into small groups. Members of each group will write and act out a short one-act play about the American Revolution. The play could focus on certain episodes such as the signing of the Declaration of Independence, Benedict Arnold's treason, the Battle of Yorktown, Benjamin Franklin's trip to Paris, and so on. Each group can have a parent assist them with research, costumes, sets, and production. The play can be put on for parents, or for other students in the school.

2. How could a short pamphlet like *Common Sense* change the minds of a whole country? Would it have changed people's minds if the war had not already begun? Can you think of any ideas, books, plays, or letters written in recent history that have changed people's minds about something?

The American Larder

In New England, and especially around Boston, fish was a main staple of the larder. As a sea town, Boston was utterly dependent upon its fishing trade, and soups made of fish or clams were very popular. New England clam chowder was made with a harvest of clams simmered with onion, bacon, and clam juice; thick cream was then added to make a delicious white soup. Today, shellfish like oysters, clams, shrimp, and lobster are expensive and rare. However, in eighteenth-century Boston it was the poor people who ate shellfish (especially oysters and lobster), because it was plentiful and easy to harvest, while the wealthier folk ate fish and meat.

Chapter 9 How We Got Our Constitution

Troubles after the Revolution

Shays' Rebellion

Though the colonies had won their independence from Great Britain, all was not well in America. This was especially true for farmers, who had done quite well for themselves throughout the war selling crops to the Continental army. When the war ended, these farmers could not make as much money, since there was no longer an army to feed. So it was that many farmers could not pay back money they owed, nor could they pay their taxes.

In those days, people could go to jail for not paying their debts, and so many a farmer found himself thrown into debtor's prison. Other farmers lost their lands and property, for the people to whom they owed money were allowed to seize property as payment.

Some states took measures to help the farmers, but not Massachusetts. The wealthy men in the state assembly blocked bills that were aimed at helping the farmers. The Massachusetts

A debtor's prison. A jail for people who could not pay their debts

**Shays' Rebellion.
A mob of discontents
seize the Massachusetts
court house.**

assembly even passed a stamp tax. Throughout the state, farmers began gathering to protest what the assembly was doing (or not doing) to help them. When the assembly still refused to listen to their complaints, farmers began setting up committees to resist the government. Sam Adams, who had done the very same thing against the British government 10 years before, said the rebellious farmers should be hanged.

Such threats did not frighten the farmers. In the fall of 1786, farmers in western Massachusetts kept local courts from trying cases, so that no one could be tried for not paying his debts. The leader of the rebellious farmers was Daniel Shays, who had been a captain during the Revolutionary War. When Massachusetts Governor James Bowdoin ordered the farmers to disperse (or else he would send out the state militia against them), Shays and his men did not run for cover. Instead, they set out for the town of Springfield to keep the state supreme court from meeting.

When Shays and his men arrived at Springfield on January 25, 1787, they found the state militia under General William Shepherd already there, guarding the town. Shepherd, who had fought side by side with Shays at Bunker Hill, did not want to hurt the farmers. He ordered his men to fire over the farmers' heads, but Shays and his men showed no signs of fear. They kept on advancing against the militia. Shepherd, knowing the farmers meant business, then ordered his men to shoot to kill. A loud explosion of muskets and artillery followed, and the air was filled with black smoke. This was too much for the farmers; they broke and fled.

It was bitter winter, and Shays and his men trudged through ice and snow until they reached the town of Petersham, northeast of Springfield. On February 4, they fought another battle with state militia under General Benjamin Lincoln. Shays was defeated and fled to Vermont. Another of the rebel leaders, Eli Parsons, fled to New York, where he was again able to gather a force. In late February, Parsons and his men marched again into Massachusetts, gathering more men as they went. At Stockbridge they seized supplies, but at Springfield they were defeated by a larger force of state militia. In this skirmish, two of the rebels were killed and 30 were wounded.

So ended Shays' rebellion. Though it was short and unsuccessful, it did accomplish something. In the spring of 1787, the people of Massachusetts elected a new assembly and a new governor who passed laws to help the farmers. The rebellion also frightened many. What if it had been larger and better organized? Could the government of Massachusetts have stopped it? And if Massachusetts could not control such a rebellion, could the government of the United States in Philadelphia do anything to help? This last question, as we shall see, was the most important of all. By 1787 many had come to think the Continental Congress a very weak and incompetent government.

A blacksmith expresses anger over a legal writ foreclosing his shop.

The Articles of Confederation

To create a common, or federal, government over all the states had not been easy. Back in 1776, a constitution for just such a government, called the **Articles of Confederation,** had been written; but it took three years for all the states to agree to it. Even then, one state, Maryland, would not sign the articles. It was not until March 1, 1781, that Maryland signed the articles, seven months before the battle of Yorktown.

Articles of Confederation: the first American constitution, which established a single-house congress with very limited powers

The Articles of Confederation set up a one-house legislature, called the Congress of the United States of America, to which each state sent representatives. The Congress had these powers: to make war and peace, to approve treaties with foreign nations, to control the coining of money, and to referee disagreements between states. Each state had one vote in the Congress.

After winning independence from Great Britain, people in the states were unwilling to give over too much power to the federal government. Thus, under the Articles of Confederation, the federal government had very little power over individual state governments. Congress could not tax people in the states, but had to ask state governments for contributions. If Congress wanted to declare war or to make a treaty, it had to get the agreement of representatives of nine of the 13 states, and that was hard to do. But if it was hard to do these things, it was even harder to make any changes in the Articles of Confederation. For that to happen, Congress had to get the approval of all the state legislatures—an almost impossible task.

Because state legislatures were unwilling to pay the contributions they owed to the federal government, Congress was always lacking money to pay its debts. During the Revolutionary War, this meant that the Continental army was always short of supplies, and soldiers went without pay. Worse than this, Congress did not have enough power to keep peace between the states, and the states were continually squabbling. Many feared that the United States would split up into a number of small nations with no common government, whose disagreements might turn into wars that would destroy the peace of America.

Treaty of Paris (1783): the Treaty between the Americans and British, which gave the United States all the lands between the Atlantic Ocean and the Mississippi River

The weak congress, moreover, could not earn the respect of foreign governments. Though in the **Treaty of Paris,** which ended the Revolutionary War, Great Britain gave the United States all the lands between the Atlantic Ocean and the Mississippi River, Great Britain still had forts in those territories. When Congress complained that keeping these forts was against the treaty, the British government replied that the United States had also not kept the treaty. Congress had not protected the property of loyalists in the states, nor had it paid the debts it owed to Great Britain. This was true, for Congress was powerless to stop the states from taking loyalist property and was always short of money.

Even before Shays' rebellion, many in the states had realized that something had to be done to strengthen the federal government. The states of Virginia and Maryland were the first to call for a convention to discuss how this might be done. Soon Congress agreed, and in February 1787 called for a convention of all states to meet in Philadelphia in the spring.

A New Constitution

The Constitutional Convention

George Washington had wanted only one thing after the war—to spend the remainder of his life with his wife, Martha, on their Mount Vernon plantation. He wanted nothing more of war, and he certainly wanted nothing to do with politics. The life of a gentleman farmer was what Washington desired; but as before, if his country asked for his services, he would gladly give them.

The country did ask for Washington's services. This time, he served as the president of the convention that would meet in Philadelphia to draw up a new constitution. Though as president, Washington could not participate in the convention's decision making, he would serve a very important function. It would be his task to bring unity to a

Benjamin Franklin at the Constitutional Convention of 1787. He was instrumental in bringing together warring factions within the new republic. His humor and political skill brought about vital compromises which resulted in the adoption of the Constitution.

The United States Capitol building in Washington, D.C., where members of Congress (the Senate and House of Representatives) work and meet to make the nation's laws

group of men who had very different opinions about how to form the new government. Only Washington could do this, for he was a man all the delegates respected.

Except for Washington, who was 55 years old, and Benjamin Franklin, who was 80, the delegates to the Constitutional Convention were younger men. They were divided pretty much into two groups. The first favored a strong national government and wanted the states to give up more of their powers. The second group feared a strong national government and wanted to make sure that the states did not lose too many of their powers.

Those who favored a strong national government supported what was called the "Virginia Plan," which Edmund Randolph of Virginia introduced to the convention. According to the Virginia Plan, the new government would have a president and a supreme court. The Congress would be divided into two houses, each filled with representatives from the states. The members of the lower house would be elected by the people. The members of the upper house, called the Senate, would be appointed by the members of the lower house.

Unlike the Articles of Confederation, which gave each state one vote in Congress, the Virginia Plan gave larger states more votes than smaller states in both houses of congress. (The larger states were those with a larger population; the smaller states, those with a smaller population.) In this way, the states would not have equal representation, and laws would be passed if most of the representatives of the people in the United States wanted them, not if most of the states wanted them.

The men who supported the Virginia Plan at first controlled the convention. Those delegates who wanted to protect state power did not have a plan to match the Virginia Plan. So, most of the discussions were about how to adjust the Virginia Plan. Should there be one president, or two? Some of the delegates thought having one president was too much like having a king. Should members of Congress be elected by the people or appointed by state legislatures? James Madison of Virginia thought the people should elect members of both the lower house and the Senate, while men like Roger Sherman of Connecticut thought the people could not be trusted to

The United States Supreme Court building in Washington, D.C.

elect members of the federal government. Though George Mason of Virginia agreed with Madison that the people should elect the members of the lower house of Congress, he and others thought state legislatures should appoint members of the Senate.

If the supporters of the Virginia Plan thought no one at the convention would oppose them, they were wrong. On June 9, William

The Mothers of the Constitution

Behind the men who shaped the American Constitution, were the women who influenced them. Wives, mothers, and daughters discussed the new government and its constitution with the men of their families. It was a momentous time: no other country in the world had ever had the chance to choose, freely, the kind of government that it thought best for the common good. Abigail Adams, the wife of John Adams, wrote to her husband, who had written the Massachusetts constitution and was very involved in the shaping of the American Constitution. Both learned and intelligent, Abigail and John discussed everything that happened during the Constitutional convention, and left a record in the extensive correspondence between them. Together, they envisioned a classical form of government, tempered by practical nobility that insisted on liberty and justice for all. Although Abigail was never present at the discussions on the new constitution, her influence was carried through her beloved husband, John.

Paterson spoke out in favor of the small states and of those who wanted to protect state power. His own state of New Jersey, he said, would never accept the Virginia Plan. On June 15, he surprised the delegates by offering another plan for the constitution—the New Jersey Plan. This plan stated that only small changes should be made to the Articles of Confederation. More importantly, it said that all states should continue to have equal representation in the federal government: one vote per state.

Those delegates who wanted a strong federal government thought it was unfair for smaller states to have the same power as larger states. When the New Jersey Plan was brought up for a vote on June 19, it was defeated. This did not discourage the delegates from small states like New Jersey, Delaware, and Maryland; they declared they would never enter into a union that had a constitution based on the Virginia Plan. For many days both sides argued and fought, but they could come to no agreement on the chief question: should states be treated equally in Congress, or should states with more people have more representatives than states with fewer people? Unless the delegates could agree on this question, it looked as if the convention would break up without having written a constitution.

It was Roger Sherman who saved the convention with what was called the Connecticut Compromise. Sherman had offered this compromise in June, after Paterson presented his New Jersey Plan, but no one was then interested in it. Now, in July, when it was clear that the delegates from small states and the delegates from large states could not agree, all were ready to listen. The Connecticut Compromise said that in the lower house, larger states should have more representatives than smaller states. But in the Senate, each state should have the same

The White House, where the United States president lives and works

number of representatives as any other state (two senators per state). The convention voted on the Connecticut Compromise and passed it on July 16.

The Writing of the Constitution

The next step was actually to write up the new constitution. For several weeks a committee worked on the document. On August 6 they were finally finished, and presented it to the Constitutional Convention. The following were the most important parts of the new constitution.

House of Representatives: the house of Congress elected by the people
Senate: the house of Congress appointed by the state legislature. Today the Senate is elected by the people.

1. A congress would make all the laws for the new government. This Congress would be divided into two houses: the **House of Representatives** and the **Senate.**
2. In the House of Representatives, the larger states had more representatives than the smaller states. In the Senate, each state had two representatives. The people elected the members of the House, while state legislatures appointed the members of the Senate. (Nowadays, the people elect the members of the Senate.)
3. Members of the House of Representatives were elected every two years. Members of the Senate were appointed (by state legislatures) every six years.

bill: a proposed law to be rejected or approved by the Congress
veto: the act by which a president refuses to allow an approved bill to become law

4. There was a president, whose job was not to make laws but to make sure that the laws made by Congress were enforced. Yet, before a **bill** passed by both the House and the Senate could become law, the president had to sign the bill. If he refused to sign the bill (called a **veto**), it could not become a law, unless two-thirds of both the House and Senate rejected the president's veto. If both houses rejected the veto, the bill became a law whether or not the president agreed to it.
5. The president was also commander in chief of the army and navy of the United States.

Preamble to the Constitution

We the people of the United States, in order to form a more perfect union, establish justice, insure domestic tranquillity, provide for the common defense, promote the general welfare, and secure the blessings of liberty to ourselves and our posterity, do ordain and establish this Constitution for the United States of America.

6. The president was *not* elected by the people. Instead, the people voted for **electors,** who in turn voted for the president. Each state had a different number of electors; larger states had more electors, smaller states, fewer electors. A president could not be removed from office unless the House of Representatives **impeached** him (accused him of serious crimes) and three-fourths of the Senate convicted him of those crimes.

7. There was also a **Supreme Court.** The president appointed the members of the Supreme Court; the Senate, though, could reject any of the men the president appointed. Supreme Court justices could serve as long as they wished, unless they were impeached and convicted of serious crimes by the House of Representatives and the Senate.

8. The federal government could tax the people in the states directly without asking the states' permission. Still, the federal government could only do certain things: declare war, make treaties, coin money, judge between states when they had a disagreement, and make sure one state did not treat the citizens of another state unjustly. All other tasks belonged to the states or to the people.

electors: representatives of the people, who were qualified to elect the president
impeachment: the act by which the Congress accuses a president or Supreme Court justice of serious crimes
Supreme Court: the highest court in the land, which would decide cases that had not been settled by local judges

The Convention Approves the Constitution

The draft of the Constitution did not entirely please any of the delegates. Some thought it gave the federal government too much power. Others thought it did not give the federal government enough power. Even though he was a slave owner, George Mason wanted the Constitution to make the foreign slave trade (bringing slaves from other countries to America) illegal. But delegates from South Carolina and Georgia did not like Mason's idea. These states would not accept the Constitution if it forbade the slave trade. Because of these delegates, the Constitution did not outlaw the slave trade. Instead, it said the slave trade could continue for another 20 years. After that time, it would be illegal to bring slaves to America.

Another important question was, what could the federal government do to make sure a state would obey its laws? Some of the delegates thought the federal government should have the power to gather an army from the various states to force a disobedient state to obey its laws. Others, like James Madison, thought this gave the federal government far too much power. The delegates finally decided

Slaves working in
a cotton field

that the federal government could not use force to make a state obey federal laws. It could only bring the disobedient state to court.

When the day came for the delegates to sign the new Constitution (a sign that they approved it), some of them refused. Only a few who did sign the Constitution liked it, but most figured it was simply the best agreement they could get. They certainly did not want to spend any more time in Philadelphia arguing with *other* stubborn delegates. They knew they had plenty of fights ahead of them, for many people in the states would not want to accept the new Constitution. Indeed, no one was sure that the states would accept it, or, if some did and others did not, that the United States would remain a federal union.

The Fight for the Constitution

Many men opposed the new Constitution in the states. Because those in favor of the Constitution were called federalists, those who opposed it became known as anti-federalists. They fought hard and long to keep their states from approving the Constitution.

Why were they so against it? Some of them did not want a strong government outside their own states. Others were afraid they would be taxed more by a federal government. Still others feared the federal government would get so strong that it would become worse than the government of Great Britain. What was the point of fighting a

Independence Hall in Philadelphia, Pennsylvania, was built in 1732 as the Pennsylvania State House. It was here that the Declaration of Independence was adopted and the United States Constitution was debated, drafted, and signed.

The Federalist Papers

A series of 85 essays on the proposed new Constitution of the United States and on the nature of republican government, published between 1787 and 1788 by Alexander Hamilton, James Madison, and John Jay in an effort to persuade New York state voters to support ratification. Seventy-seven of the essays first appeared serially in New York newspapers, were reprinted in most other states, and were published in book form as *The Federalist* on May 28, 1788; the remaining eight papers appeared in New York newspapers between June 14 and August 16.

long war with Great Britain, they thought, only to end up just as bad off as before?

Many famous and powerful men became anti-federalists. In Virginia, Richard Henry Lee (of the powerful Lee family) opposed it; so did Patrick Henry. Even George Mason, who helped write the Constitution, ended up turning against it.

The federalists also had many famous men among them. James Madison of Virginia supported the Constitution. He and two New Yorkers, Alexander Hamilton and John Jay, wrote a series of newspaper articles, later published as *The Federalist,* defending the Constitution. The federalists also included another Lee—Henry (called "Lighthorse Harry") Lee—as well as John Adams, Edmund Randolph, and, most important of all, General George Washington.

Most of the small states were in favor of the Constitution. The only one against it was the always stubborn Rhode Island. The first state to ratify the Constitution was Delaware, on December 7, 1787. But the second state was a large state, Pennsylvania, on December 12. By the end of February 1788, four more states had ratified the Constitution: New Jersey, Georgia, Connecticut, and Massachusetts.

The Constitution needed the approval of 9 of the 13 states before it could become the law of the land. In the spring of 1788, when Maryland, South Carolina, and New Hampshire approved the Constitution, the federalists had the nine states they needed. Yet, the Constitution was still in trouble. The two most powerful and influential states, Virginia and New York, had not ratified it. Without them, it was unlikely that there could be a federal union.

In Virginia, Patrick Henry led the fight against the Constitution. The Constitution, he said, would destroy American liberty. Calling for a single man to be president, said Henry, was the same as calling for a king, and Henry did not want any kings. Edmund Randolph spoke against Henry. Without the Constitution, said Randolph, the states would become nothing but small, quarreling countries. America, instead of a strong and great country, would become the laughingstock of the civilized world.

Back and forth went the arguments, for and against the Constitution. No one could be certain how Virginia would vote. It was probably George Washington who won the day for the Constitution in Virginia. With his support, Virginia finally voted to ratify the Constitution on June 23, 1788.

In New York, the battle for the Constitution was just as difficult. Rich landowners controlled the state government in New York, and they feared that a strong federal government would tax them too much. But it was probably their snobbery that finally convinced these rich men to approve the Constitution. Besides New York, only Rhode Island had not ratified the Constitution. And Rhode Island was run by poorer sorts of people. Since the rich New Yorkers did not want to be stuck outside the federal union with only Rhode Island for company, they finally, after much fighting, agreed to ratify the Constitution on July 26, 1788.

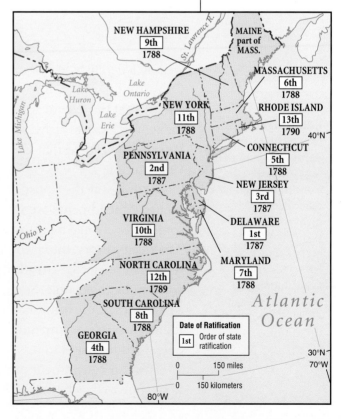

Map showing when each state ratified the Constitution

Washington's inauguration

Bill of Rights: a list describing the rights of citizens and states, added to the Constitution so that the federal government could not take them away

amendments: new laws, added to the Constitution, that sometimes change a part of the Constitution

The First President and the Bill of Rights

No one had any doubt about who would win the first presidential election in 1788. Only one man could unify the nation, and that man was General George Washington. Both federalists and anti-federalists respected and loved Washington. No one ran against him in this, our country's first presidential election; and so, in the spring of 1789, Washington was inaugurated as the first president of the United States.

Washington knew he could not ignore the anti-federalists if he wanted truly to unite the country. Many anti-federalists as well as federalists had wanted a **Bill of Rights** to be added to the Constitution. This bill would list the rights that citizens and states had, so that the federal government could not take them away. In his inaugural address (the speech he gave when he took office), Washington hinted that Congress should add a Bill of Rights to the Constitution.

The only way the Constitution can be changed is through **amendments.** Amendments are new laws, added to the Constitution, that sometimes change a part of the Constitution. For instance, later in American history, there would be an amendment that changed how senators are elected—no longer appointed by state legislators, but voted in by the people. Sometimes an amendment does not change a part of the Constitution, but adds something new to it. The Bill of Rights, a series of amendments, did not change the Constitution, but added new laws to it.

Before an amendment can become part of the Constitution, it has to be approved by both the House of Representatives and the Senate.

If the amendment passes both houses of Congress, it is sent to the states. If at least three-fourths of the states approve the amendment, then it becomes part of the Constitution.

By November 1791, Congress and the states had approved 10 amendments, called the Bill of Rights, and they became part of the Constitution. The basic shape and form of the Constitution had been completed. That same year, Rhode Island voted to accept the Constitution and so entered the federal union—the last state to do so. So it was that the 13 colonies that had revolted against Great Britain were finally united in a common nation—the republic of the United States of America.

The Bill of Rights

The Bill of Rights contains 10 amendments that deal with the rights Americans cherish the most. For instance, the First Amendment says that Congress is not allowed to make any particular religion the official religion of the entire United States. It also says that Congress cannot keep people from saying or printing what they wish to say or print. The Second Amendment states that since states need militias to defend themselves, the government cannot take away the right of citizens to bear arms. According to the Tenth Amendment, the federal government does not possess all power in the United States. This amendment states that all powers the Constitution does not give to the federal government belong to the states or to the people.

The Oval Office in the west wing of the White House, where the president conducts the day-to-day business of the nation

Chapter 9 Review

Summary

- The survival of the new American nation was hanging in the balance. Farmers led by Colonel Daniel Shays rebelled against unjust debt laws and high taxes in Massachusetts. Although Massachusetts put down the rebellion and finally changed its laws, many patriots who had protested the king's high taxes were unsympathetic. Meanwhile, the states were not paying their contributions to the Congress, which weakened its power to keep peace at home and gain the respect of nations abroad. The new nation was being torn apart by squabbles and injustices that were unbecoming of a free people.
- In 1787 the Constitutional Convention gathered in Philadelphia. The delegates were fiercely divided, supporting two different plans of

government—the strong Virginia Plan and the weaker New Jersey Plan. The nation almost dissolved at this convention, but was saved by the Connecticut Compromise. Slowly and sometimes reluctantly, nine states ratified the Constitution that established a presidency, a two-house Congress, and a Supreme Court. A new government was born.

- In 1789, Revolutionary War hero George Washington was elected as America's first president. The people trusted him to lead the country justly. While Washington was president, the Bill of Rights was passed, which ensured that the national constitution would protect freedom of religion, the right to bear arms, the right to a free press, and the right for states and people to govern themselves through the federal system.

Chapter Checkpoint

1. Why did Shays' rebellion take place? Did Samuel Adams support the rebels?
2. How many years did the United States rule itself by the Articles of Confederation? Was there a president then?
3. Who was the first president of the United States?
4. Summarize the laws of our constitution. List at least eight points that define our way of government.
5. Who were the federalists? Who were the anti-federalists?
6. Why were some of our founding fathers afraid of the Constitution?
7. Who was the only man who could unify the nation, which was divided into federalists and anti-federalists?
8. When was the Bill of Rights added to the Constitution? What rights did it protect? Did the Bill of Rights reassure the anti-federalists that America would be governed justly?

Chapter Activities

1. As a class, learn about the history of farming in early America. Were most of the American people farmers? What was the difference between gentleman farmers, small landowners, and indentured servants? What kinds of crops did they grow? Where did they sell their crops after the colonies were set free, and colonists no longer had to send crops to Britain? Were there too many crops and not enough people to eat them?
2. As a class, led by your teacher, read parts of the American Constitution. Focus on the preamble, the powers of the three branches of government, and the original Bill of Rights.

3. Many democracies have written and discarded two, three, or even 20 constitutions. What is special about our Constitution that has made it last so long?

The American Larder

The early Americans used butter for medicine and cosmetics as well as for food. They poured lots of butter on their vegetables, fish, eggs, bread, and sweets; just about everything they ate was doused in butter. Every American locale had its own unique taste of butter, depending upon what the cows ate and what time of year it was; winter butter was almost white in color. Butter could be produced and sold in round, cubed, or rectangular shapes, all stamped with a wooden stamp to state when it was made. Some butter was passed through a tube and sold by the yard; elsewhere it was sold in pieces, about the size of an egg. Many eighteenth- and nineteenth-century recipes called for the addition of "butter the size of an egg."

Chapter 10 The Early Days of a New Nation

Under President Washington

Political Parties—What They Are and How We Got Them

The Constitution of the United States of America says nothing about **political parties.** The founding fathers of our country hoped that America would have no political parties, so they did not make them part of government. George Washington, especially, disliked political parties because he feared that they would split the country apart. He knew people would disagree about laws and such, but he hoped they would not form little groups that fought with each other over their disagreements. He wanted people to think of themselves as Americans, not as members of parties.

Yet, no sooner had Washington become president than political parties began to form. In his

> **political party:** a group that shares similar ideas about what is best for society. Political parties spread their ideas and elect candidates who will form laws that agree with those ideas.

Citizens rally to support their political party.

cabinet: the group of people who advise the president

own **cabinet** (the group of people who advise the president) were two men who disagreed over what was good and how the country should be run. One of these was the secretary of the treasury, Alexander Hamilton. The other was the secretary of war, Thomas Jefferson.

Hamilton and Jefferson were two very different men. Hamilton had been born poor; Jefferson was the son of a wealthy Virginia plantation owner. Hamilton had a warrior's spirit and had fought bravely during the Revolution; Jefferson was a peaceful man and had served as governor of Virginia during the Revolution. Hamilton was impetuous and energetic; Jefferson appeared somewhat slow and easygoing.

politics: the art by which people live together in society

Where Hamilton and Jefferson differed most was in their opinions on **politics.** Hamilton had always favored a strong federal government; during the Constitutional Convention he said he wanted to get rid of the old states entirely. He also said that the United States should have a king of its own. Hamilton also believed that the United States should have a strong army and navy and should wage wars to gain more land. He wanted the United States to become a great manufacturing nation, with great cities built around great factories. Moreover, Hamilton believed the government should favor the rich. Though born poor himself, he had a deep distrust of the common people.

Alexander Hamilton

Jefferson, on the other hand, feared a strong federal government. He thought Americans needed strong state governments in order to remain free. Jefferson also was opposed to a large army and navy, for he feared the government would use them to oppress the states and the people. The armed forces, he thought, should only be large enough to defend the country from invasion. Jefferson deeply disliked large cities and factories. The only truly free men, he thought, were small family farmers, who did not have to please customers or work for other men. Jefferson hoped that the United States would remain a country of

What Is Politics?

Politics is the art by which people live together in a society. In families there are those (the father and mother) who make the rules for the family's good, and there are those who obey the rules (the children). In the same way, in societies, there must be rules (called laws) and people who should make those rules for the good of everyone. Those who make the rules are, in some countries, called kings or queens; in others, they are legislatures, presidents, or prime ministers. But most of the time, people have different ideas about what is good for society; or they disagree about what sorts of laws to make. When different groups of people have very different ideas about these things, they often form different political parties. In a country like the United States, political parties work to spread their ideas about what is good for society. They also, in elections, run candidates for public offices. Party members hope that if their candidates are elected, they will work to make laws that agree with the ideas of their political party.

farmers. Finally, the privileged Jefferson, who was born into wealth, distrusted the rich; he wanted the government to follow the wishes of the common folk.

At first, Jefferson and Hamilton worked together. Jefferson admired Hamilton, because he had been a war hero. Hamilton respected Jefferson, who was an inventor, an architect, an amateur scientist, and had written the Declaration of Independence. Thus, Jefferson and Hamilton worked together on planning the new capital of the United States, which would be named Washington in honor of the first president. Their first disagreement was over whether the federal government should have its own bank. Jefferson said it should not, because the Constitution had not given the government the power to found a bank. Hamilton said it should, because a bank would be a good thing for the government to have, and besides, the Constitution never said the federal government *could not* found a bank.

Jefferson and Hamilton began to disagree on other matters as well. Soon, they became bitter enemies. Hamilton was able to

Thomas Jefferson

James Madison

Republicans:
a political party founded by Thomas Jefferson; Republicans opposed a strong federal government, favored strong state governments, and preferred farming over manufacturing.
Federalists:
a political party founded by Alexander Hamilton; Federalists favored a strong federal government, a strong defense, and manufacturing.

convince not only Washington of his ideas but also Washington's vice president, John Adams. Hamilton became Washington's most trusted advisor, and this made Jefferson so angry that he resigned from his office of secretary of state.

But Jefferson was not alone in disliking Hamilton and his ideas. James Madison, who had written *The Federalist* with Hamilton, became another of Hamilton's political opponents. So did many farmers and old antifederalist people throughout the country. All these men gathered around Jefferson and began to call themselves **Republicans,** because they believed the government should be a republic —a government controlled by the people.

Men like John Adams and others who agreed with Hamilton's ideas also gave themselves a name. They called themselves **Federalists** because they believed in a strong federal government. The Federalists became the party of the wealthy, while the Republicans became the party of the common people. Thus were born the first political parties in the United States.

In many ways the Federalists and the Republicans were unlike political parties of our time, but in other ways they were alike. They argued with each other, both in speeches and in newspapers. They called each other names, and they sometimes got into actual fights with each other. Each party thought the other did not really hold true American ideas.

The Trailblazer of Kentucky

Ever since he was a young man, Daniel Boone had dreamed of exploring the West. When he was about 20 years old, while fighting for the British in the French and Indian War, Boone met a man who had traded with the Indians on the western side of the

Republican Became Democrat; Federalist Became Republican

The Federalists and the Republicans were the ancestors of the political parties of our day. However, Jefferson's Republican party is not the same as today's Republican party, even though it has the same name. In fact, the modern Democratic party is a descendant of Jefferson's Republicans, while our Republicans come from the Federalist party.

Appalachian Mountains. Daniel Boone was a hunter, a restless man, with a curiosity about these wild lands that gnawed at him like a great hunger. He longed to see the western lands, to explore the beautiful country that was called Kentucky.

But Boone did not set out right away on his western explorations. Instead, he got married and moved with his wife to North Carolina's western frontier; yet, this was not the wilderness that Boone longed for. In 1767, when he was 33 years old, Boone crossed the Blue Ridge Mountains. For the first time, he camped and hunted on the edge of Kentucky. But this trip only whetted his hunger to see more of the wild lands.

Boone and five other hunters set out on May 1, 1769, to explore the wilderness. In early June, while standing on a mountaintop, Boone saw for the first time the beautiful level lands of the Bluegrass region of central Kentucky. In Kentucky a farmer could find rich soil for cultivating his crops, and the hunter could find an abundance of game. Kentucky, Boone discovered, was full of wild animals, especially buffalo. Large herds of these beasts grazed the rich grasses or clipped the leaves of the wild cane plants. It was also a land of flowers and wild fruit trees, as well as other trees of all sorts and sizes.

Appalachian Mountains: a low range of mountains, stretching from Maine to Georgia, that divides the coastal plain of the eastern United States from the middle of the country

Daniel Boone

Buffalo Blaze the Trail

As anyone knows who has visited it, the Daniel Boone National Forest in eastern Kentucky is a vast sea of green, tall trees and dense underbrush. Plants like rhododendron and mountain laurel, though beautiful, still make thick and nearly impassable barriers, as they did in Daniel Boone's time. How did he get through? He discovered the ancient trails made by migrating herds of buffalo that once roamed throughout Virginia and the Carolinas. Over hundreds of years of migration before they became extinct east of the Appalachian Mountains, the buffalo moved through Cumberland Gap, knocking down underbrush and pounding the earth to a hard and easy-to-follow road. This was the path that Daniel Boone followed from North Carolina into Kentucky.

But lurking among the beauties of this land, death awaited explorers in many forms: savage Indians, attack by wolves and mountain lions, disease, a sudden fall down a sheer cliff. Only the bravest left civilization to face such dangers. One evening, on a journey near the Kentucky River, Indians attacked Boone and his companion, John Stewart. The Indians took them captive and treated them with great savagery. Hourly, they expected death. Finally, on the seventh night of their captivity, Boone and Stewart escaped while their Indian captors slumbered. But when Boone and Stewart returned to their old camp, they found that their other two companions had already departed.

Despite these hardships, Boone continued his journey; he was determined to explore Kentucky. He had to be most wary, for Indians followed his path. When John Stewart was killed by the Indians, he was all alone. One day, climbing a high hill, Boone surveyed the wide country. On one side stretched the wide plains of

Kentucky; on the other rolled the broad Ohio River. Far to the east, Boone saw the dim purple line of the Appalachian Mountains. How beautiful it all was. Strong and industrious men could turn it into a garden of delights.

After two years in Kentucky, Boone returned home to his wife, Rebecca, and their family. In 1773, he tried to settle Kentucky with his family and some friends, but Indians turned them back at the Cumberland Gap—the pass through the Blue Ridge. Two years later, Boone led an expedition to cut the Wilderness Road over the Appalachian Mountains into Kentucky. This time, despite attacks by Shawnee Indians, Boone founded a settlement and fort called Boonesborough in Kentucky. Boone returned to North Carolina and brought his family to Boonesborough.

In August 1776, the settlers in Boonesborough received a copy of the Declaration of Independence. Their continued war with the Indians now became a part of the Revolutionary War, with the Indians fighting for the British. In February 1778, Shawnee Indians captured Boone and his companions. Treating their captives with unexpected kindness, the Shawnee took them to the British Fort Detroit in Michigan. Though the British offered to ransom Boone from the Shawnee, the Indians refused to give up their respected captive. Instead, they carried him off to their settlement, called Old Chelicothe, from which Boone escaped in June.

Thinking her husband dead, Rebecca Boone and her family returned to North Carolina. Reaching Boonesborough after his escape from the Shawnee, Boone was saddened to find that his family had gone. But he was unable to follow them because the Kentucky settlement was soon under siege by a combined force of Shawnee and British. For 11 days, the siege continued. Finally, the attackers, unable to take Boonesborough, withdrew. Shortly after, Boone returned to North Carolina to find his wife and family. A year later, in

A Legend in His Own Time and Beyond

Though he lived to be a very old man (he died in 1820), Daniel Boone had become a legend as early as 1784. That year, a man named John Filson published an "autobiography" of the frontiersman, called *The Adventures of Colonel Daniel Boone.* Other stories of Boone's life followed, making Daniel Boone one of our most famous national heroes.

1779, Boone led more settlers into Kentucky and founded the settlement of Boone's Station in the region north of the Kentucky River. For many more years, Daniel Boone continued his adventures, exploring the wild lands, hunting, and battling Indians.

The Victories of "Mad Anthony"

Continuous warfare still raged between the settlers and the Indians. Even after the Treaty of Paris, which ended the Revolutionary War, the fighting did not let up. Part of the problem was that it seemed as if the British would not give up their forts (like Fort Detroit) in what was called the Northwest Territory of the United States. Even worse, British Governor Simcoe of **Upper Canada** (now called Ontario) built a brand new fort on the Maumee River, deep within United States territory. Worse, he gave the Indians guns and ammunition that they could use to attack American settlements.

> **Upper Canada:** modern-day Ontario

This state of affairs did not please President Washington, but what was he to do? He could tell the British to leave the Northwest Territory, but what if they refused? Since he could not risk another war with Great Britain, Washington knew he could do nothing directly against the British. But he could protect the American settlers who, in greater and greater numbers, were settling the lands west of the Appalachians.

> **During the Battle of Miami in 1791, United States soldiers battled Miami and Wabash Indians.**

At first, however, it seemed that Washington was unable even to do this. In 1790, Brigadier General Josiah Harmar led over 1,300 Americans against the Miami and Wabash Indians in the Northwest Territory. On October 22, Indians led by Chief Little Turtle ambushed Harmar and his men and defeated them. But worse was yet to come. After Harmar's defeat, even more

troops were sent west under Major General Arthur St. Clair in November 1791. Chief Little Turtle led a surprise attack against these reinforcements and defeated them; nearly 900 men were lost in this battle near what is now Fort Recovery, Ohio.

After these defeats, it appeared that the United States government was unable to defend American settlers in the West. Even more serious, if the United States could not protect its western territories against Indians, how could it hope to defend them from powerful nations like Great Britain, Spain, and France? Washington and others worried that the country might in due course lose all its western territories.

Washington chose to send yet another general, who turned out to be the right one. Major General Anthony Wayne had been a brave and successful general during the Revolutionary War. So brave was General Wayne and so careless about his own safety that his men called him Mad Anthony. General Wayne was, moreover, very skilled in forest warfare, and he trained his men to be so, too. More importantly, his men grew to love their rather odd, but very capable, general. They would follow him wherever he led them.

Major General Anthony Wayne

But Mad Anthony did not attack the Indians right away. In the summer of 1793, he moved his army to the area of what is now Cincinnati, Ohio, but waited to see if Washington would be successful in convincing the Indians to allow American settlers on their lands. Fearing that white settlers would eventually drive their people from their homeland, the Indians refused. In September, Washington sent word to Mad Anthony to attack.

In the spring of 1794, Mad Anthony began his war on the Indians. Leading only a small number of men deeper into what is now Ohio, he built Fort Recovery. In June 1794, Indians under Chief Little Turtle attacked the fort; but Mad Anthony's well-trained men finally forced them to retreat.

Chippewa Indians and a Chippewa lodge

After their victory at Fort Recovery, Mad Anthony and his men continued their march north, fighting Indians in the dense forests of what is now Indiana and Ohio. Reaching the region around Lake Erie, Wayne and his men built Fort Defiance. In the lands around the new fort, the Indians had log cabins and small farms. Instead of attacking these Indian settlements, General Wayne offered the Indians peace. The Indians refused, and retreated to the area around the British fort on the Maumee River. Mad Anthony and his men pursued them.

On August 20, 1794, Mad Anthony found the Indians he was chasing behind a stockade made of fallen trees. There were gathered warriors of the Miami, Shawnee, Chippewa, Potawattomi, Sauk, Fox, and Iroquois peoples, along with a contingent of 70 Canadians under an old loyalist commander. Mad Anthony and his men attacked the Indians, and in less than an hour, defeated them. As the Indians fled in all directions, Wayne proceeded to destroy their farms and houses in the region. At the forks of the Maumee River in Indiana, he raised another fort and named it **Fort Wayne,** after himself.

The so-called Battle of Fallen Timbers convinced the Indian tribes that they could not fight against the Americans. A year later, the Indians and Wayne signed a **treaty,** the Treaty of Greenville, in which the Indians agreed to sell to the United States the lands that make up Indiana and Ohio, as well as the areas that are now Chicago and Detroit. Now in safety, the number of white settlers in the West began to expand.

Fort Wayne: a fort built by Mad Anthony Wayne and a modern-day city in northeastern Indiana

treaty: an agreement made with a foreign country or group of countries. In the United States, the Senate ratifies treaties and they become the law of the land.

Washington's Farewell

By 1796, Washington was so tired of public life that he decided not to run again for president. All he wanted to do was retire to Mount Vernon and, once again, live the life of a farmer. In the election that year, for the first time, candidates from the different parties ran against each other. Vice President John Adams was the candidate for the Federalists, while Thomas Jefferson was the candidate for the Republicans. Adams defeated Jefferson and became president. In those days the candidate with the second highest number of votes became vice president. So it was that, when Adams became president in 1797, Thomas Jefferson, Adams's political enemy, became vice president.

John Adams, the second U.S. president

In his farewell address to the nation on September 17, 1796, Washington said he hoped that the happiness of the United States would continue to grow in the years to come. He warned his countrymen against forming factions and parties because these could destroy the independence and liberty of America. Americans, he said, should be prouder of being Americans than of being Virginians, New Englanders, New Yorkers, or the citizens of any other region. He warned against changing the Constitution unless the people clearly wanted to, and he praised religion because it made men good citizens.

In March 1797, after John Adams was sworn in as the second president of the United States, George Washington returned to his beloved Mount Vernon. There, on his estate that overlooks the broad Potomac, Washington lived the peaceful life he loved so much, experimenting with the planting of crops and trees, raising horses, and taking care of his family and slaves. One early December day in 1799, he mounted his horse and rode out (as he always did) to inspect his plantation. In spite of the rain, hail, and snow falling that day, Washington completed his rounds. When he returned home, he had a bad cold. The cold developed into pneumonia, and two days later the **Father of His Country** died peacefully in his bed at Mount Vernon. He was buried in the soil of his beloved home.

Father of His Country: a complimentary nickname given to our first president, George Washington

Fighting and Bickering

President Adams

One of the issues upon which Republicans and Federalists disagreed had nothing to do with America. It had to do with France. France had had a revolution, but unlike the American Revolution, France's revolution had been far more bloody. In Paris, French revolutionaries had not only overthrown the king and queen, but beheaded them. Not only the king, but thousands of aristocrats, priests, monks, nuns, and ordinary Catholics were killed. Setting up a guillotine at the beautiful cathedral of Notre Dame in Paris, the leaders of the French Revolution tried to destroy not only the king and nobles, but the Catholic Church as well.

President Adams, Alexander Hamilton, and other Federalists hated the French Revolution because it gave total power to the common people and led to great injustices. A nation could have true liberty, the Federalists thought, only if it had a constitution and its government was controlled by men from old

The storming of the Bastille during the French Revolution

and wealthy families. The French Revolution was destructive and bloody, they said, because mobs of common people controlled the country.

However, Thomas Jefferson and the Republicans praised the French Revolution, for they said it had brought liberty and republican government to France. Republicans thought of the French Revolution as a continuation of the American Revolution. While Jefferson did not like the violence he saw when he was in France during the

The American merchant ship *Planter* beats off a French privateer ship of 22 guns, July 10, 1799.

Revolution, he decided, nevertheless, that the violence was necessary to bring liberty to France. Two years earlier, Jefferson had written (concerning Shays' rebellion): "A little rebellion now and then is a good thing; the tree of liberty must be refreshed from time to time with the blood of patriots and tyrants." Jefferson and John Adams became bitterly opposed on this matter.

Adams and the Federalists had other reasons to be against France. In 1793 France was at war with other nations in Europe, and French ships began attacking American merchant ships on the high seas. By 1797, when Adams became president, French ships had captured more than 300 American ships. That same year, the French government told three American ambassadors in France that they had to pay a large sum of money before they could speak to the French foreign minister. This was no way for one government to treat another government, and the government and people of the United States were insulted. Because of these events, President Adams convinced Congress to build up the United States army and navy in case of a war with France.

War with France—the Republicans were angry and shocked! How could President Adams go to war against another free government? France was fighting for its freedom against "tyrant" countries such as Great Britain. If the United States declared war on France, it would be fighting on the side of Great Britain and the kings and princes of Europe. In their many newspapers, Republicans began attacking Adams and the Federalists in Congress. And most of these attacks were rude, indeed.

Adams and the Federalist-controlled Congress responded to the Republicans by passing three laws, called the Naturalization and the Alien and Sedition Acts. Two of these laws or acts were directed against foreigners (called **aliens**) in the United States. The third punished **sedition,** that is, acts that men do to overthrow a government. The Sedition Act made it a crime to write or speak in an insulting way against the government. Anyone who did such things, said Adams, destroyed the respect people should have for the government.

alien: a foreigner who lives within the boundaries of a another country

sedition: spreading ideas that seriously undermine a government's authority

Because of the Sedition Act, 25 men (many of them Republican editors) were arrested; 10 of them, one of whom was a member of Congress, actually went to prison or paid a fine. But the Republicans were not frightened, and they continued to speak out against President Adams and the Federalists. Though he was the vice president, Jefferson wrote a document called the Kentucky Resolves, in which he attacked Adams. In it, Jefferson said that the Sedition Act was against the First Amendment of the Constitution, which protected freedom of speech. Because the federal government was committing an unconstitutional act by passing the Sedition Act, Jefferson wrote that the states had the right to refuse to enforce it. Jefferson said the states had just as much right as the federal government to decide whether laws were constitutional or not.

Thomas Jefferson arrives at his inauguration.

Election of 1800

The Alien and Sedition Acts were the last straw for the Republicans. They were determined to take control of Congress and throw out President Adams in the election of 1800. For their presidential candidate they chose Thomas Jefferson; for their vice presidential candidate, Aaron Burr of New York State.

In those days, candidates did not go about speaking to people to get their votes, as candidates do today. Other people did this for them, while the candidates went about their own business as if they did not care about winning. But, though other people did Jefferson's talking for him, they talked only about his ideas. Jefferson wanted the federal government to do nothing more than what the Constitution had spelled out for it to do. He said the government should not spend any more money than it collected in taxes, and he wanted to get rid of the army. State militias, he said, were enough to protect the country, while only a small navy was needed to guard the coasts of the United States. He also believed that the Federalists had gone against the right of freedom of speech by passing the Sedition Act.

Aaron Burr, vice president under Thomas Jefferson

In the election of 1800, Adams lost to Jefferson by only a few electoral votes; but the Republicans took control of both the House of Representatives and the Senate. Never again would the Federalists control either Congress or the presidency. But the Republican victory was not complete. Shortly before leaving office in 1801, President Adams named several Federalist judges to federal courts; more importantly, he appointed John Marshall to be chief justice of the Supreme Court. Though he was Jefferson's cousin, Marshall was a Federalist. With the Supreme Court in his control, Marshall would give Jefferson trouble in the years to come.

In March 1801, Jefferson was in the new capital city, Washington, for his inauguration as president. Washington City, as it was then called, was not a very cheerful place in those days. The Capitol, the building where Congress and the Supreme Court met, was still unfinished. Between the Capitol and the president's mansion (called the **White House**) lay a tract of swampy land. Along with the Treasury building, the Capitol and the White House were the only government buildings in the city.

White House: the presidential mansion in Washington, D.C.

On the day of his inauguration, no parades or fanfare surrounded Jefferson as he went to the Capitol where he would take his oath of office. Instead, dressed in simple but dignified clothes, the new president rode alone on horseback to the Capitol building. Arriving there, he dismounted and hitched his horse, like any common rider. This was not the way Washington or Adams had come to their inaugurations; they had come in carriages and with attendant fanfare. Jefferson wanted to make the point that he was a citizen, just like any other American.

A plan of the streets of Washington, D.C., three years after the original plans by L'Enfant, shows the planned sites of the Capitol and White House.

The Choosing of a Capital City

Since July 4, 1776, when the united colonies declared themselves independent from Great Britain, several cities had served as capitals for the government: Philadelphia; Baltimore, Maryland; as well as Lancaster and York, Pennsylvania. In 1783 Congress again returned to Philadelphia, but moved to Princeton, New Jersey, when angry soldiers of the Continental army marched into Philadelphia to demand the pay that the government owed them. In 1784 the government moved to New York City, where, under a new Constitution, Washington was inaugurated as the first president of the United States.

Since 1783, Congress had been talking about founding a new federal city that could serve as the capital of the United States. The problem was that northern states wanted this federal city to be in the north while southern states wanted it in the south. Two sites were finally chosen: one on the Delaware River near Trenton, New Jersey, and the other on the Potomac River, near Georgetown, Maryland. Congress favored the Delaware River site, but the southern states were opposed to it. Nothing further was done until after the states adopted the new Constitution in 1789.

When the first Congress met in New York in 1789, the question of a new capital came up for a vote. The Senate was split; the current vice president, John Adams, cast the final vote, not for the Potomac or for the Trenton area, but for Germantown, Pennsylvania. (The vice president also serves as president of the Senate. In split votes, he can cast the final vote.) This angered the southern states, and they threatened to leave the union. But Thomas Jefferson and Alexander Hamilton joined forces and were able to convince Congress to vote for a southern site for the capital, on the eastern banks of the Potomac River.

Congress gave President Washington the authority to find a suitable place for the capital somewhere on the Potomac River. The new president chose the area around Georgetown. He hired the gifted French architect, **Pierre-Charles L'Enfant,** to design the city, which would be a great square with sides that were 10 miles long. The plans were completed, and construction on the capital and president's mansion began. However, by 1799, when Washington died, the capital had not been completed; Congress was holding its sessions in Philadelphia. But that year, Congress voted that the government should be in the new capital by the first Monday in December 1800. Thus in June of 1800, President Adams moved the presidential offices to the federal city.

> **Pierre-Charles L'Enfant:** the architect who designed the city of Washington, D.C.

After taking his oath of office to protect the Constitution of the United States, Jefferson gave his inaugural speech. Like Washington, he asked the citizens of the United States to "unite with one heart and one mind" and restore, once again, their affection for one another. He admitted that Americans had different political opinions; but, he

Aaron Burr Kills Alexander Hamilton

In 1804, when Aaron Burr—an old political enemy of Alexander Hamilton—was running for governor of New York, Hamilton led the fight against him. One night at a dinner party, Hamilton made a speech against Burr in which he said something very insulting about Burr's private life. That statement came out in a newspaper. Burr thought that Hamilton had ruined his reputation. The only way Burr thought he could restore his reputation, his "honor," was by challenging Hamilton to a duel, a fight to the death. Hamilton could not turn down Burr's challenge without losing *his* honor, so both met at Weehawken, New Jersey, on the morning of July 11, 1804. As the two men stood 10 paces from

each other, Hamilton fired first, but shot wide as if he intended not to hit Burr. Burr was unwounded. Then came Burr's chance; he aimed, and fired. Hamilton fell to the ground, mortally wounded. So, Burr had killed his old political enemy. But the duel ruined Burr's remaining reputation. When his term as Jefferson's vice president ended, he left New York and headed into the western frontier, there to stir up trouble.

said, those opinions should not cause them to hate one another. Americans had fought together against a common enemy and they had, together, shed their blood. In the end, said Jefferson, all Americans agreed on the kind of government they wanted to have. Compared to that agreement, any other differences they had were small and of no account. "We are all republicans," said Jefferson. "We are all federalists."

Chapter 10 Review

Summary

- Although the founding fathers feared that political parties would split the country apart, two parties developed quickly. The Federalists, including Alexander Hamilton and John Adams, became the party of the wealthy. The Republicans, led by Thomas Jefferson, became the party of the common people.
- During and after the Revolutionary War, Daniel Boone explored and settled the rolling lands of Kentucky, braving the attacks of Indians fighting for the British. After the Revolution, the British refused to abandon their forts in the Northwest Territory, and were finally driven out by Mad Anthony Wayne. General Wayne also defeated the Indians who were attacking American settlers in the West.
- George Washington bade farewell to the nation after serving two terms. He warned that the people should be prouder of being Americans than of being New Englanders or Virginians, Federalists or Republicans. But bickering continued during John Adams's presidency, as the Federalists and Republicans disagreed about the morality of the French Revolution, French aggression against America, and the Alien and Sedition Acts. In 1800 the people elected the Republican Thomas Jefferson to be the third president of the United States.

Chapter Checkpoint

1. What does the Constitution of the United States say about political parties?
2. What were the first two political parties? What ideas did each party believe in?
3. Why did the Federalists disapprove of the French Revolution? Were they right or wrong? Explain your answer.
4. What did the Constitution say about a national bank?
5. When did Daniel Boone make his first journey to the Kentucky wilderness? When did he settle Kentucky?
6. Where did the founding fathers decide to build a federal city? What Maryland town was it near?
7. How did the Alien and Sedition Acts change the law? Why did the Republicans dislike them?
8. Who was elected president in 1800? How did he dress at his inauguration? Why did he dress this way?

Chapter Activities

1. Thomas Jefferson thought the killing of nobility, royalty, and clergy during the French Revolution was a necessary evil in the French struggle for liberty. Alexander Hamilton and the Federalists opposed the injustices of the Revolution and its elevation of the common person. Look up the Catholic teaching on the difference between just and unjust wars. Was the French Revolution just or unjust?

2. Look up the Catholic social teachings about the rights of the common people, and about the responsibilities of more wealthy and educated people toward society. Imagine you are in a room with Alexander Hamilton and Thomas Jefferson, and they are arguing about whether the educated people or the common people should dominate the country. Write a short speech to Hamilton and Jefferson about the proper place of the educated and the common people in ruling a country.

The American Larder

From the early nineteenth century on, ice harvesting became popular in America, though it did not catch on in Europe. Farmers, fishermen, and other country folk who could not work the fields or fish in the winter months would harvest ice to be stored and used during the summer. It took lots of hands to help with the many steps of ice harvesting. Ice surfaces had to be kept clear of snow, which was not desirable in the ice, and of horse manure, which was even less desirable. When the surface was frozen to the depth of a foot or more, horses (wearing spiked shoes so that they would not slip) were taken onto the ice. The horses dragged a toothed plow over the surface to mark out the blocks of ice (22 inches by 32 inches), which were then cut again and again with a plow until almost through to the unfrozen water below the ice. Large ice sheets were then cut free with handsaws and picks, and the horses pulled the sheets of ice off to the icehouses. There they were broken into blocks and stacked up for use in the warm months ahead.

Catholics in the Early United States

A Bishop for America

Newfound Freedom

M any Catholics did not join in the American Revolution. A large number simply did not take sides in the war. Others were loyalists because, like Protestant loyalist Americans, they believed they could not break oaths to remain faithful to the British king. However, many other Catholics felt morally justified in joining the American Revolution. One of these Catholics was Charles Carroll, the lord of Carrollton Manor in Maryland. Carroll was more than a wealthy plantation owner; he was one of the wealthiest men in the colonies.

Being Catholic had not been easy in the English colonies before the Revolutionary War. Most Americans were Protestant and, unfortunately, they feared or despised the Catholic Church. This was true also of many of the founding fathers of the United States. Many colonies had laws forbidding Catholics from holding a public office. Even Maryland, where most Catholics lived, had anti-Catholic laws. Only in Pennsylvania did Catholics have complete freedom of religion.

Charles Carroll, a signer of the Declaration of Independence, and a revolutionary leader

227

Charles Carroll signed "Charles Carroll of Carrollton" on the Declaration of Independence.

Charles Carroll said he had joined the Revolution in order to win religious freedom for Catholics. Indeed, he became an important founding father of the United States. Carroll not only signed the Declaration of Independence but also was responsible for getting Maryland to join the Revolution. His cousin Daniel Carroll was present at the Constitutional Convention in 1787.

The number of Catholics in the colonies was small. Yet, even among so small a group, religious life was not strong. Most of the priests were old. In Maryland, they tried to remain as hidden as possible because they feared the laws made against them would deprive them of their rights as citizens. Further, there were too few priests to serve the Catholics of the colonies. Those priests who could do so traveled long distances through forests and swamps to minister to their flocks.

Following the Revolution, anti-Catholic sentiment among Americans began to change. Because of men like Charles and Daniel

Carroll, and other Catholics who had supported the Revolution, Protestant Americans were no longer so certain that Catholics were enemies of liberty. Fewer Protestants than before continued to believe that Catholics would try to bring America under the control of a "foreign ruler," the Pope. Catholics, they began to think, were really not *too* different from other Americans.

Father John Carroll

Another famous Carroll was to play an important part in American history; he was John Carroll of Maryland, Daniel Carroll's older brother. John Carroll was born in 1735. With his cousin, Charles, he attended a Jesuit-run school at Bohemia Manor in Maryland. In 1748, both Carroll cousins went to a Jesuit seminary called St. Omer's, in France. While Charles decided to study law, John remained in the seminary and entered the Society of Jesus, the Jesuits. Ordained a priest, Father John Carroll taught in France and in Belgium. Later, he was a chaplain to a Catholic nobleman in England. In 1774, he returned to Maryland and resided at his mother's house in Rock Creek.

Bishop John Carroll

Like his cousin Charles and his younger brother Daniel, Father John Carroll believed in the cause of American independence. Along with Charles Carroll and Benjamin Franklin, he traveled to Quebec to convince French Canadians to join the Revolution. On that trip, Father Carroll earned Benjamin Franklin's deep respect and friendship. Throughout the remainder of the Revolution, Father Carroll remained in Maryland, ministering to his flock.

After the war, Catholics in America realized that they needed strong leadership to unite them, since they had never had a bishop. But, curiously, many Catholics in America were opposed to having a bishop. They feared that their Protestant neighbors would think a bishop un-republican and un-American, since he would be appointed by the Pope and not elected by the people. In 1783, Father Carroll and five priests wrote to Rome to ask that one of them be appointed the leader (but not the bishop) of the rest. Rome agreed to the request and made John Carroll "Prefect Apostolic" of the Church in the United States. This meant that Carroll had authority to make rules for the Church in America and could administer the **sacrament of confirmation.**

sacrament of confirmation: the sacrament in which the Holy Spirit is given through the laying on of hands and the anointing of the forehead with holy oils

As Prefect Apostolic, Father Carroll had to deal with many problems. First, there were not enough priests to minister to all the Catholics in America. To solve this problem, Father Carroll brought priests over from Europe; but some of these turned out to be troublemakers. In America, too, parishes belonged to a group of laymen called "trustees." These trustees controlled the money and the parishes and paid priests' salaries. In some instances, the trustees simply refused to obey Father Carroll.

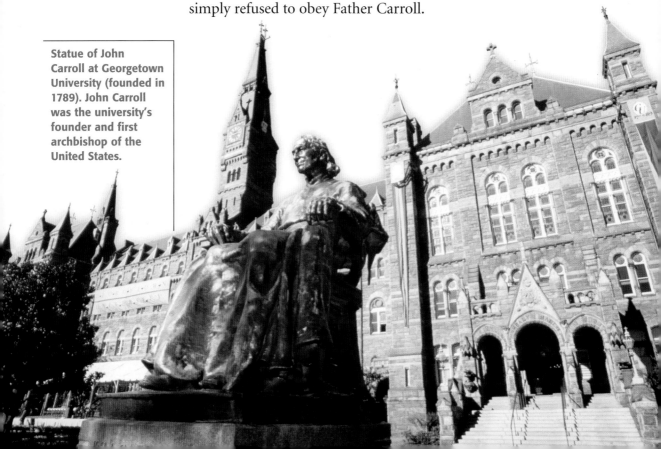

Statue of John Carroll at Georgetown University (founded in 1789). John Carroll was the university's founder and first archbishop of the United States.

Bishop Carroll and Georgetown University

Georgetown University in Washington, D.C., was originally founded by the Jesuits in 1789, the same year that the United States Constitution was instituted. Construction began on the first building in 1788, although the deed to the property on which it sat was not actually obtained until the following year. The original structure was first called the Carroll Building, and it had 10 or 11 rooms, which served as dormitory, classroom, and dining room. This original building—which encompassed the whole of the original university—was named after John Carroll, who was at that time a priest and not yet bishop.

It was Father John Carroll who first proposed the school, and it is to him that the college owes its existence. Appointed superior of the American Mission by the Pope in 1784, Father Carroll realized that American Catholics needed an American Catholic academy of higher learning. While still just a priest, Fr. Carroll published formal plans in 1786 for an "academy, at George-town, Patowmack-River, Maryland." Even after Father Carroll was elevated to Bishop of Baltimore in 1789 and then to Archbishop in 1808, he continued to be interested in and to influence the academy that he had founded.

In 1814, civil recognition for Georgetown was sought in the form of a federal charter. United States Congressman William Gaston of North Carolina, who had been the first student at Georgetown, proposed the federal charter. William Gaston had arrived at Georgetown in 1791, before the first building was even completed; his own son and grandson also attended Georgetown. The federal charter was signed by President Madison on March 1, 1815, allowing the college to "admit any of the students . . . to any degree in the faculties, arts, sciences, and liberal professions, to which persons are usually admitted in other Colleges or Universities of the United States . . ." Now, there existed an American Catholic college that (along with the Protestant institutions like Harvard, Yale, and William and Mary colleges) could confer the degrees of bachelor of arts and of sciences.

Such problems convinced Father Carroll and others that the Catholic Church in America needed someone with more authority than a Prefect Apostolic. The Church in America needed a bishop. Normally, the Pope would appoint a bishop for what was called a mission church, as America then was. In 1785, Carroll wrote to the Pope asking that he allow the priests in America to elect the bishop for the United States. He feared that Americans would think the bishop was the servant of a foreign prince if the Pope appointed him. The Pope agreed to this request, but said it was an exception. The American priests then chose John Carroll to be their bishop. In November 1789 Pope Pius VII appointed him bishop of Baltimore. The following spring, in 1790, Father John Carroll sailed to England, where he was ordained as bishop.

Even with his new authority, Bishop John Carroll had difficulties with rebellious priests and trustees. For instance, German-speaking Catholics were not satisfied; they wanted a German, not an Englishman, to rule as bishop. Yet, Bishop Carroll had some successes. In 1791, four Sulpician priests (from the Society of St. Sulpice in France, which was dedicated to the teaching of seminarians) came to America and opened the first Catholic college in the United States in Georgetown, Maryland.

Converts and Missionaries

Mother Seton

Everyone who knew her would have said that Elizabeth Ann Bayley had had a happy life. She was loved, and her upbringing had been comfortable. Dr. Richard Bayley, her father, was a physician, who also worked as the health officer for the port of New York City. He was a loving father who made sure his children had a good education. His daughter Elizabeth Ann was a good student who diligently studied all her subjects, but especially religion and history. Probably because of her mother, Catherine, whose father was an **Episcopalian** minister, Elizabeth Ann learned to love the Sacred Scriptures, especially those songs of praise to God, the Psalms.

Episcopalian: a member of the Protestant Episcopal Church, as the Anglican Church has been known in the United States

More happiness came to Elizabeth Ann when, in 1794, at about the age of 20, she married William Magee Seton at St. Paul's Episcopal Church in New York City. William was a good man and a loving husband; their marriage blossomed in the births of five children—two sons and three daughters.

Through William, Elizabeth found an additional source of happiness: her friendship with William's sister, Rebecca Seton, whom Elizabeth called the friend of her soul. Moved by their love for God and neighbor, Elizabeth and Rebecca did so much charitable work among the poor of New York City that people began to call them the

Protestant Sisters of Charity. In 1797, they formed the Society for the Relief of Poor Widows with Small Children.

Like his father before him, William Seton was a prosperous businessman, and for the first several years of the marriage he provided for his family very comfortably. Sadly, however, the business failed and the family was left bankrupt. Worse, in 1798 William's father died, leaving several small children who came to live with William and Elizabeth. Then, in 1801, Elizabeth's beloved father died, too. With many tears and prayers she begged God for his salvation. Two years later came the greatest sorrow of all; William fell seriously ill, and it looked as if he would not recover. Elizabeth spent most of the hours of every day in caring for him. Even in these terrible times, Elizabeth tried to bring happiness to her family, and spent time in playing and skipping rope with her daughters when she was not nursing her husband.

In great anxiety for William's health, Elizabeth and her eldest daughter took him to Italy where, they hoped, the warmer climate might help him regain his health. When William arrived in Italy he had to be kept confined in quarantine at the docks of Livorno, so that his sickness would not spread to others. These trials were too much for William, already very weak from his sickness. Despite Elizabeth's attempts to cheer him, he slowly grew weaker and weaker and, in a few weeks, died. Elizabeth's beloved husband was dead, and she and her daughter were left alone in a foreign land.

Yet, in this darkest time, God was watching out for the Setons and was preparing for them a far greater joy than any they could have imagined. They were not left helpless. The Filicchi family, devout Catholics who had been William's business associates in Italy, took care of the widow and her daughter. For two years they remained in Italy where, for the first time, Elizabeth discovered the beauty of the Catholic Church. Going to Mass with the

Elizabeth Ann Seton. She was canonized as America's first native-born Roman Catholic saint.

Filicchis, Elizabeth saw not only how beautiful the Italian churches were, but also she witnessed the glories of Catholic worship. The Latin Mass, the singing, the incense, the devotion to the Blessed Virgin moved Elizabeth's sorrowful soul and gave her a taste of true joy. Through conversations with Antonio Filicchi, Elizabeth began to understand the truth of the Catholic faith and soon decided that the Catholic Church was where she belonged. She knew that to embrace Catholicism would be to bring the **censure** of her friends and relations; it could also mean extreme poverty as well.

censure: criticism and reproach

When Elizabeth Ann Seton returned to New York in 1804, she fasted and prayed that God would lead her to the truth. She began a correspondence with the bishop of Boston, Jean-Louis Lefebvre de Cheverus. Bishop de Cheverus was a wise man; but more important, he was very holy. Bishop de Cheverus lived like the poor of the city. His house was a two-room shack; he chopped his own wood; he gave what little money he had to the poor. The prayers and work of this holy man for the soul of Elizabeth Ann bore fruit. On Ash Wednesday, March 14, 1805, she confessed her sins to the priest at St. Peter's church in New York City and was received into full communion in the Catholic Church.

But becoming Catholic brought Elizabeth even more troubles. First, her Protestant friends and relatives abandoned her, and she was forced to find work to support herself and her five children. For a time she taught at a school in New York operated by an English Catholic; but that school had to close

This picture from 1863 shows Mount St. Mary's College in Emmitsburg, Maryland, founded in 1808.

because of a rumor that it was trying to make the Protestant students Catholic. Elizabeth Ann then opened a boarding house for boys who attended a Protestant school; but when William's youngest sister became Catholic through Elizabeth's influence, threats were made to have the New York legislature force Elizabeth to leave the state. In the midst of these troubles, God did not abandon Elizabeth Ann and her children. Her educational gifts came to the attention of Bishop Carroll of Maryland, who invited her to begin a teaching order for girls. She kept her daughters with her and sent her sons to the seminary high school.

Elizabeth Ann opened her school for girls in Baltimore in 1808. She and other women who joined her in running the school began living like religious sisters. They lived together and prayed together. A Catholic man from Virginia heard about their work and gave them $10,000 to open a school for poor children. Elizabeth Ann and her community used the money to buy a farm in Emmitsburg, Maryland, where they moved in June 1809. For several years they lived like religious sisters at Emmitsburg, caring for and teaching the children that came to live with them. There were many challenges to the school. Sometimes the snow even fell right through the drafty roof onto their beds. Despite it all, in 1812 the women took religious vows and formed a religious congregation called the Sisters of Charity. They elected Elizabeth Ann to be their first mother superior.

Even living in a convent, Mother Seton had great sufferings, despite her capacity for great joy. She experienced the sadness of seeing two of her young daughters die. Yet, she was both trusting in God and simple in her motherliness to others. Even though she lost her own children, she gained spiritual children. Her congregation grew until, by 1821, 50 Sisters of Charity were working not only in

Sisters of Charity minister to sick and dying victims of yellow fever.

Emmitsburg but also in Philadelphia and New York City. Toward the end of her life, Mother Seton herself grew sickly from tuberculosis; still, she carried on her duties as superior. She passed from this life in 1821, at the age of 46. She is now buried in the basilica church at Emmitsburg, where the Sisters of Charity pray every day, still carrying on the religious mission she began. She was canonized a saint by Pope Paul VI on September 14, 1975. She is the first native-born American to be declared a saint.

Foundling Hospital of Sisters of Charity

The Frontier Church

How many people would take a job that offered no salary and no holidays, but did offer much hard work and a poor house to live in, as well as sickness and a violent and lonely death? Not many, one would think. Yet a "job" advertisement in France offered just these things. It was advertising to recruit men to work in the missions in the western United States (which, in those days, meant places like Tennessee, Kentucky, Illinois, and Louisiana.) And, despite the advertisement's threatening words, there were men who answered its call.

One of these was a French Sulpician priest named Benedict Joseph Flaget. After spending several years as a professor at Mt. Saint Mary's in Emmitsburg, Maryland, much to his surprise, Father Flaget learned not only that he was to be a missionary, but that he had been chosen to be the first bishop of the frontier outpost of Bardstown, Kentucky. The thought of being a bishop, and a bishop of such an uncivilized outpost as western Kentucky, frightened poor Father Flaget. Was he worthy of such an honor? Would he be able to accomplish such a mission in the wilderness of far-away America? Falling down on his knees before his superior, he begged that someone else be made bishop. His superior only replied, "My lord bishop, you should be in your diocese."

When Bishop Flaget arrived in Bardstown in 1808, he saw that the American West not only lacked a bishop, but had very few priests. Catholics (most of them French) who lived along the Mississippi River had only about eight priests to minister to them. Only two of these priests had permanent parishes. The rest traveled from place to place through thick forests and uncivilized lands, in danger from savage Indians, wild animals, robbers, and sickness. Bishop Flaget spent most of his time on horseback, riding to minister to the Catholics in his enormous diocese. When at home, he lived in a small log cabin that had room enough only for his bed and a writing desk. Bishop Flaget's life was hard; he suffered sickness, cold, hunger, and probably loneliness. Yet he embraced all these sufferings to bring the Gospel and the sacraments to the Catholics of the western United States. Catholics in Kentucky and Tennessee met in 10 small log-cabin churches. Most Sundays they did not have Mass, but a layman read lessons and prayers for the congregation. Laymen also took over other functions, such as emergency baptizing.

Early Catholic churches in Maryland would have resembled this old frontier church in Idaho.

After Bishop Flaget, the Pope appointed other bishops for what was then the western United States: all the land west of the Allegheny Mountains to the Mississippi River. One of these bishops was another Frenchman, Simon Bruté de Remur, who became bishop of Vincennes in Indiana in 1834. Bruté de Remur had lived through the French Revolution; he was only 14 years old when the Reign of Terror began in France. During the Reign of Terror, the French revolutionary government imprisoned and executed countless nobles, faithful lay Catholics, priests, brothers, and nuns. The young boy Simon accompanied disguised priests as they ministered to the prisoners.

The late eighteenth-century church of Old Bohemia, the St. Francis Xavier Jesuit Mission in Warwick, Maryland

Though he had studied medicine, Bruté de Remur decided to answer God's call to the priesthood. Ordained a Sulpician priest, he went to America, where for many years he taught at Mount St. Mary's Seminary in Emmitsburg, Maryland. In 1834, when he was in his fifties, he became bishop of Vincennes, Indiana. Despite his age, he rode on horseback across his wide diocese, which included the entire state of Indiana and eastern Illinois. He lived like the poor, giving away whatever wealth he had to help those who lacked worldly goods. Even though he was bishop for only five years, because he died in 1839, Simon Bruté de Remur in that time set up two new seminaries to train priests for his diocese.

One of the most interesting of the missionary priests in America at this time was a man who called himself Mr. Smith. (In those days, some priests in America were called not Father, but Mister.) Mr. Smith's real name was Demetrius Augustin Gallitzin, and he was a prince; so his full name and title was Prince Demetrius Augustin Gallitzin. It is no wonder that, when he came to America, he called himself simply Mr. Smith. Prince Gallitzin's father was the Russian ambassador to the Hague in Belgium. Though Gallitzin's father was an agnostic (an agnostic is someone who doubts that God exists), his German mother, in addition to being kind and loving, was a very devout Catholic who went about doing good works. So, it is not surprising that Prince Gallitzin followed his mother's example, not his father's, and himself became a Catholic in 1787 when he was 17 years old.

Prince Gallitzin's father, the Russian ambassador, cared very little about his son's conversion. He was concerned only that Demetrius Augustin would earn wealth and honor in the world. Through his father's influence, Prince Gallitzin was able to enter the Austrian army as an officer. He would have continued to rise in the ranks of the Austrian army if he had not visited the United States in 1792. There he decided to serve a greater king than even the Emperor of Austria; in 1792, Prince Gallitzin entered Bishop Carroll's seminary to study for the priesthood. After Gallitzin was ordained a priest, he turned his back on titled rank and fame and, instead, set out across the Allegheny Mountains to minister to the poor Catholic farmers in western Pennsylvania.

In western Pennsylvania, as Mr. Smith, he used his wealth to buy land for Catholic farmers to settle on. He also built a flour mill where the farmers could grind their grain and a saw mill where they could turn their tree trunks into usable lumber. Gallitzin spent all his wealth on this settlement, which he called Loretto. Loretto was a haven where Catholic laypeople could live and raise their families in a Catholic atmosphere. Gallitzin's mother also gave her son money for his project, as did the King of Holland, who gave Gallitzin $10,000 to pay off all his debts. Once, the Russian ambassador to the United States loaned Gallitzin $5,000 for Loretto. Gallitzin could not pay the baron back. But one night at dinner, the Russian ambassador took out the note on which Gallitzin had written his promise to repay him and used it to light his cigar. In doing so he showed that he had forgiven Gallitzin's debt.

Prince Gallitzin was the ruler of Loretto, and he ran it like a general runs an army. But though he was very strict, the people of Loretto loved him. Later in life, the prince-priest fell and became paralyzed; but despite his sickness, he continued to ride about in a sled, ministering to his people. Anyone seeing Prince Gallitzin on his daily rounds would not have known he had been raised in a noble family and was a prince, for he dressed like any peasant. He wore an old, threadbare overcoat and a beaten hat. Like so many of the pioneer clerics, he preferred to store up treasure in heaven; and so he lived, served and died, simply, as Mr. Smith.

Dedication of America to Mary

Even though for the previous 300 years, Spanish America had been blessed by Catholic devotion to the Blessed Virgin Mary, it was Bishop John Carroll who made the first official dedication to Our Lady of the young Republic of the United States. In his first pastoral

Bishop Carroll and the Litany of Loreto

Bishop Carroll loved Our Lady, the Blessed Virgin Mary. He ordered that the Litany of Loreto (named for a town in Italy) be recited before every High Mass in American churches. The Litany of Loreto is a prayer invoking Mary under various titles:

The Litany of Loreto

Lord have mercy on us.
Christ have mercy on us.
Lord have mercy on us.
Christ, hear us.
Christ, graciously hear us.
God the Father of Heaven, *have mercy on us*
God the Son, Redeemer of the world,
  have mercy on us
God the Holy Ghost, *have mercy on us*
Holy Trinity, one God, *have mercy on us*
Holy Mary, *pray for us*
Holy Mother of God, *pray for us*
Holy Virgin of virgins, *pray for us*
Mother of Christ, *pray for us*
Mother of divine grace, *pray for us*
Mother most pure, *pray for us*
Mother most chaste, *pray for us*
Mother inviolate, *pray for us*
Mother undefiled, *pray for us*
Mother most amiable, *pray for us*
Mother most admirable, *pray for us*
Mother of good counsel, *pray for us*
Mother of our Creator, *pray for us*
Mother of our Savior, *pray for us*
Virgin most prudent, *pray for us*
Virgin most venerable, *pray for us*
Virgin most renowned, *pray for us*
Virgin most powerful, *pray for us*
Virgin most merciful, *pray for us*
Virgin most faithful, *pray for us*
Mirror of justice, *pray for us*
Seat of wisdom, *pray for us*
Cause of our joy, *pray for us*
Spiritual vessel, *pray for us*
Vessel of honor, *pray for us*
Singular vessel of devotion, *pray for us*
Mystical rose, *pray for us*

Tower of David, *pray for us*
Tower of ivory, *pray for us*
House of gold, *pray for us*
Ark of the covenant, *pray for us*
Gate of Heaven, *pray for us*
Morning Star, *pray for us*
Health of the sick, *pray for us*
Refuge of sinners, *pray for us*
Comforter of the afflicted, *pray for us*
Help of Christians, *pray for us*
Queen of Angels, *pray for us*
Queen of Patriarchs, *pray for us*
Queen of Prophets, *pray for us*
Queen of Apostles, *pray for us*
Queen of Martyrs, *pray for us*
Queen of Confessors, *pray for us*
Queen of Virgins, *pray for us*
Queen of all Saints, *pray for us*
Queen conceived without original sin, *pray for us*
Queen assumed into heaven, *pray for us*
Queen of the most holy Rosary, *pray for us*
Queen of peace, *pray for us*
Lamb of God, Who take away the sins of the world:
  spare us, O Lord.
Lamb of God, Who take away the sins of the world:
  graciously hear us, O Lord.
Lamb of God, Who take away the sins of the world:
  have mercy on us.
Pray for us, O holy Mother of God,
  That we may be made worthy of the promises of Christ.

Let us pray.

Grant, we beseech Thee, O Lord God, unto us Thy servants, that we may rejoice in continual health of mind and body; and, by the glorious intercession of blessed Mary ever Virgin, may be delivered from present sadness, and enter into the joy of Thine eternal gladness. Through Christ our Lord. Amen.

letter written on May 28, 1792, Bishop Carroll wrote a dedication of our country to the Mother of God, only three years after the U.S. Constitution was established. In the following words, Bishop Carroll called down the blessings of Mary upon his fellow Americans and placed the Church in the United States under her patronage:

> I shall only add this my earnest request, that to the exercise of the sublimest virtues, faith, hope and charity, you will join a fervent and well regulated devotion to the Holy Mother of our Lord and Saviour Jesus Christ; that you will place great confidence in Her intercession; and have recourse to Her in all your necessities. Having chosen Her the special patroness of this Diocese, you are placed, of course, under Her powerful protection; and it becomes your duty to be careful to deserve its continuance by a zealous imitation of Her virtues, and reliance on Her motherly superintendence.

Chapter 11 Review

Summary

- Catholics were persecuted for their faith in the English colonies. The colony of Pennsylvania did allow Catholics religious freedom, and it had a large population of Catholics in it. The participation of Catholics such as Charles Carroll in the American Revolution softened Protestant Americans' views toward Catholicism.
- Fr. John Carroll was a priest during the American Revolution. He saw that Catholics in America needed a leader but did not want to increase the Protestant suspicion of Catholics as un-republican by having Rome appoint a bishop for America. Pope Pius VII allowed the American priests to elect the first American bishop; they elected Fr. Carroll in 1789.
- Elizabeth Ann Seton was the first American-born Catholic to be canonized. A convert to Catholicism and the mother of a large family, she was particularly concerned with the need to educate children of all classes. She opened a Catholic boarding school for girls in 1808. She became the mother superior of a religious order and is considered the mother of the parochial school system. She was declared a saint in 1975.
- Catholics lived scattered on the western frontier. They had few priests, and these priests had to travel long distances to minister to their flocks. These men, however, braved the dangers of the West and served Catholics as priests and bishops.

2/4 - 2/5

Chapter Checkpoint

1. Which of the original colonies allowed Catholics complete freedom of religion?
2. Who were Charles Carroll and Fr. John Carroll? What role did each play in American history?
3. What was the first Catholic college founded in America? When was it founded?
4. Who was Elizabeth Ann Seton? Briefly recount her life and deeds.
5. What did "Mr. Smith" do for frontier Catholics?

Chapter Activities

1. Think about what you would have done as a Catholic colonist. Would you have moved to Pennsylvania to practice your faith freely? Would you have been a Catholic in secret? Would you have been like Charles Carroll and been a proud Catholic and American despite persecution?
2. Think about the result of Mother Seton's work with education. Imagine the United States without a parochial school system—how would life here be different?

The American Larder

The churning of butter was essentially the same for hundreds of years, from medieval Europe up to nineteenth-century America. Churning was a precise operation; it had to be done in the morning when the temperature was cool. The churning was done by the woman of the house, and it took a light hand and patient rhythm to "make the butter come." Even though Abigail Adams was the wife of the second president, she preferred to churn her own butter. The American butter churn, like the European, looked like a cylinder with a wide base and narrow neck. This narrow wooden tub had a lid with a hole in the center. Through this lid was inserted a plunger, a wooden pole fixed with a perforated flat attachment at the bottom. The woman stood and thrust this plunger up and down in the cream that had been poured into the tub. Her skilled "light hand" told her when the cream was beginning to form into globules of butter. Those who could afford to do so fed the buttermilk (which was left after the butter had been made) to their pigs; it made the pork meat very tasty.

Chapter 12 The Young Republic Grows

A New Frontier

2/8

The Louisiana Purchase

Napoleon Bonaparte, who ruled France, planned aggressively to conquer the rest of Europe and then, perhaps, all the world. As part of these grand plans, he dreamed of an American empire for France. Since the end of the French and Indian War, Spain had controlled the vast territory called Louisiana. Napoleon Bonaparte wanted to take this territory, and Spain (eager to keep Napoleon's friendship) was willing to give it to him. In 1800, Spain gave Louisiana back to France, but kept Spanish troops and a Spanish governor there.

Napoleon was not the only one who wanted a great empire in the lands west of the Mississippi. President Thomas Jefferson wanted these lands, too. Jefferson thought the United States should expand ever westward, all the way to the

The ceremony of land transfer for the Louisiana Purchase in 1804. U.S. Commissioner Captain Amos Stoddard takes a document from Lansat, Napoleon's representative.

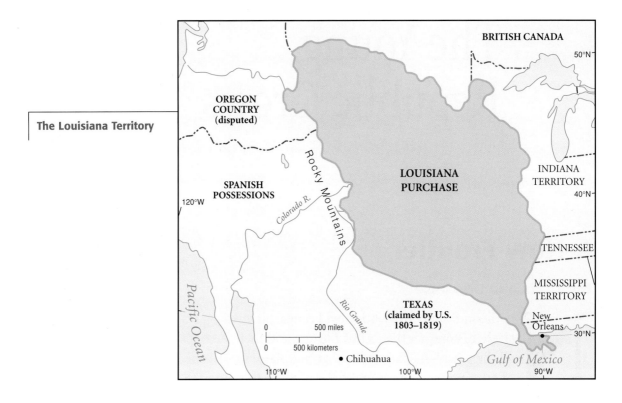

The Louisiana Territory

Pacific Ocean. He thought that the great western lands (about which he knew very little, actually) could be settled by sturdy American farmers. Their sense of independence, he believed, could eventually make North America an empire for liberty.

Despite wanting an American empire for France, Napoleon first wanted to establish a French empire in Europe. He desperately needed money to build his army, and probably thought that after conquering all of Europe, he could reclaim the lands of America for France once again. So in 1803, Napoleon offered to sell all of Louisiana to the United States and for a rather small sum of money. Jefferson was very eager to obtain the territory, and he pushed for the purchase of Louisiana. The United States Senate was in favor of the deal and approved the treaty with France. In December 1803, France transferred all of the Louisiana Territory to the United States. With this new territory, the country was now twice as big as it had been before. Thirteen states or parts of states have been carved from the territory gained in the Louisiana Purchase: Louisiana, Oklahoma, Arkansas, Kansas, Missouri, Iowa, Minnesota, North Dakota, South Dakota, Nebraska, Wyoming, Colorado, and Montana.

The Lewis and Clark Expedition into the Great Plains

To Americans in the early 1800s, the lands that lay between the Mississippi and the great Rocky Mountains were a mystery. Except for a few trappers who paddled up the great muddy Missouri River in search of furs, no European man had explored the vast Louisiana Territory. Even the trappers had not explored the full length and breadth of the plains that rolled from the forested lands of the East to the barren crags of the Rocky Mountains.

Few Americans were more curious about this great country than President Jefferson. He wanted to know as much as he could about it: the people, plants, animals, and land. He hoped the Louisiana Territory would have lands as rich and fertile as those of the great Ohio Valley in the east.

Jefferson organized an expedition into the Louisiana Territory to scout out the territory. His plan was for the expedition to follow the Missouri River westward to its source high in the Rocky Mountains. From there, Jefferson wanted his expedition to explore the British territory of Oregon—primarily to see if there was a water route to the Pacific Ocean. He also hoped Oregon would one day belong to the United States and so thought it was important to explore the area.

Jefferson chose his 29-year-old personal secretary Meriwether Lewis, a gifted natural scientist and writer, to lead this expedition. The 33-year-old William Clark, who had long lived on the frontier as both an explorer and Indian fighter, was also part of the expedition. Lewis and Clark were to lead a Corps of Discovery numbering over 40 men.

Meriwether Lewis

William Clark

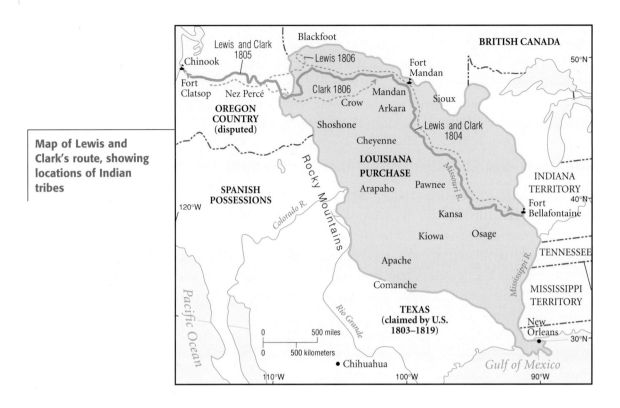

Map of Lewis and Clark's route, showing locations of Indian tribes

Lewis and Clark's task was not just to map out the lands through which they passed; they were also to gather information on the soil, plants, and animals in the Louisiana Territory. Jefferson was also curious about what sorts of Indians the explorers found. He wanted Lewis and Clark to describe in detail the religion, customs, and language of each Indian tribe they encountered. Jefferson thought such facts most interesting, but he also wanted to use them to help the government to civilize the Indians. He hoped that the Indians could eventually become productive farmers and good citizens of the United States.

On May 14, 1804, Lewis and Clark (with their party, the Corps of Discovery) set out from St. Louis on their long journey up the Missouri River. For hundreds of miles from St. Louis, the Missouri is a wide, swift-moving, muddy brown river. Traveling in a 55-foot **keelboat** and two smaller boats, the expedition would have found

keelboat: a large, flat-bottomed boat without sails

going upstream on the Missouri difficult at any time of year. In the spring, though, it was doubly difficult, because the river was swollen from the floodwater draining into it from the melting snow. Not only did the men have to struggle against the rushing river, but they were also soaked to the skin by the cold May rains. At most, they could go only three to four miles a day—not even one mile per hour.

After passing the French Catholic settlement of St. Charles, Missouri, Lewis and Clark traveled into regions where no Europeans dwelt, and that no Europeans had officially explored. The explorers kept extensive notes and diaries. As they continued along the Missouri River, they met many different Indian tribes: the Kickapoo, the Osage, the Missouri, the Sauk, and the Fox tribes. These tribes often waged wars with each other. Lewis and Clark crossed on into the Great Plains and saw the enormous herds of buffalo that grazed there. They met more Indian tribes who were nomadic hunters of the buffalo: the Pawnee and the Sioux. The Plains Indian tribes lived in curious shelters that no one traveling with Lewis and Clark had ever seen: teepees, cone-shaped dwellings made of sticks and buffalo hides.

Lewis and Clark hold friendly council with the Indians and distribute presents to win their good will.

In the region of what is now North Dakota, Lewis and Clark met two trappers, who joined the expedition. One of these trappers, a Frenchman named Toussaint Charbonneau (TOO•SAN SHAR•bo •NO), had bought and married an Indian woman name Sacagawea. Sacagawea had been stolen from her people, the Shoshone, by a war party of enemy peoples and sold to Charbonneau. With him, and with their infant son, "Pomp," strapped to her back, Sacagawea also joined the expedition. She would be of great help to the Corps, for she knew the land and its inhabitants; she also knew which plants and roots were safe to eat and which could be used for medicine. She also spoke the language of the Shoshone Indians who lived in the mountains where the expedition team was about to cross. The presence of an Indian woman in the group of white men also made other strange tribes less hostile and suspicious toward the group, because no Indian war party would have been traveling with a woman.

Over the Rocky Mountains

When the snow melted in the early spring of 1805, Lewis and Clark continued their journey up the Missouri River. Gradually the lands around them changed, becoming hilly and then more and more rocky and barren. As it neared the Rocky Mountains, the Missouri grew narrow and ran through deep canyons. The cliffs towered over 1,000 feet on each bank of the river. In this desert land, the herds of buffalo disappeared. The travelers saw fewer and fewer elk and antelope. In late May the expedition saw the snow-capped Rocky Mountains in the distance. In June they reached the great falls of the Missouri in what is now Montana.

In August, Lewis and Clark reached the Continental Divide, which splits the rivers of North America. Rivers on the eastern side of the divide flow east, while those on the western side flow westward, into the Pacific. The next day after crossing the divide, Lewis's party met a band of Shoshone Indians. Sacagawea quickly learned to her joy that their chief was her own brother, Cameahwait. Through Sacagawea, Lewis asked Cameahwait to give him horses with which the Corps could climb

Sacagawea guides the expedition from Mandan through the Rocky Mountains.

down the mountains. Happy to be reunited with his sister again, Cameahwait agreed.

With the aid of the Shoshone horses, the Corps began their long climb down the western face of the Rocky Mountains. They passed through the lands of the Nez Percé nation (so called because they had pierced noses) and of the Flathead Indians, who it was said used two boards to compress the foreheads of their infants to give them a flattened appearance.

After descending the Rocky Mountains, the Corps followed the path of the Snake River until it flowed into the Columbia River. Passing into the region of the Pacific Coast, Lewis and Clark discovered a different sort of Indian. The people of the Pacific Coast tribes—the Chinook, Tillamook, Klamath, and Clatsop—were shorter than the Plains Indians and (according to Clark) bowlegged. They were wood-carvers, and they built longhouses (lodges made of long wood planks). They also carved out redwood canoes from which they hunted salmon, and they created tall, wooden totem poles.

It was fall when Lewis and Clark reached the mouth of the Columbia River. After so many hardships, on November 15 they saw a long-awaited sight, the great Pacific Ocean. At the Columbia River's mouth, surrounded by the misty forests of the Oregon coast, the men of the Corps built their winter quarters, which they named Fort Clatsop, after the local Clatsop Indian tribe. There they would await the coming of spring when snow would not hinder their return passage over the Rockies.

The Homeward Journey

At the end of March 1806, the Corps of Discovery began their journey homeward. The journey back would not be as long or as hard as the journey into the wilderness because, after crossing the Rockies, they could float down the Missouri instead of beating upstream against it. After crossing the Continental Divide, Lewis and Clark again split up. With part of the company, Lewis went north and

A totem pole

Sacagawea and "Pomp"

The 2000 commemorative silver dollar depicts Sacagawea and her son, little "Pomp," who was later baptized as a Catholic and named Jean-Baptiste Charbonneau. After the death of Sacagawea, Jean-Baptiste was cared for by William Clark, who became his guardian. When he grew up, Jean-Baptiste also became a famous guide, hunter, and trapper. He knew well all the major travel routes between the Mississippi River and the Rocky Mountains. He was a gentle, well-mannered, cultured man who, when young, had been to school in Europe. He could speak many languages; he knew the dialects of many tribes as well as European languages. In the 1840s, he became a member of an expedition led by a wealthy Scotsman named Sir William Drummond Stewart, who wanted to explore for the fun of it. By a curious coincidence, among the Stewart party was Jefferson Clark, who was the son of Jean-Baptiste's own guardian, William Clark. More than thirty years before, it was Sacagawea who had helped guide the Lewis and Clark Expedition through uncharted western lands. Now Jean-Baptiste, Sacagawea's son, was guiding Clark's son on his own journey through the West. He also sought gold in California and went on many other western expeditions. On May 16, 1866, Jean-Baptiste Charbonneau died of pneumonia in Oregon.

explored the Marias River, while Sacagawea led Clark along the Jefferson and Yellowstone Rivers to the south. The Corps were reunited where the Little Missouri River flows into the Missouri. Farther down the Missouri river, they said good-bye to Sacagawea.

Floating down the muddy Missouri, Lewis and Clark met few adventures. On September 23, 1806, they reached St. Louis, from which—two years and four months earlier—they had set out on their long expedition. In February 1807 they went to Washington to report their important discoveries to the president, Thomas Jefferson.

The Path to War

Trouble with Great Britain and France

After he had been crowned Emperor of France in May 1804, Napoleon Bonaparte made plans to conquer all of Europe. The wars that Napoleon fought brought not only such European powers as Prussia, Austria, and Russia against him, but Great Britain as well. In October 1805, the British fleet destroyed the French and Spanish fleet at Trafalgar, off the coast of Spain. Though Napoleon's armies won every battle they fought in Europe, Great Britain still controlled the seas.

Great Britain's control of the seas caused trouble not only for France, but for the United States as well. Because America fought for neither France nor Great Britain, American ships continued to trade with both countries. In 1805, British ships began stopping American ships at sea, seizing cargo and **impressing** American sailors into the British navy.

impress: to force someone to serve in the military or navy

These acts made Americans very angry, but worse was to come. In June 1807, only 10 miles off the coast of Virginia, the British ship HMS *Leopard* shot at the American ship USS *Chesapeake*. This was an act of war, and the Federalists demanded that Congress declare war on Great Britain. Then France began to seize American merchant ships. President Jefferson thought he could not go to war with Great Britain and hope to win; he certainly could not go to war with both Great Britain *and* France. Instead of war, Jefferson asked Congress to place an embargo on all American ships, which forbade them from trading with either Great Britain or France.

Thomas Jefferson probably could have been elected to another term as president, but he did not want to run. Like Washington, he wanted to serve no more than two terms. The new president was Jefferson's close friend, James Madison. Madison promised that he would follow in Jefferson's footsteps and keep the United States out of war.

Keeping the United States from going to war would be very hard to do. After James Madison became president, Congress passed a new law forbidding American ships to trade with either Great Britain or France, but both of those countries continued to seize American ships. Great Britain, too, continued to force sailors on American ships to serve in the British navy. Such acts were an insult to the United States. How long could the country bear such insults without going to war?

Triumph of the War Hawks

Though the United States continued its refusal to trade with Great Britain, the British did not cease to board American ships and force sailors to serve in the British navy. Napoleon, however, promised the

Napoleon Bonaparte, emperor of France, in coronation robes

United States government that French ships would no longer bother the American ships. With this promise, President Madison asked Congress to permit Americans to trade with France, but not with Great Britain. Congress agreed.

President Madison commanded naval captain John Rodgers to protect American shipping. One evening, sailing the 44-gun USS *President* out of Chesapeake Bay, Rodgers saw a British warship, the HMS *Little Belt.* The *Little Belt* fired on the *President,* striking the American ship's mainmast with a cannon ball. The President returned fire and crippled the *Little Belt,* killing or wounding 32 British sailors.

The news of the naval battle angered many Americans. The British had attacked an American ship in American waters. In Congress, a group of representatives and senators called the War Hawks demanded that the United States declare war on Great Britain. Other congressmen and senators opposed the War Hawks, fearing that the United States was not strong enough to carry on a war with Great Britain. The War Hawks prevailed, and in June 1812, Congress declared war.

Only 31 years had passed since the end of the Revolutionary War. Once again, Americans were at war with their mother country, Great Britain.

The War of 1812

Victory at Sea, Defeat on Land

The United States was not very well prepared to go to war with Great Britain. The British had a much larger army and the largest and most powerful navy in the world. Fortunately for the Americans, the British could not send many troops to America, since most of them were fighting Napoleon's armies in Europe. Even so, in the early part of the war, the Americans lost most of their battles against the British.

The War Hawks hoped that the United States could conquer Canada in this war. On July 12, American General William Hull marched his untrained troops out of Detroit across the river into Ontario, Canada. There, without even firing a shot, he called on the Canadians to surrender and join his forces. Hull was jumping the gun, as it turned out. British general Isaac Brock, leading a force of British and Indians, pushed Hull back into Detroit. On August 16, Hull surrendered his troops and Detroit itself to Brock. Far from surrendering to the Americans, the British now had a military base in the United States.

Two other American attempts to invade Canada also failed. The problem was not only that the American generals were inept but also that the American volunteers were stubborn. They had not joined the army, they said, to invade Canada but to defend their country. To lead them into Canada was against their constitutional rights, they said.

The loss of Detroit was serious, for the British and their Indian allies could now easily invade the American frontier. The Shawnee chieftain Tecumseh, who earlier had attempted to unite the midwestern Indian tribes against the encroaching European settlers, but

Battle between the USS *United States* and the HMS *Macedonian* during the War of 1812

Tecumseh, chief of the Shawnee tribe, and British general Proctor

whose warriors had been defeated at Tippecanoe, led raids against frontier settlements, striking terror into the hearts of settlers. General William Henry Harrison gathered a force of regular army troops and volunteers to fight Tecumseh. Leading a part of Harrison's army, General James Winchester at first had some success against the British and the Indians in northeastern Indiana. But in January 1813, the British and the Indians defeated Winchester at Frenchtown, forcing the Americans to surrender.

With Winchester out of the way, the British general Proctor—with 1,000 Canadians and 1,200 of Tecumseh's Indians—went hunting for Harrison. Proctor first attacked Ft. Meigs and lay siege to it. But unable to take the fort, in August he continued his hunt for Harrison. In his path lay Fort Stephenson, which was defended by only 160 Americans under George Croghan. Harrison had told Croghan to abandon Fort Stephenson, but Croghan had bravely replied, "We are determined to maintain this place, and by heaven we will!" And maintain it they did. Though surrounded and vastly outnumbered by 500 British regulars and 700 Indians, Croghan and the Americans stoutly defended their fort.

Gate leading into a frontier fort

Firing from behind their log walls, the Americans targeted the British officers and killed them all, as well as many of the regular soldiers. Unable to capture Fort Stephenson, the British retreated. Because of Croghan's brave defense, Harrison's army was safe.

During the first year of the war, the American navy had more luck than the army. Under Commodore John Rodgers, the small American fleet set sail from New York harbor into the North Atlantic. By the end of summer, two American ships, the USS *Constitution* and the USS *United States,* had captured or sunk three British ships of war. These were not great victories; but they humiliated the British, who were very proud of their sea power. They also showed that the American navy, at least, had some skill and daring.

Don't Give Up the Ship!

Still, the small American fleet was no match for the British navy on the high seas. In 1813, the British sent even more ships to America. The British ships, bristling with cannons, kept American merchant ships and others from sailing out of American ports, and the small American navy could do little about it.

The British even had ships on the Great Lakes. On Lake Erie, British captain Robert H. Barclay commanded the HMS *Detroit,* which had 19 guns, and the HMS *Queen Charlotte,* which had 17 guns. But throughout the winter and spring of 1813, American Commodore Oliver Hazard Perry was at work building two large ships, the *Niagara* and the *Lawrence,* each with 20 guns. They would soon meet the British enemy in open battle on the water.

Hoping to control Lake Erie, the British invaded Ohio in the early spring of 1813. By summer they had come as far as the Sandusky River, which flows into Lake Erie. If the British army joined up with the British naval fleet on Lake Erie, they would be an unstoppable force. Commodore Perry knew this, and with his small fleet attacked Barclay's British fleet on September 10. During the battle, the British ships *Detroit* and *Queen Charlotte* attacked Perry's flagship, the

Lawrence. Flying a flag with the words, "Don't Give Up the Ship!" Perry and his men fought long and hard; but, finally, the *Lawrence* had been so damaged by the British ships that Perry was forced to abandon her. Then, taking command of the *Niagara,* Commodore Perry performed a very daring maneuver. He sailed his ship right between the *Detroit* and *Queen Charlotte.* Firing from both sides of the ship at once, Perry so crippled the British ships that the British commander was forced to surrender. "We have met the enemy and they are ours," declared Perry.

With the Americans in control of Lake Erie, the British army was forced to retreat into Canada. It was already autumn when Perry transported General Harrison and the American army across Lake Erie into Canada. On October 5, the Americans attacked the British and their Indian allies on the banks of the Thames River in Canada, forcing the British to retreat. The Americans next attacked the Indians; Chief Tecumseh, Harrison's old enemy, was among them. Though his people were dying all around him, Tecumseh stood firm, guarding the British retreat. The chieftain died bravely that day, surrounded by 33 of his warriors.

Commodore Perry at the Battle of Lake Erie

More American victories followed. On April 27, 1813, American Commodore Chauncey, commanding 14 ships, took the city of Toronto (then called York) on the northern banks of Lake Ontario. After the British there surrendered, the Americans burned the provincial capital buildings and several houses. Next, the Americans drove the British from Fort George.

Battle of the Thames: the American army fights the Indians. Chief Tecumseh is shot in the chest.

Washington in Flames

When Napoleon Bonaparte gave up the throne of France on April 11, 1814, Great Britain's war in Europe came to an end. The British could now send more troops to America, and they sent the very best troops they possessed.

The British planned a two-pronged attack on New York City and the United States capital, Washington City. After retaking Canadian areas seized by the Americans, British General Prevost planned an invasion of New York. With 10,000 troops, Prevost's plan was to move along Lake Champlain and then down the Hudson River Valley to New York. At the same time, British Major General Robert Ross planned an attack on Washington.

Unfortunately for Prevost, matters did not turn out as he wished. The fleet that was to carry the British down Lake Champlain met a much smaller American fleet under 30-year-old Thomas Macdonough at Plattsburgh. Though the British fleet had more guns than Macdonough's fleet, he did not shrink from joining battle with it. In the fight that followed, Macdonough lost many men, but he finally forced the British to surrender. Without a fleet, General Prevost gave up his plan to invade New York and retreated to Canada.

At about the same time the Americans and British were fighting on Lake Champlain, farther to the south, British Admiral Cochrane was sailing his fleet into Chesapeake Bay. Landing at the Patuxent River, British troops under General Ross marched 50 miles inland until they reached the village of Bladensburg, Maryland, only seven miles from Washington City. Knowing of the approaching British, President Madison tried desperately to defend the capital. He sent 5,000 men to block the road to the city; but the commander returned to Washington soon after setting out. In desperation, President Madison and James Monroe, his secretary of state, rode out from Washington themselves to command the small American force defending Bladensburg.

Important government papers (including the Declaration of Independence) had already been removed from Washington. Many citizens had fled, including the president's wife, Dolly Madison, who took with her a portrait of George Washington. No American troops stopped the British from marching into Washington. Entering the capital, General Ross's troops set fire to the White House, the treasury building, and the navy yard. Angry flames licked the sky and would have utterly destroyed the White House had not a sudden thunderstorm extinguished them. Still, the fact that the British had been able to take the United States capital was a great humiliation to the Americans.

The Flag Was Still There

Having punished Washington, General Ross returned to the British fleet. Their next target was the city of Baltimore, Maryland. In the British plan, Ross was to attack Baltimore by land, while Admiral Cochrane and his fleet destroyed Fort McHenry, which guarded Baltimore from the sea. Samuel Smith, who commanded the American forces in Baltimore, prepared a defense of the city by placing over 10,000 men around it and by strengthening Fort McHenry. As a defiant sign against the British and as a rallying sign for the

Americans, Smith raised an enormous American flag over the fort.

The British Admiral Cochrane began his attack on Fort McHenry on the morning of September 12. On board one of his ships was a young American, Francis Scott Key, who had been detained by the British. All day long, and into the night, Key watched as volleys of British bombs burst in tremendous explosions over Fort McHenry. That night he wondered if the great American flag would still be flying over the fortress; or whether, by morning, a smaller British one would be flapping there in its place. All night long, the light of the exploding bombs showed that the Stars and Stripes was still waving. And in the morning, tattered and torn, the flag was still there. The British had failed to take McHenry. In great joy, Key wrote a poem to honor the great event. He named it the "Star-Spangled Banner."

The British attack by land also failed. Though the British had forced the American army to retreat, they did not move into the city. General Ross had been killed, and his men were too weary to continue the attack. On September 13 the British fleet and army sailed down the Chesapeake Bay into the open sea.

But Cochrane had not given up. He sailed to the West Indies, where he was to join a powerful land and sea force. The next British target would be New Orleans, in Louisiana.

Fort McHenry National Monument, where American forces held off a British attack during the War of 1812

Francis Scott Key observes the bombardment and the U.S. flag over Fort McHenry.

The Star Spangled Banner

O say, can you see, by the
  dawn's early light,
What so proudly we hail'd at
  the twilight's last gleaming?
Whose broad stripes and bright
  stars, thro' the perilous fight,
O'er the ramparts we watch'd,
  were so gallantly streaming?
And the rockets' red glare, the bombs bursting in air,
Gave proof thro' the night that our flag was still there.
O say, does that star-spangled banner yet wave
O'er the land of the free and the home of the brave?

On the shore dimly seen thro' the mists of the deep,
Where the foe's haughty host in dread silence reposes,
What is that which the breeze, o'er the towering steep,
As it fitfully blows, half conceals, half discloses?
Now it catches the gleam of the morning's first beam,
In full glory reflected, now shines on the stream:
'Tis the star-spangled banner: O, long may it wave
O'er the land of the free and the home of the brave!

And where is that band who so vauntingly swore
That the havoc of war and the battle's confusion,
A home and a country should leave us no more?
Their blood has wash'd out their foul footsteps' pollution.
No refuge could save the hireling and slave
From the terror of flight or the gloom of the grave:
And the star-spangled banner in triumph doth wave
O'er the land of the free and the home of the brave.

O thus be it ever when free-men shall stand
Between their lov'd home and the war's desolation;
Blest with vict'ry and peace, may the Heav'n-rescued land
Praise the Pow'r that hath made and preserv'd us a nation!
Then conquer we must, when our cause it is just,
And this be our motto: "In God is our trust!"
And the star-spangled banner in triumph shall wave
O'er the land of the free and the home of the brave!

Old Hickory

The British advance on New Orleans would be no surprise to the American commander there, General Andrew Jackson. Hearing about the British fleet gathering in the West Indies in September, Jackson wasted no time in preparing for the defense of New Orleans. In December he arrived in the city with 5,000 men, just in time. A British fleet of 50 ships, said to be carrying 15,000 men, had arrived in the Mississippi delta, only 10 miles south of the city.

Because he was hard and tough as the wood of the hickory tree, Jackson's men gave him the nickname, "Old Hickory." Jackson had lived the hard life of a frontiersman. A born fighter, he had been in several duels. In one of these duels, he killed his opponent but also received a gunshot wound. Jackson received another wound in another duel in a tavern. The bullets from both duels remained in his body until his dying day.

Old Hickory had become a hero in his war with the Creek Indians in southern Alabama. In the summer of 1813, the Creek Indians went on the warpath with about 2,000 warriors, who were called Red Sticks because of the red war clubs they carried. In August, the Red Sticks captured a fort in southern Alabama and brutally killed over 500 settlers who had gathered there for protection.

Jackson led some 2,500 volunteers from Tennessee, Georgia, and Louisiana, and some Cherokee and Creek Indian allies, against the murderous Red Sticks. At first Jackson was unsuccessful, for his men would not follow orders. Gathering a new army, Jackson attacked a Red Stick fortress on the Coosa River in Alabama and killed about 600 Indians. He then led his men farther south, destroying any Creek villages they found. By the spring of 1814, Jackson had utterly crushed the Red Sticks.

With the same pluck and courage, Jackson then faced the invading British at New Orleans. He gathered a hodgepodge army of all the able-bodied men he could find to defend the city: French noblemen in blue and red uniforms, free blacks, frontiersmen from Tennessee and Kentucky, and sailors who had been with the pirates Pierre and Jean Lafitte. Hearing that 1,688 British soldiers were advancing on the city, Jackson marched downriver to meet them.

The Battle of New Orleans

In late December 1814, British guns fired hot shot into the USS *Carolina,* a ship that had supported Jackson's attack, and the ship sank in a fury of flame. On January 8, 1815, the British commander, Major General Sir Edward Pakenham, was ready for his major attack on the American lines. In well-formed lines, the British in their bright red uniforms prepared for the assault. Hiding behind barricades built of wood, mud, and cotton bales, Jackson and his men awaited them.

Marching into the open, with no protection but their guns and their own courage, the British were an easy target for the unseen

Major General Andrew Jackson with his troops defends New Orleans against British forces during the War of 1812.

American guns. In their first charge against Jackson's defenses, the British soldiers were mercilessly cut down. Leading the second charge, Pakenham himself was shot and killed along with many of his men. Seeing that a third attack was hopeless, the British general who had taken over from Pakenham ordered a retreat. In the battle, the British lost 2,000 men, including three generals and 86 officers. The Americans lost only 45 men.

The British army and fleet withdrew from New Orleans and Louisiana. Taking to sea, they were preparing to attack Mobile, Alabama, when they heard that the war was over. On December 24, 1814, the United States and Great Britain had signed a peace treaty two weeks before the Battle of New Orleans. Because, in those days it took so long for news to travel, neither the British nor Jackson heard news of the treaty until after the Battle of New Orleans had been fought.

The Treaty of Ghent

Representatives of the United States and Great Britain had been meeting in the city of Ghent in Belgium since August 1814 to discuss how to end the war. At first the British demanded a great deal from the Americans, including giving a large part of Maine to Canada. But as the months passed, less was asked because the British people were growing sick of the war. Finally, the two nations signed a treaty that simply ended the war. Neither Great Britain nor the United States won any more lands from each other, and Great Britain did not promise to stop boarding American ships and taking their sailors into British naval service. Matters stood exactly as they had been between the two nations when the war began.

But there was one change. The war actually brought the United States and Great Britain closer together. Both nations realized that they depended on each other for trade, and the British had come to respect American soldiers and sailors. The war also helped Americans to think of themselves as citizens of the same nation. All the states, in one way or another, had helped to fight the war; they had all been united in a common cause to save the honor of their nation.

Chapter 12 Review

2/11 - 2/12

Summary

- Thomas Jefferson was the president when the United States purchased the territory of Louisiana from Napoleon Bonaparte's France in 1803. Napoleon needed money for his war with the European countries and Great Britain, so he sold the land for a relatively small amount of money.
- The Lewis and Clark expedition began in 1804 and lasted almost three years. Lewis and Clark met many different Indian tribes, most of whom were friendly. With the help of a Shoshone Indian, Sacagawea, Lewis and Clark traveled across the Rocky Mountains to the Pacific Ocean. They brought back detailed maps and information about the western lands and people. Their expedition allowed later groups of settlers and explorers to travel more easily to the West.
- Despite having fought and won a war for its independence, the United States continued to be threatened by Great Britain. British warships persisted in attacking U.S. merchant ships, taking cargo, and impressing American citizens into the British navy. To defend its independence, the United States again declared war on Britain in 1812. On the water, Commodore Perry successfully defeated British ships in the Great Lakes. On the land, however, British troops marched on Washington and partially burned down the White House. Yet, at the battle of Ft. McHenry, U.S. troops again defeated the British, and Francis Scott Key was inspired to write the "Star-Spangled Banner" in honor of the victory. The final battle of the war took place in New Orleans, where Andrew Jackson, losing only a handful of men, repulsed a British invasion of the town.

Chapter Checkpoint

1. What is the Louisiana Purchase? Which modern states were once part of the Louisiana Purchase territory?
2. What areas did Lewis and Clark explore? Why is their expedition important?
3. What events preceded the second declaration of war by the United States on Great Britain?
4. Who wrote the "Star-Spangled Banner," and why?
5. Describe the two military encounters, one by Commodore Perry and the other by General Jackson, of the War of 1812.
6. What were the positive effects of the War of 1812 on the United States and Great Britain?

Chapter Activities

1. Explore your own neighborhood, and keep an explorer's journal. Take notes about interesting bugs or leaves that you find.
2. What if France had not sold the Louisiana Territory to the United States? Draw a map of what you think the United States might look like today, and briefly explain your reasons for drawing it the way you did.

The American Larder

Louisiana's famous and unique food is a blending of many cultures and flavors. What is now known as Creole cuisine was mainly the creation of the aristocratic Spanish and French settlers of Louisiana in the seventeenth century. In Louisiana cooking, European flavors blended with those of the native American Indians as well as with the African flavors brought into the port city of New Orleans by the Haitians and the African servants of the European settlers. Then the arrival of the Acadians (known as Cajuns) gave an additional influence to the cooking—meals, usually prepared in a single pot, and called Cajun cooking. The Acadians came to Louisiana because of a tragic effort to relocate exiled French Catholics who were deported from Protestant Nova Scotia in 1755; most of the Acadian families were never reunited after they were deported. The Acadians settled in the bayous of Louisiana; they were a tough people who had previously lived under the adverse conditions of Nova Scotia. While Creole and Cajun cooking are different, rice is a staple of both, and many have common ingredients like fish, shellfish, crawfish, frogs, and turtles, plus squirrels, wild turkeys, ducks, pork, homemade sausages, beans of all kinds, yams, pecans, tomatoes, okra, and oranges.

Chapter 13 # In the Days of Old Hickory

The Postwar Years

2/22

Frontier Hero and Troublemaker

Because of his crushing defeat of the British at the Battle of New Orleans, General Andrew Jackson became a national hero. He was a tough, freedom-loving frontiersman who could "whup" the British as well as the Indians. Old Hickory was the sort of fellow many Americans wished they themselves could be. As congressman, Andrew Jackson had represented Tennessee in the United States House of Representatives, then in the senate and, later, had served as a judge on the Tennessee supreme court. A Republican, Jackson had been an opponent of President Washington.

For two years after the end of the War of 1812, Jackson remained in New Orleans, even though President Madison's secretary of war had told him to leave the city. Because of his insubordination, Jackson could have been removed from the command of the army, but he

Statue of Andrew Jackson, also known as "Old Hickory"

was not removed. Jackson was widely recognized as the best general in the United States army, and he was much too popular to challenge. So it was that General Jackson did what he wanted, whether or not the secretary of war or the president liked it.

One thing Jackson wanted to do was to get rid of "undesirables" and to take care of certain problems in Florida. Florida was still Spanish land, but the Spanish did not have enough soldiers there to take care of "troublemakers": Seminole Indians and black slaves who had escaped from plantations in Georgia, Alabama, and Mississippi. Throughout the War of 1812, the white settlers in Florida had fought bloody skirmishes with the Seminoles and escaped slaves, who kept raiding the white settlements. Then, in 1814, some runaway slaves built a fort on a bluff on the banks of the Apalachicola River in western Florida. From this fort, they raided white settlements in Georgia.

In 1816, General Jackson told the Spanish governor that he must do something about this fort. When the Spanish authorities did nothing, Jackson sent his own troops into Florida and destroyed it. In the spring of 1817, Seminole Indians in Florida began attacking white settlements to the north, in Georgia. General Jackson sprang into action again and invaded Spanish Florida, marching all the way

General Andrew Jackson with his troops during his invasion of Pensacola, Florida, in 1818

to the coast. When the Spanish governor in Pensacola protested against Jackson's invasion, Old Hickory did not bandy words with him. Instead, he led his own troops to Pensacola, captured the city, and took the Spanish governor prisoner.

The Spanish government was very upset that Jackson had dishonorably captured and imprisoned one of its governors. The new American president, James Monroe, knew that if he did not punish Jackson, Spain might declare war on the United States. Most of Monroe's cabinet agreed with him, except the secretary of state, John Quincy Adams, son of former President John Adams. Ultimately, Monroe did not punish General Jackson. John Quincy Adams said that Jackson had acted out of necessity; after all, the Spanish government could not keep the escaped blacks and Indians in order.

John Quincy Adams

Jackson's invasion of Florida made him an even more popular hero with the American people than he had been before. War with the Seminoles continued until 1818. In 1819, Spain agreed to sell all of Florida to the United States. In 1821, Florida became a United States territory, and General Andrew Jackson became the territory's first military governor.

Slave State, or Free?

As Americans moved west, they formed new states that in time became parts of the Union. The forming of these new states made Americans again reconsider a troubling question: What to do about slavery?

In 1787, Congress had formed the Northwest Territory from the lands that lay west of the Appalachian Mountains and north of the Ohio River. The lands that made up this early Northwest Territory included Indiana, Ohio, Illinois, Michigan, Wisconsin, and a part of Minnesota. Congress did not allow slaves in this Northwest Territory, and so the states that formed the territory came into the Union as free states. Slaves, however, were allowed in the territories

The Accursed Institution of Slavery

Slavery is almost as old as the history of mankind. The ancient world was filled with slavery. The Old Testament speaks of slavery and tells how even holy patriarchs like Abraham, Isaac, and Jacob owned slaves. Slavery could be found in Asia, Africa, Europe, and among the natives in the Americas. Even a great Greek philosopher like Aristotle thought slavery was natural—simply because, wherever one found human society, there was slavery.

But with the coming of Christ, things changed. Even though St. Paul told slaves to obey their masters, he told a Christian slave owner named Philemon to receive back his escaped slave, Onesimus, not as a slave, but as a brother in Christ. Knowing that all men, even slaves, were their brothers, the early Christians raised money to buy slaves from their masters—to free them. Because slavery and the Christian faith did not mix, gradually and over centuries, slavery withered away in Christian Europe. The slave became the serf and the serf became the free peasant. Finally, through the Christian faith, Europeans learned that all men have human dignity, and so no man can use another man for his own profit.

But things changed again when the faith of Europeans grew cold. Exploring Africa in the 1400s, Europeans found slavery among the Arab Moslems and the black tribesman there. African chieftans were very willing to sell slaves and the Europeans were eager to buy them. When the Spanish settled America, they enslaved many of the Indians, but when the Indians began to die off in great numbers, the Spanish brought black African slaves to America to work on plantations and in gold and silver mines. Later, the English and the Dutch also shipped slaves from Africa to America to do the work that white Europeans did not want to do. So it was that black slavery became established in the northern and southern English colonies and throughout Latin America.

Not all Europeans approved of slavery. In Latin America, men like the Dominican friar Bartolomé de las Casas condemned enslaving the Indians and blacks. Eventually, the Spanish government passed laws to protect the rights of slaves to marry and to buy their way into freedom. The English American colonists at first protested bringing slaves into America but could do nothing about it because the British government wanted slavery in the New World. After a while, British Americans grew used to slavery and even some freed blacks who had become wealthy bought lands along with the slaves to work them.

Gradually, however, in both the northern and southern British colonies, some people remembered their Christian faith and began to condemn slavery. Northerners gradually rid themselves of their slaves; many freed them, but others sold their slaves to new owners who lived farther south. By the time of the American Revolution, most slaves were held in the South. This caused great difficulties during the convention which wrote the United States Constitution in Philadelphia in 1787. Most of the delegates thought slavery was opposed to the principles of freedom and equality for which they had fought. But, in order to keep the southern and northern states together, the Constitutional Convention had to keep this issue in the background. They even had to allow the foreign slave trade to continue for another twenty years because both northern and southern merchants made so much money off the trade. Everyone at the convention knew slavery would be confronted someday. They agreed to put it off, however, hoping to avoid what came 73 years later—a civil war, the most terrible war in American history.

south of the Ohio River, and so states formed from those territories came into the Union as slave states. These states were Kentucky, Tennessee, Alabama, Mississippi, and Louisiana.

In the years before the Revolution, it looked as if slavery might die a natural death, even in the South. While many Americans in both the North and the South hated the institution of slavery, it was not so much because of concern for human rights that slavery began to end; it was because of money. It was actually quite expensive to keep slaves, since a slave owner had to feed and clothe his slaves even when they were too sick or too old to work. When an employer hired free workers, he had only to pay them for work done; he did not have to pay for the free workers' meals and lodging for their whole lives. It began to seem that owning slaves cost more money than paying for the labor of free workers.

The original cotton gin of Eli Whitney, on display in the Smithsonian Institution

All that changed in 1793 when Eli Whitney, a man from New Haven, Connecticut, invented the cotton gin. Being a cotton farmer had always been difficult. Separating the hard, clinging cotton seeds from the cotton was laborious. The cotton gin was a machine that made this easy. One machine could do the work of many men, and these men could then be put to work growing and harvesting cotton. With more men in

A working cotton plantation

Slaves using the first cotton gin

the fields, the cotton grower could farm more fields of cotton. So it was that slavery once again became profitable in the parts of the South where cotton grew.

In the years just before and just after the War of 1812, few Americans paid any attention to slavery. In fact, the only magazine that called for an end to slavery was the *Philanthropist,* published in the South. But in 1819, slavery became an important issue when the Missouri Territory asked to be allowed into the Union as a state. Most of the people who had settled Missouri were Southerners, many of whom owned slaves. Thus, Missouri wanted to become part of the Union as a slave state.

Some northern congressmen wanted Missouri to be admitted into the Union as a free state. They proposed that no new slaves be allowed into Missouri and that all children born to slave parents become free when they turned 25. Southerners in the Senate and in Congress were angry. They feared that if no more slave states were allowed into the Union, the free states—that is, the northern states—would sooner or later outnumber the slave states and be able to control Congress. If that happened, the northern states would be able to control the southern states.

Maine was seeking statehood at the same time that Missouri was, only Maine wanted to come into the Union as a free state. This allowed the Senate to draw up a compromise bill in 1820. To make the South happy, Missouri could become part of the Union as a slave state, while Maine, to make the North happy, could join as a free state. The bill also drew a line that divided the western part of the country in half. Every territory north of that line would be free; every territory south of that line could admit slaves. Many had thought the fight over Missouri would split the country in two, but this "Missouri Compromise" saved the union of the states.

But some prominent Americans thought that dangers still lay ahead. John Quincy Adams believed that the slavery question would eventually lead to a splitting of the United States into northern and southern republics. Two former presidents, the elderly John Adams and Thomas Jefferson, also believed disunion would come because of the slavery question. Their only comfort was that they would not live to see it happen.

The First Western President

Elections Lost and Won

Many Americans thought that the war hero, General Andrew Jackson, had become too powerful. Some people worried that Old Hickory might even lead his soldiers to Washington and try to take over the government by force. It was true that Jackson wanted to take over the government, and eventually he did so, but not by war. In 1824, he announced that he would run for president against John Quincy Adams, President Monroe's secretary of state.

The election in 1824 was very close. Though Jackson won the popular support of most of the people, neither Jackson nor Adams won a majority of the electoral college votes. When that happens, it is the House of Representatives that must decide who will be president, and the House of Representatives preferred Adams to Jackson. So it was that in 1825, John Quincy Adams came to live in the White House.

A man of honor and fairness, John Quincy Adams brought dignity to the office of president. He also tried to make sure the federal government treated the Indians with justice. He

When he was 13, Andrew Jackson joined the army to fight in the American Revolution. He was given the duty of messenger. Captured by the British, he was ordered to clean an officer's boots. When he refused, he was struck in the face with a saber, leaving a scar that he carried with him the rest of his life.

2/23

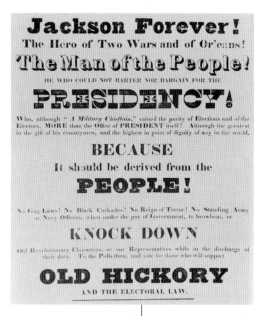

A Jackson campaign poster

worked to make Washington City a center of learning, but he found that Congress did not agree with him.

Jackson was very angry that he lost his first bid for the presidency. After all, he thought, he had received the highest number of votes. As soon as he heard that he had lost the election of 1824, Jackson began planning for the election of 1828. The second time around, Jackson easily beat President Adams. Those who supported Adams were generally wealthy, while the less wealthy and the poor supported Jackson, whom they saw as a poor man who had risen in the world. He also had strong support in the West, for he himself was a westerner, the first man from west of the Appalachians to become president.

Old Hickory Beats Down Opposition

Politics in bygone times. Andrew Jackson speaks to a crowd after his election.

One of the first things everyone learned about President Jackson was that he was a fighter. He was not about to let anyone stand in the way of what he wanted done. Those who disagreed with him or tried to block him had to be ready for a beating, because Jackson never backed down.

The first to learn this was Jackson's own vice president, John C. Calhoun. Like many other men from South Carolina, Calhoun thought that the Congress was passing laws that were unfair to the South. Calhoun believed that if the federal government passed a law unfair to a state, a state government had the right to ignore that law.

With Calhoun's encouragement, the government of South Carolina threatened to ignore a particular federal law that they thought was unjust to the south.

Many Northerners and Southerners in Congress thought that what South Carolina threatened to do was unjust. Daniel Webster, a Massachusetts senator and native of New Hampshire, said that if every state ignored federal laws it did not like, the union of the states would break apart. Webster believed that if the union were destroyed, freedom in America would end. South Carolinians, though, said that if a state could not ignore certain federal laws, then states would lose all their freedom to the federal government.

Usually President Jackson was on the side of the states; but this time, he defended the federal government. Those from South Carolina had said that if Jackson tried to force their state to obey the federal law, they would secede from the federal union. These were fighting words to Jackson. He sent more federal troops to Fort Moultrie and Fort Sumter, which lay in Charleston harbor. When South Carolina began raising an army, Jackson declared he would send the federal army into the state. For a time it looked like there might be war between the United States and South Carolina. But finally South Carolina backed down when Congress voted to allow the president to send an army into South Carolina if the state continued to ignore federal laws it did not like.

Jackson also showed he was hickory-tough in his battle against the Bank of the United States. Jackson hated this bank, which Hamilton and Washington had founded, because he thought it favored the rich and cheated the poor. But many powerful congressmen and senators were on the side of the bank and did not want it destroyed.

As ever, Jackson knew how to appeal to common people, and he had the common people on his side. For the election of 1832, Jackson and those who supported him formed a new political party, which they called the Democratic

Political cartoon of Andrew Jackson brandishing an "Order for the Removal of the Public Money deposited in the United States Bank," sending small figures running. In 1832, Jackson vetoed the recharter of the Bank of the United States.

On January 30, 1835,
Richard Lawrence,
a deranged house
painter, attempted to
assassinate President
Andrew Jackson as
he was leaving the
U.S. Capitol building.
Although Lawrence
tried to shoot two
pistols at Jackson at
close range, neither
gun discharged.

Party. The Democrats declared themselves against the national bank. Jackson's enemies formed another party, called the Whig party, which supported the bank. Once again, Jackson easily won the election, and many Democrats were elected to Congress. With such a victory, Jackson knew he could do what he wanted with the bank. Even before his second term as president began, Jackson removed all the federal government's money from the national bank. Without these funds, the bank was forced to close its doors. Jackson had destroyed the national bank.

Indian Wars

Black Hawk

A mighty warrior from his youth, Chief Black Hawk had fought many battles against the United States. In the War of 1812 he and his people, the Sauk and Fox tribes, fought on the side of the British. After the war, Black Hawk and his people could do nothing to stop white American settlers from moving onto Sauk and Fox lands, where the Rock River in Illinois flows into the mighty Mississippi. When the United States government asked the Sauk and Fox to leave Illinois and cross the Mississippi into the western lands beyond, many chiefs agreed. But Black Hawk and his Indian band refused to abandon the beautiful lands that had been their home.

In 1831, white settlers began moving into the area around Black Hawk's village. When the governor of Illinois heard that Black Hawk was threatening to drive out the settlers, he sent out volunteer militia to protect the settlements. Unable to fight the better-armed and more numerous whites, Black Hawk and his people escaped across the Mississippi into Iowa. Later, Black Hawk met with the governor of Illinois and agreed that he and his people would leave Illinois forever. The once-proud chief had been defeated.

But the winter of 1831–32 was a bitter one for Black Hawk's people. Since they had been forced to leave their corn crop in Illinois, the Indians had little food and began to starve. They also feared attacks from the more powerful Sioux Indians, who lived in those western lands. Faced with these dangers, Black Hawk led his people back over the Mississippi into Illinois in the spring of 1832. In Illinois Black Hawk thought he could grow the corn to feed his people in safety.

But the Indians could hope for no safety in their old homeland. Indian enemies of the Sauk and Fox told the governor of Illinois that Black Hawk was planning to drive out European settlers who lived in the lands around Rock River. Believing these reports, the governor sent out the state militia, which was joined by United States army troops, to drive Black Hawk out of Illinois. With the army went volunteer soldiers from Illinois; among them was a young man from Springfield, Illinois, named Abraham Lincoln.

Chief Black Hawk

In May 1832, Black Hawk, leading 40 warriors, clashed with a group of Illinois volunteer soldiers. Defeating these soldiers, Black Hawk and his warriors began attacking white settlements. In June, Black Hawk again battled with Illinois volunteers; but even though he was victorious, the chief lost many warriors. Knowing they could no longer defend themselves in Illinois, Black Hawk and his people fled north into Wisconsin.

The journey north was bitter for the poor, starving Indians. When Black Hawk and his people tried to cross the Wisconsin River, a band of volunteer soldiers attacked them. Losing 68 warriors in this battle, Black Hawk and the rest of his people continued pushing north. When they reached the place where the Bad Axe

River flows into the Mississippi, the Indians were trapped. A gunboat on the Mississippi kept them from crossing the river while, from behind, the United States army cut off their retreat.

Black Hawk knew he was defeated and sent out a white flag of surrender. But the American soldiers ignored the chief's offer. Wantonly, they attacked the Indians, killing not only warriors but old people, women, and children as well. At the battle's end, even though Black Hawk survived, his band of Indians had been destroyed. The old warrior, proud and brave, was imprisoned. Later, he was released and sent to a reservation prepared for the Sauk and the Fox on the Des Moines River, in Iowa. There, Black Hawk died, on October 3, 1838, at the age of 71.

The "Trail of Tears"

The differences between the white American settlers and the native Indians were vast: religion, culture, family structure, and behavior. In time, some Indian tribes began living like the American settlers. These Indians mostly gave up hunting and became like the white farmers, with plowed fields, cattle, and permanent houses. More important, many of these Indians became Christians and learned to read and write. The tribes who lived in this way were known as the Five Civilized Tribes: the Choctaw, Creek, Chickasaw, Cherokee, and Seminole tribes.

The most civilized of these Civilized Tribes were the Cherokee. The Cherokee not only had farms and houses, but they also built roads and churches like other American settlers. They developed an advanced network of tribal government with a constitution and a congress. The Cherokee even invented a written language, had printing presses, and began making books. There had been no written language among the North American Indian tribes, but one Cherokee, named Sequoia, had invented an alphabet for the Cherokee language. The Cherokees were the only Indian tribe to have books, two newspapers, and the Bible printed in their own language.

Sequoia, Creator of the Written Word for His Cherokee People

Although the Aztec and the Maya Indians had developed a kind of -hieroglyphic writing system, Sequoia, a Cherokee with little knowledge of English, is the only man known in history to have invented a complete syllabary, a type of alphabet.

Sequoia was born in a Cherokee village near Loudon, Tennessee, around 1770. Raised by his Cherokee mother, Sequoia grew up without knowing how to speak English. As a young man, he met white people and became fascinated by the way they could write out their ideas. Sequoia's father was probably an English scout and trader named Nathaniel Gist. Later, Sequoia took the English name of George Gist.

Determined to preserve his Cherokee culture, Sequoia began to develop an alphabet for the Cherokees around 1809. He was thought foolish and even irreverent to want to do such a thing. It might anger the Great Spirit, who did not give writing to the Cherokee people. If, they thought, the Great Spirit had wanted them to do so, the Cherokee would already have had the ability to write. Even Sequoia's wife opposed him because she was so strongly convinced that he was going against the will of the Great Spirit. In fact, one day, in an effort to stop Sequoia, she burned every scrap of rawhide and tree bark on which he had

Sequoia, inventor of the Cherokee alphabet

written his notes. Still he persevered, and by 1821 he had developed a syllabary of over 80 characters for the sounds of the Cherokee language. The alphabet allowed the Cherokee to publish newspapers and books in their own language, and thousands learned to read and write in the new written language.

Cherokee has few individual words, but it has a precise formula for enlarging each word base. Verbs are short phrases that say when and how an event happened. Nouns are descriptive; for example, a turtle would be "he walks with house on his back." The word *Cherokee* actually means "Creek Indians with another language." The Cherokees' word for themselves is Tsalagi; there is no letter *r* in Cherokee.

Sequoia became a very learned man and read every book possible; many he had translated and printed for his own people. He trusted President Jackson, but his trust was betrayed. Even so, Sequoia's learning was instrumental in advising his people in a path of wisdom and prudence, not revenge; this counsel probably saved many lives during the dark days before, during, and after the Trail of Tears and the shameful Cherokee Removal. The Cherokee language split into two main dialects after the Trail of Tears in 1839, when most Cherokee were forced from their native land in North Carolina, Tennessee, and Georgia to territory in Oklahoma and Texas.

The giant redwood trees in Sequoia National Park in California are named after this influential Cherokee man.

Though the Cherokee lived in their areas just like their neighboring American settlers did, there was a big problem. Gold had been discovered on the Cherokee lands in 1828, and the settlers wanted it. By 1830, about 3,000 non-Cherokees had moved into Cherokee lands, looking for gold. Though settling on Cherokee lands was against the law of the United States, the state of Georgia did nothing to stop the white settlers. Instead, the government of Georgia began giving away Cherokee lands to the whites.

The Cherokees tried to stop their land from being taken, but they could do nothing against the power of the state of Georgia. They received no help, either, from the federal government and President Jackson, who sided with the settlers who had begun destroying Cherokee property. They beat Cherokee men and women and, in some cases, murdered them. Things grew so bad that the federal

Map of the Trail of Tears

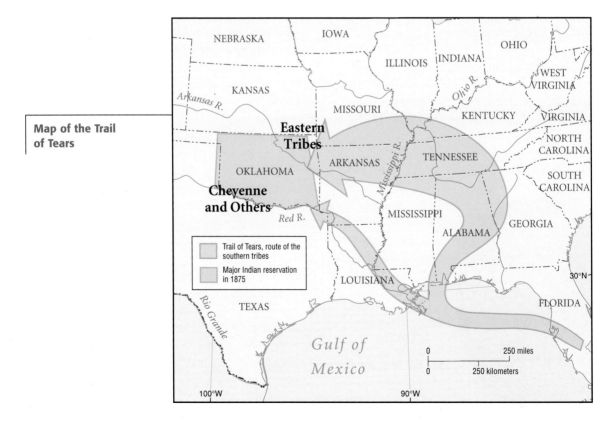

government decided the only way to save the Cherokees from the settlers was to force them to leave their lands and move west.

In May 1838, U.S. Army forces arrived in Cherokee lands to force the Indians to move west across the Mississippi to Indian Territory, into what is now Oklahoma. Soldiers carrying guns with bayonets rounded up women from their houses, children from their play, and men from their fields, forcing them to make the long, sad journey to the West. This journey, during the fall and winter of 1838–39, became known as the Trail of Tears, since thousands of Cherokee died on the long journey to Indian Territory.

Osceola and the Seminole Resistance

2/24

The Cherokee were not the first of the civilized tribes to follow the Trail of Tears. The Choctaw, the Creek, and the Chickasaw had already been forced to leave their lands and settle in Indian Territory. But Seminoles in Florida, under their chief, Osceola, fought back against the United States government. Though President Jackson said that he would drag the Seminoles in chains to Indian Territory if they did not go willingly, the Indians were determined to stay on their lands or die.

| Chief Osceola of the Seminole Indians |

The Seminole war was very bloody. The U.S. troops were much more powerful than the Indians, but the warriors could hide in the swamps and thick forests that everywhere covered Florida. With his warriors, Osceola attacked forts and raided plantations, forcing their owners to flee to the cities. The Indians made their attack and then vanished; they were able to melt back into the forests and swamps before the United States military could arrive.

After many months of fighting, the American general Thomas Jesup realized he could never capture Osceola in battle. So, he turned to trickery. Jesup invited Osceola to meet him under a flag of truce, which meant

American soldiers capture Osceola, leader of the Seminole warriors.

that Jesup promised not to harm or capture the Indian chief. Osceola and Jesup met in the fall of 1837. While the chief and general were talking, U.S. troops silently surrounded the Seminole camp. Osceola and his men were taken captive and sent as prisoners to Fort Moultrie near Charleston, South Carolina.

The capture of Osceola, though, did not end the war. For five more years, the Indians fought the U.S. army until the army just gave up the struggle. Some Seminoles finally followed the Trail of Tears to Oklahoma, though many remained in hiding in the swamps of Florida. For about 100 years, the Seminole in Florida signed no peace treaty with the United States. To this day, their descendants still live in the swamps of the Florida Everglades.

The Texas War for Independence

On to Texas

The Republic of Texas flag

One of the first Americans to settle in Texas was Stephen F. Austin. In 1823, the government of Mexico had given Austin permission to settle three hundred families in the lands watered by the Brazos, Colorado, and Trinity rivers in Texas. Austin and the settlers received thousands of acres of this rich land to farm. In return, they had to become Mexican citizens and be baptized into the Catholic Church.

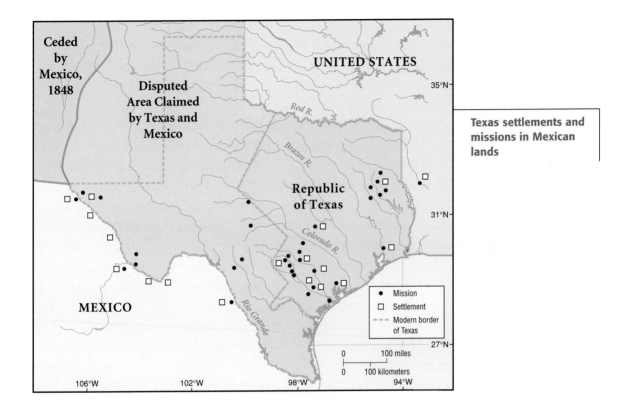

Ceded by Mexico, 1848

Disputed Area Claimed by Texas and Mexico

UNITED STATES

35°N

Red R.

Brazos R.

Republic of Texas

31°N

Colorado R.

MEXICO

Rio Grande

Texas settlements and missions in Mexican lands

• Mission
□ Settlement
--- Modern border of Texas

27°N

0   100 miles
0   100 kilometers

106°W   102°W   98°W   94°W

For several years, Stephen Austin governed the Americans in Texas, who became known as Texians. The Texians conducted themselves as good citizens of Mexico, and most of the Americans (though not all) became Catholic. Many of the American settlers came to Texas to grow cotton and brought their slaves with them. Austin did not like slavery, but allowed it in Texas.

More and more people from the United States came and settled in Texas. One of these was a man named James Bowie. Born in Kentucky, Bowie moved with his family to Louisiana. Bowie was said to be a great hunter; he trapped bears, rode wild horses, and even wrestled alligators. He was also a fighter. Once Bowie got into a fight with a man who shot him in the chest. Injured, but still able to fight, Bowie pulled out a big butcher knife and stabbed the man to death.

A Bowie knife

Because of this fight, Bowie became a famous knife fighter. His knife also became known far and wide as the Bowie knife. In 1830, James Bowie moved to Texas, where he became a Mexican citizen and entered the Catholic Church. He later married the daughter of a rich Mexican family in San Antonio.

Another settler in Texas was Sam Houston. The six-foot, two-inch tall Sam Houston was an old friend of Andrew Jackson; they had fought together in the War of 1812 against the Creek Indians. When he was in his teens, Houston had lived with the Cherokee in East Tennessee. In 1829, after serving both as a congressman and as governor of Tennessee, Houston went again to live among the Cherokees, who adopted him as a member of their tribe. In 1832, at the age of 39, he moved to Texas, where he soon became a leader of the Texians. Like other Americans, Houston became a Mexican citizen and, of course, a Catholic.

American settlers like James Bowie and Sam Houston soon began to dislike living under Mexican laws. Even though they had chosen to become Mexican citizens, many of the settlers wanted to have laws like the ones they were used to in the United States. For one thing, the settlers wanted their own legislature to represent the people and to make laws for them. When the Mexican government refused to allow them to have a legislature, they set up one anyway.

For a while, the Mexican government had too many troubles of its own to do anything about the rebellious Texians. But in 1835 the new president of Mexico, Antonio López de Santa Anna, decided that he would force the Texians to obey the government. He sent General Martín Perfecto de Cós to Texas with 1,200 Mexican troops. Cos, thought Santa Anna, would teach the Texians that they had to obey the laws of Mexico.

Remember the Alamo!

Hearing that Santa Anna had sent an army to Texas, Stephen Austin and Sam Houston called on the Texians to take up arms. Made general of the Texian army, Sam Houston ordered them to march against the city of San Antonio where General Cos and the Mexican army had arrived in October 1835. On December 4, the Texians attacked the Mexican army. For five days the battle raged until General Cos finally surrendered. The Texians fortified the old Franciscan mission church there, which people in San Antonio called the Alamo. Hearing of the defeat of Cos, President Santa Anna led his own army into Texas. There they found the Texians waiting for them behind the mud walls of the Alamo.

Commanding the Alamo was Colonel William Barret Travis. With him stood James Bowie and about 150 Texians and Mexicans born in Texas. Another famous defender of the Alamo was David Crockett from Tennessee. Crockett was already a well-known frontiersman by the time he reached the Alamo. He left his home state of Tennessee for Texas and arrived in San Antonio just in time to join Travis and his Texians at the Alamo.

The Alamo in San Antonio, Texas

In February 1836, Santa Anna came with his army of 3,000 and laid siege to the Texians in the Alamo. For two weeks the siege continued, Colonel Travis refusing to surrender. Finally, in the early morning hours of March 6, Santa Anna ordered his army to attack the Alamo. He ordered his trumpeter to play the *deguello*, a signal that told the Mexican soldiers that they were to kill every man within the Alamo.

The fight for the Alamo lasted only a few hours. Colonel Travis died early in the battle from being shot through the head. James Bowie, who lay sick in bed, was also shot. Crockett, it was said, killed many enemy gunners and almost shot Santa Anna himself. At the battle's end, nearly all the defenders were dead. Crockett and four other men were taken prisoner and led to Santa Anna. Angry that his soldiers had not obeyed his orders to kill every man in the Alamo, Santa Anna commanded that Crockett and his companions be run through with bayonets and then shot. Crockett, wrote one Mexican soldier, died bravely and without complaining.

Victory at San Jacinto

After conquering the Alamo, Santa Anna led his army against Sam Houston and the Texians, 200 miles to the east. Hearing that Santa Anna was coming, Houston ordered his army to retreat.

With Houston fleeing before him, Santa Anna believed he was victorious. Santa Anna followed Houston to Harrisburg, on the San Jacinto River. The two armies met at a place called Lynchburg Ferry but did not fight. For a day the two armies did nothing. The next day, Santa Anna, confident that he would destroy the Texian army, lay down to take an afternoon nap in his tent. He was certain that the Texians would not dare to attack his army. How very wrong he was.

Loud cries of "Remember the Alamo!" woke Santa Anna from his sleep. Sam Houston was leading a surprise attack against the Mexican army. Rushing from his tent, Santa Anna saw his men fleeing before

The captive Santa Anna is brought before General Sam Houston April 22, 1836, the day after the great Texas victory at San Jacinto.

the Texians. Santa Anna himself mounted his horse and fled, for he was fearful that he would be captured. The next day the Texians found Santa Anna, dressed in a blue shirt, white pants, and red slippers, hiding in tall grass. He soon learned that the Texians had utterly destroyed his great army. A prisoner of the Texians, Santa Anna knew he had no choice but to recognize the independence of Texas.

Though many (including President Jackson) wanted Texas to become a part of the United States, people in the northern states objected. They did not want another slave state to enter the union. For several more years, the "Republic of Texas" remained an independent nation, with its own legislature and president. Not until 1845 did it become a part of the United States.

Chapter 13 Review

Summary

- The conflict over slavery increased as more territories entered the Union as states. The invention of the cotton gin by Eli Whitney seemed to secure the permanency of the institution of slavery, thus ending many people's hopes that it would die naturally. The southern states worried that the northern states would overpower their political and economic interests. These concerns led to the Missouri Compromise, which was an agreement that the balance of free and slave states would be maintained with the entrance of new territories.

- Andrew Jackson became the first western president. He strengthened the United States' hold on territories such as Florida, and he fought against Indian incursions on European settlements. While ending such federal powers such as a national bank, Jackson supported the strength of the federal government over states such as South Carolina, which was threatening to secede from the Union.

- Conflicts with Indian tribes increased. Chiefs such as Black Hawk and Osceola attempted to maintain their lands for their tribes, but both were captured. The Cherokee tribe, despite conforming the most to western European culture, was forced off its land and followed the Trail of Tears to Oklahoma. The Seminole tribe was somewhat successful in staying on their lands in Florida, but they had to live in the Everglades to remain safe in Florida.

- Pioneers continued to move into western lands, and many began settling in the northern territories of Mexico. The Mexican government granted settlers land as long as they became Mexican citizens and converted to Catholicism. As more American settlers came to Texas, the more Americans wanted the land for themselves. The Texians, under the leadership of such men as Stephen Austin and Sam Houston, fought off the attacks of the Mexican army led by General Santa Anna. Though many famous frontiersmen lost their lives in the defense of the Mission of San Antonio—or the Alamo—the Texians were finally successful in defeating the Mexican army, capturing Santa Anna, and creating the Republic of Texas. Texas became a state in 1845.

Chapter Checkpoint

1. Who invented the cotton gin? What impact did this invention have on slavery in the United States?

2. What is the Missouri Compromise?
3. What is the Trail of Tears, and which tribes were involved?
4. What does "Remember the Alamo!" mean? Name the men who were involved at the Alamo.

Chapter Activity

Though the Indian tribes were driven from their native lands, Americans adopted the Indian names for towns and rivers. Look on a map of your state or town, and find at least five things named by Indians or for the Indians of your area. Try to find out how one of those things was named.

The American Larder

America has an abundance of sugar maple trees, especially in the northeast part of the country and in Canada. These trees did not grow in England or Europe. Sugar maples had brilliant red leaves in the autumn, but even more important, they yielded delicious maple syrup. In February, when the sap began to rise in the trees, but before any sign of green had appeared, the sugar maple trees were tapped. Tapping meant that a small hole was bored into the trunk of a sugar maple, and into the hole a wooden spigot was tapped with a hammer; the wooden spigot could be turned on and off. At night, buckets were hung over the spigot and by morning were brimming with clear sap. A single sugar maple tree produced a gallon or more of sap per day. Many sugar maples yielded an enormous amount of sap, which was boiled down until a golden syrup formed. This syrup was thick, sticky, and very sweet. It was a favorite for pouring on Indian griddlecakes, then, even as we enjoy it on our pancakes today. The methods of making maple syrup have changed very little since the founding of our country.

Chapter 14 The Fight for the Far West

Americans West

Mountainy Men

Texas was not the only place west of the Mississippi River that attracted Americans. Since the expedition of Lewis and Clark, American adventurers had been crossing the Great Plains and climbing the high Rocky Mountains. These mountainy men, as they were called, went west to hunt and trap beaver along the banks of rivers and mountain streams. Beaver skins sold for much money in the East, where they were turned into hats, gloves, and other items of fashionable clothing.

The mountainy men were not simply interested in money, but also in the life of freedom, and adventure that trapping gave them. Mountainy men did not live like civilized men; they dressed in skins, let their beards grow wild, and sometimes took Indian women for their wives. Spending the fall, winter, and spring in the wilderness trapping beaver, trappers gathered together at a rendezvous (a French word meaning "meeting place"), where they sold their furs to fur companies. Usually trappers did not save any of the money they earned from the sale of their furs, but spent it recklessly at the rendezvous. When fall came

Typical clothing and gear of a mountainy man

A grizzly bear

again, the mountainy men returned to their isolated lives of trapping in the mountains.

If life in the mountains was free, it was also very dangerous. Trappers suffered from the bitter cold of mountain winters or from hunger. The Indian tribes that wandered in those regions were not always friendly, and the woods were filled with fearsome beasts, like the grizzly bear.

Because of this hard life, trappers had to be strong and tough. A grizzly bear attacked one trapper, Jedediah Smith, who was trapping in the Rockies in the winter of 1823. Smith survived the bear attack, and his fellow trappers tended to his wounds. But before he could recover, Indians attacked the party and killed everyone but Smith, who had hidden in some bushes. Left alone with only his knife, a flint, and a Bible, Smith kept himself from starving by eating the beavers he found in the traps.

Trapper and Explorer

After Jedediah Smith recovered from his injuries, he spent some time trapping beaver in the Green River region of what is now Utah. By 1825, Smith and his partner, William Sublette, had made so much money trapping beaver that they were able to buy a fur trading company. But Smith had other interests besides trapping. He wanted to explore and see what wonders lay farther west.

In the summer of 1826, Smith set out with 18 men and 50 horses to find a route through the Rocky Mountains to California. From the Great Salt Lake in northern Utah, Smith and his party followed the Sevier River through the Wasatch Mountains. From the Wasatch

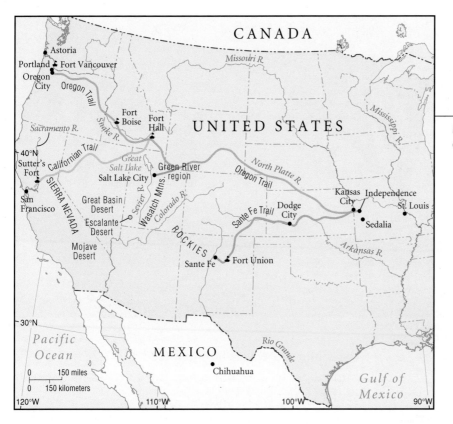

Map of the westward expansion

Mountains they descended to the Escalante Desert and passed westward across the dry, hot Great Basin desert. There the explorers met the primitive Paiute Indians, who lived by hunting and gathering seeds and nuts. Arriving at the Colorado River, Smith and his party met the Mojave Indians. Unlike the Paiute, the Mojave were farmers, growing crops of squash, corn, beans, and melons in the fertile soil of the Colorado River Valley. The Mojave told Smith that the Spanish settlements of California were only a 10-day journey away.

Crossing into the dry, desolate Mojave Desert, Smith soon found that the Mojave had lied to him: the Spanish settlements were not as close as they had said. Without a guide, Smith knew his party would quickly become lost in that hot, barren, waterless land. Returning to

Landscapes of the
Mojave desert

the Colorado River, Smith forced the Mojave to give him guides to lead him across the desert to the Spanish settlements.

Two Indians who had run away from San Gabriel Mission guided Smith and his men across the desert. They followed the dry bed of the Mojave River to the San Bernardino Mountains. Crossing these rugged mountains, the Indians led the trappers to San Gabriel Mission where, several weeks after starting out, the party was greeted with great hospitality by the Franciscan friars.

Smith remained with the friars at San Gabriel until December, when he went to San Diego to meet with the Mexican governor. The governor, who did not want Americans wandering around California, told Smith to leave California by the way he had come. He and his men ignored the governor's orders and went north into the great San Joaquin Valley, where they found rivers full of beaver. Smith then sent word to fellow trappers and friends about the beaver hunting grounds he had found in California.

Pioneers to Oregon and California

Jedediah Smith was the first of many American trappers to cross the deserts and the mountains into California. Just as Smith had said, these trappers found the mountain streams and valley rivers full of beaver. The Mexican governor of California did not want the trappers in California, and he ordered them to be imprisoned. But it was hard to catch the trappers, because they easily vanished into the mountains and mainly went to places where few Californians lived. So, whether the governor liked it or not, the trappers kept coming to California.

If trappers needed supplies while in California, they could go to a fort on the Sacramento River owned by a man named John Sutter. Sutter had come from Switzerland to the United States in 1834. In 1839 he arrived in California, where the Mexican governor gave him some land on the Sacramento River. Though Sutter was supposed to help the governor keep Americans out of California, he quickly became friendly both with the trappers and with other Americans who were crossing into the Mexican territory.

Part of the Sierra Nevada mountain range

A wagon train avoiding a buffalo stampede

These other Americans were not coming to California to hunt beaver, but to farm the rich land. In the 1840s they began crossing the plains in wagon trains from St. Louis, following the Missouri and Platte rivers all the way to the Rocky Mountains. Passing over the Rockies, they crossed the Nevada deserts, following the trail Jedediah Smith took on his homeward journey, along what is now the Humboldt River. They then passed over the tall, rugged Sierra Nevada mountain range, suffering many hardships until they arrived at Sutter's fort on the Sacramento River.

Many American pioneers also headed for Oregon. Unlike California, Oregon was not a Mexican territory; it was held by both the United States and Great Britain. In 1834, the first group of American pioneers led by Protestant missionaries settled in Oregon's Willamette Valley. There they established farms where they grew wheat and raised cattle.

Whether they were going to California or Oregon, pioneers faced many dangers on their journey. Unfriendly Indians sometimes attacked wagon trains. Pioneers faced bitter cold, extreme heat, **dehydration,** and starvation. Since trails were not well marked, wagon trains sometimes took the wrong paths and wandered in the wilderness. If all went well, the wagon trains reached California or Oregon after a six-month journey that began in the spring and ended in the autumn.

dehydration: a condition caused by lack of fluids in the body

War with Mexico

The Pathfinder

The government of Mexico was not happy that so many Americans were moving into California. Mexicans remembered what had happened in Texas. Americans had moved there and were finally able to separate Texas from Mexico. The Mexican government did not want the same thing to happen in California. However, the Mexican authorities were not powerful enough to keep Americans out of California. Each year, American pioneers continued to pour over the Sierra Nevada into the fertile valleys of the Mexican territory.

John Charles Frémont, nicknamed the "Pathfinder"

More and more Americans began to think that California should belong to the United States. These Americans thought the United States should stretch from the Atlantic to the Pacific Ocean. But most of the lands west of the Rocky Mountains belonged to Mexico, and Oregon was held by both the United States and Great Britain. The United States, many Americans thought, should take control of these western lands, even if they had to go to war to do it.

John Charles Frémont was one of those Americans who thought it was the destiny of the United States to stretch from sea to shining sea. A captain in the United States army, Frémont led an expedition into California, arriving at Sutter's fort in 1844. Frémont wrote a description of his journey, including all the animals and plants he found along the way and in California. He also described how weak the Mexican forces in California were, and how easy it would be for another country to conquer that rich land. Because of this journey, Frémont earned the nickname of the Pathfinder.

In 1845, Captain Frémont again visited California with about 60 men, including 12 Delaware Indians. The explorer and trapper Christopher "Kit" Carson accompanied Frémont. Frémont's second expedition was supposedly another exploring trip, just like the first one. It was really much more warlike. He had come to help stir up rebellion among the Americans in California.

The Mexican general in command in California, José Castro, was disturbed by Frémont's expedition. What was a U.S. army officer doing in Mexican territory? Frémont, however, told Castro he had entered California just to get supplies, and that he would continue on to Oregon. At first Castro believed Frémont; but when the captain stayed on in California well into the autumn, Castro grew suspicious. The Mexican general finally ordered Frémont to leave California. The captain obeyed, but took his time traveling through the Central Valley toward Oregon.

On May 8, 1846, a lieutenant of the United States Marines named Archibald Gillespie caught up with Frémont near Mount Shasta in the northern part of California. Gillespie carried messages for Frémont from the United States government. No one knows what these messages said, but after reading them Frémont discontinued his journey to Oregon and returned to the Sacramento River, against the direct command of General José Castro.

The Bear Flag Revolt

The Americans who had settled in California were not happy living under Mexican laws and government. Since the Americans had settled in California without permission, they were worried that the Mexicans might force them to leave. Besides, like the Texians, Americans in California wanted to live under the laws of the United States. They thought, as well, that the Mexicans had no right to California, since, the settlers believed, it was the destiny of the United States to possess the land. So it was that at least some of the American settlers were looking for an opportunity to revolt against Mexico, just as the Texians had done several years earlier.

The opportunity came in early June 1846. News had reached Frémont, who was then at Sutter's fort, that General Castro had sent some of his soldiers to a ranch near Sonoma to gather 200 horses. The ranch was owned by a wealthy Mexican Californian named Mariano Vallejo. The Americans thought that Castro was gathering the horses in order to attack them. To stop Castro, an American named Ezekiel Merritt rode out with some of Frémont's men to capture the horses from the Mexican soldiers. After capturing the horses, Merritt returned with them to Frémont's camp. There, gathering 21 men, Merritt again rode out, this time toward Sonoma.

In the early morning hours of Sunday, June 14, Mariano Vallejo awoke to find his house surrounded by Ezekiel Merritt and his men. The Americans were a mean-looking group, and Vallejo decided he had no choice but to surrender to them. Merritt made Vallejo a prisoner and led him to Frémont at Sutter's fort.

William Ide leads a revolt to raise the bear flag and claim California as an independent country.

The capture of Mariano Vallejo was the beginning of a revolt, led by an American settler named William Ide. Ide declared that California was now an independent country. He also made a flag for this new country; it was white, with one red stripe along the bottom and a red star in the upper left-hand corner. To the right of the star was the image of a grizzly bear, under which were written the words, "California Republic." Because of this flag, Ide's revolt became known as the Bear Flag Revolt. Ide raised this flag over the plaza (or public square) in Sonoma on the same day Mariano Vallejo was taken prisoner by Merritt.

General Castro heard of the revolt three days after the raising of the bear flag and began gathering an army to crush the rebellion. Meanwhile, Frémont left Sutter's fort and came to Sonoma, where he took command of the "Bears," as the Americans were called. On July 4, Frémont and the Bears celebrated American Independence day in Sonoma with the booming of a cannon, a Spanish dance, and the reading of the Declaration of Independence.

In joining the Bears, Frémont had not had the open support of the United States government. Like the Texians, the Americans in California had carried out their revolt all by themselves. Perhaps Castro could have crushed the Bear Flag Revolt, but on July 7, 1846, everything changed. Commodore John Drake Sloat, who commanded the Pacific squadron of the United States Navy, sailed into Monterey harbor and took control of the Mexican capital of California. The fact that an American naval commander did this could mean only one thing: the United States and Mexico were at war. How did this war begin?

Blood on the Rio Grande

The United States and Mexico had not been friendly with each other. One reason for this unfriendliness was Texas. Ever since the revolution in 1836, Texas had been an independent republic. It had its own president, its own congress, and its own laws. Still, many Texians wanted to join the United States. Many people in the United States wanted this, too, but Mexico was against it. The Mexicans still said that Texas belonged to Mexico and so it would be unjust for the United States to take it. But the United States government ignored Mexico and in 1845 accepted Texas as part of the United States.

James K. Polk, who became president of the United States in 1845, was one of those who thought the United States should spread from the Atlantic to the Pacific. He hoped Mexico would want to sell its lands west of the Rocky Mountains—especially California—to the United States. But the Mexican president was so angry about the

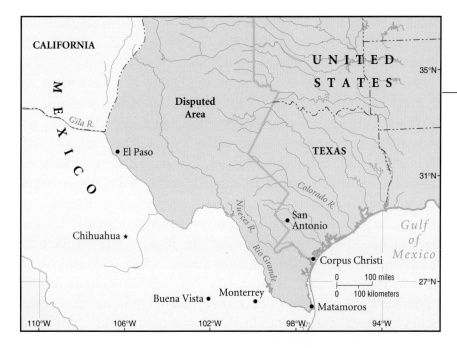

CALIFORNIA

MEXICO

Gila R.

● El Paso

Chihuahua ★

UNITED STATES

Disputed Area

TEXAS

Colorado R.

Nueces R.

Rio Grande

35°N

31°N

27°N

● San Antonio

● Corpus Christi

Buena Vista ●   Monterrey ●

● Matamoros

Gulf of Mexico

0   100 miles
0   100 kilometers

110°W   106°W   102°W   98°W   94°W

The Texas/Mexico border showing the disputed river lines

United States having taken Texas that he refused to sell those lands. The United States and Mexico also disagreed over the southern boundary that divided Texas and Mexico. Mexico said it was the Nueces River, but the United States said it was the Rio Grande, a river lying 150 miles south of the Nueces River.

If President Polk could not buy California from Mexico, he was willing to go to war to get it. In January 1846, he ordered General Zachary Taylor to lead his army across the Nueces River and march to the Rio Grande. Polk knew that Mexico would think this an act of war, for the American army had crossed over into Mexican territory. He hoped that the Mexican army would attack the American army. If this happened, Polk was sure the American people would become so angry that Congress would declare war on Mexico.

Everything happened just as Polk wished. General Taylor led his troops to the Rio Grande and laid siege to the Mexican border city of Matamoros, which lay across the river. For one month Taylor

cavalry: soldiers on horseback

remained across the river from the city. Finally, on April 25, 1846, Mexican **cavalry** crossed the Rio Grande and skirmished with American soldiers, killing several of them.

On May 11, President Polk appeared before Congress. Mexican soldiers had attacked American soldiers on American soil, he declared. This was, of course, not quite true, since there was no agreement that the land between the Nueces River and the Rio Grande belonged to the United States. It made just as much sense to say that the American army had invaded Mexico. If that was so, then, Mexico had the right to attack. But most people in the United States did not care about this; they were angry that American soldiers had been killed. So that same day, Congress declared war on Mexico. James Polk had gotten the war he wanted.

News traveled slowly in those days. When the Bears in California began their war of independence, they did not know that the United States had been at war with Mexico for two full months.

The Invasion of Mexico

Though most Americans were in favor of the war with Mexico, some opposed it. Antislavery people thought that adding more western territories to the United States would mean that southern slavery would spread to new areas. These people had been against making Texas part of the country for the same reason. Some pro-slavery Southerners also opposed the war because they wanted no more fights with antislavery advocates over slavery in the new territories. Some Americans opposed the war because they thought it was unjust. President Polk, they said, had picked a fight with Mexico. One of these was the young congressman from Illinois, Abraham Lincoln. Lincoln said that since the Rio Grande had never been the southern boundary of Texas, it had been wrong for Polk to send General Zachary Taylor across the Nueces River. The United States, not Mexico, Lincoln said, had started the war.

But most Americans cheered as General Taylor crossed the Rio Grande and forced the Mexican army to leave Matamoros. The

Mexicans were brave fighters, but their weapons were not as good as those of the Americans. After taking Matamoros, though, General Taylor stopped. Old Rough and Ready, as Taylor was called, waited in Matamoros for more troops and supplies. In September of 1846, he led his army south to Monterrey in the Mexican state of Nuevo León. There, in a three-day battle, he again defeated the Mexican army. From Monterrey, Taylor marched into the state of Coahuilla and set up his camp at a place near Saltillo. There again he halted. Old Rough and Ready would not move for another four months.

President Polk did not think Taylor was moving fast enough and was very displeased. He was also displeased by the victories Taylor did win, for Polk feared the general was using his fame to promote himself as a candidate in the next presidential election. So it was that Polk gave the command of the army in Mexico to another—Major General Winfield Scott, whom his men privately called Old Fuss and Feathers, because he cared so much about how he looked in his handsome dress uniform. Besides his preening, however, Scott was making a daring plan to invade Mexico. He would sail his army to the port city of **Vera Cruz** and march his men overland to capture the capital of Mexico, Mexico City. He was to follow the same route Hernán Cortés took about three hundred years earlier.

Vera Cruz: meaning "True Cross" in Spanish. Today it is spelled as Veracruz. The name can refer to both the city and the state.

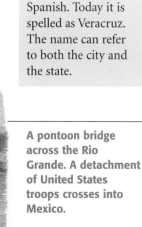

A pontoon bridge across the Rio Grande. A detachment of United States troops crosses into Mexico.

While Scott was preparing to invade Mexico, the Mexican army under the command of General Santa Anna (the same one who had been defeated in Texas) marched to fight Taylor at Saltillo. Old Rough and Ready did not expect that he would be attacked. Hearing, in February 1847, that Santa Anna was marching against Saltillo leading 25,000 men, Taylor retreated to a mountain pass near a hacienda called Buena Vista. Santa Anna followed Taylor and attacked his army at Buena Vista. It was a bloody battle. At first it looked like the Mexicans would defeat the Americans, but the Americans had much better guns, which cut down the Mexicans in great numbers. When night fell, Santa Anna ordered his men to retreat.

General Taylor expected Santa Anna to attack again the next morning. When dawn came, however, the Americans saw that the Mexicans had abandoned their camp. In messages sent back to the United States, Taylor claimed he had won a great victory over Santa Anna at Buena Vista. Yet, even though the Mexican general had retreated, Taylor did not follow him. Perhaps he feared that in another battle, his army might not be so fortunate as it had been at Buena Vista.

General Scott's Advance

About two and a half weeks after Taylor's battle at Buena Vista, General Winfield Scott, with about 12,000 men, landed at Vera Cruz. Scott laid siege to the city and began bombarding it. After about two weeks, the Mexican forces surrendered; Scott had taken Vera Cruz.

Taking Mexico City, however, would be more difficult. To reach the capital, Scott had to travel 350 miles, first through swampy country and then up into the high mountains. At any time, the Mexican army could get between Scott and his source of supplies in Vera Cruz. The Mexicans, too, could block the mountain passes the United States army had to pass through to reach the capital. Scott's plan was a daring one, and it might easily have failed. But he was helped by the fact that the Mexicans were not united. While the

Americans were invading their homeland, Mexican leaders were busily fighting among themselves.

From Vera Cruz, Scott and the army marched to a mountain pass called Cerro Gordo. Santa Anna and the Mexican army had blocked Cerro Gordo so well and fought so courageously there that it seemed the Americans could not pass through. Fortunately for Scott, one of his officers, Captain Robert E. Lee (later to be the famous Civil War general), discovered a way to get around the Mexican army. On one side of the Mexican army was a steep mountain slope that seemed impossible to climb, but Captain Lee found a way. Placing men on this slope, the Americans were able to attack the Mexicans from the front and the side. Unable to withstand this assault, the Mexican army retreated.

General Winfield Scott, also known as "Old Fuss and Feathers," entering Mexico City— the final act of the Mexican War.

The Mexicans were unable to stop the American advance through the mountains and on to the beautiful valley where Mexico City lay. On August 9, 1847, the bells of the cathedral of Mexico City sounded the alarm: the Americans were coming. The next day, for the first time, the American army beheld, through the mountain mists, the glorious capital of Mexico.

But they would not find it easy to conquer the city. Forgetting all their differences, the Mexicans united themselves under the leadership of General Santa Anna. The Americans had to fight for every inch of ground against the courageous Mexicans. At the battle at the convent of Churubusco on August 20, nearly 10,000 Mexicans died while the Americans, with a much smaller army, also suffered losses: 179 killed, 879 wounded. Finally the

Captain Robert E. Lee

Americans arrived at the fortress of Chapultepec, which guarded Mexico City. There, General Scott told Santa Anna that he must surrender.

When Santa Anna refused to surrender, General Scott began his assault on Chapultepec. But Santa Anna did not stay to defend the fortress; as before, he fled. Those who stayed fought bravely, but they were too few. Finally, the Americans scaled the walls of Chapultepec and captured the fortress. That evening, they broke through the gates of Mexico City.

Santa Anna had fled far from Mexico City, but still the Mexicans fought on. The Americans had to fight bloody battles in the streets of the city against the Mexican defenders. When it became clear that all was lost, the Mexicans surrendered. Led by two generals (one wearing only one boot), the ragged American army marched into the plaza in front of the cathedral, which, hundreds of years before, Cortés had built. Finally, General Winfield Scott entered the city. Dressed in a splendid uniform, Old Fuss and Feathers rode into the plaza, leading a company of soldiers. The Americans had conquered Mexico City.

Zócalo Square and the Cathedral of Mexico City

St. Patrick's Brigade

At the battle of Churubusco, many American soldiers fell to the bullets of the San Patrício Brigade. The San Patrícios were not Mexican, but mostly Irish, though some of them were German, English, Italian, French, Scottish, and Polish. Like many Irish who came to America, they had joined the United States army at the beginning of the Mexican-American War. But unlike most of the Irish who served in the army, the San Patrícios had deserted and joined the Mexican enemy. Why did they do this?

The chief reason was that Protestant officers in the U.S. army mistreated these Irish-born men because they were Catholic. The Irishmen and their leader, John Riley, also did not want to fight on the side of Protestants against a Catholic nation. Having just come to America from Ireland, Riley and his men felt no special love for the United States. They thought that it was more important to be faithful to their holy Catholic faith rather than to a nation that persecuted them for their faith.

In every battle they fought for Mexico, the San Patrício (or "St. Patrick") Brigade fought with courage and skill. Their bravery, though, could not save them at Churubusco. At the end of the battle, the American army captured 83 San Patrícios, including John Riley. Many of these were sentenced to be hanged.

The American army, under the command of General Scott, defeats the Mexican army at the fortress of Chapultepec.

The War's End

Everywhere the Americans had been successful. Though the Mexican Californians had tried to drive out the Americans, they were too few and inadequately armed. Many fought on horseback using the traditional Spanish lance. After the battle of Mexico City, Santa Anna tried to cut Scott off from Vera Cruz, but failed. For months, small bands of Mexicans fought the United States army, but could not drive them from Mexico.

Finally, several months after the Americans had taken Mexico City, the Mexican government agreed to surrender. On February 2, 1848, the Mexican government signed the Treaty of Guadalupe Hidalgo, which ended the war. In this treaty, Mexico agreed to sell its northern lands to the United States for $15 million. The American states of New Mexico, Arizona, Colorado, Utah, Nevada, and California were cut out of these lands. In return, the United States government promised that it would respect the religion and property of Mexicans living in those territories. Mexicans in those territories could choose to become United States citizens or go to live in Mexico.

Because of the Mexican-American War, Mexico lost half of its territory. The victorious United States now spread from sea to shining sea. Americans moved freely into the new lands. In the coming years, the new American territories would bring not only great wealth to the United States but many problems, as well.

Chapter 14 Review

Summary

- Rugged mountain men who trapped beavers and hunted other animals for survival were the first Americans to explore the western lands. Figures such as Jedediah Smith blazed trails across the Rockies and the western deserts. Wagon trains full of farmers later followed these paths. However, the entrance of so many Americans into the Mexican territory of California made the Mexican government angry and concerned.
- Many Americans believed America was destined to stretch from sea to shining sea. Americans in California, led by such men as John (the Pathfinder) Frémont revolted against the Mexican government in California in what is called the Bear Flag Revolt.
- The United States declared war on Mexico in 1846 under the presidency of James Polk. Polk believed that the United States should own California, and when Mexico refused to sell it to the United States, Polk asked Congress to declare war on Mexico. The Republic of Texas had been received into the Union in 1845, despite Mexico's objections, and in 1846, the U.S. army invaded Mexico. The U.S. army drove the Mexican army to the capital of Mexico City, where the Mexicans finally

were defeated. In 1848 the Mexican government signed the Treaty of Guadalupe Hidalgo, in which Mexico agreed to sell half its territory to the United States.

Chapter Checkpoint

1. Which was the first group of American pioneers to begin really exploring California and Oregon?
2. What was the Bear Flag Revolt? What was its outcome?
3. What were the causes of the Mexican-American War? What were a few reasons some opposed the war? Be sure to include names of significant figures in your answer.
4. What did the Treaty of Guadalupe Hidalgo gain for the United States? Which U.S. states were once in Mexican territory?

Chapter Activities

1. Imagine you are a member of a wagon-train party going across the western mountains. Keep an imaginary journal of what you might meet on the trek—Indian tribes, weather, wild animals, and so forth.
2. Pretend you are a trapper in the Pacific Northwest. Make a list of the supplies you would need to survive in the wilderness. How would *you* trap a beaver?

The American Larder

Sugar was scarce and very expensive throughout the eighteenth and nineteenth centuries. When it was available, honey was the precious sweetener of most households, not sugar. For a special event, mountain folk of the nineteenth century liked to go on what was called a honey sup. When one of the hunters discovered a wild honeycomb, families would make a party of gathering it and enjoying it together. Families would ride in their wagons as near as possible to the site of the wild honeycomb. They baked several loaves of bread and took it with them, along with cider or lemonade. The women would prepare the eating area while the men went out to gather the honey. This was not so easy. The honeycomb was always in a hollow tree, and there were many bees about to guard it. The men did not want to kill the bees, so drove them away by making smoke inside the tree. Then a brave youth would climb up in the tree to the comb and cut it away with a knife. He had to be careful not to break the comb and so lose the precious honey. The other men would help lower it and then carry the comb back on a large wooden plank. The families would then have a mountain feast on honey and fresh bread.

Chapter 15 America Between the Wars

Gold in California

Discovery on the American River

California had become a United States territory, but it seemed that nothing much would change there for a long time. As before the war, most inhabitants of California were Indian and Mexican. They lived on ranchos and raised cattle for their meat, hides, and fat; the fat they boiled down to make tallow for candles. These ranchos were enormous, covering thousands of acres and containing as many head of cattle. California had only a few pueblos (or towns), some of which were named after saints. These included El Pueblo de Nuestra Señora La Reina de Los Angeles (meaning "The Town of Our Lady, Queen of the Angels") and San Jose ("Saint Joseph"). In those days, California was a quiet, pastoral land.

The Franciscan missions started by Junipero Serra were no more. The churches and some buildings remained, but the Mexican government had

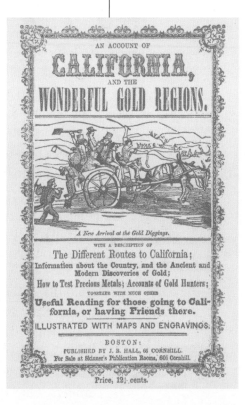

An old gold mining manual

AN ACCOUNT OF
CALIFORNIA,
AND THE
WONDERFUL GOLD REGIONS.

A New Arrival at the Gold Diggings.

WITH A DESCRIPTION OF
The Different Routes to California;
Information about the Country, and the Ancient and Modern Discoveries of Gold;
How to Test Precious Metals; Accounts of Gold Hunters;
TOGETHER WITH MUCH OTHER
Useful Reading for those going to California, or having Friends there.
ILLUSTRATED WITH MAPS AND ENGRAVINGS.

BOSTON:
PUBLISHED BY J. B. HALL, 66 CORNHILL.
For Sale at Skinner's Publication Rooms, 60½ Cornhill.

Price, 12½ cents.

Gold nuggets

long ago divided the mission lands among the Indians who lived on them. But the mission Indians did not keep these lands for long; the owners of Spanish ranchos took control of them. The mission Indians remained as workers on the ranchos. In addition to the California mission Indians, there lived many "wild Indians," who had never been Christianized by the friars.

Over time, the number of American settlers from the East moving to California was bound to grow. However, the journey over plains, mountains, and deserts, or by ship was a long and dangerous one, so it would probably have been many years before the number of Americans in California became very large. But one event changed all that: the discovery of gold.

John Sutter had hired a carpenter named John Marshall to build him a sawmill on the American River, which flows from the Sierra Nevada into the Sacramento River. While working on the mill in January 1848, John Marshall saw something shining in the water. Reaching down, he picked up a gleaming yellow nugget, about the size of a pea. Marshall knew right away it was gold. Looking again in the water, he found another piece; it was certainly gold.

When Sutter heard of the discovery, he wanted to keep it quiet, but soon the news spread until Sam Brannan, who ran the *California Star* newspaper in San Francisco, heard about it. The *Star* declared the stories about gold to be "humbug." But finally, Brannan traveled out to Sutter's fort to see for himself—and indeed, the rumors about gold there were true.

But Sam Brannan was uncertain that there was much gold in California. Even so, he hoped the news of gold would sell copies of the *California Star*. He also bought up large quantities of picks, shovels, and gold pans which, he hoped, he could sell to would-be miners. One day in May, Brannan walked through San Francisco holding a bottle of gold nuggets over his head and crying, "Gold! Gold! Gold on the American River!" When the citizens of San Francisco heard the news, they left their homes and businesses and went to search for gold on the American River. The same thing happened wherever else in California the news of gold came. It seemed as though everyone in California wanted to get rich quickly by becoming a gold miner.

The Gold Rush

Over the summer of 1848, news of the gold strike traveled swiftly outside of California. Between December 1848 and January 1849, about 3,000 gold seekers set sail in 61 ships bound for California. A few months later, by the end of 1849, nearly 45,000 Americans had sailed to California in search of gold.

Other gold seekers loaded their belongings into Conestoga wagons, or even pushcarts and wheelbarrows, and made the long journey overland to California. Though led by expert trappers and explorers, these Forty-Niners (so called because they began coming in 1849) suffered many dangers and hardships. One group took what it thought was a shortcut and ended up in a vast, hot, dry desert valley in California; this below-sea-level desert came to be called Death Valley.

When the Forty-Niners set out to seek their gold fortunes, they followed the American River into the Sierra Nevada mountain range; there they panned for

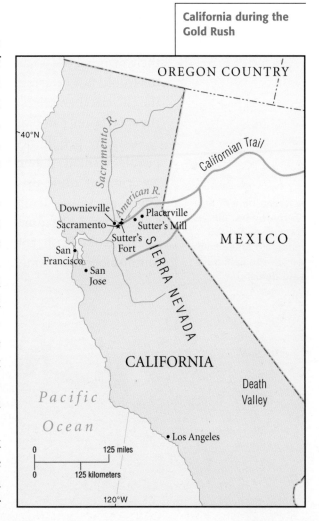

California during the Gold Rush

boomtowns: a town that grows very suddenly because of some local resource

gold in rivers and streams or tried to hammer it out of rocks. Soon, other gold discoveries were made farther north, all the way to the Oregon border. Wherever miners went, new **boomtowns** sprang up. These were rough, brutal, and lawless towns with names such as Murderer's Gulch, Whiskey Diggings, Hangtown, and You Bet. There was no rule of law in these towns, nothing to correct the runaway greed, and crimes such as robbery and murder were frequent.

Older California towns also grew. The little town of San Francisco had only 500 inhabitants, but by 1850 it had grown to more than 40,000. Like the boomtowns and mining camps, San Francisco had a good deal of crime. To control the crime, citizens took justice into their own hands. If caught while committing a crime, the perpetrator would not be arrested and tried before a judge and jury. Instead, the citizens themselves would condemn the person and hang him on the spot. Soon, San Francisco had less crime than many eastern cities.

So many people flooded into California that in June 1849, the people wanted the territory to become a state. The territorial government drew up a constitution and sent it to Congress for approval. In September 1850, Californians received word that California had become the first state on the Pacific Coast.

The Gold Rush completely changed life in California society. Outnumbered by Americans, the Spanish Californians either fled to

A wagon train of the "Forty-Niners" passes through an Oregon mountain range on its way to the California gold fields.

California boom-towns would have been similar to this one (a Nevada boom-town in 1902). Prospectors from all over the country would rush to the scene to stake out claims.

Mexico or remained like strangers in their own country. The newly arrived, gold-crazy Americans were cruel to many of the Indians of California, including the mission Indians as well as the wild Indians; both groups of natives died in great numbers. Because of the Gold Rush, California became a very different place. Instead of a quiet, pastoral society, it was now a rough and wild American frontier settlement.

Slavery Divides the Nation

The Abolitionists

Many Americans had hoped that the Missouri Compromise had ended the fight over slavery. The compromise drew a line across the western part of the country: every territory north of that line would be "free," but every territory south of that line could admit slaves. But the Missouri Compromise could not end the problem of slavery. Many people began to ask how a country that believed that *all*

An engraving titled "Human Flesh at Auction," from an anti-slavery book published in 1864

men are created equal could allow slavery. Did not the words of the Declaration of Independence include all people, everywhere, including black and Indian peoples? Surely, the Declaration did not mean equality only for the descendants of the Dutch, French, German, and English settlers.

Many Americans opposed slavery, not only because it was against the Declaration of Independence but also because they believed slavery in itself was a cruel and vicious institution. Slaves had to work long hours in the fields, for no pay; they could be harshly beaten by their masters or overseers. Slaves had no legal rights, not even the right to life or the stability of a family. If a slave owner wanted to do so, he could sell off family members to different owners. Even young children could be torn from their mothers at slave auctions, events where human beings were bought and sold like farm animals.

There were, of course, vast differences in how slaves were treated. Not all slave owners were cruel. In fact, many masters were kind to their slaves, claiming them as if they were family and refusing even the thought of splitting slave families. Because most Southerners were not wealthy, except in owning land, they worked in the fields side by side with their slaves. Everyone worked, and everyone ate, sometimes at the same table. When a slave was injured, his master cared for him. When the slaves grew old and could no longer work, their master still fed and clothed them. Household slaves sometimes became trusted counselors of the family. Slave women not only cared for the master's children, but actually nursed the infants right along with their own babies. Names of endearment for slaves, like "Uncle Ben" or "Aunt Jemima," were common throughout the South.

Yet despite it all, slavery was and is a cruel and inhumane institution, even at its best. And despite the exceptions, slavery's dark side was very dark indeed. It was so dark that many Americans, both in the North and the South, thought slavery had to be abolished and done away with altogether.

There were many in the South who wanted to end slavery. However, these antislavery Southerners could not see how they could abolish slavery without destroying the whole society of the South. Cotton plantations needed slaves, and cotton growing had become all-important to the South. Without cotton growing, many southern states would fall into deep poverty. In most parts of the South, the black slaves outnumbered the whites. Many worried that if slaves were freed, there would be chaos, as the blacks would come to control whites. The thought of such a thing happening was very frightening to white people living in the South.

CAUTION!!
COLORED PEOPLE
OF BOSTON, ONE & ALL,

You are hereby respectfully CAUTIONED and advised, to avoid conversing with the

Watchmen and Police Officers of Boston,

For since the recent ORDER OF THE MAYOR & ALDERMEN, they are empowered to act as

KIDNAPPERS
AND
Slave Catchers,

And they have already been actually employed in KIDNAPPING, CATCHING, AND KEEPING SLAVES. Therefore, if you value your LIBERTY, and the *Welfare of the Fugitives* among you, *Shun* them in every possible manner, as so many *HOUNDS* on the track of the most unfortunate of your race.

Keep a Sharp Look Out for KIDNAPPERS, and have TOP EYE open.
APRIL 24, 1851.

THEODORE PARKER'S PLACARD

A placard cautions slaves to be careful.

Fugitive slaves ride toward liberty.

Northerners did not have so much to lose by abolishing slavery. True, free blacks in the North were not treated as equals to whites, and they often lived in great poverty. Nevertheless, antislavery sentiment began to spread; many Northerners saw slavery was wrong and thought it had to end. The most outspoken of these northern abolitionists was a young printer and writer from Boston, named William Lloyd Garrison. In 1829 Garrison moved to Baltimore and began helping to write and edit an abolitionist journal, *The Genius of Universal Emancipation.*

emancipated: freed

After only about a year, however, Garrison parted ways with the journal, because the journal's official position was for a slow abolishment of slavery. It also declared that **emancipated** slaves should be sent away, preferably back to Africa. Garrison strongly disagreed with this. He thought slavery should be abolished immediately and that freed slaves should become full citizens of the United States. To spread his ideas, Garrison returned to Boston in 1831 and began editing his own journal, called the *Liberator.* Throughout the 1830s and 1840s, other voices joined Garrison in calling for an immediate end to slavery.

Garrison had harsh words for both the North and the South. Both sections of the country, he believed, were responsible for slavery. Yet, Garrison's strongest condemnation was directed at slaveholders in the South, because that is where slavery had become an institution in society. Southern leaders feared that Garrison's ideas and harsh language would lead to slave revolts in the South.

Another abolitionist, Harriet Beecher Stowe of Connecticut, became well known for her novel, *Uncle Tom's Cabin*, which was published in 1852. *Uncle Tom's Cabin,* a story of the cruelty of slavery, convinced many in the North that slavery was evil. Southerners, however, said Stowe's description of slavery was false. They said she knew nothing about slavery, since she had never visited the South.

Among the most powerful spokesmen against slavery were black men and women. One of these was Frederick Douglass, who had once been a slave in Maryland. As a young boy, Frederick was taught how to read by his master's wife. Reading opened a new world for Douglass, and he longed to be a free man. Douglass attempted to escape in 1836, but failed. But two years later he was successful. Disguised as a sailor, Douglass escaped from a Baltimore shipyard to New York City. Eventually, he made it to New Bedford, Massachusetts.

In 1841, Douglass gave a speech at an antislavery meeting in Nantucket, Massachusetts. The people who heard him were enthralled by this young black man. How learned they thought he was, and how well spoken! Soon he was speaking at other antislavery meetings. But some thought Douglass had always been a freeman, that he had never really been a slave; so to prove it, he wrote a book about his life: *The Narrative of the Life of Frederick Douglass, An American Slave.*

American abolitionist and former slave Frederick Douglass wrote a book about his life.

Isabella Baumfree was another former slave who fought slavery. Baumfree had been a slave in New York until that state abolished slavery; her master then set her free. Calling herself Sojourner Truth, Baumfree wandered from place to place preaching against the evils of slavery. Sojourner Truth believed that God had told her directly to speak out against slavery. She was a powerful and moving speaker who drew many listeners. Both Frederick Douglass and Sojourner Truth were devout Christians, and they based their strongest arguments on the Christian teaching that all people are children of the same God.

NARRATIVE

OF THE

LIFE

OF

FREDERICK DOUGLASS,

AN

AMERICAN SLAVE.

WRITTEN BY HIMSELF.

BOSTON:
PUBLISHED AT THE ANTI-SLAVERY OFFICE.
No. 25 CORNHILL
1845.

Frederick Douglass

However, speaking out against slavery could be dangerous, even in the North. In 1835, William Lloyd Garrison was nearly hanged by an angry mob. In Philadelphia, a mob attacked the Pennsylvania Hall for Free Discussion, where an antislavery meeting was being held. The mob burned down the hall and then began beating free blacks in the city.

The Underground Railroad

Like Frederick Douglass, Harriet Tubman had been born a slave in Maryland; and like Douglass, she had escaped to the North and freedom. In 1849, when Tubman learned that she was to be sold following her master's death, she fled to Philadelphia. Though free, Tubman was not content: her brothers, cousins, mother, and father were still slaves in Maryland. She was determined to bring her family out of slavery. A year after she had escaped from slavery, Harriet Tubman returned to slave territory. In the following years she went back and forth between the free and slave states, leading 300 slaves to freedom.

Harriet Tubman was one of many brave souls who operated what became known as the Underground Railroad. The Underground Railroad was, of course, not a real railroad, but routes that ran from Kentucky and Virginia into the northern states. Escaping slaves followed the North Star until they found a "conductor" for the railroad. The conductors secretly led them from house to house until they crossed into the North and freedom. Ultimately, many slaves went to Canada, where they had no fear of being captured. Even in the northern states, escaped slaves were not secure because slave catchers had the right to pursue slaves into free territory.

Harriet Tubman helped hundreds of slaves escape the South by means of the Underground Railroad. She nursed Union troops during the Civil War and took on spying missions at great personal risk. She is known as the "Moses of Her People."

Elijah Lovejoy was one of those who paid the ultimate price for speaking out against slavery. Lovejoy had been living in St. Louis, Missouri, where he began publishing antislavery articles. The people of St. Louis were angry at his articles; after all, Missouri was a slave state. Lovejoy finally fled across the Mississippi to Alton, Illinois, and set up a printing press there. In a free state like Illinois, he thought, he would find less opposition to his antislavery ideas.

But the people of Alton were as opposed to abolition as the people of

Harriet Tubman (far left, holding a pan) with a group of former slaves whose escape she assisted during the Civil War

St. Louis. In 1837, a mob destroyed Lovejoy's printing press. When he bought a second press to replace the first, another Alton mob destroyed it. Lovejoy then bought a third press, and this time placed it in a warehouse under armed guard. The mob attacked the warehouse, but withdrew when one of them was shot by Lovejoy's guards. But when Lovejoy himself opened the warehouse doors, five shots rang out. Lovejoy fell to the ground dead. The death of Elijah Lovejoy attracted even more people to the antislavery cause. By 1840, antislavery societies had about 150,000 members.

The South Fights Back

Attacks by William Lloyd Garrison and other abolitionists against slaveholders did not make Southerners more willing to free the slaves. Garrison, and others, wrote outrageous stories about the wickedness of Southerners; these stories were often untrue, but they did their damage. The North began to think of itself as virtuous and to fear the South as a place of blackest vice, crimes, and cruelties. Garrison even said that the northern states should break away from

Sojourner Truth, one
of the leaders of the
Underground Railroad

the southern states because they were so evil. Such dishonest attacks deeply offended the Southerners. So, instead of inspiring the South to give up slavery, abolitionist attacks only stirred the Southerners to defend it even more strongly.

Southern congressmen and senators also fought back. Abolitionists had been sending petitions against slavery into Congress. Some of these petitions asked Congress to abolish slavery. Congress alone could not abolish slavery; that would require a Constitutional amendment approved by three fourths of the states. In 1836, the Southerners in Congress convinced other representatives to ignore any petitions against slavery. Such petitions were not even to be considered. Some congressmen (especially John Quincy Adams, then a representative from Massachusetts) thought such a rule was against the citizens' right to freedom of speech.

Not all Southerners defended slavery, but those who did were loud. Some said that the Bible defended slavery. Others said that there could be no civilization without slavery. Still other Southerners argued that they had the moral superiority over the Northerners; Southern slave owners, they claimed, treated their slaves better than factory owners in the North treated their workers. This was often true, for factory workers were treated very badly, sometimes much worse than slaves. But despite all the pro-slavery arguments, many Southerners felt deeply guilty about slavery.

But the biggest disagreement between Northerners and Southerners was over the western territories the United States had obtained after the Mexican-American War. Should these territories be open to slavery or not? Congressman David Wilmot of Pennsylvania said no. Congress, he said, should not allow slavery in any new territories. Southern representatives, of course, protested Wilmot's plan. President Polk suggested that Congress extend the Missouri Compromise line to the Pacific. Territories north of that line would be free, while those south of the line would be open to slavery. Yet, by the time Polk left office in 1849, no one had agreed about what to do in the new territories.

General Zachary Taylor, who became president in 1849, was not sure what to do about slavery in the West. He just wanted those lands and California to become United States territories with governors and legislators. The new Congress, however, fought bitterly over the question. Finally, in January 1850, Senator Henry Clay of Kentucky came up with a plan. California, he said, should enter the Union as a free state, while slave owners should be allowed to settle in the territories of New Mexico and Utah. (Oregon had already been made a free territory in 1846.) Knowing that neither abolitionists nor Southerners would like this plan, Senator Clay added some points to please both. For Southerners, Clay offered a law that would make it easier for slave owners to capture escaped slaves in the North. For abolitionists, Clay said that the slave trade should be abolished in the District of Columbia, the area around the nation's capital.

Arguments over Clay's compromise lasted for weeks and weeks. Abolitionists said that because slavery was wrong, it should not be allowed in the territories. Southerners declared that they were not being treated as equal members of the Union and threatened to leave the Union if things did not go their way. In the middle of all this fighting, President Taylor died (on July 4, 1850) and his vice president, Millard Fillmore, became president. Finally Clay, with help from Illinois senator Stephen Douglas, was able to get Congress to

Slave quarters on a Southern plantation

pass his compromise. President Fillmore signed this compromise, called the Compromise of 1850, into law in September. It was the last great compromise between the northern and southern states before the Civil War broke out.

From Words to Bloodshed

Working on the Railroad

Senator Stephen Douglas was the Democratic nominee for president in 1860, an election he lost to Abraham Lincoln.

Northerners and Southerners disagreed not only on slavery, but on other issues as well. One of these issues had to do with where to build a railroad that could connect the eastern states with California. By the 1850s railroads had been built all over the eastern United States, but especially in the North. In the 1850s, many Americans dreamed of a railroad that would join the Atlantic with the Pacific. The question was: should the railroad run through the "southern" territory of New Mexico, or farther north?

Franklin Pierce, a Democrat, had become president in 1853 after defeating Winfield Scott in the election. Pierce's secretary of war was Jefferson Davis, a powerful politician from Mississippi. Davis was a slave owner, but a kindly one; yet he dreamed of a great Southern empire that included slavery. He hoped to include New Mexico Territory in this empire, so he worked to get the new railroad to run from New Orleans, Louisiana, through Texas and New Mexico and into California.

Davis's opponent was Illinois Senator Stephen A. Douglas. Douglas was a powerful

Democratic senator. He was small in stature, yet so influential he was called the Little Giant. Douglas wanted the new railroad to run from St. Louis, Missouri, across the central part of the country to San Francisco. Because this route favored the northern states, it was opposed by Southerners. Without southern support, Douglas knew he could not get his plan past Congress.

To get southern support, Douglas in 1854 introduced into Congress the Kansas-Nebraska Act. This act proposed the formation of two new territories in which the settlers would decide whether slavery would be permitted or not. But the act went against the Missouri Compromise, since both territories were north of the line the Compromise had established for slave or free states. Though objected to by many, the act passed Congress, and President Pierce signed it into law in 1854.

The Kansas-Nebraska Act did not help Douglas get the railroad route that he wanted; that question would not be settled for many more years. But it did stir up much anger and controversy. Many in the North were angry because the act ended the Missouri Compromise, which had been in place since 1820.

Groups from both sides of the slave issue organized to send settlers into Kansas who would support one side or the other of the slavery issue. These groups were so opposed to one another morally and politically that **hostilities** and violence quickly broke out among them.

hostilities: angry conflict

The Foundation of the Modern Republican Party: Antislavery

The Republican Party was formed in response to objections to the Kansas-Nebraska Act. Abolitionists wanted a new antislavery party. John Quincy Adams's son, Charles Francis Adams, wrote out a party platform declaring that no man has the right to own slaves, and that Congress should forbid slavery in all United States territories. Such was the beginning of today's Republican Party.

Bleeding Kansas

Though Kansas was settled by a majority of antislavery settlers, pro-slavery groups from Missouri illegally crossed the border and voted to elect a pro-slavery legislature. The antislavery citizens, or free-soil settlers, of Kansas elected a competing antislavery legislature. Members of the Free-Soil party took up arms to defend themselves from pro-slavery volunteer soldiers from both outside and inside the state. Fights began between Free-Soilers, abolitionists, and pro-slavery, pro-South forces.

Kansas erupted into a small civil war. Bands of free-soil men, called Jayhawkers, fought with pro-slavery "border ruffians" from Missouri. Both sides were brutal and cold-blooded. Both sides committed robberies and murders; they burned down settlements and seized whatever property was not destroyed. The fight over slavery had become a murderous war, filling people in the eastern states with horror. No one could say how the violence would end in the state which became known as "Bleeding Kansas."

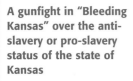

A gunfight in "Bleeding Kansas" over the anti-slavery or pro-slavery status of the state of Kansas

John Brown's Body

The Rise of the Republicans

The election of 1854 was a bitter surprise to the Democrats. In that election, more Republicans than Democrats were elected to Congress. If the Republicans were so successful in 1854, what might they do in the presidential election of 1856?

In 1856, the Democrats nominated James Buchanan for president rather than the current president, Franklin Pierce. Buchanan had been a friend of Andrew Jackson, his ambassador to Russia, and had served as Pierce's ambassador to England. The Republicans nominated a candidate they thought more interesting than Buchanan; he was John C. Frémont, the Pathfinder. It was a lively election campaign. Democrats declared that the Black Republicans (as they called them) wanted to stir up a slave revolt in the South. Republicans said that Congress should forbid all slavery in the territories. Though Buchanan won the election, Frémont and the Republicans won many votes.

Former congressman Abraham Lincoln was one of those who had campaigned for Frémont during the election. Because of sentiment in favor of the Mexican-American War, and because he was against it, Lincoln had not been reelected to Congress. Since then, he had practiced law in Springfield, Illinois, and had not been involved in politics. The election of 1856 changed that. Lincoln went around Illinois giving speeches for Frémont and the Republicans. He told people that Congress should not allow slavery in the territories, because it was a moral evil. Slavery, said Lincoln, also contradicted the Declaration of Independence, which said that all men are created equal.

Lincoln was a popular speaker; large crowds gathered to hear him. Two years later, in 1858, Lincoln decided to run against the Little Giant, Stephen Douglas, for United States Senate. Lincoln

John Brown, an abolitionist who led the raid on Harper's Ferry

Abraham Lincoln and
Stephen Douglas
debate slavery

challenged Douglas to debate him in public, and Douglas accepted. The Lincoln-Douglas debates grew to be famous examples of public oration over the slave issue. In one of these debates, Lincoln declared that the United States could not be divided and could not remain half-slave and half-free.

Though Lincoln drew many people to his speeches, he could not beat the Little Giant. Douglas returned to the Senate, but he was a less powerful senator. During the debates with Lincoln, Douglas indicated he did not strongly support the Dred Scott decision of the Supreme Court. In the Dred Scott decision, the Supreme Court ruled that slaveholders could bring their slaves to any territory they pleased without fear of seeing their slaves gain freedom. Because Douglas did not support this decision strongly enough, he lost the support of southern Democrats in Congress.

Death at Harper's Ferry

John Brown was an abolitionist who took part in the bloody battles in Kansas. He had grand plans to free the slaves, plans that he shared with abolitionists he had met in Canada. Brown wanted to lead the slaves in an armed rebellion against their masters in the South. Brown thought that in order to begin the rebellion, he only needed to find guns to arm the slaves.

Dred Scott

Dred Scott had been the slave of a military doctor whose job forced him to travel to different military posts in the West. In the early 1840s Scott accompanied his master, Dr. John Emerson, to Fort Snelling, which sat on the west bank of the Mississippi River. According to the Missouri Compromise, Fort Snelling was in a territory where slavery was not allowed. After Emerson's death in 1843, Scott said he was no longer a slave because he had lived for a time in free territory.

Dred Scott's claim to freedom was brought before a judge in Missouri, who ruled that Scott was indeed free, because of the Missouri Compromise. Dr. Emerson's wife, however, took the case to the Missouri Supreme Court, which, after six long years, declared that Scott was still a slave. Dred Scott's lawyer asked the Supreme Court of the United States to hear the case, and the Supreme Court agreed, in 1856.

The following year, the Supreme Court gave its decision: Dred Scott was still a slave. Chief Justice Roger Taney wrote that no black man could ever be a citizen of the United States and that when the Declaration of Independence said, "all men are created equal," it did not mean black men. Taney also wrote that a slave is property, much like a horse or a dog or a house is property. Since the Constitution protected a man's property, Taney said that Congress could not keep slave owners from taking their "property" into free territory. Both in slave and free territory, a slave was still a slave.

The Dred Scott decision of the Supreme Court meant that no one had the power to keep slaves out of the territories. Congress did not have that power. The people who lived in those territories did not have that power. The Dred Scott decision not only destroyed the Missouri Compromise but also put an end to Stephen Douglas's Kansas-Nebraska Act.

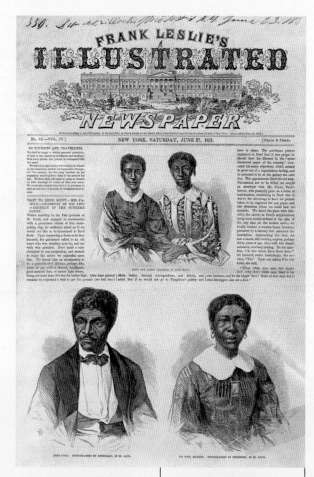

A front page news article on the Supreme Court's anti-abolitionist Dred Scott Decision of 1857. The story includes illustrations of Dred Scott and his family.

John Brown returned to the United States and moved to a farm near the town of Harper's Ferry, Virginia, which had a federal arsenal and a gun factory. Brown hoped to make Harper's Ferry the center of his slave revolt, but first he had to seize the arsenal and the factory.

On the night of October 16, 1859, John Brown—with 18 men, including his own sons—attacked the federal arsenal at Harper's Ferry. Killing the major, Brown and his men took control of the arsenal. They then took several prisoners and freed the slaves in the town. Fifty of these slaves joined Brown and his men, who took cover in the **engine house.**

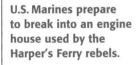

engine house: a large, circular building for switching locomotives

The news of Brown's deed spread over the countryside. The next morning, members of the Virginia militia surrounded the round-house where Brown and his men were. A gunfight followed in which, one by one, Brown's men fell dead around him. Though he lost two sons in the battle, Brown fought on into the night.

By the next morning, the United States Marines, commanded by Colonel Robert E. Lee, arrived and defeated Brown. Lee took Brown and three others prisoner and sent them to Charles Town, Virginia, to stand trial for treason.

U.S. Marines prepare to break into an engine house used by the Harper's Ferry rebels.

No slave revolt followed Brown's action. In Richmond, the court that tried Brown condemned him to death; he was executed by hanging on December 2, 1859, in Charles Town.

What Brown did at Harper's Ferry filled many in the South with fear; if Brown had actually stirred up a slave revolt, many Southern men, women, and children would have died horrible deaths. Some abolitionists praised John Brown, and this made Southerners fear and hate them even more. Many Southerners began to think that they would be safe only if their states left the Union and formed their own country.

John Brown's Body

John Brown's act set the stage for the Civil War, in which northern soldiers marched into battle singing this song (to the tune of "The Battle Hymn of the Republic"):

> John Brown's body lies a-mould'ring in the grave,
> John Brown's body lies a-mould'ring in the grave,
> John Brown's body lies a-mould'ring in the grave,
> His soul goes marching on!
> Glory, glory, hallelujah!
> Glory, glory, hallelujah!
> Glory, glory, hallelujah!
> His soul goes marching on!

The Election That Split the Nation

Abraham Lincoln's speeches and debates with Stephen Douglas had made Lincoln very popular in Illinois and other western states. In February 1860, he traveled to New York and spoke before Republicans there. After hearing the tall, homely lawyer from the West, the eastern Republicans were very impressed, indeed.

Lincoln's message was that slavery was morally evil, and so Congress had to keep it from spreading into the territories. Lincoln did not think Congress had the right to end slavery in the southern states, but he thought that it would gradually die there if it was not permitted to spread anywhere else. Even though he was against slavery, Lincoln condemned John Brown's raid, since such an action was against the law.

The Democrats were so split over slavery that they ended up choosing two candidates for president. The northern Democrats chose Senator Stephen Douglas as their candidate, while the southern Democrats chose John C. Breckenridge of Kentucky.

Abraham Lincoln was elected president of the United States for his anti-slavery stance.

secede: to separate from

When the Republicans met in Chicago to choose their candidate, they chose Abraham Lincoln. As the year went by, it seemed more and more likely that Lincoln might win the election. Many Southerners threatened that if Lincoln were elected, the southern states would **secede** from the Union. A Republican president, they thought, would harm the South beyond repair.

Abraham Lincoln, a "Black Republican," as Southerners called him, did win the election of 1860. What would the Southerners do now? Would they secede from the Union as they had threatened? Many Northerners, including Lincoln, said they would not.

However, they were wrong. On December 20, 1860, legislators at a state convention in South Carolina voted to secede from the

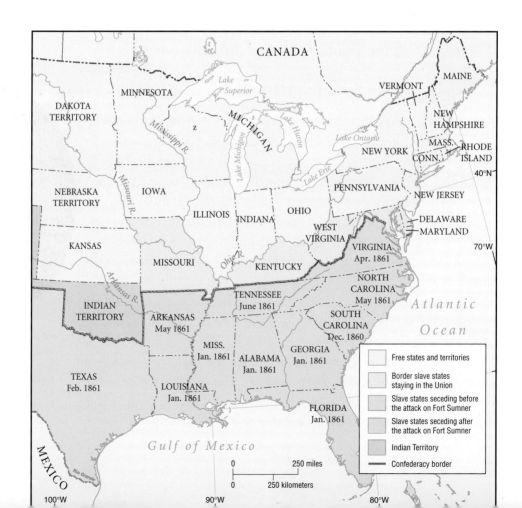

Union. With this vote, the state of South Carolina became an independent nation. Soon after, representatives at state conventions in Alabama, Mississippi, and Florida voted to leave the Union, followed by Georgia, Louisiana, and Texas. As they had threatened, the states of the Deep South had cut off their ties with the Union. Representatives from these states met in Montgomery, Alabama, wrote up a constitution, and formed a new government for the seceded states. They called this government the Confederate States of America. On February 9, 1861, the delegates elected Jefferson Davis of Mississippi as the president of the new nation.

After seceding from the Union, the Confederate states elected Jefferson Davis as their president.

Chapter 15 Review

Summary

- The discovery of gold in 1848 in California brought a rapid migration of people into the territory. In some towns, such as San Francisco, the population soared in a very short time. Lawlessness and crime became large problems for the people of California, so citizens often took law and justice into their own hands. With such a growth in population, California petitioned to become a state in the Union. In 1850, California became the first state on the Pacific Coast.

- Division over the slave issue continued to increase. Ex-slaves such as Frederick Douglass won many over to the cause of abolition of slavery. Harriet Tubman began the Underground Railroad to help runaway slaves reach the free North. The Compromise of 1850 extended the "line" of the Missouri Compromise all the way to the Pacific, so that any new territories north of the line would be free territory, and any south of the line would be slave territory. But the Kansas-Nebraska Act in 1854 ended both the Missouri and 1850 Compromises by allowing the new territories to decide the slave issue for themselves. The first large-scale bloodshed over the slave issue began in Kansas, which came to be called Bleeding Kansas.

- The victory of Abraham Lincoln in the presidential elections of 1860 and the victory of the antislavery Republican Party in Congress caused the South to finally secede from the Union. Led by South Carolina, the southern states formed their own government. Lincoln had been vocal about his opposition to slavery, and the southern states feared the new president would work to destroy the South's economy by freeing all slaves. Secession seemed the solution.

Chapter Checkpoint

1. How did the discovery of gold in California in 1848 transform the western territories?
2. Who were Frederick Douglass and Harriet Tubman?
3. How did the Underground Railroad work?
4. What was the Kansas-Nebraska Act supposed to do? What problems arose from the act?
5. What impact did the Dred Scott decision have on the slavery issue?
6. What role did John Brown have in setting the stage for the Civil War?
7. Which state was the first to secede from the Union? When did this occur?

Chapter Activities

1. Using clay (or a flour and water paste), create a topographical map of California.
2. With a small group of your class members, prepare a problem-solving drama. First, choose one of the following situations, and then perform a skit to show what might happen: (a) a slave family is about to be separated because the father has been sold; (b) a white family in the South believes that slavery is wrong but is worried that its slaves, who are like family members, will have nowhere to go and no money to live on if they are freed; (c) a family of Northerners that has never owned slaves has to decide whether it should help the Underground Railroad bring slaves to freedom; (d) a Catholic order of priests owns slaves and believes that they should be freed; but how can this be done to make sure the slaves can survive in freedom?

The American Larder

From a distance, a sorghum field looks like an expanse of enormous corn stalks. Sorghum was grown in nineteenth-century America both for its sweet syrup (made from boiling down the sap) and because it could be made into efficient brooms. These thickly bound, flexible, round brooms were a real help to housekeeping. The brushes were made from the "broomcorn" of the sorghum, which were the long bristles sprouting from the sorghum ears. Later, flat brooms replaced the round brooms. These flat-based brooms covered more area in a single sweep than did the round brooms.

Chapter 16 The Civil War, Part 1

The War Begins

Fort Sumter

After seceding from the Union, the southern states began taking over any Federal (or Union) forts that lay on their lands. Soon, only two forts in the Deep South remained in Federal hands: Fort Pickens in Pensacola, Florida and Fort Sumter in Charleston Harbor, South Carolina. James Buchanan, who was still president when the Union forts were being seized, did nothing to stop the seizure.

President Buchanan did try to send supplies to Fort Sumter, which was a Federal army garrison (held by the U.S. government). But members of the South Carolina militia would not allow Buchanan's ships to enter the harbor. When Abraham Lincoln was inaugurated as president in March 1861, at first nothing much changed. In his inaugural address, Lincoln said

The bombardment of Fort Sumter by Confederate troops at Fort Johnson—the first shots of the Civil War

Cannons at Fort Sumter

Confederate general Toutant Beauregard

that because secession was against the Constitution, what the southern states were doing was illegal. Though he would not send an army into the South, Lincoln said he would not give up any U.S. government property that lay in the states that left the Union.

So it was that Lincoln sent a message to Governor Pickens of South Carolina, telling him that a supply ship was on its way to Fort Sumter. This did not please Pickens or General Pierre Gustave Toutant Beauregard, who commanded the Confederate States of America's forces around Charleston. The generals and the president of the Confederate States, Jefferson Davis, thought that Lincoln's decision to keep United States troops in Fort Sumter was an act of war against the Confederate States of America.

So, on April 11, 1861, some of General Beauregard's staff officers crossed Charleston Harbor to the small island on which Fort Sumter sat. The officers came to ask Major Robert Anderson, the U.S. commander of Fort Sumter, to surrender the fort. Major Anderson replied that he could not surrender the fort without the permission of the United States government. At 3:20 in the morning of April 12, General Beauregard sent a message to Anderson announcing that Confederate cannons would open fire on Fort Sumter.

Fort Sumter was not the only fortress on Charleston Harbor. Fort Moultrie protected the entrance to the harbor, and Fort Johnson lay across the harbor from Sumter. Fort Johnson fired the first shot against Fort Sumter. At 4:30 A.M., a mortar gun sent a missile arching over the bay. When the missile exploded directly over Fort Sumter, all the guns from the Confederate batteries opened fire.

The attack on Fort Sumter continued throughout the day and into the night. In spite of all the exploding missiles, no one inside the fort was killed. However, the next day, April 13, Major Anderson ran out of ammunition. He sent a message of surrender to General Beauregard, who allowed Anderson and his men to fire a last salute to the flag of the United States before they lowered it.

The first shot of the war had been fired. What would President Lincoln do now? How would he respond to the attack on Fort Sumter? In both the North and the South, people waited and wondered.

Other States Secede

Confederate president Jefferson Davis thought he knew what Lincoln would do. Even before the attack on Fort Sumter, Davis asked for 100,000 volunteers to join the new Confederate army. Two days after Fort Sumter surrendered, President Lincoln called for 75,000 volunteers to join the United States army. He said these men were needed to end the rebellion in the South.

As we have seen, not all the southern states had left the Union. Only the states of the Deep South (South Carolina, Alabama, Mississippi, Georgia, Florida, Louisiana, and Texas) had seceded. Virginia, one of the most important of the southern states, would not secede if the United States government would just let the Confederate states alone. But when Lincoln asked for 75,000 volunteers, Virginia

Major Anderson's command at Fort Sumter

saw that he meant to crush the southern states by arms. Virginia could not stand by and allow this to happen to her sister states, so a state convention voted that Virginia secede from the Union and join the Confederate States of America.

With Virginia went one of the best military men in the country, Colonel Robert E. Lee. Lee was deeply attached to the Union and disagreed with secession. (He was also opposed to slavery.) But when Lincoln offered him the command of the United States army, Lee refused it. He believed he could not fight against his native state, Virginia, nor against his friends and family who lived there. To do so would violate his sacred honor. At Arlington, from his house overlooking the Potomac River and Washington, D.C., Lee resigned from the United States army.

Virginia also provided the Confederate States of America with a new capital. Soon after Virginia's secession, Jefferson Davis moved the entire Confederate government to Richmond, a city that stood only 100 miles south of Washington, D.C.

The southern states of Tennessee, North Carolina, and Arkansas followed Virginia's lead and seceded. The only southern states that remained in the Union were the so-called border states of Maryland, Delaware, Kentucky, and Missouri. Each of these states had a large number of people who wanted to secede, but also a good number who did not. In Missouri, Union forces drove the pro-Confederate governor out of the state. Kentucky decided not to secede, but to support neither the Union nor the Confederacy. Lincoln used the United States army to keep Maryland from seceding from the Union. The army jailed many pro-southern members of the state legislature, so Maryland could not vote for secession.

Confederate general Robert E. Lee and his men

The War's First Battles

On May 24, 1861, Union forces crossed over the Potomac River from Washington, D.C., into Virginia and took Arlington Heights (where Lee's house stood) and the town of Alexandria. A month later, General George Brinton McClellan led the Union army into the mountains of western Virginia, where lived many people who were against secession. The Confederates had a small army under General Robert E. Lee, but McClellan was able to drive it out of western Virginia. Lee went to Richmond, where President Jefferson Davis gave him a job working behind a desk. Southern newspapers mocked Lee for his defeat, calling him such names as "Granny Lee" and "Evacuating Lee."

Union general George Brinton McClellan (second from left) and his staff in Washington, D.C.

People in the North, angry over what had happened at Fort Sumter, wanted Lincoln to crush the southern "rebellion" quickly. So Lincoln told General Irvin McDowell, commander of the Union army in Washington and northern Virginia, to attack the Confederate army—and soon. About 22,000 Confederates under the command of General Beauregard were at Centreville, Virginia, only 25 miles from Washington, D.C.

On a hot, humid day in July, McDowell with 37,000 Union troops marched out of Washington against the Confederate army. Following the soldiers were carriages full of congressmen, senators, ladies, and other important citizens who wanted to watch the battle. It was almost as if the soldiers and those who followed them were marching out to a picnic rather than a battle.

After three days, on July 21, 1861, the Union army reached Bull Run (a creek) near Manassas Junction, Virginia. The onlookers perched on the outskirts of the army. From there they could see that the Confederates were drawn up on the other side of Bull Run. As they watched, General McDowell led 18,000 men across the run and crashed into the left flank of the Confederate army. What joy the onlookers felt as the Confederates retreated before McDowell and his boys, who shouted, "We've whipped them! We'll hang Jeff Davis to a sour apple tree! They are running. The war is over."

Confederate general Joseph E. Johnston, who had taken over the command of the army from Beauregard, saw how his army was fleeing before the Union forces, and he sent reinforcements to Henry's Hill, where the home of the Henry family stood. When the fleeing Confederates reached the hill, they found South Carolina and Georgia troops waiting for them and stopped their retreat. Soon, five Virginia regiments under Brigadier General Thomas J. Jackson arrived to join those who defended Henry Hill. About noon, the Union troops attacked the hill. The Confederates, hit hard, were about to break and again retreat.

The First Battle of Manassas, or Bull Run

In desperation the South Carolina general, Barnard Bee, rode up to General Jackson.

"General, they're beating us back," declared Bee.

Coolly Jackson responded, "Sir, we will give them the bayonet."

Riding back to his men, General Bee cried, "Look! There is Jackson standing like a stone wall! Rally behind the Virginians!" After Bee said this, a bullet struck him in the stomach and he fell to the ground, dead.

But with "Stonewall" Jackson and his men, the Confederates held their line and retreated no farther. About 4 P.M., Jackson ordered an attack. "Yell like furies!" he cried, and his men sent up a chilling cry—the rebel yell. Soon, it was the Union troops who were running, casting aside their weapons in their terror. They fled across Bull Run to a road called the Warrenton Turnpike, which ran from Manassas to Washington. There they became mixed up with the carriages of the onlookers, who were also fleeing to Washington.

With the Union army fleeing, General Jackson wanted to attack and capture Washington; but General Johnston said no. Johnston thought his men were not prepared for such an attack. Instead, he remained at Centreville and trained his men.

Confederate general Stonewall Jackson and his troops at the Battle of Manassas

A New General

So, the First Battle of Manassas (or of Bull Run, as the Federals called it) ended in defeat for the Union. Lincoln saw that he had to strengthen the Union army and, maybe, find a new general to lead it. So the president asked the states to send him 100,000 fresh soldiers, and then he removed McDowell from command of the army and replaced him with Major General George McClellan. It had been McClellan who had chased Robert E. Lee out of western Virginia.

At first, it seemed that McClellan was just the general Lincoln needed. McClellan took the Federal army, trained it, and gave it confidence and pride. And the men loved him. Their young, handsome general was not very tall, but they did not mind. Instead, they gave him the friendly nickname, "Little Mac." Not only his men, but people throughout the North, loved the new commander of the army that became known as the Army of the Potomac.

But Lincoln soon became impatient with McClellan. The summer of 1861 passed, autumn came, and McClellan showed no sign that he was going to attack the Confederates at Centreville. Though McClellan had over 120,000 men in his army, he thought the Confederates at Centreville numbered 150,000. McClellan said he could not attack such a large Confederate force, but that he needed more men. In reality, the Confederate army was much smaller than McClellan's. Johnston had fewer than 60,000 men.

New Year's Day of 1862 came and went, and still McClellan would not move out of Washington. Lincoln, finally, had had enough of McClellan. On January 27, 1862, he told the general that he must march against General Johnston and the Confederates at Centreville. McClellan told Lincoln that it would be very dangerous to attack

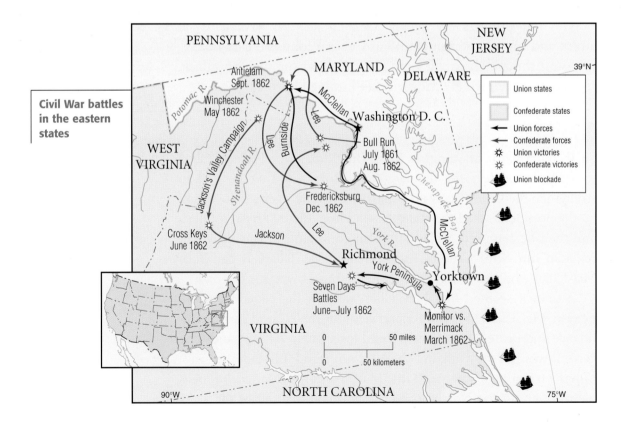

Civil War battles in the eastern states

Centreville. He asked, instead, if he could march his army down to the Rappahannock River, which lay between Centreville and the Confederate capital, Richmond. Lincoln agreed to this, and McClellan prepared to lead his army south.

Confederate general Johnston, though, knew that McClellan's army was much bigger than his own. Johnston decided he had better abandon Centreville and march to the Rappahannock River himself. So it was that McClellan had to come up with another plan of attack. He decided he would move his army, by sea, down to the York Peninsula, the peninsula between the York and James rivers, along which he could march to the James River and on to Richmond. Then, if he could capture the Confederate capital, the war would be over. President Lincoln agreed to McClellan's plan.

War in the West

While General McClellan was deciding what he should do in Virginia, Union general Ulysses S. Grant was scoring victories farther west. Grant was moving down the Tennessee River, through Kentucky into Tennessee. With him, on the river, were steam-powered gunboats commanded by Commodore Andrew Foote. On February 6, 1862, Grant and Foote conquered the Confederate Fort Henry on the river in Tennessee. While Grant attacked the fort from the land, Foote's cannons hammered its walls from the river.

Grant's next target was Fort Donelson, which lay only 15 miles away from Fort Henry on the Cumberland River. Since Foote's gunboats could not cross by land, they sailed all the way back up the Tennessee River to the Ohio River. From the Ohio, the gunboats entered the Cumberland River and sailed south until they reached Fort Donelson. There, Foote fired again and again at the walls of Donelson, but with no success. His cannons could not break down

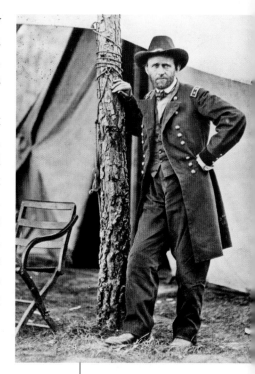

Union general Ulysses S. Grant

Battle of the Ironclads

On March 8, 1862, one of the strangest ships ever seen by man came steaming down the Elizabeth River in southern Virginia. This ship looked like a giant turtle covered with iron, except that along each of its sides were 10 holes from which poked the mouths of cannons. This ship, named the C.S.S. *Virginia,* was following the Elizabeth River into Hampton Roads, a waterway that led to the sea. In Hampton Roads were several Union ships, floating at anchor near the port city of Norfolk, Virginia.

Unlike the Union, the Confederates had no navy, so early in the war the Union troops were able to take control of Hampton Roads. The Confederates, though, thought that if they could come up with a boat made of iron, it could destroy the Federal ships, which were made of wood. At the Virginia port city of Norfolk, up the Elizabeth River, the Confederates had salvaged the hull of a sunken ship called the U.S.S. *Merrimack.* After placing iron plates on its sides and fixing a sharp iron beak on the ship's prow, they then renamed it the C.S.S. *Virginia.*

So on that day, March 8, the *Virginia* struck a number of Federal ships in Hampton Roads. With her iron beak, the *Virginia* rammed the side of the Union ship *Cumberland* and then fired a broadside at her. The *Cumberland,* whose guns could do no damage to the ironclad ship, was so badly damaged that she sank in shallow water. The *Virginia* set fire to one ship and disabled another, the *Minnesota,* and then returned up the Elizabeth River to Norfolk.

But the next morning when the *Virginia* sailed again down the Elizabeth River to finish off the crippled *Minnesota,* she discovered another ironclad, the *Monitor.* The Federals had known about the *Virginia* for some time and had built their own ironclad. The *Monitor* looked like an oversized toy boat, only it was covered with iron. Instead of having guns along its sides, the *Monitor* had a revolving gun on her deck that could move in circles. In the battle, the two ironclads fired again and again at each other, but neither could sink the other. Finally, after four-and-a-half hours of fighting, the *Virginia* returned up the Elizabeth River. Two months later, the Confederates blew her up when they had to give Norfolk up to the Union.

The battle of the *Virginia* and the *Monitor* was the first battle ever fought between ironclad ships driven by coal instead of by sails.

the stout walls of that fortress. So General Grant just lay siege (blocked the Confederates from leaving or entering) to the fort, and waited.

Since the Confederate generals in Fort Donelson could not escape and did not know if help would be coming, they discussed whether they should surrender to Grant. Three of the generals agreed to surrender the fort, but the fourth wanted to fight it out. This was Nathan Bedford Forrest, a cavalry officer. Taking 70 of his men, Forrest broke out of the fort and escaped to Nashville. The only general who remained (the other two fled by themselves) agreed to surrender Fort Donelson to Grant.

After the conquest of Fort Donelson, Admiral Foote and his gunboats continued to push up the Cumberland River. Soon they were only a day's journey from Nashville, the capital of Tennessee. Nathan Bedford Forrest, who commanded Confederate troops in Nashville, knew this. He also knew that another Union general, Don Carlos Buell, was marching toward Nashville from Kentucky. Since he did not have enough men to fight both Buell and Grant, Forrest abandoned Nashville. A day later, General Buell's Union forces marched into the city and took it.

A Battlefield Named Peace

While Foote and Buell moved toward Nashville, General Grant led his army of 42,000 men south along the Tennessee River. He got as far as Pittsburgh Landing, near the Tennessee-Mississippi border. There he waited for General Buell to arrive with 25,000 more men.

Only 22 miles away in Corinth, Mississippi, were about 40,000 Confederates under the command of General Albert Sidney Johnston. General Johnston knew that once Buell joined forces with Grant, the Union army would greatly outnumber his own army. For that reason, Johnston had to attack Grant before Buell arrived.

General Beauregard, who had been at Fort Sumter and in northern Virginia, was now in Mississippi with General Johnston. Under

Union general
Tecumseh Sherman
(leaning on the breach
of the gun) with
his staff

Johnston and Beauregard's leadership, the Confederates marched to Pittsburgh Landing. Unknown to the Federal army, on the night of April 5, 1862, the Confederate camp lay only one mile away from their own at Pittsburgh Landing.

The morning of April 6 was a pleasant one. The Union soldiers enjoyed the spring weather as they polished their muskets and cleaned their shoes and uniforms. Suddenly, the sound of gunfire and the roar of artillery broke the stillness. Confederate soldiers broke into the Federals' camp. Unprepared to fight, the Union soldiers fled.

William Tecumseh Sherman commanded a brigade from Ohio. On a hill around a small Methodist church called Shiloh (which means "place of peace"), Sherman and his men prepared to meet the Confederate attack. As more than 400 Confederates from Mississippi under General Hardee tried to take the hill, Sherman's muskets and artillery cut down rank upon rank of them. But the Confederates would not give up; they kept pushing up the hill. Finally, even after most of the 400 Confederates had been killed or wounded, the Federals broke and fled. General Hardee had taken the hill and Shiloh church.

Elsewhere on the battlefield, Union troops from Iowa and Illinois were fighting under the cover of a sunken road. Again and again, Confederates under General Braxton Bragg attacked the sunken road; again and again they were fended off, and thousands of Confederates died. So bitter was the fighting at the sunken road that it was called the Hornet's Nest.

General Johnston himself led the attack against Union forces who were lined up in a peach orchard. General Johnston's charge was successful—the Union line broke. Rejoicing over his victory, Johnston did not notice that he himself had been struck by a bullet behind his knee. Johnston continued fighting while blood spurted from his wound. Finally he reeled and fell from his horse, for he had lost too much blood. Later that afternoon, he died.

Union troops under General Grant and Confederate troops under General Beauregard engage at Pittsburg Landing, Tennessee, during the Shiloh campaign.

General Beauregard now took command of the Confederates. He ordered more attacks on the Hornet's Nest. Though the Union soldiers fought fiercely, by evening they were forced to retreat. The Confederates took the sunken road, but because darkness was coming, they could not utterly destroy Grant's army. That night General Buell arrived at Pittsburgh Landing with 20,000 more men for Grant. Beauregard, who knew he could not defeat so large an army, ordered the Confederates to retreat to Corinth. Because of this retreat, the Battle of Pittsburgh Landing was considered a victory for Grant.

The Fall of New Orleans

Despite the victories of Forts Henry and Donelson and the Battle of Shiloh, General Henry Halleck, who commanded all Union armies in the West, was not pleased with General Grant and removed him from command. General Halleck himself took command of the Federal army at Pittsburgh Landing and marched it south. Arriving at Corinth, Mississippi, after a month, he found no Confederate army, for Beauregard had moved farther south into Mississippi. Halleck sent a message to President Lincoln saying he had won a great victory over the Confederates.

Debris litters the battlefield at Port Hudson, Louisiana.

This was not the only Federal victory. Union general John Pope, with Commodore Foote's gunboats on the river, had marched down the Mississippi, taking all the Confederate forts between St. Louis and Memphis, Tennessee. After General Halleck arrived in Corinth, General Pope captured Memphis as well.

But an even greater victory was to come. Twenty-four Federal ships under the command of Flag Officer David Farragut had arrived at the mouth of the Mississippi River at a place where it flows into the Gulf of Mexico. About 100 miles north lay New Orleans, Louisiana, one of the South's most important port cities. Farragut was aiming to capture this city.

But between the mouth of the Mississippi and the city of New Orleans were Forts Jackson and St. Philip, located on both sides of the river 75 miles south of New Orleans. Farragut and his ships had to pass these forts before they could reach New Orleans. When he reached the two forts, Farragut began to bombard them. For six days, he tried to destroy the forts; but it was no use. Finally, Farragut sailed his fleet past the forts, losing only four ships. New Orleans did not resist Farragut, and he captured the city on April 25, 1862.

From New Orleans, Farragut moved on and took Baton Rouge and Port Hudson, Louisiana, as well as Natchez, Mississippi. The Confederates then had only one fortress on the Mississippi, at Vicksburg. If the Union forces could take Vicksburg, they could cut off the eastern half of the Confederacy from the western half: Arkansas, the Indian Territory, and Texas. The only problem was that Vicksburg sat on top of high river bluffs, and it was surrounded by swamps. It would be very hard, indeed, to take that fortress.

General Lee Turns the Tide

On to Richmond

While Union armies in the West were winning victories, General George McClellan with his enormous Army of the Potomac was camping near Yorktown, Virginia. Richmond was only a few miles away and was protected by a Confederate army much smaller than McClellan's. But McClellan thought the southern army was much larger and refused to attack it.

Finally, on the morning of May 4, 1862, McClellan decided to attack Yorktown. To his surprise, General Joe Johnston and the Confederates had abandoned the city. The next day Union troops and Confederates fought a small battle near Williamsburg, and the Confederates retreated. General Johnston moved his army outside of Richmond in order to protect the capital. On May 24, McClellan moved the Army of the Potomac to the battle lines six miles from Richmond. But he did not attack. He still believed Johnston's army was far too large.

It was Johnston who attacked first. On Saturday, May 31, the Battle of Seven Pines (or Fair Oaks) was fought. It was a bloody battle, and the Confederates got the worst of it. General Johnston himself was wounded and was forced to give up his command of the Confederate army in Virginia.

Who would replace Johnston? President Jefferson Davis decided on Robert E. Lee, but many in Richmond thought Lee a bad choice. Many still called him "Evacuating Lee," because McClellan had driven him out of western Virginia and "Granny Lee" because they thought him an overly fussy general. But those who laughed at Lee did not know him. When Lee took command of the Confederate army he renamed it: it was now the Army of Northern Virginia,

Union troops inspect a destroyed Confederate water battery in Yorktown, Virginia.

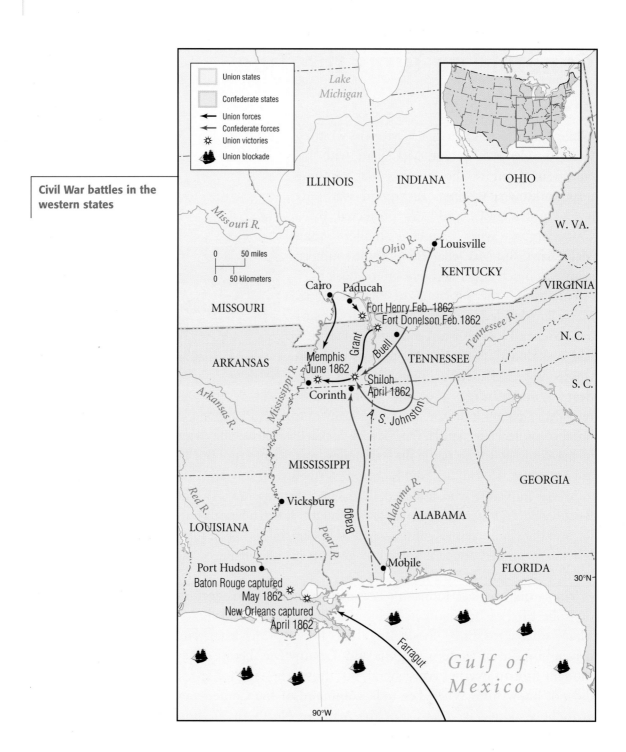

Civil War battles in the western states

because Lee was determined to drive the Yankees out of Northern Virginia. As for Richmond, Lee said, it "must not be given up. It *shall* not be given up."

To find out where the different parts of the Federal army lay, Lee sent James Ewell Brown (J.E.B., or "Jeb") Stuart with 1,700 cavalrymen to ride around the Union army. Stuart was a dashing fellow: he had a great beard and wore a large white feather stuck in his hat. He was also a very good cavalry officer. He rode 150 miles, completely around the Union army, and returned to Richmond with 170 prisoners as well as 300 horses and mules.

On June 26, Robert E. Lee's army attacked McClellan's. In this battle, the Army of Northern Virginia nearly destroyed one part of the Union army, though the Confederates themselves lost many men. The next day, Lee again attacked McClellan, forcing the Union troops to retreat. Every day for seven days, Lee attacked until he had pushed McClellan to the York River, where the guns from Union warships protected McClellan's army.

Both the Confederates and the Federals lost many men in this struggle, called the Battle of the Seven Days. The battle was such a disappointment to Lincoln that he sailed to the York River to visit McClellan. Though his army was much larger than Lee's, McClellan told Lincoln he would not attack Lee unless he received 50,000 or 100,000 more men. Lincoln told him this was impossible and ordered him to bring the Army of the Potomac back to Washington.

Old Granny Lee had saved the capital of the Confederacy.

Union soldiers visit the headquarters of Revolutionary War hero Lafayette in Yorktown, Virginia. Historic places from the Revolutionary War were popular with soldiers during the Civil War.

Pope vs. "Old Blue Light"

Abraham Lincoln very much wanted a victory in Virginia, but George McClellan was not giving him one. So, after the Seven Days' Battles, Lincoln took a part of McClellan's army and gave it to General John Pope. Pope had won victories in the West; maybe he could win some in the East.

General Pope certainly thought he could. In the West, Pope told his men, the Union forces only saw the backs of the Confederates, because they always had them on the run. But General Pope would meet a different enemy in Virginia. Robert E. Lee was a fighter who was determined to drive Pope and his army out of Virginia.

General Lee sent General Stonewall Jackson with about 20,000 men to fight Pope. A hard fighter who was tough on his men, Jackson was about the best general Lee had. A deeply religious man, Jackson led his men every day in worship and prayer. Though he worked them hard, Jackson's men were proud to serve him. They called themselves Old Jack's boys, and Jackson they named "Old Blue Light."

Now they were marching with him to fight Pope, who—they had heard—had been taking the property of the people of Northern Virginia. After fighting Pope at Cedar Mountain, Jackson led his men around Pope's army to Manassas. Pope thought Jackson was retreating and followed him. He found Jackson on a stony ridge that overlooked the old Manassas battlefield. Pope tried to drive Jackson from the ridge, but could not. That night, both sides received more men, with Generals Lee and Longstreet joining Jackson.

The next morning, Pope again attacked Jackson. General Lee ordered General James Longstreet and his over 30,000 Confederate troops to attack Pope. Pope could not stand up against both Jackson and Longstreet; he retreated to Henry House hill where, over a year before, Jackson had stood like a stone wall. The next day, Pope retreated to Centreville. Lee had again defeated the Federal army, and President Lincoln decided to replace General Pope with McClellan.

**Union general
John Pope**

A group of soldiers from General John Pope's federal army in Virginia gather near a damaged railroad line after General Stonewall Jackson's men sacked Manassas.

Lee Goes North

General Lee wanted to draw the Union army out of Virginia. To do this, he decided he would cross into the North. If he went north, he thought McClellan would follow him.

The Federal army was far larger than Lee's army. The Federals had more and better food; they had factory-made uniforms and boots. Lee's army, on the other hand, was ragged and hungry. His soldiers were often barefoot and wore tattered uniforms, or any clothes they could get, including cast-off Union coats and trousers. But despite all this, McClellan feared Lee and his men and followed them into Maryland very cautiously.

While McClellan was cautious, Lee was daring. Crossing into Maryland, Lee sent Stonewall Jackson with nearly half the army to Harper's Ferry to capture a Federal garrison. With Jackson gone, Lee had only 18,000 men, while McClellan had 95,000. McClellan, moreover, found a copy of Lee's orders to his men, which a Union soldier found wrapped around three cigars. Consequently, McClellan knew all of Lee's plans. He could have attacked Lee and

easily destroyed his army, but again McClellan waited. Even when only the small Antietam Creek near Sharpsburg, Maryland, separated the armies, McClellan did nothing. He waited two days before attacking Lee, and by that time Jackson had returned.

But even with Jackson, Lee's army was far smaller than McClellan's. General Longstreet said the Union army looked like a "field of blue" which stretched "as far the eye could see."

The battle for the hill overlooking the stone bridge above the Antietam stream

In the early morning of September 17, 1862, McClellan finally began his attack. He sent General Joseph Hooker against Stonewall Jackson's men, who were on a hill on which stood a small church. Between the Federals and the Confederates stretched a field of corn. For four hours, Jackson and Hooker fought over this cornfield until 8,000 men from both sides lay dead.

Elsewhere, Confederates held a sunken road that became known as Bloody Lane. For hours the Federals tried to drive the Confederates from Bloody Lane, but at each attack the Confederates drove them back. Finally, some Federals found a hill from which they could fire

The infamous sunken road that the soldiers termed "Bloody Lane." Thousands of soldiers on both sides lost their lives in the battle.

down on the Confederates. The Confederates could not stand up under such fire. They broke and fled.

The victory at Bloody Lane could have destroyed the Confederate army if General McClellan had ordered his men to follow up on it. But he did not, and Lee's army was saved; but only for the moment. On another part of the battlefield, Confederate general Robert A. Toombs, with only 400 men, was fighting for a small hill overlooking a stone bridge that crossed Antietam stream. Against Toombs were 12,500 Federals led by General Ambrose Burnside. For four hours, Toombs and his men held the hill and the bridge against Burnside, but finally the Federals were too much for them. The Confederates retreated, and Burnside captured the stone bridge and the hill.

Map of the Sharpsburg (Antietam) battlefield, where the bloodiest battle of the Civil War took place

At this point Lee was worried. If Burnside were not stopped, he could destroy the Confederate army. Lee had no more men to send against Burnside—what could he do to stop him? Then, in the distance, Lee saw a cloud of dust. "Whose troops are those?" he asked one of his men. He feared they might be more Union troops. Looking through the **spyglass,** the soldier saw that many of them wore blue Union jackets. But then he saw something else that gave him hope. The soldier said to Lee, "They are flying the Virginia and Confederate flags, sir."

spyglass: a small telescope

It was General A. P. Hill, leading 3,000 Confederates from Harper's Ferry. Hill and his men crashed into Burnside, forcing him and his

Confederate general Stonewall Jackson directs his troops during the Battle of Sharpsburg (Antietam).

men back to the stone bridge. Burnside asked McClellan for more men, but McClellan refused to send any. When night fell, Lee led his army back across the Potomac into Virginia. He had not defeated McClellan at Sharpsburg, but at least he had saved his army.

In this Battle of Sharpsburg (or Antietam) Lee lost 10,318 men; McClellan lost 13,000. It was the bloodiest day of the war.

Freedom for Some Slaves

President Abraham Lincoln did not believe that states had the right to secede from the Union, so he fought to keep the southern states in the Union. Though Lincoln thought slavery was evil, he did not think the federal government had the right to end slavery in the states where it existed. But the president saw that he could use the war as a way of freeing the slaves. If he did this, the North would fight not just to keep the South in the Union, but to free the slaves as well.

Lincoln could not free all the slaves, though. He could not force slave states (like Kentucky, Maryland, and Missouri) that had remained in the Union to give up slavery. But he could declare that slaves in the rebellious states were free. So it was that he wrote a document called the **Emancipation Proclamation,** which declared that all slaves in the Confederate states were free men.

But Lincoln had a problem. He could not issue the Emancipation Proclamation while Union armies were losing battles in Virginia. The Battle of Sharpsburg, however, changed things. Even though McClellan had not destroyed Lee's army, he had driven Lee out of Maryland. This was a victory for the North that Lincoln badly needed.

On September 22, 1862, President Lincoln issued the Preliminary Emancipation Proclamation. (The word *preliminary* meant it would not go into effect right away.) Lincoln gave the states that had seceded until January 1, 1863, to lay down their arms and come back into the Union. If they did not do so, Lincoln said the slaves in those states would be "forever free."

Many people, not only in the South but in Europe as well, condemned the Emancipation Proclamation. They said Lincoln was using it to stir up slaves so that they would rebel against their masters. In other places, like Haiti, slave rebellions had been bloody; white men, women, and children had died cruel deaths at the hands

> **Emancipation Proclamation:** a statement issued on January 1, 1863, declaring the freedom of all slaves living in the territories still at war with the Union

President Lincoln reads the Emancipation Proclamation to his cabinet.

of their slaves. Many feared that the same would happen in the South if slaves found out that Lincoln said they were free.

Many people in the North did not like Lincoln's proclamation, for they did not particularly like black people. These northerners were willing to fight a war to save the Union, but not to free the slaves. Even some abolitionists were not pleased, because the proclamation did not free slaves everywhere—only in the rebellious states. Other northerners welcomed the proclamation. For them it gave the war a new meaning. It was now a fight for human freedom.

Indeed, the soul of John Brown was marching on—but whether to victory or defeat, no one knew.

Slaves who were freed after the Emancipation Proclamation

Chapter 16 Review

Summary

- After South Carolina seceded from the Union, the Civil War began on April 12, 1861, at Fort Sumter in Charleston, South Carolina, when Confederate cannons fired upon the Federal fort. Southern states soon followed South Carolina's lead and seceded from the Union. The capital of the Confederate States of America was placed first in Montgomery, Alabama, then in Richmond, Virgnia.

- The southern forces won many of the initial battles of the Civil War, and at first it appeared that the South would be victorious in seceding from the Union. The Confederacy maintained its military leadership with competent generals, such as Robert E. Lee and "Stonewall" Jackson, while the North suffered from the appointment of a succession of generals. The first major battle of the war occurred at Bull Run and was won by the Confederacy.

- Ulysses S. Grant was a very able Union general who scored many victories on the western frontier of the war. An important victory for the North occurred at the Battle of Shiloh. Under the command of Grant and William Sherman, Federal troops defeated the Confederate General Pierre Beauregard. The northern troops were then able to continue pushing against the Confederate army on the western front. The port city of New Orleans soon also came under Federal control.

- Jefferson Davis chose Robert E. Lee to take command of the Army of Northern Virginia, which was the Confederate army in the East. The Confederate capital in Richmond was under attack, and Lee—with the aid of other military leaders such as Jeb Stuart—beat back the Federal army, nearly destroying it. The Federal army was not only much better supplied than the Confederate army, but it had more soldiers. However, under Lee's command, the Army of Northern Virginia defended the Confederate capital and then marched into the northern territory of Maryland. At the Battle of Sharpsburg, also known as Antietam, Lee met the Federal general, George McClellan. A bloody battle followed, in which Lee's army was overpowered by the larger Federal army and forced to retreat. At the battle, both sides together lost nearly 23,000 men; it was the bloodiest single day of the war.

- The victory at Sharpsburg gave Abraham Lincoln the opportunity he needed to issue the Preliminary Emancipation Proclamation, which said

that if the "rebellious" southern states did not lay down their arms by January 1, 1863, the slaves in those states would be forever free.
• On January 1, 1863, Abraham Lincoln issued the Emancipation Proclamation, which proclaimed that all slaves in the South were free.

Chapter Checkpoint
1. Where was the first shot of the Civil War fired?
2. Who were the presidents of the Union and the Confederacy?
3. Where was the capital of the Confederacy?
4. Why did Robert E. Lee refuse the command of the U.S. Army?
5. Where was the first major battle of the War? Which side won?
6. At what battle did the bloodiest day of the war occur?
7. What was the Emancipation Proclamation?

Chapter Activities
1. Pick one military leader from each side of the War and research his life. Write a brief description of the character and deeds of each man.
2. Research the events of either the Battle of Antietam or the Battle of Shiloh. Write a one-page report including information about who commanded each side, how many men were killed or wounded, and how the battle was won.

The American Larder
When away from a supply center, Civil War soldiers often made and ate what was called critter burgoo. Because food was always scarce, especially in the wilderness, the soldiers were always on the lookout for wild animals that could be killed with a slingshot or small rock; they did not want to use their precious ammunition to bring down small game. These critters— squirrel, opossum, raccoon, rabbits, rats, and mice—were skinned and put into stew, or burgoo. Out of their own packs, the men would take hardtack (very hard, flat biscuits) and soften it up by dipping it into the stew broth. Usually, insect larvae (little worms) were living in the flour of the hardtack. Instead of picking these worms out, the soldiers knocked them from their biscuits right into the hot broth, where the worms joined anything else edible (wild onions and herbs) that could be added to make up a critter burgoo.

Chapter 17 The Civil War, Part 2

Confederate Victories and Defeats

New Generals for Lincoln

Union general
Ambrose Burnside

The states that formed the Confederacy did not surrender by Lincoln's deadline of January 1, 1863; so on that day, Abraham Lincoln issued the Emancipation Proclamation. On New Year's Eve, 1862, the men and women who had fought slavery for many years gathered in Music Hall in New York City to await the coming of midnight and the new year. William Lloyd Garrison was there, as were Frederick Douglass and many others. When the clock struck midnight, all rejoiced. Douglass shed tears of joy, for at that moment slaves throughout the South were proclaimed free.

But the Emancipation Proclamation was just words, for Lincoln still had to destroy the southern armies before any slaves could actually be freed. After the Battle of Sharpsburg, things had not been going well for the Federal armies. Lincoln finally grew so tired of General McClellan that he replaced him with General Ambrose Burnside.

Since the Battle of Sharpsburg, General Lee and the Army of Northern Virginia had been marching farther and farther south. Burnside and the Army of the Potomac followed Lee, hoping to chase him all the way back to Richmond. By early December 1862, Burnside had reached the Rappahannock River. The Army of Northern Virginia stood on the other western side of the river, encamped on hills called Marye's Heights above the town of Fredericksburg, Virginia. The Federal army was encamped on the eastern side of the Rappahannock, across the river from Fredericksburg.

On December 11, the Federal cannons opened fire on Fredericksburg. Most of that town's citizens had fled, but the cannons did great damage to buildings. Laying floating bridges (called pontoon boats) across the Rappahannock River, the Federals began to cross into the town. As they passed through Fredericksburg, Federal soldiers destroyed and stole property.

General Burnside's pontoon boats at Fredericksburg

To attack the Confederates, Burnside's army had to climb the long slope of Marye's Heights. The Confederates could fire at the Federals from behind a stone wall at the top of the heights, so when the Federals attacked, they were cut down by Confederate gunfire and artillery fire. The Battle of Fredericksburg was a Confederate victory, but Robert E. Lee did not rejoice. Seeing the thousands of dead on the hills and hearing the cries of the wounded for help, he said: "It is well that war is so terrible, or we should grow too fond of it."

During the winter months of 1863, the Army of the Potomac camped along the banks of the Rappahannock River. The Federal soldiers were discouraged. The weather was cold and rainy, and the roads had turned to mud. After the Battle of Fredericksburg, the soldiers no longer trusted General Burnside. But when spring came, they received news that pleased them. President Lincoln had replaced Burnside with General Joseph Hooker. Called "Fighting Joe," Hooker gave his men confidence. If anyone could beat Bobby Lee, they thought, it was Hooker.

Hooker had 130,000 men, while Lee had only 60,000. Hooker's plan was to divide his army in half and lead one part to attack Lee from behind, while the other part attacked Lee from the front, at Fredericksburg. But General Lee had figured out what Hooker would do and planned a very daring strategy. Lee divided his army as well, even though his army was far smaller than Hooker's to begin with. Lee left 10,000 men to fight at Fredericksburg while he led the rest westward to fight Hooker.

On May 1, 1863, Hooker and his part of the Army of the Potomac crossed the Rappahannock into a thick and tangled forest, called the Wilderness. Hooker set up his headquarters at a large house called Chancellorsville.

Meanwhile, Lee was moving his army against Hooker. Stonewall Jackson, who was with Lee, asked the general to divide his army again. Lee agreed, and Jackson led 26,000 men against Hooker. The Federals did not know of the Confederate plan; so on the evening of May 2, when Jackson attacked the Federal camp, the Federals retreated in confusion.

But Jackson was not satisfied with this small victory. That night he rode out with other officers to find out where the Federals were encamped. When he returned to his own camp, shots rang out; Jackson fell from his horse, shot through his left arm and right hand. In the darkness the Confederates had not known it was Jackson. They shot at what they thought were Yankee soldiers.

Jackson was not dead, but he was too badly wounded to fight. Lee knew that without Jackson the battle would be harder to win, but still he fought on. On May 3, Federals under General Sedgwick drove the Confederates from

Personal items that belonged to Stonewall Jackson

Marye's Heights. But the next day, Lee's men drove Sedgwick back across the Rappahannock River. Lee then reunited his entire army to attack Hooker; but Hooker did not want another defeat. On May 6, he retreated across the Rappahannock. Lee had beaten Fighting Joe.

Both Lee and Hooker lost thousands of men in this Battle of Chancellorsville. But Lee suffered another great loss—Stonewall Jackson. Because of his wounds, Jackson had to have his left arm **amputated.** It seemed he would recover, but then he became very sick. On Sunday, May 10, he died with his beloved wife Anna by his side. Before his death, Jackson opened his eyes one last time, smiled slightly, and said his final words: "Let us cross over the river and rest under the shade of the trees."

amputated: cut off

Gettysburg

The Battle of
Gettysburg

The defeat at Fredericksburg was a great disappointment to Abraham Lincoln. Fighting Joe was not the general Lincoln had hoped for. But whom would he get to replace Hooker? For the time being, Lincoln was stuck with Fighting Joe.

Meanwhile, Lee was again leading his army north. He wanted to go into Pennsylvania, where he could find food to feed his army. Though many of his men wanted to destroy Pennsylvania just as the Federals had destroyed Virginia, Lee said his army had to respect property. If his men took anything to eat or to wear, they had to pay for it. Not all of his men obeyed Lee, but most did.

While Lee marched into Pennsylvania, General Hooker wanted to go south and attack Richmond. But President Lincoln would not allow this. He told Hooker to follow Lee and to destroy his army. Hooker, however, did not remain the commander of the Army of the Potomac. In June, after Lee had crossed the Potomac and taken the town of York, Pennsylvania, Hooker resigned. Lincoln replaced him with General George Meade.

The road to Gettysburg, December 1862– July 1863

Lee did not know exactly where Meade's army was, so he was surprised to learn that Confederates and Federals had begun a small battle in the town of Gettysburg, Pennsylvania. The Confederates had gone to Gettysburg because there was a supply of shoes there. To their surprise, they met Federal cavalry in the town, and a battle began. Soon, other Federal forces came up, but the Confederates were able to drive them out of the town. Then, more Federals arrived and took a position on Culp's Hill and Cemetery Ridge, south of Gettysburg.

**General
George Meade**

Since the battle had already begun, Lee moved his whole army to Gettysburg. Lee saw that the Federals held the hills, and he knew that to defeat the Federals, he had to drive them from those hills. Lee sent General Longstreet to attack the hill called Little Roundtop. The Federals held Little Roundtop, but with only a few men. These were 350 soldiers from Maine under the command of Colonel Joshua Lawrence Chamberlain.

Longstreet sent 3,500 men to attack the Federals on Little Roundtop. Of these, about 700 men from Alabama tried to take the hill. It was a fierce battle, but the Maine men were able to hold off the Confederates. When the Federals ran out of ammunition, Colonel Chamberlain told them to fix bayonets to their guns. He commanded his men to charge the Confederates. They did, and the Confederates were so surprised by this attack that they fled.

Elsewhere, the fighting was fierce and thousands died; but at the end of the day, Lee had been unable to drive the Federals from the hills. The next day Lee planned a daring attack. He would send 13,000 men across a wide, open field to attack the Federals on Cemetery Ridge. This was a dangerous plan, for Federal guns and cannons on Cemetery Ridge could easily cut Lee's men to pieces. But

**Soldiers' National
Cemetery at Gettysburg
National Military Park**

if Lee could drive the Federals from Cemetery Ridge, he could destroy their army.

Lee chose General George E. Pickett of Virginia to lead the charge. Pickett was eager to obey, for he longed to win honor in war. At about one in the afternoon on July 2, 1863, Confederate cannons began firing at the Federals on Cemetery Ridge to destroy as many Federal cannons as possible. The Confederate guns caused much destruction behind Federal lines, and the Federal soldiers were frightened. To calm his men, Federal general Winfield Scott Hancock rode on horseback in front of the lines. When one of his men told Hancock that he should climb down from his horse because he could easily be hit by cannon fire, Hancock bravely replied, "There are times when a corps commander's life does not count."

After about two hours, Pickett received orders to begin his charge. To his 13,000 soldiers he cried, "Up, men, and to your posts! Don't forget today that you are from old Virginia!" Forward they marched from the woods where they had been hidden into the open field. So beautiful was the sight of their red flags waving and their arms glistening in the sun that the Federals were amazed. And Pickett's men kept marching, on and on. It seemed nothing could stop them.

Suddenly, the Federal cannons opened fire, cutting large holes in the Confederate lines; but that did not stop Pickett's Virginians. With perfect discipline and courage they marched on. When they were 200 yards from Cemetery Ridge, all the Federal guns opened fire on them. The brave Confederates fell before the cruel fire. Most never reached the wall behind which the Federals fired, except General Lewis A. Armistead and his men. They fought hand to hand with the Federals, and even broke through their lines; but in the end, Armistead was shot and his men were captured or killed.

So ended Pickett's Charge. Over half the men who set out had been killed or taken prisoner. As Lee watched his shattered army returning, he cried out, "All this has been my fault—it is I who have lost this fight." The next day, July 4, Lee's army retreated in pouring rain. Once again they crossed the Potomac, back into Virginia.

A group of black sailors aboard the USS *Vermont.* The United States Navy employed thousands of freed slaves during the Civil War.

The Victories of Ulysses S. Grant

Gettysburg was not the only bad news the Confederacy received. On July 4, 1863 (the very day Lee retreated from Gettysburg), Vicksburg fell to Generals Grant and Sherman. Vicksburg was the last Confederate fortress on the Mississippi River. Now that this stronghold was in Union hands, the Federals controlled all of the Mississippi. They had also cut off Arkansas, Indian Territory, western Louisiana, and Texas from the rest of the Confederacy.

The victory at Vicksburg, like Gettysburg, gave hope to people in the North that the Union could win the war. Since 1862, things had not been going well for the Federals in the west. The Confederate army had been able to invade Kentucky, and though the Confederates had retreated again to Tennessee, they were not defeated. At the Battle of Murfreesboro, Tennessee, on December 31, 1862, it was unclear who had won: Federal General William Rosecrans could not defeat Confederate General Braxton Bragg, nor could Bragg defeat Rosecrans. Bragg retreated, but Rosecrans did not follow.

For months afterward, General Rosecrans did nothing to defeat Bragg. Like McClellan, "Old Rosy" (as Rosecrans's men called him) said he needed more men and supplies. Finally, in June 1863, when Rosecrans learned that Lincoln was thinking of removing him as

Federal troops march into Vicksburg, Mississippi.

general, he began driving Bragg and the Confederates southward, through Chattanooga.

The Confederate president, Jefferson Davis, worried about the situation in the west, and sent General Longstreet and 12,000 men from Lee's army to Bragg's. On September 20, 1863, Bragg attacked Rosecrans on the Chickamauga Creek in southern Tennessee. General Longstreet broke through Rosecrans's lines of men and forced the Federals to run. Were it not for the bravery of Federal General George Henry "Pap" Thomas, who kept the Union lines from breaking, Longstreet and Bragg might have destroyed the Federal army.

Union infantry practice forming for an assault. During the assault on Missionary Ridge, Tennessee, in 1863, these troops struck the center of the Confederate line.

Longstreet thought that if Bragg had attacked the Federal army again after the Battle of Chickamauga, he might have destroyed Old Rosy's army. Bragg did nothing, which made Longstreet ask President Davis to remove Bragg from command. Yet Davis, who visited the western army, decided to keep Bragg as general—which was a great mistake.

Lincoln, too, was not pleased with his general, Rosecrans; he made U.S. Grant general over all the armies in the West. When Grant came to Chattanooga, he saw that Bragg's army held a strong position on some hills called Missionary Ridge, east of Chattanooga. Though it was dangerous, Grant ordered an attack against Missionary Ridge on November 24. General Hooker, who was fighting under Grant, attacked Lookout Mountain, where the Confederates had many cannons. The mountain was covered with thick fog, but Hooker led his men up its slopes. In this Battle Above the Clouds, Hooker drove the Confederates from the mountain and took their cannons.

The next day, General Pap Thomas attacked the Confederates in the center of Missionary Ridge, where the Confederates had dug trenches from which they fired at the Federals. Thomas was able to drive the Confederates from the first line of these trenches, but then he stopped to await more orders from General Grant. While Thomas waited, one of his generals, Philip Sheridan, the son of immigrants from Ireland, pulled out a flask of whiskey and drank a toast to the Confederates. "Here's at you," he shouted to them. The Confederates answered the toast by firing their cannons. This angered Sheridan, and he cried, "*That* was ungenerous! I'll take your guns for that!"

Without orders from anyone, Sheridan and his men began climbing Missionary Ridge. Though Confederates were firing guns and

The Gettysburg Address

Four score and seven years ago our fathers brought forth, upon this continent, a new nation, conceived in Liberty, and dedicated to the proposition that all men are created equal.

Now we are engaged in a great civil war, testing whether that nation, or any nation so conceived, and so dedicated, can long endure. We are met here on a great battlefield of that war. We have come to dedicate a portion of it as a final resting place for those who here gave their lives that that nation might live. It is altogether fitting and proper that we should do this.

But in a larger sense we can not dedicate—we can not consecrate—we can not hallow this ground. The brave men, living and dead, who struggled, here, have consecrated it far above our poor power to add or detract. The world will little note, nor long remember, what we say here, but can never forget what they did here. It is for us, the living, rather to be dedicated here to the unfinished work which they have, thus far, so nobly carried on. It is rather for us to be here dedicated to the great task remaining before us—that from these honored dead we take increased devotion to that cause for which they here gave the last full measure of devotion—that we here highly resolve that these dead shall not have died in vain; that this nation shall have a new birth of freedom; and that this government of the people, by the people, for the people, shall not perish from the earth.

cannons at them, the Federals kept coming. So unstoppable were Sheridan and his men that the Confederates turned and fled. Sheridan had taken Missionary Ridge, and Grant now controlled the town of Chattanooga.

Lincoln at Gettysburg

Five days before the Battle of Missionary Ridge, Abraham Lincoln came to Gettysburg. A cemetery had been placed on the battlefield to honor the Federal soldiers who had fallen there. Lincoln had come to dedicate the cemetery and, for the occasion, had penned a short speech. On November 19, 1863, he delivered what has gone down in history as a masterpiece—the Gettysburg Address.

The Last Year of the War

Lincoln Finds His General

Though General Meade had stopped Robert E. Lee at the Battle of Gettysburg, he was not the man to chase the Army of Northern Virginia and defeat it. Lincoln had had many generals in command of the Army of the Potomac, and all of them had been disappointments. There had been McClellan, Pope, Burnside, Hooker, and Meade. Would the president be able to find a general who could do any better than they had done?

After the Battle of Missionary Ridge, Lincoln believed he had found the right man. In March 1864, Ulysses S. Grant came to Washington to command not only the Army of the Potomac, but all the armies of the United States. Grant had new plans for

> General Grant leads his troops during the Battle of the Wilderness in 1864.

battle and even a new name for the army. After Grant took command, the Army of the Potomac became known as the Grand Army of the Republic.

Grant had a grand plan. In the West, General William Tecumseh Sherman and his army would march through Georgia and to the sea. At the same time, in the East, General Franz Sigel would invade the Shenandoah Valley of Virginia, where much of the food for the Confederate army was grown. Finally, Grant would lead 110,000 men south to Richmond.

In early May 1864, Grant and the Grand Army of the Republic (110,000 strong) marched from Brandy Station, Virginia, in pursuit of General Lee. Lee and his ragged, hungry army were encamped in a place called the Wilderness outside of Chancellorsville, where the Confederates had defeated Hooker and Stonewall Jackson had lost his life. Lee had only 60,000 men.

On May 5, Grant's army attacked Lee's men in the Wilderness. It was a hard-fought battle. There were so many trees, and the smoke from guns and cannons was so thick, that soldiers fired on their own men instead of the enemy. On the second day of the battle, Federals broke through the center of the Confederate army. Lee was worried, but General John Gregg from Texas led his men to drive the Federals back. Lee rode to the front to lead General John Gregg and his Texans against the Federals.

"Attention, Texas brigade," shouted Gregg. "The eyes of General Lee are upon you, forward march!" But when the Texans saw that Lee intended to lead them and to risk his life, they cried "Lee to the rear!"

Hearing the men's cry, Lee, after much hesitation, agreed to go to the rear of the battle. Standing up in his stirrups, he took off his hat, and exclaimed to the troops, "Texans *always* move them." When the Texans heard Lee's words, they sent up a fierce yell. One man, weeping, declared, "I would charge hell itself for that old man." The Texans did charge and drove the Federals back.

Lee defeated Grant at the Battle of the Wilderness. But unlike other Federal generals, Grant did not retreat. He knew he had far more men than Lee, and so he just pushed south around Lee's army. Lee knew this was Grant's plan, so he too moved his army south. He wanted to keep between Grant and Richmond.

Grant next attacked Lee on May 12, at Spotsylvania Courthouse. Confederates and Federals fought at a place called the Bloody Angle. For hours, until midnight, the men fought, but no one was victorious; 12,000 men died. Grant again had not destroyed Lee. But instead of retreating, Grant moved his army south once more.

Lee again kept ahead of Grant. On June 3, the two armies clashed at Cold Harbor on the Chickahominy River, only a few miles from Richmond. The battle was brutal and bloody. In the first eight miutes of fighting, about 7,000 Federals were killed. Cold Harbor was the third time Lee had defeated Grant. Indeed, in one month of fighting, Grant had lost 50,000 men; but the North had more men to send to the Grand Army of the Republic, and Grant again moved south.

But Grant did not attack Richmond, as Lee thought he would. Instead, he marched against Petersburg. This was a smart move, for a railroad ran through Petersburg on which trains brought food to Richmond. If Grant could take Petersburg, he could keep food from getting to Richmond and so starve the city until it surrendered.

Lee, however, beat Grant to Petersburg, digging trenches around the city from which his men could fire at the Federals. For the next nine months, the Grand Army of the Republic camped in front of Richmond, trying to find a way to break through Lee's lines.

The Battle of Cold Harbor

Union troops at a Confederate fort near Atlanta that was captured by General Sherman's armies in 1864. General Sherman is in the background.

Sherman Marches to the Sea

While Lee and Grant were fighting in Virginia, Federal general Sherman with his three armies, totalling 112,000 men, was pushing into Georgia. Sherman's goal was to take the city of Atlanta, Georgia—an important city, because it had factories that manufactured many things for the Confederacy. The only thing that kept Sherman from marching directly to Atlanta was General Joe Johnston and the Confederate army. But Johnston never attacked Sherman, and Sherman kept pushing Johnston closer and closer to Atlanta.

After about two months of this sort of warfare, President Jefferson Davis grew tired of Johnston's fighting strategy. Davis wanted a general who would boldly attack the enemy and destroy his army. So it was that on July 17 he replaced Johnston with General John Bell Hood. Though Hood had lost one leg and the use of one

General Sherman orders all civilians to leave Atlanta.

arm in battle, he was a fighter. Unfortunately, however, he was not a very good general.

Hood attacked Sherman on July 20, 1864, at Peachtree Creek near Atlanta, but Sherman's men drove the Confederates back. Two days later, Sherman again defeated Hood in the Battle of Atlanta. The final battle at Ezra Church was yet another defeat for Hood. For a month, the Confederates were in Atlanta, surrounded by the Federal army. Finally, thinking he could not save both the army and the city, Hood abandoned Atlanta. On September 2, Sherman and the Federal army marched triumphantly into the city.

William T. Sherman orders the destruction of railroads and buildings during the march to the sea.

General Sherman wanted to punish the people of the South, so they would never again rebel against the Union. In September he said that all the civilians had to leave Atlanta; when the civilians had gone, Sherman ordered his men to burn down one-third of the city. On his march from Atlanta to the sea, Sherman would be harsher still. On that march, Sherman's troops destroyed everything in their path. Wherever Sherman's men passed, they destroyed fields and burned houses. The soldiers destroyed the property of both whites and blacks, rich and poor. Scores of black men, women, and children followed Sherman's army, for they hoped to be set free.

Sherman had no Confederate general to stop him; General Hood had gone into Tennessee, hoping that Sherman would follow him. Near Nashville, Tennessee, General Pap Thomas fought Hood's army and destroyed it on December 5, 1864. Meanwhile, Sherman continued on to the sea. On December 21, he reached Savannah, Georgia, a port city. Sherman had conquered Georgia from the Tennessee border to the Atlantic Ocean.

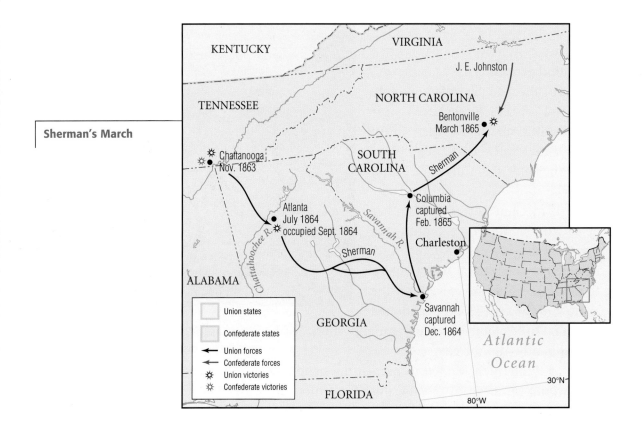

Sherman's March

Into South Carolina

Even though winter rains had turned the dirt roads to mud, General Sherman was determined not to remain in Savannah for the winter. He had punished Georgia for rebelling against the United States, and he now wanted to do the same thing to South Carolina. The tireless Sherman ordered his men to cut down forests of trees. Using the tree trunks, they built roads on which they could march into South Carolina.

As in Georgia, Sherman and his army destroyed the areas of South Carolina through which they marched. After all, they thought, South Carolina was especially guilty, because it had been the first state to secede from the Union. On February 17, Sherman captured Columbia, South Carolina—the state capital. Like Atlanta, Columbia was set on fire. Sherman blamed the fire on the Confederates who had retreated from the city, but Columbia citizens blamed Sherman's soldiers.

On the same day that Sherman captured Columbia, the Confederacy suffered another loss. The Federal navy took Fort Sumter. Now even Charleston, South Carolina, was under Federal control.

From Columbia Sherman began his march into North Carolina—he was on his way to Virginia to join Grant. A small army of Confederates under the command of General Johnston tried to stop Sherman. At Bentonville, North Carolina, Johnston attacked Sherman. The battle lasted three days; but at the end of it Johnston and his army retreated. Sherman once again was victorious.

Surrender at Appomattox

Only Robert E. Lee and the Army of Northern Virginia lay between Lincoln and complete victory. But Lee's army was shrinking day by day; many of his soldiers were leaving and returning home. It would not be long before General Grant learned just how small and weak Lee's army had become.

That day came on April 2, 1865. In the early morning, Grant's army attacked Lee's trenches. Though the Confederates fought bravely, they could not stand up against the Federals. Some of the Confederate defenders were old men; others were boys as young as 14. Only a few hours after the attack, General Lee sent a message to President Davis in Richmond. "Richmond must be evacuated this evening," said the note.

General Robert E. Lee surrenders to General Grant at Appomatox.

That evening, the Confederate president and Congress left Richmond by train. As Confederate soldiers left Richmond, they set fire to the city. When the Federal army entered Richmond the next day, April 3, they found many smoking ruins instead of buildings.

Meanwhile, Lee's army had left Petersburg and marched south-westward along the Appomattox River toward the Appalachian Mountains. Lee hoped he could escape Grant's army and make it to North Carolina, where he could join up with Joe Johnston's army. For several days, Federal forces attacked Lee's army. Lee hoped he could reach Appomattox Court House before Grant did, for there he could find food and arms for his men.

But General Sheridan beat Lee to Appomattox and seized the supplies. Though surrounded by the Federal army, Lee thought he would try one more time to escape. On April 9, Lee attacked Sheridan's lines and broke through them. But beyond, he saw thousands upon thousands of Federals. Lee knew he could not fight his way through them all.

"There is nothing left for me to do but go and see General Grant," said Lee, "and I would rather die a thousand deaths." A messenger carrying a white flag delivered Lee's note to Grant. When Grant read it, one of his men jumped up on a log and called for three cheers. A few cheered, but the rest broke down in tears. The horrible war, it seemed, would soon be over.

Grant and Lee met at a house at Appomattox. Lee was dressed in his dress uniform; Grant wore a dirty shirt and pants, and his boots were spattered with mud. Lee showed great dignity, and Grant was kind. Grant said Lee's men could keep their personal weapons and their horses. He also declared that they could return home, and that he would provide food for Lee's hungry men. Lee surrendered to Grant; the two generals then stood and shook hands. When Lee returned to his men, various Federal soldiers began to cheer, but Grant angrily stopped them. The Confederates are again "our countrymen," said Grant. "We do not want to exult over their downfall."

Lee was extremely sad. But when he rode into his camp and heard his weary, ragged men cheer for him as he passed, the general lifted his head, removed his hat in salute to his men, and rode by them with eyes ablaze. Some of his men reached out to touch the sides of Lee's horse, while others broke into tears. One old man declared what all the men felt: "I love you just as well as ever, General," he cried.

Good Friday at Ford's Theater

When news reached Washington that Lee had surrendered, there were fireworks and much rejoicing. No one was happier than Abraham Lincoln. He could now begin to rebuild the nation. Lincoln said he did not want to punish the southern states, but to receive them back into the Union as equals. He hoped the nation would learn to forget the bitterness of the Civil War.

John Wilkes Booth shoots President Abraham Lincoln as he watches a play at Ford's Theater in Washington, D.C, in 1865.

But Lincoln had enemies in Washington. Their leader was a man named John Wilkes Booth, a famous stage actor of the time. Booth believed in the southern cause and hoped that if he could get rid of Lincoln and General Grant, the South could have another chance to win the war. It was Good Friday, April 14, 1865. Booth learned that President and Mrs. Lincoln, with General and Mrs. Grant, were going to Ford's Theater to watch a play that night. Because he was an actor, Booth could get into the backstage. From there he could find his way to the theater box where the Lincolns and Grants would be watching the play.

Though the Lincolns attended the play, the Grants were unable to attend. The play that night at Ford's Theater was a comedy. While the Lincolns and the rest of the audience enjoyed the play, John Wilkes Booth arrived at the theater. He climbed the steps to the president's box and waited. In Booth's hands were a small pistol (called a derringer) and a dagger.

Booth waited for the audience to burst out laughing; then he jumped into Lincoln's box. At close range, Booth shot Lincoln in the back of the head and slashed at someone else with his dagger. Then, while leaping from the box to the stage below, Booth broke his left leg. Waving his dagger, the assassin cried out to the astonished audience, *"Sic semper tyrannis!"* ("Thus ever to tyrants!") Then, stumbling offstage, he mounted his horse and rode away. Federal troops caught up with Booth more than a week later (April 26) at a barn in Virginia where he was hiding. It is not clear whether Booth attempted to surrender or not, but he was shot by one of the soldiers and soon died. Officials buried his body under the penitentiary in Washington, D.C.

The injured Lincoln was carried off to a nearby house. There he lay, noticing nothing and no one around him. He did not live long. The following morning—April 15, 1865—Abraham Lincoln died.

The War's End

Though Robert E. Lee had surrendered, other Confederate generals had not. President Davis, too, had not yet been captured, but he continued to flee south. He hoped he could reach Texas and there continue the war for southern independence. But that was not to be. On May 10, Federal cavalry captured Jefferson Davis in Irwinville, Georgia. The Federals imprisoned the Confederate president at Fortress Monroe.

General Joe Johnston surrendered his army on April 17 to General Sherman. Like General Grant, Sherman was kind and generous to Johnston and his men. They could return to their homes in peace.

But in Texas, citizens decided not to surrender. They called meetings to encourage men to sign up for the army. On May 13, Federals and Confederates fought a battle at Palmito Ranch, near Brownsville, Texas. The Confederates beat the Federals, but it was the last victory for the South. Indeed, it was the last battle of the war. Thirteen days later, the Confederate army in western Louisiana and Texas surrendered to the Federals.

More than 558,000 soldiers on both sides, or 2 percent of the total U.S. population, were killed during the four years of the war. The long, bloody conflict was finally over.

Chapter 17 Review

Summary

- The Federal army slowly progressed southward against the Confederate troops. Stonewall Jackson, the Confederate leader, was killed at the Battle of Chancellorsville, along with thousands of men on both the Union and Confederate sides. Robert E. Lee made one last push into the North and marched into Pennsylvania. A great battle took place at Gettysburg, Pennsylvania, in which Lee's whole army faced the northern forces. Thousands and thousands of troops on both sides were killed; but in the end, the North was victorious. Lee's Army of Northern Virginia retreated into Virginia. Abraham Lincoln made his now-famous Gettysburg Address at the dedication of the cemetery at the battlefield of Gettysburg.

- The U.S. army, under the leadership of Ulysses S. Grant and William Sherman, continued to have victories in the South. Grant planned for Sherman to take the army to the southwest and move eastward across the South. At the same time, Grant would press his forces from the north to the south, thus forcing the Confederacy to fight the war on two fronts. This plan was very successful. Sherman's "March to the Sea" was disastrous for the South; Sherman burned and destroyed everything in his path, including the cities of Atlanta, Georgia, and Columbia, South Carolina. Grant pursued Lee's army into the South, and despite a few victories of Lee over Grant, the Union army was too powerful for Lee's ragged men to defeat. When Lee surrendered to Grant at Appomattox in April 1865, everyone knew the war was essentially over.

- A Southern sympathizer, John Wilkes Booth, assassinated President Abraham Lincoln at Ford's Theater on April 14, 1865. Lincoln and his wife were attending a play at the theater when Booth entered the president's theater box and shot him at close range. Shouting, *"Sic semper tyrannis!"* the assassin escaped, only to be caught a week later and killed. The president died from his gunshot wound on April 15, 1865.

Chapter Checkpoint

1. At what battle did Stonewall Jackson receive the wound from which he died?
2. List three reasons that the Battle of Gettysburg was important.
3. How did Ulysses S. Grant change the course of the war?
4. What was Sherman's March to the Sea? Why did Sherman act so harshly?
5. Where and when did Robert E. Lee surrender to Ulysses S. Grant?
6. Describe the assassination of President Lincoln: Who? Why? When? Where? How?

Chapter Activities

1. Memorize and recite the Gettysburg Address.
2. Consider the actions of Robert Lee and Ulysses Grant at the surrender at Appomattox. How would you have felt if you were a Confederate soldier? A Union soldier? How would you have felt as a commander, and how would you have acted?

The American Larder

Coffee and tea, both imported goods, were expensive and scarce on the frontier—especially so during the Civil War. The coffee and tea had to be carried by packhorse to the interior from the ports. Because coffee and tea were so expensive and rare, all sorts of substitutes were used. In place of real tea, mint, chamomile, sassafras, birch bark, and spice bark were used as herbal drinks. In place of coffee, roasted chicory roots and corn, burned bread crumbs, peas, and locust tree seeds were baked and used instead. These beverages, along with homemade cider and lemonade, were the usual drinks of nineteenth-century Americans. Milk was not considered a healthy drink; it was stored in open wooden containers and was probably highly contaminated with bacteria. Glass bottles for milk were not made until the 1880s. In that same decade, Louis Pasteur discovered that heating milk (pasteurization) would destroy harmful bacteria. After the 1880s, milk became a very popular American drink.

Chapter 18   The Wild West

Big Changes After the War

Changes in the South

The United States after the Civil War were, in many ways, very different from what they had been before the war. For one thing, Congress declared all slaves free, not only those in the former Confederate States. Secondly, the South had been a very powerful and important part of the country. After the war, the South was defeated and crushed. Even though Andrew Johnson (who became president after Lincoln) wanted the southern states to enter the Union again, many Republicans in Congress opposed this. These Radical Republicans, as they were called, wanted to protect the newly freed black people from any kind of ill treatment shown them by whites. They wanted to make sure that new state governments protected blacks and whites equally, and that black people had the right to vote in the South.

Freedmen voting in New Orleans

Some white people in the South were cruel to blacks after the war. These whites were afraid that blacks would end up in control of the southern states and harm whites. Many thought this because Congress allowed only blacks, and not whites who had fought for the South, to vote. When Congress eventually allowed some southern states back into the Union, blacks took control of the government and black representatives were sent to Washington, D.C. Many whites in the South did not like having their former slaves rule over them.

To keep blacks from voting, and to prevent them from exacting vengeance on their former masters, some southern whites formed secret groups like the Knights of the White Camelia and the Ku Klux Klan. Dressed in white sheets and wearing white masks, members of these groups rode out to black settlements at night to frighten blacks. In many cases, these white-sheeted men beat up and even killed black people.

To protect blacks, federal troops were kept in the South after the war to guard against violence from white people. The federal government formed the Freedman's Bureau to teach blacks how to read and do arithmetic so they could function as citizens. The Bureau also distributed food to both black and white Southerners. To

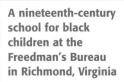

A nineteenth-century school for black children at the Freedman's Bureau in Richmond, Virginia

protect black citizens, Congress passed two amendments to the Constitution: one said that black people have the same rights as white people, and the other gave black people the right to vote. When these amendments were approved by most of the states, they became part of the Constitution.

Yet southern whites suffered greatly after the war. The Radical Republicans passed laws to punish them for fighting against the Union. Many Southerners were poor and hungry and were not treated justly—such as not having the right to vote. Many white people from the North came to the South to take advantage of the misfortunes of white Southerners. These Northerners were called "carpetbaggers,"

A political cartoon depicts a woman as the South being crushed under the weight of the carpet-bagger, who is pro-tected by federal military support.

because they came south with all their belongings in a bag made from two pieces of carpet. The carpetbaggers bought up southern plantations and other property that white Southerners were too poor to hold onto. Carpetbaggers could vote and serve in government when many white Southerners could not. White Southerners were treated like foreigners in their own land.

But Radical Republicans in Congress could not control the South forever. Eventually, southern whites gained control of their state governments. Former Confederate officers even became governors of states. At first, this did not mean that southern blacks lost all their rights. For many years, many blacks in the South continued to vote; some even served in state legislatures. (P. B. S. Pinchback, the son of a white planter and a freed slave, served as governor of Louisiana for a month in 1872–73.) But, eventually, this would change, and once again blacks (both in the South and the North) suffered from great injustices.

The Homestead Act motivated people, like the family shown here in Custer County, Nebraska, to leave the East and settle in frontier country.

Homesteaders and Cowboys

In 1862, during the Civil War, Congress passed an important law called the Homestead Act. This act gave settlers 160 acres of land if they paid a small fee and lived on that land for five years. Because of the Homestead Act, many settlers began moving out into the Great Plains after the war. There they set up farms, where they grew grains such as wheat and corn.

Many settlers traveled to these new lands by wagons, on horseback, or by foot. But another act passed by Congress in 1862 gave settlers another way of traveling: the railroad. There were already many railroads in the eastern United States, especially in the North. But in the 1862 law, Congress said that a railroad should be built, stretching from the Mississippi River to the Pacific Ocean.

On May 10, 1869, at Promontory Point, Utah, the last spike is driven into the ground, connecting the Union Pacific and Central Pacific railroads.

The railroad was built in two parts. One part, called the Central Pacific, began in Sacramento, California, and crossed the Sierra Nevada mountain range into the deserts of the Great Basin. The other part, called the Union Pacific, began in Omaha, Nebraska, and crossed the Great Plains and the Rocky Mountains. The two railroads met on May 10, 1869, at Promontory Point, near Salt Lake City, Utah. There, railroad officials and workers drove a golden spike into the ground to mark the completion of the first railroad to connect the eastern United States with the Pacific coast.

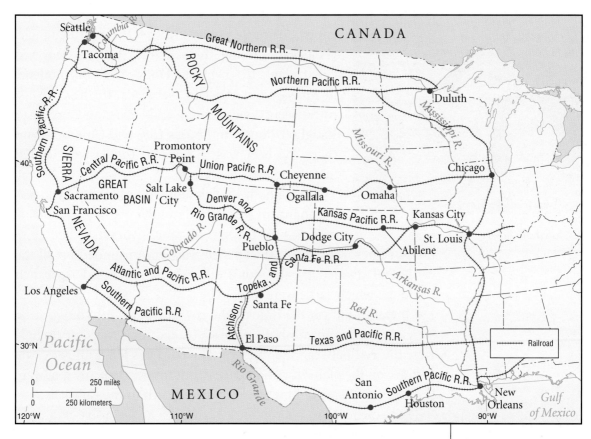

Railroad routes across the western United States

With the completion of this railroad, many settlers rode on trains to their new homesteads. Congress gave the railroad companies thousands of acres, some of which in turn were sold to the settlers. On account of the **transcontinental** railroad, and other railroads built soon after, many parts of the Great Plains filled up with settlers and new towns.

Railroads also made it possible for western ranches to get their cattle to markets in midwestern and eastern cities. The Spanish had brought longhorn cattle to Texas in the 1700s. When the Spanish left Texas, the herds of longhorns remained and wandered the wide plains. The Confederate soldiers who returned to Texas after the war began herding the longhorns, and soon west Texas was divided into

transcontinental: stretching across the continent

A longhorn steer

enormous cattle ranches. To sell their cattle, ranchers began driving them across the grass-covered Great Plains to towns like Dodge City and Abilene, in Kansas, and Ogallala, Nebraska. In these towns, cattle were loaded onto train cars and taken to slaughter houses in Kansas City and Chicago; from there the beef was shipped to the eastern United States and even to Europe.

Throughout the fall and winter, enormous herds of longhorns were left to wander over the vast plains of Texas. In the spring, ranch workers called cowboys or buckaroos (from the Spanish *vaqueros*) rounded up all the cattle and divided them among the various ranches. Each ranch could tell which cattle were its own by a mark they had made with a hot metal brand on the hide of the cows or bulls. All young cattle were branded, and motherless calves (called mavericks, or dogies) were divided between the ranches. The cowboys left younger cattle to graze on the plains for another year, but rounded up any that were three or four years old for the long drive north to the railroads.

Every cattle drive had about 12 cowboys and a horse wrangler, who managed their horses. These cowboys, who drove their cattle (about 2,500 longhorns) over 1,200 miles of rich grassland, lived

Cowboys herd longhorn cattle.

a hard life. Under his broad-rimmed *sombrero* (Spanish for "hat"), the cowboy had to ride around the herd day and night to guard it from various dangers, which included prairie fires and **stampedes.** Rustlers (men who stole cattle) also endangered the herd, as did wild Indians. Only when the herd finally reached the "cow towns," where the cattle were taken onto the trains, did the cowboy get any rest.

stampedes: sudden headlong rushes of startled animals

But when more and more settlers began farming the Great Plains, it became harder for cowboys to have cattle drives. Settlers, who did not like large herds of cattle crossing through their fields, put up barbed-wire fences to keep them out. Moreover, since the number of railroads had increased, ranchers did not have to drive their cattle as far to ship them by train. A harsh winter in 1886–87 (when thousands of head of cattle froze to death) and the loss of good pasture for so many cattle on the plains also took their toll. So the great cattle drives of the West came to an end.

Indian Wars on the Great Plains

Troubles in Montana

The building of railroads soon brought on trouble with the Indians of the Great Plains. The Union Pacific Railroad had to run across lands on which the Plains Indians hunted buffalo. The United States government did not simply take Plains Indians' lands; they made peace treaties with the Indians. If the Indians agreed to give up some of their lands, the United States promised them other lands in return. The government promised that it would never take these lands, called reservations, away from the Indians.

Even before the Union Pacific was built, the United States was having trouble with the Indians. Gold had been discovered in Montana, and miners and settlers, following the Bozeman trail, were trespassing on Indian Lands to get to the gold fields. To protect the

Oglala Sioux warriors on horseback

Chief Sitting Bull of the Sioux tribe

miners and travelers from Indians, the U.S. army built forts on the Bozeman Trail. Red Cloud, chief of the Oglala Sioux, wanted to protect Indian hunting grounds, and he began attacking Bozeman Trail forts.

To stop the building of the forts, the Sioux attacked groups of workmen carrying timber along the Bozeman Trail. In the cold December of 1866, army Colonel Henry Carrington ordered Captain William Fetterman to guard some workmen transporting timber. Carrington told Fetterman to fight the Indians if they attacked, but not to chase them if they rode away. But Fetterman did not obey. After driving off some Sioux from the "wood train" he was guarding, Fetterman and his 80 men chased them. After crossing a ridge, Fetterman and his men were attacked by a large force of Indians. Hearing gunshots, Colonel Carrington sent some cavalry to find out what was happening. Crossing the ridge, they found Fetterman and his men. All were dead. The Sioux had massacred them.

After the Fetterman massacre, the United States government began wondering what to do about the Sioux. A Jesuit priest named Pierre-Jean De Smet, from Belgium, thought he had the answer. The United States government, wrote Father De Smet, had not treated the Sioux and other Indians justly. Many government agents had been greedy and dishonest and had cheated the Indians. The government, said De Smet, should use only honest agents and keep its promises to the Indians.

In 1868, when the U.S. government decided to call a peace conference with the Sioux, it asked Father De Smet to attend, for the Indians trusted him. Father De Smet then began a lonely journey on foot across the Great Plains to Fort Laramie, Wyoming, where the peace conference was to be held.

When he arrived at the camp of 5,000 Sioux, the Indians welcomed him. There Father De Smet met with the Sioux chiefs Sitting Bull, Four Horns, Black Moon, and No Neck and convinced them to attend the peace conference.

The peace conference seemed to be a success. The United States government agreed to give the Sioux thousands of acres surrounding the Black Hills in the Dakota Territory. The Black Hills were a sacred place to the Sioux. The government also promised to give the Indians food and clothing each year and to build schools for Indian children. No white man was allowed to settle on Indian land. In return for all this, the Indians agreed to allow the government to build railroads over the lands that lay outside Indian lands.

The government made similar agreements with other tribes. Finally, it seemed, peace would reign between the white man and the Indians.

Black Robe

The United States government would likely not have made peace with the Sioux without the help of Father De Smet. Who was this priest, and why did the Indians trust him so much?

As a young boy in Belgium, Pierre-Jean De Smet had attended a school where young men were trained to become priests. At that school, Pierre-Jean heard stories told by a missionary priest named Charles Nerinckx. Father Nerinckx told of his own work to bring Christ to people in a far-off and wild land called Kentucky. These people, said Father Nerinckx, lived in tribes that wandered and hunted in ancient forests. They were a noble people, but they were also savage and cruel. Pierre-Jean listened to these stories and decided that he, too, wanted to go to Kentucky as Father Nerinckx had done and bring the Gospel to men who had never before heard it.

Pierre-Jean De Smet came to America in 1821. He joined the Jesuits in Whitemarch, Maryland, but after

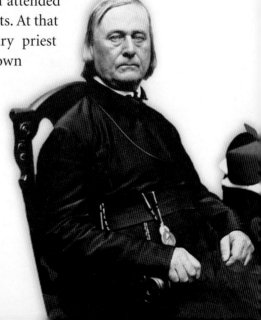

Father Pierre-Jean De Smet

two years he was sent to help set up a new Jesuit house near St. Louis, Missouri. There he was ordained a priest in 1829. Two years later, some Indians from the far West arrived in St. Louis looking for "blackrobes." Some Iroquois Indians who had gone to live in the West told these western Indians about priests in black robes who had taught the Iroquois about Christ in the far-off years when France ruled in the New World. Now, these western Indians wanted a blackrobe to return with them to teach their people.

At first the Jesuits said they had no priests to send. But when more and more Indians came to St. Louis asking for help, the Jesuits finally agreed to send Father De Smet to them. Father De Smet had been working in the area around Council Bluffs, Iowa, where he had taught the tribes not only the Gospel, but also how to farm. In 1839, he set out to do the same good work with the Indians of the Rocky Mountains.

Over the next several years, Father De Smet set up missions among Indians in the Rocky Mountains in what are now Montana and Idaho. He also traveled into Oregon and founded a mission among the Kalispel people; he made peace between the Blackfoot and Crow tribes, and he visited other tribes on the Great Plains. In 1851, De Smet helped to bring about peace between the United States government and the Sioux, Shoshone, Assiniboine, Crow, Arikara, Pawnee, and other tribes.

But this peace did not last long. In 1862, the Sioux in Minnesota went on the warpath because the government did not keep the treaty it had signed with the Indians. The Sioux suffered terribly from hunger. They attacked white settlements in Minnesota, torturing and killing men, women and children. The government, not knowing what to do about the Indian attacks, asked Father De Smet to try to convince the Sioux to stop their murderous war.

De Smet came to Fort Berthold in Dakota Territory near where the Sioux had gathered. When Father De Smet said he would go alone to speak with the Sioux, those in the fort were surprised and fearful. Surely the Sioux would kill this foolish priest. But fearing nothing, De Smet went out to the Indians, who received him with love and respect. After three hours with the Indians, De Smet returned to the fort unharmed.

Though De Smet could have brought about peace, the government wanted only to punish the Sioux. The army finally drove the Sioux out of Minnesota. On Christmas Day of 1862, near Mankato, Minnesota, 38 Sioux warriors were executed.

On the Warpath Again

The peace De Smet helped make between the Indians and the United States government in 1868 did not last long. In a few short years, several Plains tribes were again on the warpath.

The problem was the railroads. The noisy train engines, **belching** steam and smoke, scared away the buffalo that the Plains Indians hunted for food. The Indians lived on buffalo meat and used buffalo skins for clothing and shelter. Though Indians killed buffalo by the hundreds, chasing herds over cliffs, the number of buffalo had not gone down very much. There were too few Indians to accomplish that. But with the railroads, white hunters from the East came and began killing the buffalo by the thousands. Sometimes hunters shot down the buffalos from the windows of trains and simply left them to rot.

Seeing that the number of buffalos was decreasing, tribes on the southern plains went on the warpath. The Arapaho, Cheyenne, Comanche, and Kiowa were able for a time to stop settlers from crossing the plains. The Civil War Union general Philip Sheridan led the fight against these tribes. In it, cavalry colonel George Armstrong Custer won a great victory, killing Indian chief Black Kettle and many of his warriors. Though a fierce fighter, Custer was not cruel like other army commanders, such as Colonel E. M. Baker who, in 1870, attacked an Indian village, killing 173 Indian men, women, and children.

Though many Americans wanted the government just to kill off the Indians, others wanted to help them become part of American society. Ulysses S. Grant, who had become president

belching: gushing or expelling noisily from within

General George Armstrong Custer

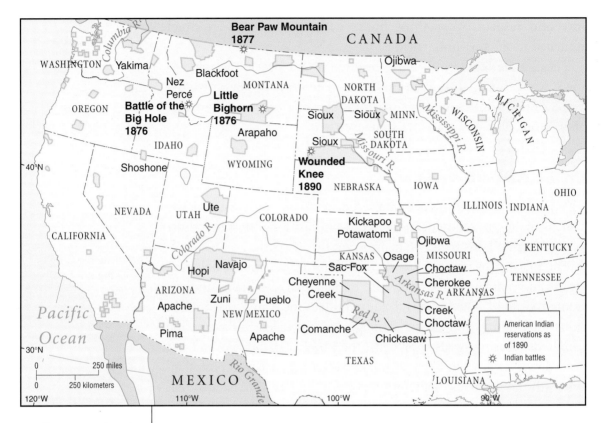

Map labels: Bear Paw Mountain 1877, CANADA, Ojibwa, WASHINGTON, Yakima, Blackfoot, Columbia R., Nez Percé, MONTANA, Little Bighorn 1876, NORTH DAKOTA, Sioux, Sioux, MINN., MICHIGAN, WISCONSIN, Mississippi R., OREGON, Battle of the Big Hole 1876, Arapaho, Sioux, SOUTH DAKOTA, Missouri R., IDAHO, WYOMING, Wounded Knee 1890, NEBRASKA, IOWA, OHIO, 40°N, Shoshone, ILLINOIS, INDIANA, NEVADA, UTAH, Ute, COLORADO, Kickapoo, Potawatomi, Ojibwa, MISSOURI, KENTUCKY, Colorado R., CALIFORNIA, KANSAS, Osage, Choctaw, Sac-Fox, Cherokee, TENNESSEE, Hopi, Navajo, Cheyenne, Arkansas R., ARKANSAS, ARIZONA, Zuni, Pueblo, Creek, Creek, Apache, NEW MEXICO, Red R., Choctaw, Pacific Ocean, Pima, Apache, Comanche, Chickasaw, 30°N, TEXAS, 0 / 250 miles, 0 / 250 kilometers, Rio Grande, MEXICO, LOUISIANA, 120°W, 110°W, 100°W, 90°W

Legend: American Indian reservations as of 1890; ☀ Indian battles

Indian reservations in Montana in 1890 and battle sites of the Indian Wars

of the United States in 1869, was willing to use the army against the Indian tribes, if necessary. But he also wanted to help the Indians. President Grant wanted to form reservations for the Indians where they could go to school and learn how to become farmers and citizens. Christian ministers, not government agents, were to direct these reservations.

Father De Smet welcomed the president's plan. The priest hoped that Catholic priests would be allowed to serve Catholic Indians, to teach them the Faith and help them form farming settlements. But De Smet was disappointed. The government appointed 43 ministers to take over the reservations, but most were Protestant. Only four were Catholic priests. With this sadness, but full of faith, Father De Smet died on May 23, 1873.

Blood on the Little Bighorn

Peace between the United States and the Sioux came to an end after only a few short years. Gold had been discovered in the Black Hills, and hundreds of miners went there to search for the precious metal. But the government had given the Black Hills to the Sioux, and so the miners were disobeying the law. Nonetheless, many began to demand that the government open up the Black Hills for prospecting. In 1875, the government offered the Sioux money in exchange for the Black Hills. Though the Black Hills were sacred to the Indians, several Sioux chiefs agreed to sell them to the United States.

Chief Crazy Horse

But some Sioux were not willing to sell their holy lands. These Sioux joined Sitting Bull and Crazy Horse, who refused to give up the Black Hills. But the United States government was determined, and General Philip Sheridan said that those Indians who did not agree to sell these lands were the enemies of the United States.

Sheridan prepared to attack those Sioux and Cheyenne Indians who had gathered around Sitting Bull and Crazy Horse. Knowing that war was coming, Sitting Bull led Sioux and Cheyenne warriors in the Sun Dance to beg the Great Spirit to give them victory. During the dance, Sitting Bull had a dream: he saw soldiers, like grasshoppers, falling into the Sioux camp from the sky. Crazy Horse, Sitting Bull, and all the Indians thought this dream meant that they would defeat the white man's army.

Sitting Bull and his family outside a teepee

The Sioux and the Cheyenne camp lay on Rosebud Creek, near the Little Bighorn River in eastern Montana. Confident that he could defeat the white men, Crazy Horse on June 16 attacked American soldiers under General George Crook,

who had been marching to attack Sitting Bull. The battle lasted the entire day. At nightfall, Crazy Horse and his warriors left the field of battle. But Crook did not pursue the Indians.

General Crook commanded one part of Sheridan's army; General Alfred Terry commanded another. Terry ordered Colonel George Armstrong Custer, who commanded the Seventh Cavalry, to ride up the Little Bighorn to find the Sioux and Cheyenne camp. Terry told Custer not to attack the camp immediately but to wait for Colonel John Gibbon to arrive with more men.

Colonel Custer found the Sioux and Cheyenne village on June 25. But instead of waiting for Gibbon, Custer decided he would attack the village by himself. The land through which the Little Bighorn ran was hilly, and Custer could not see how many warriors were in Crazy Horse's camp. He thought there were far fewer than there actually were. The warriors in the camp numbered well over a thousand, more men than Custer himself had.

Custer's last stand at the Little Bighorn, Montana, June 25, 1876

Custer divided his Seventh Cavalry into three parts. One part (about 175 men) under Major Marcus Reno attacked the northern end of the village. After crossing the Little Bighorn, Reno and his men met 1,000 Sioux and Cheyenne warriors. Unable to beat back so many Indians, Reno ordered his men to dismount and fight on foot while they retreated across the river. It was a bitter fight. By the time Reno reached the bluffs on the other side of the Little

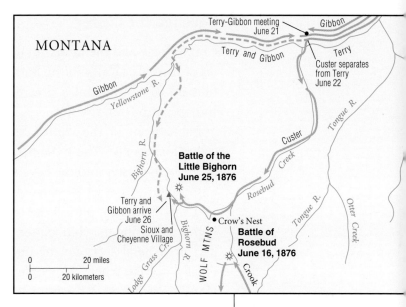

Troop movements during the Battle of the Little Bighorn

Bighorn, half of his men had been killed. Still the Indians attacked, but Reno was able to beat them off. Finally, more of the Seventh Cavalry under Captain Frederick Benteen arrived, saving Reno and his men from total destruction.

Colonel Custer and about 210 men also crossed the Little Bighorn to attack the southern end of the Indian village. While Reno was retreating farther up the river, Crazy Horse and a large number of warriors (far outnumbering Custer's small force) rose suddenly over a ridge and attacked Custer. Custer and his men fought desperately and bravely, but they could not stand up against the Indian attack. The fight lasted less than an hour.

It was not until the next day that anyone knew what had happened to Custer and his men. Scouts sent out by General Terry and Colonel Gibbon were the first to find them. All of Custer's men were dead. Their bodies had been stripped naked and were **mutilated.** Many lay behind the bodies of their horses, which they had used as shields. Only one body was not mutilated; it was Custer's. It is said the Indians did not harm Custer's body because they respected him as a great warrior.

mutilated: hacked or cut up

Revenge for Custer

Crazy Horse and the Sioux rejoiced. They believed that the slaughter of Custer's cavalry in the Battle of the Little Bighorn was the fulfillment of Sitting Bull's dream of white soldiers falling into the Indian camp from the sky.

But citizens of the United States did not rejoice. Instead, they called for revenge. The Indians must be punished for what they did to the hero Custer and the Seventh Cavalry.

In August, General Sheridan sent General Terry more men. Terry, said Sheridan, must punish the Indians for the slaughter on the Little Bighorn. During the cold winter of 1876–1877, General Crook and a part of General Terry's army pursued Crazy Horse and his people. Finally, in May, when his people were worn out and starving, Crazy Horse surrendered to Crook.

While Crook was chasing Crazy Horse, another part of Terry's army forced Chief Gall and Sitting Bull to flee into Canada. Though the government offered pardon to Sitting Bull if he returned to the United States and settled on a reservation, Sitting Bull refused to leave Canada. For four years, Sitting Bull and his Indians remained in Canada, until finally they were not able to find enough buffalo to

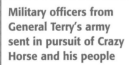

Military officers from General Terry's army sent in pursuit of Crazy Horse and his people

feed themselves. Finally, with his starving people, Sitting Bull returned to the United States and surrendered his gun at Fort Buford in North Dakota. Still proud, Sitting Bull said he wanted it to be remembered that he was the last of his people to surrender his rifle.

The Sorrows of Chief Joseph

A New Chief for the Nez Percé

As the chief named Old Joseph lay dying, he turned to his son. "This country holds your father's body," said Old Joseph. "Never sell the bones of your father and mother."

These words were the last command the old chief gave to his son, Thunder Rolling in the Mountains. Old Joseph, a Christian, had all his life kept peace with the white men who, for years, had been settling in northeastern Oregon, where his people, the Nez Percé, lived. (In French, *Nez Percé* means "pierced nose.") But even though Old Joseph told his son to keep peace with the white man, he told him never to sell the bones of his father and mother; that is, Rolling Thunder in the Mountains must never sell the Wallowa Valley, the homeland of the Nez Percé.

Young Chief Joseph (Thunder Rolling in the Mountains)

In 1855, the United States government had told Old Joseph that his people could keep the Wallowa Valley. But when whites began settling in the valley (after gold had been discovered there), the government asked Old Joseph to sell it and move to a reservation in Idaho. Though other Nez Percé chiefs agreed to the sale of their lands, Old Joseph refused to leave the Wallowa Valley, which was a holy place to him.

Rolling Thunder in the Mountains, also known as Young Joseph, became chief after his father died in 1871. While the new Chief Joseph kept peace with the white settlers as his father had done, he, too, refused to leave the Wallowa Valley. So in 1877 General Oliver Otis Howard met with Chief Joseph to convince him to move to the Nez Percé reservation in Idaho. When Chief Joseph refused, General Howard threatened him. If after a month Joseph and his people did not depart for the reservation, the army would force them to leave the Wallowa Valley.

Joseph was a wise chief. He had few warriors; he knew they could never resist the United States army. So, in sorrow, Chief Joseph and his people abandoned the bones of their fathers and mothers and crossed the Snake River into Idaho.

Flight to Canada

Trouble started almost as soon as the Nez Percé entered Idaho. Angry young warriors rode out from Joseph's band and killed 20 white settlers and burned down their farms. Though Chief Joseph was not responsible for this attack, he feared that the army would punish all his people for the actions of a few. He decided to lead his people across the Rocky Mountains and, if possible, escape with them into Canada.

When General Howard heard of the slaughter of the white settlers by the Nez Percé, he rode out with 110 soldiers in pursuit of Chief Joseph. Howard's men found Joseph and his people at White Bird Canyon. Chief Joseph offered peace to Howard, but the general refused. Instead, he ordered an attack on the Indians. Though the Indians were outnumbered, they killed 34 of Howard's soldiers and wounded 4 others. Chief Joseph then led his people farther into the mountains.

The Nez Percé followed the Clearwater River through the mountains. Now with 400 soldiers and 180 Indian scouts, General Howard pursued Chief Joseph and attacked the Indians in the Bitterroot Mountains in July 1876. But Howard was unable to stop the Indians, who continued their flight over the Rockies, finally making camp in the Big Hole Valley of Montana.

While there, Joseph and his people awoke one morning to find themselves under attack from soldiers under the command of Colonel John Gibbon. Gibbon at first killed many men, women, and children. But, gathering his warriors, Chief Joseph fought back. Gibbon and his men were forced to defend themselves, and the Indians continued their flight. This was called the Battle of the Big Hole.

The journey of the Nez Percé took them through Yellowstone in Wyoming and then north toward Canada. In October they were only 40 miles from the Canadian border when 600 soldiers under General Nelson Miles attacked them. At first the Indians beat back Miles's attack, killing many soldiers. But a few days later, when General Howard and his men joined Miles, Chief Joseph knew it was hopeless to try to escape. With his warriors and people hungry and suffering from cold, Chief Joseph surrendered at Bear Paw Mountain, Montana.

In his message to General Howard, Chief Joseph wrote: "I am tired of fighting. Our chiefs are killed . . . The old men are all dead . . . He who led the young men is dead. It is cold and we have no blankets. The little children are freezing to death. My people, some of them, have run away to the hills and have no blankets, no food. No one knows where they are—perhaps they are freezing to death. I want to have time to look for my children and see how many of them I can find. Maybe I shall find them among the dead . . . Hear me, my chiefs, I am tired. My heart is sad and sick. From where the sun now stands, I will fight no more forever."

And Chief Joseph never did fight again. The army divided his people, sending some

The surrender of Chief Joseph marks the end of the Nez Percé war.

to Idaho and others to Washington and the Indian Territory (Oklahoma). Chief Joseph himself went to a reservation in Washington, where he died 27 years later, in 1904.

War in the Southwest

Cochise

After many years of peace in Arizona, the Chiricahua Apache went on the warpath. It all began in October 1860 when some Apaches kidnapped a white child. To find out who did this deed, U.S. army lieutenant George Bascom ordered six Apaches—including Cochise, the leader of the Chiricahua Apache—to appear for questioning. Though Cochise and the other Apaches said they knew nothing of the kidnapping, Bascom said they had to go to prison. Cochise and the others then fought back, and Cochise escaped by cutting a hole through the side of Bascom's canvas tent. But Bascom held Cochise's wife, son, and two nephews prisoner.

Until this event, the Apache had lived in peace with the Americans. For centuries, this roving tribe had lived by raiding—first other Indian tribes, and then the Spanish and the Mexicans who settled in northern Mexico and New Mexico. After the Mexican-American War, the Apaches began raising cattle and selling the beef to white settlements and army forts. Then came the kidnapping and Bascom. Everything changed.

After fleeing from Bascom, Cochise attacked the Butterfield stagecoach line, wounding one white man and killing another. The same evening, Apaches killed eight Mexicans, taking two more white prisoners. Cochise kept the prisoners and told Bascom he would exchange them for the Indian prisoners. No one knows exactly what happened next; either Bascom killed Cochise's family first, or Cochise killed the captives first. But the Chiricahua Apache went on the warpath, brutally murdering white settlers and burning down ranches along the Gila River in Arizona.

Cochise

During the Civil War, when many soldiers went east to fight the Confederacy, Cochise and his warriors were unstoppable. From their strongholds in the mountains, the Apaches swooped down on white settlements to raid, **pillage,** and kill. In 1871, General George Crook told Cochise that if he ceased attacking white settlements, he and his warriors could remain on their ancestral lands in Arizona. (The government had sent other Apaches to a reservation in New Mexico.) But the U.S. government would not agree to what Crook had promised. Refusing to leave his ancestral lands, Cochise continued his war against the whites.

pillage: to steal

Finally, in 1872, the government agreed to allow the Chiricahua to remain on their lands, and Cochise surrendered. The government wanted the Indians to become farmers, but the Apache thought farming was woman's work. They continued their raiding, but only into Mexico. On one such raid, Cochise was wounded. He returned to his reservation, but his wound became infected; he died on June 8, 1874.

Geronimo

Before 1861, Cochise had kept his warriors from raiding white settlements; but after Cochise died, white settlers began complaining that the Apaches were stealing their horses and cattle. When, in 1876, the government ordered the Chiricahua Apache to leave the reservation that had been given to Cochise and move to the San Carlos reservation in a barren desert region, a medicine man named Geronimo led them in another revolt. For six years the Apaches led by Geronimo attacked white settlements, killing settlers. In 1882, General Crook with 5,000 troops set out after Geronimo. After two years Geronimo surrendered to Crook, and the Chiricahua were placed on the San Carlos reservation in Arizona.

Life on the barren San Carlos reservation was hard for the Apaches. Longing for freedom, Geronimo—with 35 men, 8 boys, and 101 women—fled from San Carlos in May 1883. General Crook again set out in pursuit of Geronimo, following the Indians

Geronimo

even into Mexico. At a canyon in Mexico, Geronimo once again surrendered to Crook. But on the return trip, near the United States border, Geronimo and a few others again escaped.

Yet another general, Nelson A. Miles, who had fought against Chief Joseph, went after Geronimo. Again the army chased the Apaches into Mexico. Finally, in September 1886, General Miles and Geronimo met for a peace conference in Skeleton Canyon in Arizona. Geronimo surrendered when Miles told him that he would be sent to Florida where, said Miles, Geronimo's wife and children were waiting for him. Eventually, said Miles, Geronimo would be allowed to return to his homeland.

The government did not keep General Miles's promise. Geronimo went to Florida, but did not see his family for several months. He remained in Florida for several years. In 1894 he was sent to the Indian Territory, where he remained until his death in 1909.

Last Battle at Wounded Knee

The wars fought with the United States by the Sioux, Cheyenne, Nez Percé, and Apaches were only a few of the Indian wars of the West. Everywhere (in Texas, the southern Great Plains, the Southwest, the Great Basin, and California), the U.S. army defeated the Indians and placed them on reservations. By the late 1880s, it was clear the Indians could not resist the whites. They had been utterly defeated.

In despair, many Plains Indians turned to a religious ceremony called the Ghost Dance. These Indians

Government troops fire on Sioux warriors at the Battle of Wounded Knee, South Dakota.

believed that the Great Spirit would come and destroy the white men and remake the world to the way it was before the white men came. The Indians believed that the Ghost Dance would give them power over the white men. The bullets of white men, it was believed, could not harm an Indian who performed the Ghost Dance.

After several years on their new reservation (the Standing Rock Reservation in what is now northern South Dakota), the Sioux were not happy. The

Some of the remaining tribe members after the Battle of Wounded Knee

U.S. government had promised to give them a certain amount of food every year, but there had been less food than promised. The Indians were no longer powerful enough to fight the U.S. army. How were they to save themselves and their families? So it was that many of the Sioux began performing the Ghost Dance.

The Ghost Dance frightened white settlers on the Great Plains, for it was a very strange ritual. The army thought that Indians would rise up and revolt against them. Police on the Standing Rock Sioux reservation were sent to arrest Sitting Bull because it was feared he would lead the Ghost Dancers in a new war. Before dawn on December 15, 1890, reservation police (who were all Sioux Indians) broke into Sitting Bull's cabin. A fight broke out between the police and Sioux who defended Sitting Bull. At the end of the fight, several lay dead, including the great chief himself. One of his own people had killed him.

When the Sioux on the reservation heard of Sitting Bull's death, they became fearful. What if the army attacked them as well? Many Sioux—warriors, women, and children—fled from the reservation, with the army in pursuit. The army finally surrounded them and moved them to a camp at Wounded Knee Creek. The Sioux were ordered to surrender their weapons. When one Sioux warrior refused, a fight broke out and the warrior's rifle fired into the air. The soldiers then opened fire. The Sioux returned fire, and in the battle that followed, hundreds of Indians fell dead. When the battle was over, more than 300 Sioux warriors, women, and children had been killed.

For two weeks, some fighting continued between the army and the Sioux, but the Indians finally returned to the reservation. Wounded Knee was the last battle the Sioux or any other Indian tribe fought against the United States.

The age of the great Indian wars had come to an end.

Soldiers leaving after the Battle at Wounded Knee

Chapter 18 Review

Summary

- Healing the wounds of the Civil War was difficult. Some Northerners wanted to punish the South for its rebellion, while some Southerners wanted to punish blacks and carpetbaggers for taking over positions of power in the South. Congress passed two new amendments to the Constitution. The first stated that black people had the same rights as white people, and the second explicitly stated that blacks had the right to vote.

- After the Civil War, many people began to move west in large numbers due to the Homestead Act of 1862, which granted settlers 160 acres of land. The completion of the transcontinental railroad made it easier for many settlers to move to the western frontier. The railroad system also made it profitable for farmers and ranchers to live in the West, for they could easily ship their goods around the country by train.

- The settlement of the western lands also created tension and friction between the white settlers and the Indians in these lands. War between the Indian tribes, such as the Sioux, and the U.S. government began because of the encroachment of white settlements into Indian territories. A Catholic priest named Father De Smet, who had worked closely with the Plains Indian tribes, tried to make peace between the Sioux and other tribes and the U.S. government, but the government did not keep its promise not to take Sioux lands.

- Throughout the West, the United States army defeated Indian tribes and placed them on reservations. The Nez Percé, under Young Chief Joseph, were forced to leave their ancestral lands in the Wallowa Valley in Oregon and settle in Idaho. In the Southwest, the Apache, under Cochise and Geronimo, fought to remain on their ancestral lands; but they, too, were finally forced onto reservations far from their homes. In many cases, the United States government broke treaties it had made with Indian tribes.

- The Battle of the Little Bighorn took place because the Sioux refused to give up their holy land, the Black Hills, to the U.S. government. Though the Sioux were victorious at this battle, ultimately the U.S. cavalry defeated the Indian tribe and forced the Sioux onto a reservation.

Chapter Checkpoint

1. Who became president after Lincoln was assassinated?
2. What two amendments to the Constitution were passed to protect black citizens after the war?

3. What were carpetbaggers, and why did Southerners dislike them?
4. How did the Homestead Act help to settle the West?
5. Explain how the railroad system helped both to develop the western frontier and to unite the western and eastern parts of the country after the war.
6. Who was Father De Smet? How did he and his fellow Jesuits assist the Indian tribes of the Great Plains?
7. In what ways did the railroad system contribute to the war between the Plains Indians and the U.S. government?
8. What was the Battle of Little Bighorn? Who was involved?
9. Why was Chief Joseph unwilling to abandon the Wallowa Valley and move his people to a reservation in Idaho? Why did he try to flee to Canada?
10. Why did Geronimo go on the warpath against the Americans in the Southwest?
11. What was the last battle of the Indian wars? When and where did it occur?

Chapter Activities

1. Discuss whether the whites and Indians could have lived in peace together on the plains? Why or why not?
2. Imagine you are a missionary to the Sioux tribe. How would you have approached them? How do you think Father De Smet was able to influence and convert many of the tribes?

The American Larder

The long cattle drives from Texas to Kansas City in the nineteenth century had food wagons, or chuck wagons, that traveled ahead of the cowboys, who rode with the herds of cattle. Ideally, food was ready to be eaten by the time the hungry, often very young, riders arrived for the evening's campsite. It is said that the chuck wagon cooks were the first to make chili. Charles Goodnight, after whom the famous Goodnight Trail was named, made the first chuck wagon; he modeled it after army wagons used in the Civil War in the 1860s. The chuck wagon had many drawers and compartments for storing food, cooking equipment, and eating utensils. The chuck wagon also stowed medical supplies and a shovel, for cooks had to act as doctors and also had to bury the cowboys who died on the trail drives.

Chapter 19 Land of Steel and Steam

Big Business

Ingenious Inventions

While settlers and the United States army were fighting Indians in the West, big changes were occurring in the East. You have already read about how, before the Civil War, many railroads crossed and recrossed the eastern states and how, after the war, a railroad was built stretching from Omaha, Nebraska, to California. This was not the end of railroad building. Soon other railroads besides the Union Pacific and the Central Pacific joined the East with the Pacific states. There was the Southern Pacific, which began in New Orleans, Louisiana, crossed Texas and the Southwest, and ended in San Francisco, California. There was the Santa Fe Railroad that stretched from Atchison,

A woman in a white robe, symbol of America's destiny to settle the West, floats over the prairie holding a school book and a coil of telegraph wire.

Kansas, to Santa Fe, New Mexico, and went from Santa Fe across Arizona and the California desert to San Diego. Far to the north, the Northern Pacific joined the Great Lakes with Portland, Oregon.

After the war, it had become much less expensive to build railroads simply because it had become much less expensive to make steel. In the 1850s, an Englishman, Sir Henry Bessemer, invented a new, less expensive way of changing **iron ore** into steel. At first, only the Europeans used the "Bessemer converter," but that changed when a young Scotsman brought the process to the United States.

iron ore: earthen material from which iron is made

Andrew Carnegie was only 13 when, in 1848, he came with his father from Scotland to America. The young Carnegie worked for the railroads and soon became a rather successful businessman. He was the first, for instance, to introduce sleeping cars for rail travel. Carnegie was shrewd. Seeing that the demand for steel would only become greater, he traveled to Europe to learn how the Bessemer converter worked. In 1875 he built the Edgar Thomson Steel Works near Pittsburgh, Pennsylvania, where he made steel rails using the Bessemer process. By 1888, Carnegie had bought the steel works in Homestead, Pennsylvania, and gained control of coal and iron fields, as well as a railway and a line of Great Lakes steamships. Carnegie was now a very rich man, indeed.

Andrew Carnegie, a businessman who invested in steel, railway lines, steamships, and other ventures

Steel was used not only for railroads but also for farm machinery. In the 1830s, Cyrus McCormick of Virginia had invented a mechanical reaper that replaced the scythe for harvesting grains. Farmers began to use steel plows, threshers (for separating grain from the **chaff**), and harvesters for other crops. In the West, barbed wire (invented by Joseph F. Glidden of Illinois in the 1870s) was used to fence in farm and cattle lands. At the end of the nineteenth century, and into the twentieth, first steam-powered and then gasoline-powered tractors with steel disc plows and other implements changed the way men farmed.

chaff: after harvest, the leftover husks that once contained seeds

But inventions were not confined to steel alone. Electric inventions began to change the face of the country. In 1832, Samuel F. B. Morse invented the electric telegraph. By the Civil War, telegraph wires, strung from poles much like electric wires are today, carried messages in code (named Morse code in honor of Samuel) to the far-flung regions of the country. Then, in 1876, Alexander Graham Bell invented the telephone. With his partner, Theodore Vail, Bell organized the Bell Telephone Company, which provided phone service to the cities. Before the Civil War, gas lamps lighted many cities; but after the war, another inventor came up with an electric generator powerful enough to power electric lamps. In the early 1870s, Wabash, Indiana, became the first city to use electric lamps instead of gas lamps.

Thomas Alva Edison of Ohio, however, came up with an even better electric light. On October 21, 1879, Edison invented the lightbulb that, with a few changes, is the same lightbulb most of us use to light

Samuel F. B. Morse, inventor of the electric telegraph

our houses today. Earlier, Edison had invented a phonograph or "speaking machine," which was a cylinder covered with tin foil and turned with a crank. When its crank was turned, the phonograph emitted recorded voices and sounds.

All these inventions, and many others, meant more manufacturing. Before the Civil War, the Northeast had factories where cotton was turned into cloth and other factories where other goods were manufactured. The invention of the sewing machine by Elias Howe in 1846 meant more and more clothing factories. But after the war, the number of factories increased. Great brick buildings with huge cylinder-shaped smokestacks belching black coal smoke and white clouds of steam began to cover not only the Northeast but the Midwest as well. Pittsburgh, Chicago, St. Louis, Akron (Ohio), and other

Thomas Edison, inventor of the lightbulb

The first commercially used electric lamp

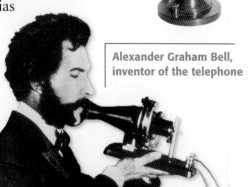

Alexander Graham Bell, inventor of the telephone

Midwestern cities joined cities like New York and Boston as great manufacturing centers. Soon, manufacturing would spread as far as the Pacific Coast.

Wars of the Captains of Capitalism

In the years following the Civil War, businessmen battled each other to get control of particular industries. Sometimes this was honest competition, but in many cases it was not. Businessmen often followed the "law of the jungle" to drive their competitors out of business. They used whatever means they could to ruin those who stood in the way of their prosperity.

Railroad companies were especially ruthless. They tried to take business from each other through competing with cheap rates. If one company lowered its rates, the other lowered *its* rates even more. Sooner or later one of the companies went out of business. The lower rates were good for the people who had to ship

Smokestacks from a factory in Pittsburgh, Pennsylvania, belch black smoke into the atmosphere in the 1890s.

goods by train, at least for a while. But, after driving its competitor out of business, a company would just raise its rates even higher than what it had charged in the first place. Farmers ended up relying on only one railroad to ship their crops and so were forced to pay very high rates.

Railroad companies sometimes became so powerful that they were able to control local and state governments. Rich railroad owners bribed lawmakers in California and New Hampshire, for example, to get laws passed that were favorable to the railroad companies. Even judges were given money, so that they would rule in favor of the railroad companies.

Not only railroad companies were involved in such activities. John D. Rockefeller, for example, tried to take control of the entire oil business in the United States. Rockefeller got into the oil refining business in 1863. In 1870, he and his brother William, and some others, formed the Standard Oil Company. The company's aim was to drive other oil companies out of business and take over their refineries. To do this, John D. Rockefeller convinced the Pennsylvania, Erie, and New York Central railways to lower their shipping prices for Standard Oil while raising them for other oil companies. Rockefeller also brought lawsuits again and again against other oil companies, so that they had to spend large amounts of money to defend themselves in court. In this way, Rockefeller forced his competitors to go out of business. He then bought out their factories, and Standard Oil became bigger and bigger.

John D. Rockefeller, a businessman and one of the founders of the Standard Oil Company

Big businessmen like John D. Rockefeller and Andrew Carnegie did many useful things, such as build railroads, produce refined oil, and manufacture inexpensive steel. Yet despite these benefits, many Americans feared that these men might rob Americans of their freedom by controlling the laws and by turning America into a land of a few rich masters and many servants. Some state governments tried to pass laws to keep men like Rockefeller from becoming so powerful. The state governments, however, were mostly unsuccessful; men like Rockefeller were so *very* powerful that the laws had no effect on them.

When the state governments failed to break the power of the rich, the federal government got involved. In 1887 it passed a law to control how much railroads could charge customers. It also passed another law in 1892 to break up enormous companies like Standard Oil. But even such federal laws were not very effective. Men like Rockefeller and Carnegie and the railroad **barons** remained as rich and powerful as ever.

barons: tycoons or those in business with a great deal of wealth and power

The Life of the Workers

But if the owners of industry were rich, the industrial workers were very poor. Because industrialists wanted to make as much money as they possibly could, they tried to pay their workers as little as possible. A typical factory worker labored 12 to 14 hours a day in

Child coal mine workers in Pennslyvania, 1911

miserable, filthy, and dangerous conditions for very little money. When business was not good, or when employers replaced men with machines, workers were fired from their jobs and then had no way of making money. This meant they and their families could go hungry and be thrown out of the houses and apartments they rented but did not own. Whole families at times became homeless.

But even when there was work, it was not just fathers who went to work. Whole families were forced to work to pay for the necessities of life: food, clothing, and a roof over their heads. Even children as young as eight years old worked long hours in the factories, or in the dark, dangerous, underground mines. They had little chance for an education and were often underfed and poorly clothed.

tenement: an apartment building

Home life was often as miserable as life at work. Whole families lived in single dark, dirty, dingy rooms that were cold in winter and hot in summer. These rooms were in **tenements** that housed many other families. Often there would be only one bathroom for dozens of people. Because of such dirty conditions, many fell sick from diseases like tuberculosis, from which both adults and children died.

Children and teenagers are supervised by adults as they clean shrimp at a cannery in Biloxi, Mississippi, 1911.

One reason workmen made so little money was that there were so many of them. A man could not demand a higher wage, because an employer could always find someone who would work for less. Blacks also came from the South to the industrial cities of the North and competed for jobs, as did immigrants from foreign countries. Large cities like New York, Philadelphia, Pittsburgh, and Chicago were filled with foreigners: Russians, Germans, Italians, Slavs, and Chinese. They had all come to America to find a new and better life. Some of them found it, but others joined the company of the poor, hungry workers.

A family makes fabric bouquets at the dining table in their tenement apartment in New York City, 1908.

Life in American cities and factories was very different from what both Americans and Europeans had been used to. All the members of a farm family had work to do on the farm; but the work was varied, and the family labored together. In the cities of the late nineteenth century, father, mother, and children all had different jobs and saw very little of each other. In the cities there had always been manufacturing shops, but these had been small and often had a family-like atmosphere. Every worker, too, did several different tasks, so the work was interesting. In the factories, however, employers often did not care about their workers. The work was also boring, with each worker repeatedly doing some small task.

Some Americans thought that the workers were poor because they deserved it. Workers were accused of being lazy or not ambitious enough. Some Protestants thought that men like Rockefeller and Carnegie were rich because God loved them more than the poor workers. Not everyone, however, believed such things. Some workers, especially, began to think that they were not being treated justly. Their answer was to band together to fight for better wages and better working conditions. The organizations they formed to do this are known as labor **unions.**

unions: organizations in which workers join together to work for what they believe are their rights

Miners pray while trapped in a collapsed tunnel at a mine in Pennsylvania.

Workers Organize

The Molly Maguires

The most dangerous and miserable places to work in the late nineteenth century were the great coal mines. The men and boys who worked deep underground to dig out the precious coal lived a dangerous life. Daily they breathed into their lungs the coal soot that also blackened their faces and clothing; many a miner died an early death from a horrible disease called black lung. Every day, the miners lived in fear of sudden death. The mines had pumps to push water out from the underground mines; if these failed, water could fill the mineshafts and drown the miners. The mines also had furnaces that created drafts to draw out the flammable methane gas found deep under the earth. If the furnaces broke down, the methane could fill the mineshafts; and if the gas caught fire, the mine would be engulfed in flames.

Such a disaster occurred in Avondale, Pennsylvania, in 1869. One of the wooden mineshafts caught fire, and soon the mine was filled with fire and dangerous gases. Raging flames leaped from mineshaft openings, and it looked as if the earth were spewing fire. When the fires finally died down, rescue crews found a sorrowful sight. Those miners who had escaped the flames had not escaped the gases. Fathers and sons lay dead, clasped in one another's arms; other dead workers were kneeling as if in prayer; still others lay facedown on the ground or were sitting with their hands clasped.

Such were the dangers miners faced for a very low wage. Some miners, however, wanted to better their lot. A group of Irish miners, called the **Molly Maguires,** began pushing for better wages and working conditions; but strong men were opposing them. One of these was Frank Gowen, who owned the Philadelphia and Reading Railroad. Gowen hired "coal and iron police" to keep the miners in

Molly Maguires: a labor group named for a legendary figure from Ireland who led poor farmers in attacks on landlords

line. Called "Pennsylvania Cossacks" by the miners, these police committed murders and other crimes to frighten the miners.

But the Cossacks could not frighten the Mollies (the Molly Maguires). They fought fire with fire. In 1875, miners in Pennsylvania went on **strike** in order to force their employers to give them better wages and safer working conditions. During this Long Strike, as it was called, the Mollies went after the mine bosses and superintendents—as well as the Cossacks—threatening them, beating them, and even murdering them. Mollies kept trains from running; they even pushed heavy engines off their tracks. The Mollies were certainly violent, but how violent is hard to say. Some say that some of the Mollies' crimes were really not done by the Mollies at all, but by the Cossacks. They were said to be Molly crimes in order to make the strikers look bad in the public's eyes.

strike: a deliberate stoppage of work to make a protest

Miners strike in Scranton, Pennsylvania, in 1922.

In the end, the Long Strike was a failure. But for two years more, fighting between Mollies and Cossacks continued. Finally, Frank Gowen hired the Pinkerton Detective Agency to undermine the Mollies. Pinkerton agents, pretending to be miners, joined the Mollies to find out what they were up to and to gain evidence that could be used in court against them. These agents themselves, it is said, committed acts of violence that were blamed on the Mollies.

Molly Maguires members on the way to the gallows in Pottsville, Pennsylvania

In 1877, evidence gathered by one Pinkerton spy led to the arrest and execution of 19 Mollies. Other Mollies were imprisoned. In this way, the power of the Molly Maguires was broken by Frank Gowen and the Pinkertons.

Workmen and firemen
drag a fireman and
an engineer from a
Baltimore freight train
during the Baltimore
and Ohio Railroad
strike in 1877.

The Great Strikes of 1877

Not long after the execution of the 19 Mollies, the Baltimore and Ohio Railroad told its workers that it was going to lower wages. The railroad workers' wages were already so low that they could barely support their families, and they pleaded with railroad owners not to cut their wages. But the owners ignored them, so on July 16, 1877, railroad workers near Baltimore, Maryland, went on strike. Soon other workers joined them, as well as railroad workers from Martinsburg, West Virginia, to St. Louis, Missouri. These Great Strikes, as they were called, stopped the railroads in the North from running. This meant the factories could not ship their goods, so all industrial production ground to a halt. The business world of the North had been paralyzed.

In the cities, not only railroad workers, but tradesmen—and even women and girls—formed angry mobs. In Pittsburgh, Pennsylvania, armed strikers pushed train engines off their tracks and dared the state militia to do something about it. When one state militia general tried to carry out his order to arrest one of the strike leaders, he found himself faced with an angry mob. When one man in the mob cried out, "At them, boys, at them!" the general, fearful of being attacked, ordered his men to fire on the mob. When the shooting stopped, 16 lay dead, including old men and children.

These killings only angered the strikers more. Soon militiamen from Pittsburgh joined the strikers, while the rest of the militia tried to protect itself in the railroad roundhouse. Four thousand strikers and others attacked the roundhouse and set fire to it, forcing the militia to retreat to save their lives. With the militia gone, strikers and others began burning railroad property and looting businesses in the city.

In the following weeks, more strikes sprang up in other cities. Coal miners, too, went on strike, which meant there would be no coal to feed the fires of industry. The strikes finally ended when the president of the United States, Rutherford B. Hayes, sent the United States army under General Winfield Scott Hancock to Pittsburgh. But by that time, hundreds of millions of dollars worth of property had been destroyed.

Yet, the Great Strikes were not a failure. The Baltimore and Ohio Railroad promised to give the families of workers who were ill, injured while working, or had died, half of the wage they would have earned if they were still working. The Pullman Palace Car Company (which manufactured passenger train cars) built a town for its workers outside of Chicago. The town included shopping centers, playgrounds, and a gymnasium. George Pullman, though, placed strict rules on the workers who lived in this town and gave them no voice in governing the town. Even so, the fact that Pullman had built the town showed the workers that if they joined together they could do much to better their condition.

The Philadelphia militia fires on the crowd during the railroad riot in Pittsburgh. People run in fear, and several lie dead.

Samuel Gompers, one of the founders of the American Federation of Labor (AFL), a labor union

Labor Unions

The Great Strikes of 1877 were effective, but workers needed a more permanent way to fight for their rights. Thus, they began to join together in unions.

There were different kinds of unions. Some were made up of workers who worked in the same industry (such as railroad workers' unions or coal miners' unions); others included workers from many industries. Some unions included only men who were skilled workmen (craft unions), and others included workers whether they were skilled or not. Some unions wanted not only to help workers, but to change society. Among these were communist unions, which wanted all property to be under the control of the government, and anarchist unions, which wanted no government at all. Most unions, however, were neither communist nor anarchist.

At first, the biggest union was the Knights of Labor, founded in 1869 by Uriah Stephens. In 1881, Terrence Powderly became head of the Knights of Labor. Powderly, an Irish Catholic, was neither a communist nor an anarchist; still, he wanted to change the way businesses worked. Powderly wanted the workers to have some part in owning the businesses they worked for—that way they could get a greater share of the profits. The Knights of Labor won some important victories for workers, but in the 1880s its membership began to shrink. Another union began to take the place of the Knights.

This union was the American Federation of Labor, or AFL, made up of skilled craftsmen from many industries. One of the AFL's most influential founders, Samuel Gompers, did not fight to change American society. He wanted very simple things, such as higher wages and a shorter, eight-hour workday. The AFL was very successful in getting businesses to shorten the workday voluntarily, going from ten, to nine, and then to eight hours. Soon, state governments began passing laws forcing businesses to give shorter workdays to women and children and to improve working conditions in workshops.

Mother Jones

Not only men, but also women took part in the fight for better wages and working hours. One of these was Mary "Mother" Jones. Mary Jones was born Mary Harris in Ireland. In those days, the British ruled Ireland; Mary Harris's grandfather fought for Irish independence and was hanged for it. Her father also fought against the British and had to flee to America to escape punishment. He brought Mary to Toronto, Canada, where, as a young woman, she taught in a convent school. When she moved to Chicago, she worked as a dressmaker. She moved again to Memphis, Tennessee, in 1861, where she married an ironworker, George Jones, who was a member of the Iron Moulder's Union.

"Mother" Jones, an early fighter for workers' rights

Mary Jones had a hard life. In 1867, her husband and their four young children died from yellow fever. When she returned to Chicago, she lost all she owned in the great fire of 1871. She again worked as a dressmaker and became involved with the Knights of Labor. From then on, she gave her life to the cause of the workers.

Mary Jones dressed in black dresses with white lace; with her gray hair pulled up in a bun, she looked like a grandmother, which was probably why she was called Mother Jones. But despite how she looked, Mother Jones fought strongly for workers' rights. Understanding the importance of women in the workers' struggle, she told workers' wives that they must stand with their husbands to keep them in the fight.

At the United Mine Workers strike at Arnot, Pennsylvania, in 1900, Mother Jones gathered the 3,000 miners' wives. When the miners went on strike, the mine owner hired other workers to take their place. (Strikers

scabs: workers hired to replace striking workers

call such workers **scabs.**) Armed with mops and buckets, Mother Jones and the miners' wives attacked the scabs. The women played drumbeats on the buckets and beat the scabs with their mops until, frightened, they ran away. "From that day on," wrote Mother Jones, "the women kept continued watch of the mines to see that the company did not bring in scabs. Every day women with brooms or mops in one hand, and babies in the other arm wrapped in little blankets, went to the mines and watched that no one went in. All night long they kept watch. They were heroic women."

Mother Jones finally helped bring the strike to an end by convincing the farmers around Arnot to join forces with miners. Met with such determined resistance, the mining company finally agreed to the strikers' demands.

During the Homestead strike of 1892, Pinkertons, escorted by armed union men, leave the barges after surrendering.

More Strikes

Andrew Carnegie had always been fairly good to his workers, at least, compared to other owners in the late nineteenth century. Though Carnegie did not provide his workers very high wages and fired men from time to time to save money, he allowed his workers to strike and refused to hire scabs to replace them. Carnegie thought workers had a right to strike. He also built the town of Homestead so his workers could have decent housing.

But by 1892, Carnegie was less involved in the management of his businesses and spent long periods living in a castle in Scotland. He left the running of his Homestead steel factory to Henry Frick. Frick had less concern for the workers than Carnegie; he was also not as charming as the Scotsman. In 1892, he told the workers at Homestead that he was going to lower their wages to $22 a month. The workers, who were organized in a union, protested. They wanted $24 a month. Frick agreed to pay them only $23 a month. Unsatisfied, the workers made a large dummy that looked like Frick and burned it in public. An angry Frick then closed the factory and brought in Pinkertons to guard it.

When the Pinkertons arrived by riverboat at Homestead in early July 1892, they found armed workers waiting for them. The Pinkertons were armed with very good rifles, but the workers had thrown up barricades behind which armed men, women, and even children awaited the Pinks, as they called them. When the Pinkertons landed, the workers rushed them and tried to seize their rifles. A gun fired, and then the Pinks fired into the workers, who fired back and forced the Pinks back into their boats.

For about 12 hours the workers kept the Pinkertons from landing. Finally the Pinks surrendered, and the workers led them in triumph into the Homestead town jail.

After the battle with the Pinkertons, the governor of Pennsylvania sent the state militia into Homestead. With state troops guarding him, Frick reopened his factory and hired scabs to work in it. Frick was triumphant. But on July 21, a young, well-dressed man entered Frick's office. The man pulled out a revolver and shot Frick. Frick fell to the ground. The young man fired two more times, but missed Frick. Soon others in the room overcame and captured the gunman. Frick survived the shooting, and the young man was sentenced to 22 years in prison.

Anarchist Alexander Berkman attempts to assassinate steel factory boss Henry Frick during the Homestead strike in 1892.

This young man, Alexander Berkman, was not one of the Homestead workers. He was a Russian anarchist who hoped his action would start an anarchist revolution against capitalists like Frick. But the Homestead workers did not want anything to do with anarchists. They were fighting for better wages, not to start a revolution. Even so, many Americans did not trust unions because it was thought they were filled with dangerous men like Alexander Berkman.

After about 143 days, the Homestead strike ended. The company won, and the workers who had lost their jobs did not get them back. Carnegie, nevertheless, gave money to the leaders of the strike and set up a fund to take care of other Homestead workers.

About a year later, workers at the Pullman Palace Car Company factory in Chicago went on strike because the owner, George Pullman, had fired a large number of workers and said he was going to lower the wages of those who remained. The workers' union went on strike in May 1894, and Pullman closed his factory. Finally, in July, President Grover Cleveland sent the United States army into Chicago. The strike was broken, and none of the striking workers were rehired.

Though many strikes failed to help the workers, they helped changed the way business was done in the country. Because of many small victories along the way, workers were able to get higher wages and better, safer working conditions. Eventually, factories and other businesses required workers to labor only eight hours a day and paid them extra if they worked longer. And, both state and federal governments passed laws to protect workers. Though some bad things came

A procession of working men march in support of the eight-hour workday.

from the labor movement, much good came, too. Among the good things was the recognition that, even though they might be poor, the workers deserved respect simply because they were human beings.

The Fight in the Fields

Even though the northern United States had always had cities and factories, most Americans in both the North and the South had been farmers. What is more, men like Thomas Jefferson had believed that it was necessary that most citizens be farmers if the United States were to remain a free republic. Jefferson even called farmers God's chosen people. Jefferson thought that since city workers relied on employers and customers to make a living, they were less free.

But at the end of the 1880s, times became hard for God's chosen people—the farmers. The price of crops like corn and wheat went down, and the farmers made less money. Farmers in the West depended on railroads to ship their crops to markets in the East, but the railroads often charged very high prices for shipping. The farmers had no choice but to pay these prices. Since they were taking in less money and paying out more, the farmers became poorer and poorer. Many even lost their farms to banks because they could not repay their debts.

Part of the problem was that farming had changed some-what since the days of Thomas

Changes in urban and rural populations

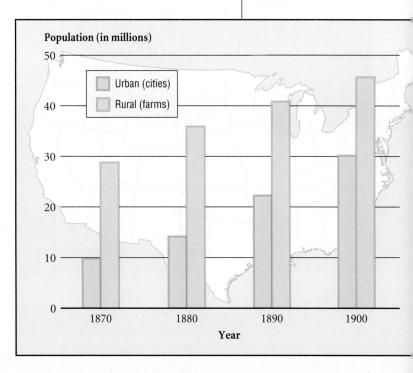

Jefferson. In Jefferson's time, most farmers grew crops to feed their families and sold only the extra on the market. Those farm families did not need money to live on, for they grew their own crops, made their own cloth from their own sheep's wool, and sewed their own clothes. They were truly independent. But the farmers of the Great Plains often grew only crops like wheat and corn for sale on the market and not, first and foremost, for their own use. Because they were trying to make money off their farms, these farmers took out loans from banks for seed and all the new farming tools and, subsequently, got into debt.

Many southern farmers after the Civil War grew only one crop: cotton. Even when they wanted to plant other crops, they were unable to. The merchants who shipped the farmers' crops often demanded that they grow cotton and nothing else. The problem was that whenever someone plants the same crop in the same fields year after year, the soil becomes less fertile. Also, the southern farmers were getting less and less money for their cotton, while the merchants who sold the cotton elsewhere were making a good deal of money. When they could not pay the loans on their farms, many farmers lost their farms to merchants who had loaned them the money to buy their farms or their machinery or their seed.

Like workers in the cities, farmers formed associations to fight for their rights against the merchants, banks, and railroads. One such farmer's association was called the National Grange of the Patrons of **Husbandry.** The Grange supported state politicians who were friendly to the farmers. Grange representatives took control of the government in some states and passed laws to keep down the rates railroad companies charged to ship crops. But most of these laws, in the end, were unsuccessful.

Convention of the National Grange of Patrons of Husbandry— a farmers' association that fought for farmers' rights

husbandry: the farming of crops and raising of livestock

Granges also built up farmer-owned businesses, so that farmers did not have to depend on merchants and manufacturers in the cities. Because the farmers in a certain area worked together to run these businesses, they were called cooperatives. The farmers had cooperative stores, cooperative ways of sending their crops to market, and even cooperative factories to manufacture farming tools. But most of these cooperatives failed, often because the railroads were opposed to them. Sometimes a railroad refused to ship anything from a town that had cooperatives.

Farmers and city workers joined together for a time in a political party called the Populist Party. The Populists ran candidates for state and federal offices, and for a time they did well. But in the end, the Populist Party could not compete with the Republican and Democratic parties.

All in all, the farmers' movements were not as successful as the union movement, which over time gained more and more benefits for workers. For various reasons, the number of farmers decreased over the years. One cause of this was farm machinery. A farmer who used reapers, tractors, threshers, and other such machines did not need as many "hands" to help him in the fields; and so, for him, farming was not as expensive as for the man who did not use

A horse-drawn combine harvester and thresher cuts wheat in a field in the 1890s. Such farm equipment was being replaced by gas-powered farm tractors which required fewer farm workers.

machines. So it was that many farmers were forced to abandon their farms, which were bought up by the farmers who remained. By the 1920s, for the first time in American history, there were more people living in the cities than on farms. Today, very few Americans live on farms; almost everyone lives either in the cities or in the suburbs and works in industries that in no way require tilling the earth and planting crops.

It is a very different America from the land Thomas Jefferson had envisioned.

Chapter 19 Review

Summary

- Andrew Carnegie brought to America Henry Bessemer's discovery of how to change iron ore into steel. Carnegie built the first steelworks plant in America. The introduction of mass-produced steel into America did several important things. The steel from this plant and others allowed the railroads that connected the country to be greatly expanded. Steel also allowed for farm machinery to be built that made the harvesting of grain more efficient, and steel made it easier for farmers and ranchers to fence off their lands.
- Many famous inventions occurred in the nineteenth century. In 1832, Samuel Morse invented the electric telegraph, which allowed messages in Morse code to be sent rapidly over long distances. Alexander Graham Bell invented the telephone in 1876, and he began telephone companies that provided telephone service to cities. Thomas Edison invented the lightbulb to replace the gas lighting of many houses and towns. In 1846 Elias Howe invented the sewing machine, which allowed for the mass production of clothing.
- Problems arose in America from the rapid growth of manufacturing and industry. Railroad and other companies tried to drive each other out in order to gain a monopoly of the market. These companies became so powerful that they were able to treat their workers poorly with little to no consequences. The life of a typical factory worker was harsh. He or she often worked 12 to 14 hours a day in dangerous working conditions for little money. Because of the large number of immigrants, the number of people wanting work was high, so a worker could not make demands on the employer for higher wages or better working conditions.

- Workers formed labor unions as a way to combat powerful companies. As a group, workers could make demands on their employer that as individuals they could not. In 1877, workers in different trades around the country began to go on strike, meaning they refused to work until their employers met their demands for better working conditions. The strikes brought industry in America to a halt and showed workers that they did have power as a consolidated group of workers. Through the power of unions, the government began to pass laws restricting the working hours and limiting the age of workers.
- Farmers also joined together in groups such as the National Grange of the Patrons of Husbandry. For a time, with laborers in the cities, farmers even established a political party. Farmers movements, though, were not as successful as the labor unions because, as the years passed, the number of farmers decreased. Finally, far more Americans lived in cities than on the land.

Chapter Checkpoint

1. How did the discovery of how to make steel change American life? Who brought this European discovery to America?
2. Name three significant inventions or discoveries of the nineteenth century that modernized the world.
3. What was life like in the large cities for working families of the late nineteenth century?
4. What are labor unions? Why and when did they begin in the United States?
5. What was the first union in the United States?
6. Describe one of the many strikes of the late nineteenth century. Why did the strike occur, and what good did it do?
7. Why did the population shift from rural to urban life occur in the late nineteenth and early twentieth centuries? What effect did this have on American families and American culture?

Chapter Activities

1. Make your own phone using two disposable paper or plastic cups, two toothpicks, and lots of string. (This is a project for two people.)

    Using a toothpick or other device, poke a small hole in the bottom of each cup (make the hole just big enough for the string to go through). Feed the string through the hole, then tie it around the middle of a toothpick. When you pull the string tight, the toothpick should lie flat against the inside bottom of the cup, preventing the string from slipping out. Feed the other end of the string through the other cup, and tie it around the other toothpick.

Have each person take one end of the telephone and walk away from the other until the string is pulled tight. Take turns talking into the telephone while the other one listens. If you make two phone lines, you can use one cup for talking and the other for listening. When you talk into the cup, the cup vibrates and then sends the vibration along the string. When the vibration reaches the other cup, it causes the other cup to vibrate, creating sound waves which you can hear.

2. The Greek philosopher Plato has often been quoted as saying: "Necessity is the mother of invention." Think about, and then describe an invention of your own.

The American Larder

John and William Kellogg were brothers who moved to Battle Creek, Michigan, in the late 1800s and developed a health spa that became one of the largest and richest hospitals in America. In 1877, the Kellogg brothers developed a toasted and ground cereal called *granola*. (A similar cereal made of baked graham loaves, broken and baked again in pieces called *granula*, had already been made in 1863 by James Jackson, a follower of Sylvester Graham, who developed the graham cracker.) The Kellogg brothers made flaked cereal almost accidentally; when they boiled the granola wheat too long, they developed a long thin flake, which turned crispy after it was baked. They began to make similar flakes out of corn, not wheat, and by 1894 had a patent on their "grain-tempering" process. Throughout the next 30 years, Will Kellogg advertised his corn flakes and by the 1930s, Americans had changed from preparing hot breakfasts to eating dry cereal with cold milk poured over it. These dry cereals became enormously popular. Similarly, what we know now as General Foods "Post Toasties" or "Cornflakes" cereal was originally called "Elijah's Manna" when it was first developed in 1904.

Chapter 20 Catholics in America

Catholic Life in the United States

The Church Grows

eing a Catholic in the United States had never been easy. Most Americans were Protestants, and Protestants did not trust Catholics. Catholic worship was strange to Protestants: the Mass was said in Latin, the priests wore strange clothes called vestments, and Catholics said the "bread" they ate at Mass was the Body and Blood of Christ. Except for groups like the Lutherans and the Episcopalians, most Protestant worship was simple, with hymn singing, Bible reading, and sermons. Most Protestant churches, too, were democratic in that the congregation selected their pastor and could get rid of him whenever they wanted. Catholics, though, had to be obedient to their priests, bishops, and the Pope. The Catholic Church was a monarchy, and American Protestants had no liking for kings or anything that looked like a king.

The Catholic Mass was more ritualistic and elaborate than the worship of Protestantism, the dominant religion in America.

The anti-Catholic "Native Americans," as they called themselves, provoked a series of riots in Philadelphia in 1844. In this illustration a "native" mob, wearing beaver hats, attacks the state militia in Philadelphia. Twenty-four people were killed and two famous old Catholic churches were burned in these riots.

uncouth: ill-mannered and uncivilized
papists: a mocking name for those who acknowledge the Pope as Vicar of Christ on Earth

The fact that Catholics obeyed the Pope was probably the thing that bothered Protestant Americans the most. In the first half of the nineteenth century, the Pope was not only the spiritual head of the Church, he was also the ruler, the king, of a large chunk of central Italy called the Papal States. Because of this, many Americans thought Catholics served a foreign government by obeying the Pope; they feared that if put to the test, Catholics would be untrue to the United States of America. Even when the Pope lost the Papal States in the late nineteenth century, many Americans still did not trust Catholics.

Protestant Americans probably could have tolerated Catholics more if the majority of Catholics had remained native-born Americans. But even before the Civil War, large groups of Catholic immigrants, especially Irish Catholics, began coming to America. Many Americans disliked and feared the Irish; they thought them dirty and **uncouth** because they were poor, were forced to work at the lowest-paying jobs, and so lived in the rundown parts of cities. After a time, northern American cities had so many Irish that they began to take over the city governments. Many of these Irish politicians were not very honest, but they were no worse than the typical native-born American politicians. Still, many an American Protestant feared that his country was being taken over by **papists,** as many called the Catholics.

The Irish were not the only Catholics to come to America. In the 1840s, many of the Germans who crossed the Atlantic were Catholic. These German Catholic immigrants were often better off than the Irish, and they settled in farming communities in the Midwest. Many of these communities were entirely Catholic. Like Loretto,

Pennsylvania (founded by Father Demetrius Gallitzin), these communities were centered on the celebration of the sacraments and had laws inspired by the Catholic Faith. The fact that the people in these German communities spoke German and not English probably disturbed many native-born Americans, but this had nothing to do with being Catholic. Even Protestant German communities were almost entirely German speaking. Most native-born Americans just figured that the Germans were stubborn people who did not give up *anything* easily.

Ellis Island, New York. Immigrants who entered the United States through the port of New York first went through legal and medical checks at Ellis Island.

After the Civil War, the number of Irish immigrants decreased, while the number of German and Central European immigrants to America increased. Many of these new immigrants were also Catholic. Later, Catholic Italians began coming to America in great numbers. Like the Irish before them, most of the Central European and Italian immigrants were poor and settled in the cities where they could find work. Unlike the Irish, though, these new immigrants did not speak English. Also, to American eyes, they had very strange customs. Because these immigrants came from countries with governments and customs very different from those of America, many Americans feared they would change the character of the American republic.

European immigrants who have passed through the entry station at Ellis Island wait for the ferry that will transport them to New York City.

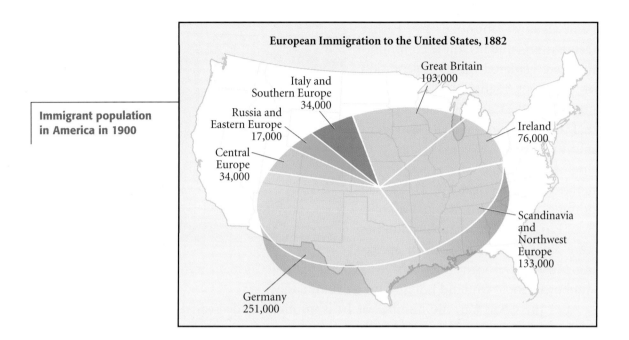

Immigrant population in America in 1900

European Immigration to the United States, 1882

Great Britain 103,000

Italy and Southern Europe 34,000

Russia and Eastern Europe 17,000

Central Europe 34,000

Ireland 76,000

Scandinavia and Northwest Europe 133,000

Germany 251,000

Since many Americans mistrusted them, Catholics faced many struggles in the United States. For a long time, some states had laws that kept Catholics from holding government offices. In other places, city governments tried to force Catholic children to attend "common" or public schools, where a kind of Protestant religion was taught. Many pamphlets and books were published that wrongly accused Catholic priests, brothers, nuns, and laymen of all sorts of horrible things.

A large number of Catholics who came to America fell away from the Faith. They left the Church for a number of reasons. Because of Protestant prejudice against them, it was hard for Catholics to find good jobs and to get ahead in the world; thus, some Catholics chose worldly success over their religion. Other Catholics settled in areas were there were no Catholic churches, and they ended up going to Protestant churches or ceased going to church altogether.

Yet, though perhaps millions of Catholics fell away from the Faith in America, the Church in America grew. In the early days of the

American republic, only a very few Catholics lived in America. By 1900, however, about 25 percent of Americans were Catholic. Not only that, but the Catholic Church was larger than any one Protestant group; there were even more Catholics than Baptists, who were the largest Protestant denomination in the United States. But despite their numbers, Catholics continued to have little power in the United States. Some Catholics became rich and influential, but most remained poor and not well educated. In the United States, the Catholic Church was the church of the poor, the weak, and the downtrodden.

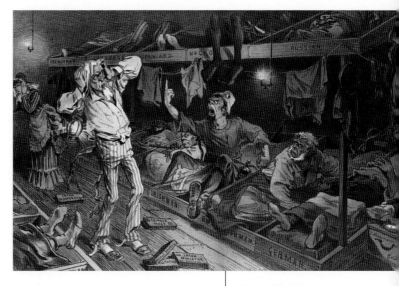

This political cartoon depicts immigrants lying in bunk beds labeled with their various nationalities. Uncle Sam says to the Irishman, "Look here, you, everybody else is quiet and peaceable and you're all the time a-kicking up a row."

Catholic Americans

A few Catholics rose to positions of importance in nineteenth-century America, and some of them became famous. Roger Taney was one famous Catholic. As Chief Justice, he handed down the famous Dred Scott decision (see Chapter 15), on account of which many have thought him a friend of slavery. Taney, however, who was born to a Virginia slave-owning family, had freed the slaves he inherited from his father and supported the older ones until their death. And, while a lawyer, he defended a Methodist minister in Maryland who had been brought into court for preaching against slavery. Taney had also said that slavery was "a blot upon our national character."

A few of the generals in both the Union and Confederate armies were Catholic. Union general Philip Sheridan, who was one of General Grant's most trusted officers, was Catholic. Later, in 1883,

agnostic: one who
doubts the existence
of God

he became commander in chief of the United States army. In that office, he succeeded General William Tecumseh Sherman. Though a priest had baptized Sherman when he was a boy, he rejected the Catholic Faith later in life and became an **agnostic.** But Sherman's wife was a Catholic, and one of his sons became a Jesuit priest. General Pierre Gustave Toutant Beauregard was among the

"The Conquered Banner," by Father Abram J. Ryan

Furl that Banner, for 't is weary;
Round its staff 't is drooping dreary;
  Furl it, fold it,—it is best;
For there's not a man to wave it,
And there's not a sword to save it,
And there's not one left to lave it
In the blood which heroes gave it,
And its foes now scorn and brave it,
  Furl it, hide it,—let it rest!

Take that Banner down! 't is tattered;
Broken is its staff and shattered;
And the valiant hosts are scattered,
  Over whom it floated high.
Oh, 't is hard for us to fold it,
Hard to think there's none to hold it,
Hard that those who once unrolled it
  Now must furl it with a sigh.

Furl that Banner—furl it sadly!
Once ten thousands hailed it gladly,
And ten thousands wildly, madly,
  Swore it should forever wave;
Swore that foeman's sword should
  never
Hearts like theirs entwined dissever,
Till that flag should float forever
  O'er their freedom or their grave!

Furl it! for the hands that grasped it,
And the hearts that fondly clasped it,
  Cold and dead are lying low;
And that Banner—it is trailing,
While around it sounds the wailing
  Of its people in their woe.

For, though conquered, they adore it,—
Love the cold, dead hands that bore it,
  Weep for those who fell before it,
Pardon those who trailed and tore it;
And oh, wildly they deplore it,
  Now to furl and fold it so!

Furl that Banner! True, 't is gory,
Yet 't is wreathed around with glory,
And 't will live in song and story
  Though its folds are in the dust!
For its fame on brightest pages,
Penned by poets and by sages,
Shall go sounding down the ages—
  Furl its folds though now we must.

Furl that Banner, softly, slowly!
Treat it gently—it is holy,
  For it droops above the dead.
Touch it not—unfold it never;
Let it droop there, furled forever,—
  For its people's hopes are fled!

Catholics who served the South in the Civil War. General James Longstreet, one of Robert E. Lee's most trusted generals, became a Catholic after the war, in 1877.

And of course, some of the soldiers who fought for the North and the South were also Catholics. Irishmen, immigrants as well as those born in America, served both in the Federal and Confederate armies. Catholic priests served as chaplains in both armies. Father John B. Bannon served as chaplain in the army of Confederate General Sterling Price in Missouri. Unlike some

A priest says Sunday Mass for troops in Washington, D.C., 1861.

chaplains, Father Bannon always accompanied the soldiers into battle, though he himself did not fight. In 1863, Father Bannon went to Rome as President Jefferson Davis's representative to convince Pope Pius IX to recognize publicly the Confederate States of America. The Pope did not do this, although he was friendly toward the Confederacy.

Another priest, Father Abram Joseph Ryan of Norfolk, Virginia, not only served as a chaplain in the Confederate army, but became a famous poet. Though Father Ryan wrote religious poetry, his most well-known poems have to do with the South and its "lost cause." Ryan's poem, "The Conquered Banner," became one of the most popular poems in the South after the war. For it and other similar poems, Ryan became known as the Poet-Priest of the Confederacy.

Unlike Catholic men and priests who served in the Federal and Confederate armies, Catholic sisters who tended the sick and wounded soldiers took no sides in the war. Though many sisters from many different orders served, all were called Sisters of Mercy by the wounded soldiers. Catholic sisters tended any who were wounded: Confederates and Federals, Catholic and non-Catholic, white men and black men. The sisters were skilled nurses, and many a soldier owed his life to the careful and merciful attention the sisters gave him. They were the best nurses on the battlefield.

Christ Bearers

The Peasant Bishop

Among the large number of Catholics who came to America, some have been remembered for their extraordinary love of God and neighbor. These men and women were truly Christ-bearers, for through the power and beauty of their holiness they brought Christ to many.

Saint John
Nepomucene
Neumann

Though he was quiet and shy, John Nepomucene Neumann was a man of strong will and determination. He was born in Bohemia (now the Czech Republic) in 1811 to a Bavarian father and a Czech mother. Longing to be a priest, John Neumann entered the seminary when he was 20 years old. At seminary, he was a diligent student who made good grades and learned to speak six languages. Offered a post in the government, John refused it, for he longed to serve God, not an earthly ruler.

John Neumann hoped to go to America, for he had heard that Catholics there were in great need of priests. He sent several letters to American bishops, asking them to consider ordaining him. When he received no answers, he decided to go to America and introduce himself in person to the bishops. Making the long journey across Europe, Neumann arrived at the port of Le Havre in France. From there he set sail to America in the spring of 1836. When Neumann arrived in New York, he discovered that Bishop Jean Dubois had sent an invitation to him; however, Neumann had left Bohemia before he could receive it. In June 1836, Dubois ordained Neumann a priest.

Bishop Dubois sent Father Neumann to a 900-square-mile parish near Buffalo, New York. The Catholics in this parish were widely scattered and of various nationalities; there were Germans, French, Irish, and Native American Catholics, all speaking their own languages. Father Neumann spent his time walking; he traveled over his vast parish on foot, Mass kit in hand, ministering to the people. Because he could speak several languages, Father Neumann was able to hear the confessions of his flock and preach to them in their own tongues.

Father Neumann carried on this strenuous life for six years. In 1840 he left parish work and entered a religious order called the Redemptorists. This brought him to Pittsburgh, Pennsylvania, where he remained until 1851, except for a two-year period when his superiors moved him to Baltimore, Maryland. In Baltimore, Neumann became the confessor to the archbishop. While serving the archbishop, Father Neumann first heard rumors that chilled his heart; people were saying he might become a bishop. Neumann thought himself unworthy of such an honor, and he even asked his friends to pray that he not become a bishop. One afternoon, however, when he entered his room, Neumann saw a bishop's ring and pectoral cross lying on an open book. This meant only one thing: like it or not, he was going to be made a bishop.

John Neumann became the fourth bishop of Philadelphia in 1852. His reign there was short, only eight years, but his accomplishments were great. During this period, Neumann built 80 parish churches for his diocese, but his chief interest was education. When Neumann became bishop, Philadelphia had only two parish schools; in eight years it had 100 schools. Neumann wanted every parish to have its own school, and his idea influenced other bishops in the United States. Over the next 100 years, parish schools spread across the United States.

Though he worked no miracles in his life, John Neumann was a holy man. As bishop he lived like one of the poor, giving to the needy whatever they asked of him. His own clothes were so shabby that once one of his priests, jokingly, told him to change them. "Today is Sunday," said the priest, "have the goodness to change your clothes."

To which Neumann replied, "What do you want me to do? I have no others."

Bishop Neumann died from a heart attack on January 5, 1860. Thousands came to his funeral, the largest Philadelphia had yet seen. No sooner had he been buried than the faithful began to say prayers at his grave, and many received answers to their prayers. Pope Paul VI proclaimed the bishop of Philadelphia a saint in 1977. He was the first American male saint.

Missionary to America

Saint Maria Cabrini

All her life, Maria Francesca Cabrini had dreamed of becoming a missionary. When she was a young girl, her favorite subject was geography, for she loved to think of the faraway lands where she could go with the Gospel of Christ. When a visiting missionary priest told of the Chinese missions, Francesca longed to go to that land in the far-off East.

But God, and the Pope, had other plans for her. In 1880, the 30-year-old Francesca founded her own missionary order for women in Italy, called the Institute of the Missionary Sisters of the Sacred Heart. As the head of this order, Francesca was called Mother Frances Xavier Cabrini. She took on the name of Xavier in honor of the great Jesuit missionary to India, St. Francis Xavier. But unlike him, Mother Cabrini was not destined to go to the East. In 1889, Pope Leo XIII told her to go to America to work with the poor Italian immigrants there.

Though she was very afraid of water, Mother Cabrini and six of her sisters set sail for New York in 1889. The sisters had been told that a house for an orphanage would be awaiting them in New York; but when they arrived in that great city, they found that the archbishop had not been able to obtain a house for them. The archbishop advised Mother Cabrini to return to Italy, but she would hear none of it. "No, Your Excellency, this I cannot do," she said. "I came here by order of the Holy See, and here I must stay."

And she did stay. Mother Cabrini and her sisters worked among the poorest of the poor and with the sick in the city slums. During the first three months of her stay in New York, Mother Cabrini opened an orphanage and a school. Over the next 30 years, she and her sisters opened hospitals, orphanages, schools, and other institutions in eight U.S. cities and in Central and South America.

Mother Cabrini was a woman who gave herself entirely to God. "Oh Jesus, I love you very much," she once wrote. "Give me a heart as big as the universe . . . Tell me what You wish that I do, and do with me as You will." She worked tirelessly for God, and God blessed her efforts. During her life God worked several miracles through her, and after her death in 1917, people from all over the world said they had received favors through her prayers. Only 29 years after her death, Pope Pius XII proclaimed Mother Frances Xavier Cabrini a saint.

A Famous Convert

She was the daughter of one of the most famous American authors, Nathaniel Hawthorne. She was born into a family that had a good reputation in society, for her father, Nathaniel Hawthorne, besides being the author of such well-known books as the *Scarlet Letter* and the *House of Seven Gables,* served as the U.S. ambassador to England. Young Rose Hawthorne spent several years of her life in England and was privileged to travel through Europe.

On one such trip to Rome, she and her family were walking through the Vatican gardens when Rose bumped into a priest. With surprise and embarrassment, Rose's mother realized that the priest was none other than Pope Pius IX. The Pope only smiled as the mother apologized; then, patting Rose's head, he gave her his blessing. Even though Rose was not Catholic, she never forgot the kindness of the great Pope.

In 1868, when she was only 17, Rose's family moved to Germany. There she met a young writer, George Lathrop. Three years later, in England, the couple was married. They then returned to the United States, where George became a well-known writer. In 1891, both Rose and George were received into the Catholic Church.

From her father, young Rose Hawthorne had learned compassion for the poor and suffering. When one of her friends, Emma Lazarus, died of cancer, Rose wondered what became of the poor who suffered from that terrible disease. Emma had been wealthy and so had had the best care money could buy. But what of those who could not afford such care?

Rose Hawthorne Lathrop decided to dedicate her life to helping the cancerous poor. Though used to the comfortable life of the well-to-do, Rose went to live among the poor and care for those stricken with cancer in their own homes. For those sick who had no place to go, Rose rented a home where they could stay. In 1897, a young art student named Alice Huber joined Rose in her work.

When George Lathrop died, Rose and Alice took up the religious life. Their life was a hard one, working with the sick poor who lived in the most dangerous and poorest sections of New York City. It was especially hard for two women who had been raised in comfort, but their prayers sustained them through the hardest times. In 1899, Rose and Alice received enough donations to buy a house for the cancer patients. In 1900 they both became Dominican sisters: Rose became known as Sister Mary Alphonsa, while Alice took on the name Sister Mary Rose.

It was not long before the sisters' house became too small for their needs. In 1901, a group of French Dominican priests sold them a large hotel with 60 rooms and nine acres of land. This the sisters turned into a hospital for poor cancer victims. Sister Mary Alphonsa was always very kind to the patients. She not only cared for their needs, but bought them things to give them pleasure. Once she bought a radio for a patient; she gave another patient a canary and another, a dog.

Rose Hawthorne Lathrop had experienced many sufferings during her life. Her father died when she was 13, and her mother not many years later. She and her husband had had a son, whom they loved dearly; but that son died of **diphtheria** at the age of four. George Lathrop developed a drinking problem, and he and Rose were separated during the last years of his life. It was then that Rose had gone to work among the poor and sick. She suffered much in caring for them, but with these sufferings came God's grace. In serving the poorest of the poor, Rose became rich in holiness. She died peacefully in her sleep in July 1926.

diphtheria: a contagious disease of the throat and lungs

Portrait of Pope Leo XIII

Into the Next Century and Beyond

Catholics Become American

Even though by 1900 many Catholics lived and worked in the United States, they did little to influence American society and government. Catholics mostly kept to themselves. This was natural, because so many Catholics were foreigners, poor, and with little education. They did not feel confident in American society. Catholics had also undergone periods of persecution in America; they were afraid to do anything to disturb or anger other Americans. Most Catholics just wanted to work and live in peace with their non-Catholic neighbors.

In the 1900s, however, Catholic priests and some laymen began trying to find solutions to the problems workers faced in the factories. These Catholics were helped by Pope Leo XIII (pope from 1878–1903), who had written an **encyclical letter** giving the Church's ideas on how employers should treat their workers, and how workers should act toward their employers. Pope Leo's work was filled with wisdom, for it was based on centuries of Catholic Church tradition.

encyclical letter: a letter on a specific subject written by the Pope to the Church and intended for universal circulation

But most Catholics in the 1900s did little more than live their daily lives and get along in a Protestant world. When the United States entered the First World War in 1917, Catholics fought alongside their non-Catholic fellow citizens. In the 1920s, when the nation entered a time of great financial prosperity, Catholics benefited with other Americans. Some Catholics became quite rich during this period. Among them was Joseph Kennedy, whose son John Fitzgerald Kennedy later became our country's first and only Catholic president. Another wealthy Catholic, Alfred Smith, ran for president as a Democrat in 1928, and he lost to the Republican Herbert Hoover. He was the first Roman Catholic to run for president. Many Americans did not vote for Smith, not only because he was a big city political boss but also because he was Catholic.

John F. Kennedy, the first and only American president who was Catholic

Since most Catholics were still poor, they suffered greatly during the Great Depression of the 1930s when millions of men lost their jobs. But during the Depression non-Catholic Americans began to listen to Catholic thinkers with respect, for they offered solutions from Church teaching to the problems the nation was facing. It seemed that the time had come for Catholics to make their contribution to American society. And Catholics, both priests and laymen, were getting involved in American life in a way they never had before.

Holiness for Catholic Laity

You have read about Catholics like Bishop John Carroll, Elizabeth Anne Seton, Demetrius Gallitzin, Bishop Neumann, Mother Cabrini, Rose Hawthorne Lathrop, and others who became well known for their holy lives. And many other Catholics became holy in their daily lives by loving God and their neighbor—mothers who faithfully raised their children, fathers who took care of their families, priests who served their flock, monks and nuns who spent their lives in prayer and in service to others. But unfortunately, too many lay Catholics thought that holiness was something only priests and the religious had to worry about. Many thought that the only thing Catholic laypeople had to do was obey Church law, go to confession and to Mass on Sunday, pray once or twice a day and at meals, and support their parishes with their offerings.

Dorothy Day

Of course, the Church has always taught that holiness is not only for priests, nuns, and religious brothers. Every Catholic is called to become holy. Sometimes, however, Catholics need to be reminded of this. In the case of our country, two of the people who reminded us of our call to holiness were people who many thought were very odd folks. Their names were Peter Maurin and Dorothy Day.

Dorothy Day was not raised Catholic; in fact, her family did not practice any religion at all. But when she was a young girl, she began attending a Protestant church, reading the Bible and praying. As a teenager, while living in Chicago, Dorothy learned how hard life was for the poor and decided that she would spend her life trying to help them in some way. When she went to university, Dorothy decided that Christians were not doing enough to better the lives of the poor. She decided that there probably was no God and became a communist. In 1915, when she was 18 years old, Dorothy moved to New York City, where she worked by writing for socialist newspapers.

Dorothy's life in New York was far from holy. Her friends were men and women who believed that Christian morals were old-fashioned. These friends were communists and anarchists who wanted to destroy American society and replace it with one in which people were all treated alike.

Dorothy first came into contact with the Catholic Church while living on Staten Island with her husband, Forster Battenham. She had always thought that the Church belonged to the rich, but she discovered that most faithful Catholics were poor. Even more, she found that the Catholic Church was a church of the poor. Dorothy began to receive instruction in the Catholic Faith from a nun, and in 1927 Dorothy had her baby daughter baptized.

But Forster, who did not believe in God, was not happy with Dorothy's interest in the Catholic Church, and he left her. Dorothy had to give up much to follow Christ. She was now left to raise her child by herself.

Dorothy continued her work as a writer both for Catholic and non-Catholic publications. But she felt that she needed to do more than just write. She still wanted to work for the poor, but she did not know how, as a Catholic laywoman, she could do this. While in a church, she knelt in prayer and asked God to show her how she could serve Him by serving His beloved poor.

God answers prayers in strange ways. When Dorothy returned to New York she had an odd visitor, a short man with a French accent who wore a rumpled suit (in which he slept) and who could not stop talking. Dorothy had met many people like this man, Peter Maurin, before. These fellows spent their days in Union Square in New York, giving speeches about how to change the world. Dorothy at first thought this Peter Maurin was as crazy as any other Union Square speechmaker, but she soon changed her mind. Peter wanted to change the world by infusing it with the wisdom of the Catholic Church and the power of the sacraments.

Peter Maurin was 55 years old in 1932 when he met Dorothy Day. He was from France, where he grew up in a large farming family.

When he was 16 years old, Peter entered a religious order of teachers called the Christian Brothers. In 1898, the French government forced him to enter the military. In 1902, Peter left the Christian Brothers, and in 1909 emigrated to Canada, where he would not be forced to serve in the military. He lived there doing manual labor and teaching French. By 1932, when Dorothy met him, Peter was working at a boys' camp outside of New York and spending whatever time he could in Union Square making speeches about how to change the world. When in the city, Peter lived and ate with the poorest of the poor.

Peter Maurin said that people could not change the world unless they first changed themselves. Each person, he said, had to become holy. Each person, he declared, had to take responsibility not only for himself but also for his neighbor. Each person had to feed the hungry, clothe the naked, and teach the ignorant. This was not a job for the government, but for individuals, families, and the Church. Peter's plan was to have "roundtable discussions" where people could come together and discuss the teachings of the Church and how to use those teachings to help others. He wanted there to be "houses of hospitality" where the poor could come to be fed, clothed, and have a place to sleep. He also wanted farms where the poor from the city could go to work and provide for themselves.

Peter told Dorothy that the first thing they needed to do was start a newspaper. "But where are we going to get the money to do that?" Dorothy asked. "In the history of the saints," said Peter, "money is raised by prayer. God sends you what you need when you need it." And God sent Peter and Dorothy what they needed. They raised the $57 they needed to print the first issue of their paper, which Dorothy named *The Catholic Worker*.

The newspaper was just the beginning of what became known as the Catholic Worker movement. Peter and Dorothy rented two buildings where long lines of poor men and women soon gathered to receive food and clothing and to find a place to sleep. Various people, even well-known Catholics from Europe and the United

States, came to the Catholic Worker house for roundtable discussions. Soon, other Catholic Worker houses were founded in other American cities by other people inspired by Dorothy and Peter's work. Other Catholic Workers started farms and retreat houses in rural areas.

The Catholic Worker was different from other Catholic movements. Unlike the groups started by Mother Seton and Rose Hawthorne Lathrop, the Catholic Worker did not become a religious order. Catholic Workers did not take religious vows, but remained laypeople. People could come to help out at Worker houses and stay as long as they wanted or leave whenever they wanted. The Catholic Worker Movement was also very American because of Dorothy and Peter's emphasis on individual responsibility and a free community life. It is one of our country's contributions to Catholic spiritual life.

The twentieth century was a time of great change for the United States. After the Second World War, the United States became a world superpower. At home, Americans focused more and more on making wealth, buying, and selling. Gradually more and more people moved away from their religious faith, and many Catholics fell away from the Church. More and more, America ought to have listened to Dorothy Day's and Peter Maurin's message (which was really the Catholic Church's message) that everyone needed to seek holiness. Each one of us, no matter who we are or what we do, is called to love God with all his heart, soul, and mind, and to love his neighbor as himself.

Only if we each take responsibility for ourselves and for our neighbor can the United States become the country that God means it to be.

Chapter 20 Review

Summary

- Catholics began immigrating to the United States in large numbers in the middle of the nineteenth century. Irish and German immigrants were the first large groups of Catholics to cross the Atlantic to America. Many Protestant Americans feared these immigrants would take jobs from native-born Americans, they did not approve of the immigrants' foreign customs, and they deeply disliked the immigrants' Catholic Faith. For these reasons and others, many immigrants were unjustly treated, particularly in the cities.

- Saint John Neumann immigrated from Bohemia to America in order to minister to Catholics there. Because he spoke many languages, he was able to minister to the various nationalities of his parish near Buffalo, New York. He became the fourth bishop of Philadelphia in 1852.

- Saint Frances Xavier Cabrini, or Mother Cabrini as she was known in her lifetime, was an Italian nun who founded the religious order, the Institute of the Missionary Sisters of the Sacred Heart. The Pope ordered her to go to America and be a missionary to poor Italian immigrants in America. She and her sisters worked in the poorest neighborhoods of New York City. During her lifetime, she and her fellow sisters opened hospitals, orphanages, and schools around the United States, and even in Central and South America. Mother Cabrini died in 1917, and Pope Pius XII proclaimed her a saint in 1946.

- Dorothy Day was a convert to Catholicism who wanted to help the poor in America. She rejected communism as a way to improve working conditions for the poor. She and a friend, Peter Maurin, discussed ways that lay Catholics could help the poor both spiritually and physically. In the 1930s they started what became known as the Catholic Worker Movement. They rented buildings from which they fed, clothed, and housed the poor. These buildings also provided a place for discussion groups to be held, where lay Catholics could talk about the Faith in their lives. Catholic Worker houses began to open around the country. The Catholic Worker Movement did not become a religious order, but remained a lay movement.

Chapter Checkpoint

1. During the first large-scale Catholic immigration to America, from what countries did the immigrants come? Discuss where these immigrants settled, and what life was like for them.
2. Name and discuss three prominent Catholics of the nineteenth century.
3. Who was Saint John Neumann, and what did he do for the Church in America?
4. Who was Mother Cabrini?
5. What is the Catholic Worker Movement, and who were its founders?

Chapter Activities

Research the history of a local Catholic church in your area. When was it built? If it was built in the nineteenth century, who built it? Was it intended for the use of specific immigrant groups? If it is a modern church, find out if it replaced an older church.

The American Larder

The German immigrants of the 1880s brought not only frankfurter sausages to America but also dachshund dogs. The name "hot dog" (or "dachshund sausage," as hot dogs were originally called) most likely began as a joke about the long, thin, little dogs that the Germans loved as their pets. Even the Germans themselves jokingly called the frankfurter a little-dog or dachshund sausage. At Chicago in 1893, the Colombian Exposition brought hordes of visitors who consumed large quantities of these German sausages sold wrapped up in bread. Also in 1893, the sausages became popular at American baseball parks, where the word *hot dog* seems to have first been used to sell this popular German American food.

Index